Offshore Tax Planning

Giles Clarke
MA (Cantab), PhD, FTII, Barrister

Seventh Edition

Butterworths
London, Edinburgh, Dublin
2000

United Kingdom	Butterworths, a Division of Reed Elsevier (UK) Ltd, Halsbury House, 35 Chancery Lane, LONDON WC2A 1EL and 4 Hill Street, EDINBURGH EH2 3JZ
Australia	Butterworths, a Division of Reed International Books Australia Pty Ltd, CHATSWOOD, New South Wales
Canada	Butterworths Canada Ltd, MARKHAM, Ontario
Hong Kong	Butterworths Asia (Hong Kong), HONG KONG
India	Butterworths India, NEW DELHI
Ireland	Butterworth (Ireland) Ltd, DUBLIN
Malaysia	Malayan Law Journal Sdn Bhd, KUALA LUMPUR
New Zealand	Butterworths of New Zealand Ltd, WELLINGTON
Singapore	Butterworths Asia, SINGAPORE
South Africa	Butterworths Publishers (Pty) Ltd, DURBAN
USA	Lexis Law Publishing, CHARLOTTESVILLE, Virginia

A CIP Catalogue record for this book is available from the British Library.

1st edition 1986
2nd edition 1990
3rd edition 1994
Reprinted 1995
4th edition 1996
Special edition 1997
5th edition 1998
6th edition 1999
7th edition 2000

ISBN 0 406 91903 8

Typeset by Columns Design Ltd, Reading, England
Printed and bound in Great Britain by The Cromwell Press, Trowbridge, Wiltshire

Visit Butterworths LEXIS *direct* **at: http://www.butterworths.com**

Preface

In this edition I have taken account of the important developments during the last twelve months. These include both recent cases such as *Billingham v Cooper* and the Finance Act changes relating to such matters as trustee borrowing and the apportionment of close company gains.

The new rules on trustee borrowing represent the change with the biggest impact. I have devoted a whole new chapter to them (Chapter 27). In terms of both drafting and policy this legislation is among the worst we have seen in recent years. Its impact goes far beyond the anti-avoidance schemes it was introduced to counter, and yet some such schemes are said to be unaffected and the legislation has almost certainly opened new avoidance loopholes.

In this edition I have introduced several chapters on some of the practical issues which arise in offshore tax planning in a new Part four. The new material reflects the paramount importance of ensuring that offshore trusts and companies are properly run.

The offshore world is in ferment on account of the many international initiatives being directed at it. The most important is perhaps the OECD's harmful tax competition programme. At this stage I have not dealt with these matters in this book, mainly because the initiatives are directed at evasion and non-disclosure rather than legitimate tax planning. However their potential for wider impact should not be underestimated.

I am grateful to the many colleagues who have made suggestions and criticisms and in particular to Mr R A Plummer, who kindly read and commented on the previous edition of this book. But as always responsibility for errors remains mine.

I have endeavoured to state the law at 1 August 2000.

Giles Clarke Associates
Rathbones
159 New Bond Street
London W1Y 9PA

Giles Clarke

Contents

Table of statutes

Table of cases

H

I

Part one

Fiscal connection

Chapter 1

Territorial limits of UK tax

Introduction

Offshore tax planning may be defined as arrangements which exploit the territorial limits of UK tax so as to minimise income tax, capital gains tax, or IHT. In the main they presuppose the ultimate owner or beneficiary achieves the intended tax minimisation while remaining resident in the UK, but in the long-term, eventual emigration may be envisaged.

This book is principally focussed on private clients and privately owned structures. In these areas, offshore tax planning has two main applications. This first is the income and asset protection which may be achieved on behalf of non domiciliaries. This relies mainly on the remittance basis and the excluded property concept and is described in Part three. Second is the sheltering of income and gains which may be achieved for UK domiciliaries through offshore trusts, companies, and other structures. This is focussed on in Part two.

Territorial limits

The territorial limits of UK tax are the foundation of offshore tax planning. Income tax, CGT, and inheritance tax each have different rules.

Income tax

The definitive statement of the territorial limits of income tax is found not in statute but in case law. The position was encapsulated in one sentence by Lord Herschell in *Colquhoun v Brooks* (1889) 14 App Cas 493 at 503, a sentence subsequently approved by the House of Lords inter alia in *National Bank of Greece SA v Westminster Bank* [1971] AC 945 at 954. Lord Herschell's words were as follows:

> 'The Income Tax Acts, however, themselves impose a territorial limit, either that from which the taxable income is derived must be situate in the United Kingdom or the person whose income is to be taxed must be resident there.'

3

As the House of Lords pointed out in *Clark v Oceanic Contractors Inc* [1983] STC 35, Lord Herschell's statement does no more than apply a general presumption of English law. That presumption was put thus by James LJ in *Re Sawers, ex p Bain* (1879) 12 Ch D 522 at 538.

> '. . . a broad, general, universal principle that English legislation, unless the contrary is expressly enacted or so plainly implied as to make it the duty of an English court to give effect to an English statute, is applicable only to English subjects or to foreigners who by coming into this country, whether for a long or a short time, have made themselves during that time subject to English jurisdiction . . . But, if a foreigner remains abroad, if he has never come into this country at all, it seems to me impossible to imagine that the English legislature could have ever intended to make such a man subject to particular English legislation.'

The application of Lord Herschell's principle may be seen in the Schedules charging investment income. Schedules A and F charge profits from UK land and dividends paid by UK companies and thus by definition are limited to UK source income. All other investment income is covered by Schedule D, which applies to the annual profits or gains arising inter alia to any person residing in the UK from any property, wherever situate, or to any person, wherever resident, from any property in the UK (TA 1988, s 18). In short, if the income does not arise in the UK it is not charged unless the person to whom it accrues is resident here. In the latter event, the charge is under Cases IV or V of Schedule D.

Capital gains tax

The territorial limits of capital gains tax are easier to define than those of income tax. Statute provides as follows:

(1) A company which is resident in the UK is liable to corporation tax in respect of its chargeable gains (TA 1988, s 6).
(2) Any other person who is resident or ordinarily resident in the UK is subject to CGT in respect of capital gains (TCGA 1992, s 2(1)).
(3) A non-resident person is not subject to tax on capital gains, even if realised on UK assets, unless the person is carrying on business in the UK through a branch or agency. In such case, the charge is in general restricted to the branch or agency assets (TCGA 1992, s 10; TA 1988, s 11(2)(b)).

Inheritance tax

Liability to inheritance tax turns not on residence but on domicile. The rules are explained in detail in Chapter 15 but in summary are as follows:

(a) An individual is subject to inheritance tax on his world assets if he is domiciled or deemed to be domiciled in the UK.
(b) Any other individual is subject to inheritance tax only in respect of assets situate in the UK.

(c)   A trust is subject to inheritance tax on world assets if the settlor was or was deemed to be domiciled in the UK when he made the settlement. Otherwise liability is restricted to UK situs assets.

The core concepts

It will be apparent from the above that the core concepts in defining the territorial limits of UK tax are as follows:

(a)   Residence (income tax and CGT).
(b)   Domicile (IHT).
(c)   The situs of assets (IHT).
(d)   The place where income arises or, to use its technical term, the source (income tax).

Since domicile and the situs of assets principally concern non-domiciliaries they are considered in Part three. Residence is examined in the remaining chapters of this part, and at the end of this chapter are a few comments on the elusive concept of source.

Transparency and characterisation

At least as regards the sheltering of income and gains there is a fifth very important issue. This is that the foreign entity to which the income or gains accrue must be opaque – i.e. for tax purposes the income or gains must be regarded as accruing to the entity rather than to the underlying owners or beneficiaries.

The question of when an entity is opaque and when it is transparent is of some difficulty. Two aspects are important in offshore tax planning:

(a)   When is a foreign organisation treated as a company and when is it not.
(b)   When is a trust or other fiduciary arrangement treated as a separate fiscal entity and when are any income or gains treated as accruing directly to the beneficiaries.

Companies

In English law a company gains its existence from statute, namely the Companies Act 1985. In other jurisdictions, corporate entities are similarly artificial creations. It is probably fair to say that two well-established principles apply in determining whether a foreign entity should be treated as a company and thus as opaque for the purposes of UK tax.

The first is that by comity of nations, English law recognises the juristic status of bodies established under foreign law. Lord Hanworth MR put the matter thus in *Dreyfus v IRC* (1929) 14 TC 560 at 576:

'if there has been a body established by foreign law, the courts will recognise the juristic status of that body and thus the Court says that the principle of the liability of members of a foreign corporation to third parties is to be referred to the law under which that corporation was established, and if the law does show it was established as a separate entity effect should be given to it.'

The second is that in determining what a foreign entity is, you look at its characteristics as determined by the foreign law and then determine what, under English law, an entity with those characteristics would be. This principle was summarised by Dyson J in *R v IRC, ex p Bishopp* [1999] STC 531 at 545 in the context of determining the status of a Jersey LLP as follows:

'It is common ground that, in determining whether a Jersey LLP is a partnership for purposes of United Kingdom taxation, the nature of the rights, obligations and other features of the organisation must be determined according to Jersey law; but the characterisation of its status, ie whether a body of that kind should be treated as a partnership or not for United Kingdom tax purposes, will be determined according to the law of the relevant part of the United Kingdom (see *Rae (Inspector of Taxes) v Lazard Investment Co Ltd* [1963] 1 WLR 555, 41 TC 1).'

Partnerships

On the face of it partnerships, or at least certain partnerships, should be treated as corporate entities for tax purposes. This is for the following reasons:

(1) A partnership is a body of persons (*Padmore v IRC* [1989] STC 493) under the Interpretation Act 1978 the term "person" includes body of persons and so arguably in the absence of special provision, a partnership should be treated as the person receiving the income or gains separate from the individual partners.

(2) Although in English law a partnership is not a separate juristic entity, in Scottish and many other systems of law it is. As the Court of Appeal held in *Dreyfus* (supra) such a partnership should on any view be taxed as a separate entity.

Historically the characterisation of foreign partnerships has been confused, so much so that the Revenue regard *Dreyfus* as wrongly decided (International Tax Handbook para 1673). However, the matter is now settled by statute, for TA 1988, s 111(1) provides that where a trade or profession is carried on in partnership, the partnership is not to be treated as a separate entity for income tax purposes. Section 111(10) extends this rule to non-trading partnerships, and the same principle applies to CGT by virtue of TCGA 1992, s 59. As a result the correct question to ask if one is dealing with a foreign body of persons carrying on business is not whether it is a company but whether it is a partnership. If it is a partnership it is transparent, whereas if it is not it will almost certainly be a company and is opaque.

Two recent cases have illustrated that just because an arrangement is called a partnership in the relevant foreign country, application of English law to the various rights and obligations may lead to the conclusion that for tax purposes it is not. In *Memec plc v IRC* [1998] STC 754 a German silent partnership gave the silent 'partner' a contractual right to share in the active 'partner's' profits and the obligation to bear a proportion of losses up to a defined amount. The Court of

Appeal held that this was not a partnership. So too in *R v IRC, ex p Bishopp* [1999] STC 531 the Revenue had indicated in an informal pre-transaction ruling that a Jersey LLP should be regarded as a company. In refusing to review the Revenue's ruling the court declined to consider the substantive issue, but the case highlights the difficulties in relying merely on foreign nomenclature. As emphasised above, it is necessary instead to see what the rights and obligations amount to in English law.

Trusts and other fiduciary relationships: income tax

Fiduciary relationships arise wherever property is held by a person who is not the beneficial owner. They run the gamut from simple nomineeship to fixed-interest trusts and ultimately discretionary or accumulation trusts. Case-law determines whether there is a separate entity for income tax purposes. The law is established by three decisions in the House of Lords, namely *Singer v Williams* [1921] 1 AC 41, *Baker v Archer-Shee* [1927] AC 844, and *Archer-Shee v Garland* [1931] AC 212. These three cases all concerned fixed-interest trusts.

In *Singer v Williams*, the trustees were UK resident and there were two life tenants, one non-resident and the other resident in the UK but not domiciled here. The trustees mandated the income to be paid direct to the life tenants but the Revenue sought to assess the trustees. The House of Lords held that the trustees were not assessable as they had not received the income, but that even if they had, they would have been assessable on behalf of the life tenants who would accordingly have been entitled to the various exemptions from tax applicable to them.

Viscount Cave encapsulated the relevant principles in the following two sentences:

> 'The fact is that if the Income Tax Acts are examined, it will be found that the person charged with tax is neither the trustee nor the beneficiary as such but the person in actual receipt and control of the income it is sought to reach.'

> 'In short the intention of the Acts appears to be that, where a beneficiary is in possession and control of the income and is sui juris he is the person to be taxed and that, while a trustee may in certain cases be charged with the tax he is in all cases to be treated as charged on behalf of or in respect of his beneficiaries, who will accordingly be entitled to any exemption or abatement which the Acts allow.'

The two *Archer-Shee* cases concerned a New York fixed-interest trust, and the issue was whether the source of the UK domiciled life tenant's income was the underlying trust investments, which did not attract the remittance basis, or a right against the trustees, which under the law at that time did. In the first case, the law of New York was assumed to be the same as that of England, and it was held that under English law, the life tenant had a specific equitable interest in each investment, thereby constituting them the source of her income. In the second case, the law of New York was proved merely to give the life tenant the right to require the trustees to pay the net income to her. As such the life tenant's source was her right against the trustees.

The following principles may be gathered from these cases:

(1) If, like a life tenant under English law, the beneficiary has a specific equitable interest in the underlying investments, the trust is transparent and the beneficiary is treated as entitled to the income of the investments.

(2)   A fortiori, if the trustee is merely a nominee, the income is plainly that of the beneficiary.

(3)   If by contrast the beneficiary merely has a right as against the trustees to net income, the trust is not transparent.

(4)   A fortiori if no beneficiary is entitled to the income at all, the trust is a discretionary or accumulation trust. Here a series of subsequent decisions have affirmed that the income is that of the trustees and that if an income distribution is made, such distribution is a new source, taxable under Schedule D Case III if the trust is UK resident and otherwise under Case V (*Kelly v Rogers* (1935) 19 TC 692; *IRC v Berrill* [1981] STC 784).

The position is not however wholly logical. If a life interest trust is governed by English or a similar law, the life tenant is not treated as receiving all the income but only such part of it as is left after deduction of the trustee's proper income expenses (cf *Macfarlane v IRC* (1929) 14 TC 532 and TA 1988, s 689A). So too if the proper law of the trust follows that of New York, the fact that the trust is opaque is of academic rather than real significance, for the life tenant is still paid the net income, thereby preventing the trust from operating as a shelter if the life tenant is UK resident.

A further important distinction may also be drawn. If a trustee holds as nominee, the source of the beneficiary's income is, as noted above, the underlying asset. But if what one party has is purely a right in contract against the other party, the latter's income is not the income of the former, any payment again being a new source derived from the contractual right. The most obvious example of this is unit-linked life assurance, where the life office's income cannot be regarded as that of the policyholder, but at most merely a measure determining the policyholder's entitlement. Failure to appreciate this fundamental point was one of the reasons why the Revenue lost *IRC v Willoughby* [1997] STC 995.

Trusts and other fiduciary relationships: capital gains tax

The CGT position as regards trusts and other fiduciary relationships is not the same as under income tax. It is however much simpler, for the position is governed by statute. There are two basic rules:

(a)   Nominee property is treated as that of the beneficial owner (TCGA 1992, s 60). Nominee property means property to which one or more persons are absolutely entitled as against the trustee (ibid). If two or more persons are so entitled, their interest must be concurrent, such as tenants in common, rather than consecutive, such as life tenant and remainderman (*Booth v Ellard* [1980] STC 555). Unit trust schemes are, however, treated as companies (TCGA 1992, s 99).

(b)   Any property vested in trustees which is not nominee property is treated as vested in a single continuing body of persons, distinct from the individual trustees (TCGA 1992, s 69). Effectively therefore trusts are separate entities for CGT purposes even where there is a life tenant and even, indeed, if the settlor is life tenant. For this reason a fixed-interest trust is a separate entity for CGT purposes but not for income tax.

Unfamiliar entities

Not all foreign entities are obviously recognisable as companies, trusts or partnerships in the sense that those terms are know to English law. In an offshore context the unfamiliar entities most often encountered are the *Anstalt* (Establishment) and the *Stiftung* (Foundation) in Liechtenstein. These entities are defined by Liechtenstein statute, but so far no case before the English courts has required an analysis of their characteristics under English law. The relevant legislation, together with commentary, may be found in *Butterworths Offshore Service*.

Following the decision in *Memec*, the Revenue published the criteria by which they characterise foreign entities. They also indicated they would publish a list of entities upon which they have formed a view, but at the time of writing that list has not appeared (*Tax Bulletin* 39 (February 1999) p 627).

Source

The concept of source is an income tax concept, and as noted above it is relevant in an offshore context in that UK source income received by a non-resident is or may be subject to UK tax whereas in the absence of anti-avoidance legislation foreign source income of a non-resident is not taxable here. In general it is usually clear as to whether or not income has a UK source. There are however certain areas which require comment.

Dividends

Dividends have a UK source and are chargeable under Schedule F if the paying company is resident in the UK (TA 1988, s 20). This is so even if the company is registered abroad (*Bradbury v English Sewing Cotton Co Ltd* [1923] AC 744). Conversely if a now rare non-resident UK registered company pays a dividend, that has a foreign source.

Interest

An area of greater difficulty is interest. The general rule is that the situs of a debt is where it can be enforced, i.e. in the case of an individual where the debtor resides (see pp 121–2). An exception is made for specialties and bearer bonds, which are situate where found. It would be logical if the rules as to source followed the rules as to situs, so that, for example, the source of interest on a simple debt is where the debtor resides. But it is clear this is not the law. The leading case is *Westminster Bank v National Bank of Greece* [1970] 46 TC 472, and, while this concerned bearer bonds, their situs played no part in determining where the source of the interest was.

A number of cases indicate that in the case of debt obligations, the source is where the debt can be enforced. In *Foulsham v Pickles* [1925] TC 261, remuneration payable to a UK employee for work done abroad was payable only in Liverpool and was held not to be derived from a foreign possession. In *Stokes v Bennett* [1953] 34 TC 337 alimony payments by a foreigner under a UK court order were held to have a UK source. In *Alloway v Phillips* [1980] STC 490 the Court of Appeal held that a one-off payment by a UK publisher to a person resident in Canada had a UK source, on the grounds that the right to payment was a chose in action in the UK.

But *Westminster Bank v National Bank of Greece* [1970] 46 TC 472 puts the matter in some doubt. Here one Greek bank had issued bonds guaranteed by another Greek bank. The bonds were secured on Greek assets and on the facts the funds to pay the interest would have had to come from Greece. Principal and interest however were payable in London or in Greece by cheque drawn on London and, by reason of default, the only place where the debts could be enforced had come to be the guarantor's branch in London. The House of Lords held that these factors did not of itself give the interest an English source and that the mere substitution of an English guarantor was not sufficient to move the source of the interest. The reasoning then concludes with the following cryptic sentence:

> 'the bond itself is a foreign document, and the obligations to pay principal and interest to which the bond gives rise were obligations whose source is to be found in this document'.

Perhaps as a result of this case, there has been a tendency to say that in ascertaining where the source of interest is it is necessary to look at a multiplicity of factors. In *Tax Bulletin 9*, (1993) 100 the Revenue, basing themselves on the Greek case, enumerated four, namely the residence of the debtor, the source from which the interest is paid, where it is paid, and the nature and location of any security. Uncontroversially, the Revenue said that if all four factors point to the UK, the interest has UK source. What is not indicated is the position if some only of the factors are in the UK.

The Revenue's *International Tax Handbook* (para 1103) is more helpful in that it describes the residence of the debtor as an 'important' factor and refers to the remaining factors as 'other factors'. It also points out that a company can be sued for a debt wherever it does business, and thus that the source of a corporate debt is where it is payable. It may be suggested that the emphasis on the residence of the debtor and where the debt is enforceable is correct. The Greek case should perhaps be seen as establishing merely that substitution of a new debtor did not of itself alter the source.

At one time the Revenue took the view that interest payable by a UK company would not have a UK source if it was paid abroad to a non-resident in foreign currency under a foreign specialty, with no security in the UK (IR letter 22 January 1980). Subsequently the Revenue revised their view and stated that a loan to a UK company normally does given rise to Case III interest (IR letter 17 February 1982), regardless of whether there is a specialty. It follows that interest on Eurobonds issued by UK companies has a UK source (cf *International Tax Handbook* para 1129 passim) although deduction at source is avoided inter alia if payment is made abroad (TA 1988, s 124).

The conclusion to be drawn from all this is that if the debtor is resident in the UK it will be difficult to contend interest does not have a UK source, save where the debtor is a company trading abroad and the interest is a debt of the foreign branch. If the debtor is not resident in the UK, the interest is unlikely to have a UK source, although there may be cause for doubt if the place of payment, the source of the funds and the security are all here. However, if the only UK element is the security there is no real basis in either case-law or Revenue practice for arguing for a UK source.

Trading income

The profits of a trade have a UK source and so are taxable under Schedule D Case I if the trader is trading in the UK rather than with the UK. The distinction between those two concepts is discussed on pp 261–2.

Chapter 2

The residence of individuals

Introduction

An individual's liability to income tax and capital gains tax (CGT) turns principally on whether or not he is resident or ordinarily resident in the UK. These terms have the same meanings for the two taxes (TCGA 1992, s 9(1)).

The issue of whether in law a taxpayer is resident in the UK is subject to certain limited statutory provisions, but otherwise the question is one of fact and degree. This means that the issue is determined by the appellate Commissioners. The taxpayer can appeal to the High Court and beyond, but the courts will only interfere if (i) the Commissioners' decision is not based on the evidence before them or (ii) they misdirect themselves in law (*Reed v Clark* [1985] STC 323, 336). The result is that the law is characterised by great uncertainty, for it consists not of clear rules, but of judgments determining whether the Commissioners were entitled to find as they did.

For years, much of the uncertainty has been removed in practice, for in IR 20 the Revenue publish a clear statement of when, and when they do not, regard a taxpayer as resident. The Revenue follow these rules as if they had statutory force, and for that reason it is sufficient for most taxpayers simply to follow them. However, the law is still important, both because Revenue practice may not be applied in tax avoidance cases, and because, with due notice, Revenue practice can and does change.

In 1993 an attempt was made to simplify the law. In the Budget of March 1993, the then Chancellor announced he was abolishing one of the most distinctive features of that law, namely the available accommodation rule. As is explained below, the actual legislation (FA 1993, s 208) did not in terms achieve this but the gap is effectively filled by Revenue practice.

The complexities of the subject make a clear exposition of the law of residence difficult to achieve. In this chapter the approach taken is first to consider the common law meaning of the terms resident and ordinarily resident. Next the limited specific statutory rules are addressed and then Revenue practice is summarised.

Residence: case law

The basic common law rule is that the term 'resident' bears its normal dictionary meaning. The matter was put thus by Viscount Cave in *Levene v IRC* [1928] AC 217, 222:

'. . . the word "reside" is a familiar English word and is defined in the Oxford English Dictionary as meaning "to dwell permanently or for a considerable time, to have one's settled or usual abode, to live in or at a particular place". No doubt this definition must for present purposes be taken subject to any modification which may result from the terms of the Income Tax Act and Schedules, but, subject to that observation, it may be accepted as an accurate indication of the meaning of the word "reside".'

The two leading cases were decided in the 1920s, namely *Levene v IRC* (1928) 13 TC 486 and *Lysaght v IRC* (1927) 13 TC 511. In both, the taxpayers were British subjects who had sold their homes in the UK. Mr Levene left the UK in December 1919, and then spent the following times in the UK:

1920–21	19 weeks
1921–22	21 weeks
1922–23	20 weeks
1923–24	20 weeks
1924–25	22 weeks

During this time Mr Levene owned no permanent home abroad, although in January 1925 he did take a lease of a flat in Monaco. Until then he stayed in hotels. His visits to the UK took place in the summer months when he also stayed in hotels. During his time in the UK he attended to family matters and took medical advice.

In *Lysaght*, the taxpayer was a director of a substantial family company in England. In 1920 he gave up his home in England and moved permanently to a house he had acquired in Ireland. However, he came to England for a week every month to attend board meetings and during these visits stayed at the same hotel in Bath. Days spent in the UK were as follows:

1922–23	101 days
1923–24	94 days
1924–25	84 days

In both cases the Special Commissioners decided the taxpayer was resident in the UK for the years in issue. In Mr Levene's case they reached this conclusion having regard to his past and present habits of life, the regularity and length of his visits to the UK, his ties with the UK, and his freedom of attachments abroad. In Mr Lysaght's case no reasons were given. The Special Commissioners' decisions were upheld in the House of Lords as being ones they could properly reach, although in *Lysaght* it is clear the House would equally have upheld the opposite conclusion and Viscount Cave actually dissented.

Levene and *Lysaght* make it clear an individual can be resident in the UK even if he is only in the UK for a relatively small part of the year and his permanent home is abroad. But it is noteworthy that both cases concerned British nationals who had emigrated from the UK. The result would very likely have been different had Mr Levene and Mr Lysaght been foreigners who had not previously resided in the UK. Such was expressly recognised by Viscount Cave in *Levene*, and it is also indicated by *IRC v Zorab* (1926) 11 TC 289. Here the taxpayer was an Indian national who had moved to Europe and spent up to six months per year staying in hotels in the UK. The Special Commissioners found he was not resident and Rowlatt J refused to interfere with their decision.

For British nationals who have emigrated it is clear *Lysaght* is close to the line beyond which in law they cannot be resident. But how close is not clear from any of the speeches in the House of Lords. Some guidance may however be obtained from two contrasting cases, namely *IRC v Brown* (1926) 11 TC 292 and *IRC v Combe* (1932) 17 TC 405. In *Brown* the taxpayer was a British national who had moved abroad in 1919 and thereafter lived in hotels in England and on the continent. In 1924–25 he spent just two and a half months in England and the Special Commissioners found he was not resident. Rowlatt J refused to inter-fere, on the grounds that the facts would have allowed a finding either way. *Brown* therefore indicates that a residence finding is possible if a British émigré spends as little as two and a half months in the UK.

In *Combe*, the taxpayer left the UK to work in New York on 3 May 1926, and returned from New York on 10 October 1928, but was abroad for much of the remainder of 1928–29. His days in the UK were 52 in 1926–27, 175 in 1927–28, and 181 in 1928–29. The General Commissioners in Scotland found he was not resident in the three years, and while this finding was not directly at issue on appeal in the Court of Session, it was not called into question. The case shows that even if a finding of residence is possible with stays of as little as two and a half months, a finding of non-residence may equally be possible with visits of close to six months.

Ordinary residence: case law

The leading authority on the meaning of ordinary residence is *Shah v Barnet London Borough Council* [1983] 1 All ER 226, which related to student grants rather than tax. The House of Lords decided that foreign students who were allowed into the UK on education visas for a limited period were ordinarily resi-dent here. Lord Scarman stated the law as follows ([1983] 2 AC 309 at 343):

> 'Unless, therefore, it can be shown that the statutory framework or the legal con-text in which the words are used requires a different meaning. I unhesitatingly subscribe to the view that "ordinarily resident" refers to a man's abode in a parti-cular place or country which he has adopted voluntarily and for settled purposes as part of the regular order of his life for the time being, whether of short or of long duration.'

Logically the term 'ordinarily resident' presupposes the individual is 'resid-ent' and then, as Lord Scarman implies, requires an added quality to make it 'ordinary'. However, certain tax legislation, most notably TCGA 1992, s 2, proceeds on the assumption that an individual can be ordinarily resident without being resident. As is explained below, the Revenue, too, take this view.

It may be suggested, however, that residence is indeed a precondition of ordinary residence. The authority for this proposition is *Levene v IRC*, which concerned ordinary residence as well as residence. Since the taxpayer was held to be resident, the issue of whether an individual could be ordinarily resident without being resident did not directly fall for decision. But Viscount Cave's speech includes the following passage ([1928] AC 217 at 225):

> 'The expression "ordinary residence" is found in the Income Tax Act of 1806 and occurs again and again in the later Income Tax Acts, where it is contrasted with usual or occasional or temporary residence; and I think that it connotes residence in

a place with some degree of continuity and apart from accidental or temporary absences. So understood, the expression differs little in meaning from the word "residence" as used in the Acts; and I find it difficult to imagine a case in which a man while not resident here is yet ordinarily resident here.'

Viscount Cave's speech was expressly concurred in by Lord Atkinson; and Lord Buckmaster concurred in the dismissal of the appeal. If, as may be suggested, this represents the law, an individual can never be ordinarily resident without being resident. It has to be accepted, however, that if this view is right, Parliament enacted such legislation as TCGA 1992, s 2 under a mistaken view of the law. But it must be pointed out that this view was shared by the Special Commissioners in *Reed v Clark* [1985] STC 323. They reviewed all the relevant authorities, including *Levene*, and concluded as follows:

'From the speeches in *Levene* and *Lysaght* we would draw the conclusion, first that to be resident in this country for a tax year a person must live here for part of that year, though not necessarily in his own place of abode, and second, that the concept of ordinary residence involves actual residence, in the sense referred to with the added quality of continuity.'

On appeal to the High Court, Nicholls J did not deal with the term ordinary residence, but his remarks on occasional residence, and specifically the passage cited on the next page, give no grounds for supposing he would have disagreed with the Commissioners.

Ordinary residence is sometimes regarded as synonymous with habitual residence. However, in *Nessa v Adjudication Officer* [1999] 4 All ER 677 Lord Slynn stated this is not necessarily so, although the two terms do have a common core of meaning. In that case the House of Lords decided that a person does not become habitually resident in a country until he has taken up residence and lived there for a period. The period may be as short as a month, but if in this respect habitual and ordinary residence are the same, *Nessa* suggests an individual cannot become ordinarily resident in the UK immediately on arrival here.

Express statutory rules

Four specific statutory rules as to residence are laid down in TA 1988, ss 334, 335, and 336.

Occasional residence abroad

Section 334 applies to an individual if:

(1)   his ordinary residence has been in the UK, and
(2)   he has left the UK for the purpose of only occasional residence abroad.

Where s 334 applies, the individual is charged to income tax as if he were still residing in the UK. The section is of very limited impact, and there is no reported case where it alone has resulted in liability to tax. This is because an individual is normally found to be still resident in the UK if he has left the UK for only occasional residence abroad. Thus in *Levene v IRC*, the taxpayer was found to have left the UK for only occasional residence abroad, but equally he was resident in the UK all along. Conversely, in *IRC v Combe* (1932) 17 TC 405, the taxpayer's three year absence in New York was not found to be for the purposes of occasional residence abroad.

The leading case on occasional residence is *Reed v Clark* [1985] STC 323. Here the taxpayer was absent for only a little over a year, but there was a distinct break in the pattern of his life and throughout his absence he had made his permanent home and place of business in California. On these facts Nicholls J decided his residence in California was not occasional. He considered that ordinary residence is the converse of occasional residence, observing that 'a person's occasional residence is contrasted with his usual (or ordinary) residence'. He then made the following comments (at 345):

> 'In my view a year is a long enough period for a person's purpose of living where he does to be capable of having a sufficient degree of continuity for it to be properly described as settled. Hence, depending on all the circumstances, the foreign country could be the place where for that period he would be ordinarily and not just occasionally resident. I appreciate that this construction may give little scope in practice for the operation of [s 334] as an independent charging provision. But having regard to the origin of the section in the earliest days of income tax at the end of the eighteenth century I do not find this consideration sufficiently compelling to require the language in [s 334] to be given some different meaning.'

Section 334 does not apply to CGT. This presumably is because ordinary residence alone (if such is possible) renders a person subject to CGT (TCGA 1992, s 2).

Full-time employment

Section 335 allows available accommodation in the UK to be disregarded in determining residence if the taxpayer works full-time abroad. For this section to apply, the taxpayer must either be self-employed and no part of his business can be carried on in the UK, or he may be an employee, in which case incidental duties may be performed in the UK. Incidental has been strictly construed, and thus a KLM pilot whose flights occasionally included a UK stop-over was held to perform more than incidental duties in the UK (*Robson v Dixon* [1972] 3 All ER 671).

'Full-time' is not defined and there is in law no fixed number of hours which is required as a minimum. If the taxpayer is an employee there is no reason why the employer cannot be a company controlled by him. But evidentially it may be harder to prove that the employment really is full-time.

The Revenue regard a working week of 35–40 hours as full-time, and may accept a lesser time commitment depending on local conditions. In certain circumstances several part-time jobs can together be regarded as amounting to full-time work. (IR 20, para 2.5; *Tax Bulletin* 6 (February 1993).) A UK directorship may not preclude full-time employment abroad but it would be scrutinised.

Temporary residents

Section 336 of TA 1988 is headed 'Temporary Residents in the United Kingdom' and it applies to any person who 'is in the United Kingdom for some temporary purpose only' and not with the intention of establishing his residence here. Such a person is not treated as resident for the purposes of Schedule E (s 336(2)), and he is not charged to tax under Schedule D as a person residing in the UK in respect of income received from foreign possessions or securities (s 336(1)). An exception to these rules is, however, made if the person has in fact resided in the UK for six months or more in a tax year. Similar provisions are made in relation to CGT by TCGA 1992, s 9(3).

Although s 336 has been in the income tax legislation since the Napoleonic Wars, it has been the subject of little case law and its meaning is far from clear. Two points in particular have arisen. The first is the meaning of 'temporary purposes' and the second is whether s 336 is a relieving section (ie relieving persons who would otherwise be taxable as residents of certain tax consequences arising therefrom) or whether by implication it enacts a substantive rule as to residence.

On this latter point, the meaning of the section itself appears clear: it does not enact a rule as to residence but merely confers relief for certain purposes. Such was affirmed by the majority of the Court of Session in *Lloyd v Sulley* (1884) 2 TC 37 and by Lord Warrington in *Levene* and it is also implicit from the facts of *Lysaght* and *Levene*. Those two cases concerned liability to tax on income of a kind not specifically mentioned in s 336, and it is noteworthy that in neither case was temporary residence a central issue. A further point is that when CGT was enacted in 1965, the draftsman did not think s 336 governed the rules as to residency. Thus, what is now the TCGA 1992, s 9(1) provided that 'resident' has the same meaning as for income tax, and then what is now s 9(3) enacted a provision exempting temporary residents from charge in the same terms as s 336.

As regards the first point, the meaning of 'temporary purposes', one authority is directly in point, namely *Cooper v Cadwalader* (1904) 5 TC 101. Here an American had taken a lease of a shooting-lodge in Scotland, and he spent a continuous period of two months there each year during the grouse-shooting season. His principal residence was in New York. The Court of Session affirmed the finding of the General Commissioners that he was resident in the UK, and upheld assessments made on him under Schedule D. The question then arose of whether he was exempted by what is now s 336(1). All three judges who gave reasoned opinions held that it did not apply as the shooting-lodge was a residence and so meant he was in the UK with the view or intent of establishing his residence here. Lords Adam and Kinnear then gave an additional reason for s 336(1) not applying, namely that coming to Scotland year after year for the shooting season was not a temporary purpose. In a significant passage Lord Kinnear observed that 'temporary purposes means casual purposes as distinguished from the case of a person who is here in pursuance of his regular habits of life'.

That this is the correct constitution of 'temporary purposes' is indicated by some of the cases concerned with individuals without available accommodation. Thus in *IRC v Brown* (1926) 11 TC 292, which concerned liability under Schedule D, the Commissioners' decision, upheld by Rowlatt J, included findings that the taxpayer's stays in UK hotels were for temporary purposes only. Similarly in *Levene*, Viscount Cave observed that Mr Levene's purposes when spending several months a year in hotels abroad were only temporary. The conclusion which may be drawn is that frequent or even lengthy visits to the UK to stay in hotels are visits for temporary purposes.

The question it would be most helpful to have an answer to is whether in *Lysaght*, the taxpayer's regular monthly visits for board meetings were for temporary purposes. This question is not however answered in the House of Lords speeches, no doubt because *Lysaght*, like *Levene*, concerned not Schedule D, but other sources of income, notably Schedule C and exempt gilts.

Available accommodation

Until 5 April 1993, the key concept in the legal meaning of residence was that of the permanent or settled abode. Thus, as repeated cases affirmed, if the taxpayer occupied a house or flat in the UK he was, in the absence of specific statutory provision, resident here. It did not matter if the house or flat was one of several homes round the world (*Lloyd v Sulley* (1884) 2 TC 37) and, indeed it was clear that a taxpayer counted as resident if he only spent a month or two in each year at his UK residence (*Cooper v Cadwalader* (1904) 5 TC 101). Provided the house or flat was available to the taxpayer he did not need to own it, and so a taxpayer could become resident here if accommodation was made available to him by a company he controlled (*Lowenstein v De Salis* (1926) 10 TC 424).

In 1993, FA 1993, s 208 introduced amendments to s 336 and TCGA 1992, s 9 with effect from 1993–94 onwards. These amendments provide that the existence or otherwise of available accommodation must be disregarded in determining whether an individual is in the UK for some temporary purpose and not with a view or intent of establishing his residence here.

As a matter of strict construction these amendments have little effect on the law of residence. Their effect is merely to reverse the principal ratio of *Cooper v Cadwalader*, namely that s 336 did not apply because the existence of the hunting-lodge meant the taxpayer did have the intention of establishing his residence in the UK. The amendments do not reverse the subsidiary reasoning of Lords Adam and Kinnear, namely that visits to the UK are not made for temporary purposes if made in pursuance of the taxpayer's regular habits of life. Strictly, therefore, the scope of the amendments may in law be limited, for in reality many foreigners with houses or flats in the UK come here regularly year in year out for business or recreational purposes. Their visits are part of the regular habits of their life, and thus, on the *Cooper v Calwalader* test, fall outside s 336.

A further issue is whether even in this limited respect the amendments changed the law as to residence. In a sense this is an absurd question, for the amendments are to ss 9(3) and 336, which, as noted above, do not as such govern the meaning of residence. But s 208(4) makes an amendment to the IHT deemed domicile rules in IHTA 1984, s 267 (see p 119). Until 1993–94, s 267(4) provided that available accommodation was disregarded in determining whether the taxpayer had been resident in the UK for 17 out of the last 20 years. Section 208(4) repealed this disregard and is comprehensible only on the basis that the rest of s 208 is concerned with the substantive law of residence. There is thus inconsistency, if not ambiguity, in s 208 and it may therefore be suggested that statements in Hansard can be taken into account in construing it (*Pepper v Hart* [1992] STC 898).

That the then Government intended s 208 to change the law of residence is indicated by the Budget Press Release on 16 March 1993, which first announced the change. This opens with the following words:

> 'The Chancellor proposes in his Budget to abolish the available accommodation rule.'

It later stated, in para 4, that:

> 'the Chancellor's proposal will mean that no account will be taken of the availability of accommodation in the UK in determining whether an individual here for a temporary purpose only is resident for tax purposes.'

That this was the intention was confirmed when the Finance Bill was in Committee stage (HC Official Report, 24 June 1993, cols 590–91). Mr Michael Stern referred to the difficulties over the scope of s 336 and asked the Financial Secretary to the Treasury, Mr Stephen Dorrell, to confirm that:

'the purpose of [s 208] as set out in the Budget Press Release is achieved by [s 208] as drafted.'

Mr Dorrell replied that the Revenue had always regarded s 336 as having illustrative value. Hence, he said:

'it is not necessary in [the Revenue's] view to go any further in [s 208] which already fully achieves its objectives.'

Mr Dorrell then referred to the available accommodation test as 'a spurious test of residence' and concluded that 'this is why it should be abolished'.

Mr Dorrell's statements were clear and unequivocal and thus satisfy the conditions laid down in *Pepper v Hart* for Parliamentary material to be taken into account. Accordingly, by this somewhat roundabout route the conclusion may be reached that s 208 indeed altered the law of residence. However, what is also clear is that it only applies to those in the UK for temporary purposes only, for the material cited above refers specifically to temporary visitors. It follows therefore that available accommodation should as a matter of law still be taken into account in relation to persons who visit the UK as part of the regular order of their life. For that reason, s 208 is in law be of only limited effect although as noted below in practice it is given much wider effect.

Revenue practice

Current Revenue practice is set out in Part I of IR 20. In one or two places this specifically refers to extra-statutory concessions and so is subject to the rubric applicable to all concessions, namely that the benefit of the concession is not given where an attempt is made to use it for tax avoidance. Otherwise IR 20 is a clear statement of practice made to all the world which can therefore be relied on by taxpayers (cf *R v IRC, ex p MFK Underwriting Agents Ltd* [1989] STC 873 at 892 per Bingham LJ).

The current edition of IR20 was issued in December 1999. It provides clear practical rules in many areas where the law is uncertain. Its overall effect is to make the number of days spent in the UK virtually the sole test of residence.

Residence

The main points of IR20 as regards residence are as follows:

(1) A taxpayer is always regarded as resident in the UK in a tax year if he is here for 183 days or more in the year (para 1.2).
(2) A taxpayer is also regarded as resident in the UK if he is here for an average of 91 or more days per tax year (paras 2.7 and 3.3). The average may be taken over a period of up to four years and is determined by a fraction of

which the denominator is the total number of days in the period under review and the numerator is the number of days in the period spent in the UK. This fraction is then multiplied by 365 to give the average number of days per year in the UK over the period.

(3) For the purposes of both the 183 and the 91 day rule, days of arrival and departure are not normally counted as days spent in the UK (para 1.2).

(4) Persons coming to the UK are divided into three categories, namely:
   (i) Those intending to live in the UK permanently or remain at least three years, who are regarded as resident from arrival (para 3.1).
   (ii) Long-term visitors, ie persons intending to remain indefinitely. They are regarded as resident from arrival if they own or lease accommodation here or have come here for a purpose which will involve remaining for at least two years (para 3.7).
   (iii) Short-term visitors, who are simply subject to the 183 and 91 day rules (para 3.3). The 91 day rule treats a visitor as resident in the UK if over a four-year period his average number of days in the UK per tax year exceed 91. In such a case, residence commences from the fifth year or, if earlier, from when the visitor decides to spend more than 91 days per year in the UK.

(5) A person is regarded as intending to remain here if he is here on a continuing basis and any departures are for holidays or short business trips (para 3.1).

(6) An individual leaving the UK is regarded as non-resident if he satisfies the 183 and 91 day rules and falls into one of the following categories:
   (i) He emigrates permanently (para 2.8).
   (ii) He or his spouse go abroad to work full time under a contract of employment which lasts at least one tax year (paras 2.2 and 2.6).
   (iii) He goes abroad for some other settled purpose which lasts for at least one complete tax year (para 2.9).

(7) An individual going abroad without satisfying any of the above three conditions is treated as remaining resident. However, if in fact he satisfies the 183 and 91 day rules for three complete tax years, his status can be reviewed (para 2.9).

Ordinary residence

IR 20 asserts that an individual may be ordinarily resident without being resident. However, the only example given is that of the individual who takes a long holiday and does not set foot in the UK during a full tax year (para 1.3). Otherwise in all cases where a departing individual is regarded as non-resident, he is also regarded as losing ordinary residence. An arrival is regarded as ordinarily resident from the date of arrival if:

(a) he is coming to the UK permanently (para 3.1);
(b) he is a long-term visitor who intends to remain in the UK for at least three years;
(c) he is a long-term visitor who owns or leases accommodation for at least three years on or in the same tax year as arrival (para 3.11); or
(d) he is a short-term visitor who intends at the outset to be in the UK 91 or more days per year over at least the next four tax years.

Revenue practice and the law

The Revenue practice is helpful and in almost all cases should be followed when questions of residence are at issue. However, in three respects it may be harsh:

(1)   It will not always be the case that a taxpayer whose average visits are 91 or more days per year will be resident. If the taxpayer has a permanent home abroad, is foreign, and has no business interests in the UK, a contrary finding would, it is suggested, be quite open to the appellate Commissioners (cf *IRC v Lysaght* [1928] AC 234 passim).
(2)   As noted above, it is doubtful in law whether it is possible to be ordinarily resident without being resident.
(3)   Also, as noted above, *Nessa* indicates ordinary residence may not commence on arrival.

A more pertinent observation is that available accommodation is hardly mentioned. In practice this is extremely important and means that available accommodation may normally be ignored. There would appear to be only two exceptions to this:

(1)   In determining whether a taxpayer has gone abroad for permanent residence. Here all that is required is that the retention of UK accommodation is consistent with living abroad permanently or for at least three years (para 2.8).
(2)   In determining whether a longer-term visitor is resident or ordinarily resident.

Compliance

Under self-assessment, individuals self-certify their residence status. The Revenue no longer give residence rulings save where such is necessary to obtain relief from foreign tax under the terms of a double tax treaty. The notes to the non-residence pages include a questionnaire to enable individuals to determine their residence status. Both these notes, and the non-residence pages themselves, echo IR 20 and emphasise that days spent in the UK are virtually the sole test.

It is open to the Revenue to check an individual's residence status as part of an enquiry into a return under TMA 1970, s 9A. The matter is immune from investigation once the 12 month period for enquiries into the return has expired unless the individual has made inadequate or fraudulent disclosure. In practice the Revenue also regard themselves as bound if they investigate an individual's residence status for PAYE coding or repayment purposes (*Tax Bulletin* 29 (June 1997) 425).

Departure and arrival

In law an individual counts as resident in the UK throughout a tax year if he is resident for part of the year. But by concession a new arrival is treated as resident only from the date of arrival if prior to arrival he was not ordinarily resident (ESC A11). This concession does not apply to CGT unless the new arrival has previously been non-resident for at least five complete tax years (ESC D2).

Those departing from the UK are by concession treated as becoming non-resident on departure if they go abroad permanently (ESC A11). This concession does not apply to CGT unless the individual was non-resident throughout at least four of the seven tax years preceding that of his departure (ESC D2). Those who go abroad to take up full-time employment which extends over at least one complete tax year are regarded as non-resident for income tax purposes from the date of their departure until the date of their return. The law and practice relating to short-term and permanent emigration are discussed in detail in Chapter 35.

Double tax treaties

A double tax treaty is material in determining residence if an individual is resident in the UK for UK domestic tax purposes and in a treaty state for the domestic tax purposes of that state. Where this happens, the treaty lays down rules for determining which state the taxpayer resides in for the purposes of the treaty.

The rules in most treaties follow those in Article 4 of the OECD Model Convention. These rules are as follows:

(1) If the individual has a permanent home available to him in only one state he is resident in that state.
(2) If he has a permanent home in both states, he is resident in the state with which his personal and economic relations are closer ('centre of vital interests').
(3) If he does not have a permanent home in either state, or his centre of vital interests cannot be determined, he is resident in the state where he has a habitual abode.
(4) If he has a habitual abode in both states or neither state, he is a resident of the state of which he is a national.
(5) If he is a national of both states or neither state, his residence is settled by mutual agreement between the two Revenue authorities.

In international tax planning treaties are often far more important than UK domestic law in determining residence, for once an individual is resident in a foreign state under a treaty, the treaty generally only allows the UK taxing rights over certain UK source income and gains. But in offshore planning, treaties are less significant, for few genuine low-tax jurisdictions have any sort of treaty with the UK. Two which do, Jersey and Guernsey, have only restricted treaties, which do not include an OECD-type residence article.

Chapter 3

The residence of trusts

Introduction

Currently different rules apply in determining the residence of trusts for income tax and CGT. Apart from one or two administrative provisions, the residence of trusts is not material for IHT purposes. As is described in Chapter 15, settled property is within the ambit of IHT unless it is excluded property, ie it is situate outside the UK and comprised in a settlement made by a non-domiciled settlor.

Capital gains tax

The basic rule is that a trust is UK resident unless two conditions are satisfied (TCGA 1992, s 69(1)):

(1) All or a majority of the trustees are neither resident nor ordinarily resident in the UK.
(2) The general administration of the trusts is ordinarily carried on outside the UK.

The trustees

The first of these conditions requires an investigation of the residence status of each of the trustees. With individual trustees this is not normally a problem, since individual offshore trustees tend to live and work in a particular offshore jurisdiction. With corporate trustees, the central management and control test described in Chapter 4 has to be watched, particularly where the corporate trustee is a subsidiary of a UK group. The residence status of offshore corporate trustees has, however, rarely if ever been attacked in practice (cf further p 129 below).

General administration

As regards the second requirement, nobody really knows what constitutes the general administration of the trusts. However, inheritance tax cases have drawn a distinction between the dispositive and the administrative powers of trustees (see especially *Pearson v IRC* [1980] STC 318, [1981] AC 753, HL). It may be suggested, therefore, that the general administration of the trusts relates to matters carried out in exercise of the trustees' administrative powers. It would thus include the making and management of trust investments, trust accounting, and the operating of the trust bank account.

Professional trustees

An exception to the general rule relating to the residence of trusts is made for trustees who carry on the business of managing trusts (TCGA 1992, s 69(2)). Such a person may be treated as non-resident in relation to a particular trust if all the settled property is derived from a person who was neither resident nor domiciled in the UK when he transferred the property to the settlement. If as a result of the operation of this rule all or a majority of the trustees are or are treated as non-resident, the general administration of the trusts is deemed to be carried on abroad.

The effect of this exception is to ensure that when it applies, the trust is non-resident. It enables trust companies and professional trustees to attract foreign trust business to the UK and should be read in conjunction with the income tax rules relating to mixed-residence trusts.

Income tax

There is no general rule determining the residence of trusts for income tax purposes. However, the various charging provisions are expressed in terms of the person receiving the income or, in the case of certain categories of deemed income, the trustee or trustees in receipt of it. Under the Interpretation Act 1978, s 6, the singular includes the plural. It follows that a trust is resident in the UK if there is one trustee and he is resident in the UK or if there are several trustees and all are resident in the UK (cf *Dawson v IRC* [1989] STC 473, HL).

Mixed-residence trusts occasioned difficulty. In *Dawson v IRC* (supra) the trust had one resident trustee and two non-resident trustees. The trustees were in receipt of foreign investment income, and the Revenue assessed the resident trustee under Schedule D Case V. Schedule D applies to foreign income if the person receiving it is resident in the UK (TA 1988, s 18). The House of Lords held that the trustees receive income jointly and that they could only be described as persons resident in the UK if all reside here.

As a result of *Dawson v IRC*, the law was changed and now FA 1989, s 110 governs the position where one or more trustees is resident in the UK and one or more is not. Such a trust is treated as UK resident if the settlor was resident or domiciled in the UK when he made the settlement or at any time when he provided funds for the settlement whether directly or indirectly. If the settlement has more than one settlor, this test is applied to each of them and the trust is UK resident if any of them was resident or domiciled in the UK when he made the settlement or provided funds. Only if none of those conditions is met is the trust non-resident, ie only if all those who have provided funds were at all material times neither resident nor domiciled in the UK.

The income tax rules as to the residence of trusts are easier to deal with than their CGT counterparts as they focus solely on the residence status of the trustees and do not require an investigation of where the general administration of the trusts is carried on. For UK domiciled settlors they are more onerous as they require all the trustees to be non-resident rather than merely a majority.

Protectors

Protectors are persons who are not trustees but have certain powers in relation to the trust. They generally have the power to appoint new trustees and often they are given the power to dismiss trustees. Their consent may be required to the exercise of major dispositive powers over capital and they may also have power to add or exclude beneficiaries.

The role of protectors has been the subject of litigation in various offshore jurisdictions. A UK tax case bearing on protectors concerned the question of whether a settlor in the position of protector had power to control the application of trust income for the purposes of TA 1988, s 742(2)(e) (*IRC v Schroder* [1983] STC 480, see further, p 171). The settlor had power to appoint members of a committee of protectors, which in turn had power to hire and fire trustees. Vinelott J held these powers were all fiduciary and decided that the settlor did not have control because both his powers and those of the trustees over income were fiduciary within s 742(2)(e).

A question which is often raised is whether, if the protector of an offshore trust is UK resident, his residence can make the trust as a whole UK resident. At present this question is academic, in that it has not been raised in any reported case, but the fear of it leads most advisers to recommend against a UK protectorship.

In fact these fears are ill-founded. Two distinct points have to be distinguished. The first is whether the protector can be classed as a trustee for tax purposes generally. It is highly unlikely that he can be so classed, for the trust property is not vested in him, and he does not have power to initiate action, but merely power to veto proposals put up by the trustees proper. Such risk as there is is reduced if the matters which require the protector's consent are restricted to major fiduciary appointments or advances of capital. The trustees should be unfettered in their discretions over income and investment.

The second point is whether the existence of a UK protector could mean, for CGT purposes, that the general administration of the trusts was not carried on abroad. In theory there could be situations where this would come about, as where a UK protector made all investment decisions and managed funds on behalf of the trustees. But this should not occur in practice, and it is difficult to see any protector, whether UK resident or not, as being involved in the general administration if, as just suggested, his consent is required only to major fiduciary dispositions.

Chapter 4

The residence of companies

Introduction

In recent years, Parliament has enacted statutory rules for determining where UK registered and dual resident companies reside. Otherwise company residence is governed by case law. In certain respects the law is unclear, but a published statement of practice gives the Revenue view on certain key issues (SP 1/90). There is an interesting discussion of the subject in the Revenue's International Tax Handbook (chapters 3 and 4).

Case law

Central management and control

The leading case on company residence is *De Beers Consolidated Mines Ltd v Howe* [1906] AC 455. Here Lord Loreburn stated that 'a Company resides where its real business is carried on'. He then offered what has become the test of company residence, namely that 'the real business is carried on where the central management and control actually abides'. In the later case of *Unit Construction Co Ltd v Bullock* [1960] AC 351, Lord Radcliffe said that this test must be treated as being 'as precise and unequivocal as a positive statutory injunction.'

The meaning of the test is illustrated by the facts of *De Beers* itself. The company was incorporated under South African law, and its general meetings took place in Kimberley. Its business involved the mining of diamonds in South Africa, and the sale of those diamonds in London. Its directors were divided between London and South Africa but a majority, including two of the three life directors, resided in England. Both under the company's regulations, and in practice, meetings of the London directors had primacy. In particular, the case stated shows instances where the South African directors referred matters to and took instructions from London.

The appellate Commissioners found that the company was resident in the UK, on the grounds that the head and seat and directing power of the company were situate here. In the House of Lords, the taxpayer argued that the company's registration meant that it resided in South Africa. Lord Loreburn, who gave the only reasoned speech, rejected this. In applying the central management and control test, the decisive factor was how the company in fact conducted its affairs rather than what was prescribed under its internal regulations or bye-laws. On this basis it was inescapable that the company was resident in the UK for, to paraphrase

Lord Loreburn, real control of practically all the important business of the company was exercised by the directors in London.

Decisions of fundamental policy

Central management and control must be distinguished from where the company's business is located. In one of the earliest cases, all the company's business was in India, where it was managed by a local director on behalf of the Board. Most of the shareholders were resident in India. The company did not own premises in London but the Board met there and on the facts the local director could only act in India by authority of the Board and could at any time be recalled. On these facts the Court of Exchequer decided that the company was resident in England (*Calcutta Jute Mills Co Ltd v Nicholson* (1876) 1 TC 83).

This point was discussed by the Court of Appeal in *R v Dimsey* [1999] STC 846. The court emphasised that the central management and control test is a composite test 'designed to identify where the decisions of fundamental policy are made as opposed to the place where the day-to-day profit earning activities are undertaken'.

Legal and actual control

The test of company residence is central management and control of the company's business rather than control of the company (*R v Dimsey* [1999] STC 846). In English and similar systems of company law, the constitutional position is that the shareholders control the company through their votes at general meeting. The directors acting as a Board exercise control of the company's business and, if matters are being conducted constitutionally, central management and control is where they meet.

In the 50 or so years following *De Beers*, several cases on company residence reached the courts. In all the cases, legal control of the company's business was vested in the directors and it was either found or assumed that what happened in practice accorded with what was required constitutionally. In *Unit Construction Co Ltd v Bullock* [1960] AC 351, the question arose of what the position is if practice diverges from the company's constitution.

The facts were that the taxpayer had incorporated three East African subsidiaries, and, under their articles, the boards of these companies had to meet locally and manage the companies. In fact losses ensued and the board of the taxpayer became so exasperated that they appointed their own man as chairman of the subsidiaries, and ran the East African operation themselves through him. Minutes of board meetings of the local board were kept, but it is questionable whether the meetings took place and at most they merely rubber-stamped decisions already taken in London.

The case arose because the taxpayer wished to set the East African losses against its own profits. This in turn meant establishing that the subsidiaries were UK resident and so the remarkable position was reached of the taxpayer arguing for UK residence and the Revenue resisting this. The Commissioners found in favour of the taxpayer on the grounds that real control and management was at all times exercised by the parent board in London.

Both the High Court and the Court of Appeal held that only authorised and constitutional management and control were material in determining where central management and control lay, and they accordingly quashed the Commissioners' decision. Their decisions were, however, themselves reversed by the House of Lords. As Lord Loreburn pointed out in *De Beers* itself, it is actual conduct that counts in determining a company's residence rather than what should happen under the company's constitution.

Dual residence

One of the most difficult issues with company residence is whether, and if so, in what circumstances a company can be resident in two territories. The problem first arose in *Swedish Central Rly Co Ltd v Thompson* [1925] AC 495. There the company was UK registered and simply received rent from a railway line it had long since built in Sweden. In 1920, taking advantage of *De Beers*, it removed decision-making powers to Board meetings in Sweden and as a result the Revenue conceded that central management and control abided there. But the secretary, the company seal, and the company's bank account remained in London, and three directors and the secretary periodically met there. The Commissioners found that the company was resident in England as well as in Sweden and the House of Lords held that such dual residence was possible in law.

The principle thus established was considered in *Egyptian Delta Land and Investment Co v Todd* [1929] AC 1. In this case, a UK registered company had removed all its functions to Egypt, save those which, as a UK registered company, it was required to have in England. Had the courts decided it was resident in England, they would have effectively decided that under the pre-1988 law, no UK company could ever be non-resident. In fact the decision of the Commissioners, affirmed by the House of Lords, was that the company was non-resident. Many people have found this case difficult to distinguish from the *Swedish Railway* case, but in fact it is not. As Lord Radcliffe pointed out in *Unit Construction Co Ltd v Bullock* [1960] AC 351, in the Swedish case the company did little, and of that little, the functions performed in London were a large part. In the Egyptian case, by contrast, the facts disclosed a large business run wholly in Egypt.

This issue of dual residence was directly in point in *Unit Construction Co Ltd v Bullock* [1960] AC 351, for it had been conceded by the Revenue that the three subsidiaries were on any view resident in Kenya. The House of Lords regretted that this concession had been made and, although not essential to the decision, discussed how the dual residence cases should be reconciled with the central management and control test. Lord Radcliffe said they were either an exception to the central management and control test, arising where the facts do not enable central management and control to be identified at all, or result simply from central management and control genuinely being exercised from two territories. It is submitted that the latter explanation is to be preferred, given that the facts in some dual residence cases are virtually identical with those in *De Beers* itself (see for example *Union Corpn Ltd v IRC* (1952) 34 TC 207, 259).

Revenue practice

The Revenue first published their practice in 1983 (SP 6/83). The present statement of practice was issued in 1990 (SP 1/90). By and large the statement accurately summarises the case law already described. However, three points are worth emphasising.

First, it is stressed that company residence is ultimately a question of fact, turning on where central management and control is in fact exercised. Such an approach is undoubtedly in accordance with the case law. It means the Revenue will, in a disputed case, investigate the facts of how the company has operated, studying Board minutes and other documents and, if available, interviewing witnesses.

Second, the Revenue indicate the approach they adopt in investigating the factual position. First, they try to ascertain whether the directors of the company in fact exercise central management and control. Next, if the directors do exercise central management and control, the Revenue seek to determine where they in fact do this. Lastly, in cases where the directors apparently do not exercise central management and control, the Revenue look to establish where and by whom it is exercised.

The final point to emphasise about Revenue practice is that they sound a warning about company residence in a tax-avoidance context. The Revenue examine the facts particularly closely where 'it appears that a major objective underlying the existence of certain factors is the obtaining of tax benefits from residence or non-residence'.

Shareholder and unauthorised control

The most difficult issue in company residence is in what circumstances involvement by the shareholders or other unauthorised persons determines company residence. This question turns on how far the *Unit Construction* case goes. The facts of the case were extremely narrow; a parent board running the subsidiaries to the exclusion of the latter's boards. Unquestionably, the parent board were the board of the subsidiaries in all but name, and they had formally resolved that the management of the subsidiaries 'must be taken over by the directors of the parent company'. At its narrowest, *Unit Construction* merely decided that the failure of the parent board to formally appoint themselves directors of the subsidiaries could not affect the latter's residence.

Recent cases

Recent case law suggests this narrow view is broadly correct. In *Re Little Olympian Each Ways Ltd* [1994] 4 All ER 561, Lindsay J had to decide whether a Jersey company had become ordinarily resident in the UK for the purposes of the law relating to service out of the jurisdiction. The company had been struck off the register in Jersey but had since been restored to conduct English litigation. The directors were four partners in a Jersey firm of lawyers, and evidence was given that half the shares were owned by the estate of a Greek intestate and the other half by a Foundation. In practice a UK resident purported to give instructions to the board, and was one of the signatories to the company's bank account. But the company's board did meet and it was the source of instructions to the English solicitors regarding the litigation.

Lindsay J found that the company was not ordinarily resident in the UK. The basis for his decision was his acceptance of evidence from one of the directors to the effect that he would act in accordance with the UK resident's instructions provided they were consistent with Jersey company law and the interests of the actual shareholders. Lindsay J also observed that the UK resident had no consti-tutional power to impose his wishes on the Board since he was not in fact a shareholder.

A similar approach was taken by Special Commissioners in a tax case, *Untelrab Ltd v McGregor* [1996] STC (SCD) 1. Here the Unigate group had incorporated an offshore finance subsidiary which over the years made loans to other group members. The loans resulted from telexed requests from the group head office and the evidence was that none of the requests were improper or unreasonable, but, if any had been, or not been in the interests of the company, they would have been refused. If the group had insisted, the directors would have resigned.

The Commissioners found that Untelrab's board did meet, in Bermuda, and transacted the company's business there. The proposals from head office were discussed and the board would have refused to carry out any proposal which was improper or unreasonable. The Commissioners also found that Unigate group policy was to devolve decision-making to the subsidiaries. On these facts the Commissioners found Untelrab was not resident in the UK, and the Revenue did not appeal.

At first sight, the Court of Appeal decision in *R v Dimsey* [1999] STC 846 is at variance with these cases. *Dimsey* was a criminal case which concerned three companies formed in Jersey by Dimsey. The companies were owned by a UK resident, Chipping. The Revenue contended on the facts that the companies were resident in the UK, with the result that Dimsey and Chipping had cheated the Revenue by causing the offshore companies not to make proper tax returns. Dimsey and Chipping were convicted and on Dimsey's appeal to the Court of Appeal his conviction was upheld.

The Court of Appeal's judgment in *Dimsey* is unsatisfactory for the Court identified defects in the trial judge's summing up and yet still decided it was safe for the jury to conclude that central management and control of the three Jersey companies was in the UK. It did not indicate which parts of the evidence ren-dered that conclusion safe. A further and perhaps more unfortunate gap is that the Court did not consider who the actual directors were and whether and, if so, where, they met. In these circumstances it is difficult to regard *Dimsey* as mak-ing any sensible contribution to the law of company residence although it is an object lesson as to the dangers in this area.

In practice

Re Little Olympian Each Ways Ltd and *Untelrab Ltd v McGregor* could be overruled in the higher courts. But they indicate that UK residence is avoided if the following conditions are met:

(1) The offshore company's board does genuinely meet at properly minuted board meetings.
(2) At those meetings it gives genuine consideration inter alia to any 'requests' being made by its owners.
(3) It is clear on the facts that the board would not agree to a request which is improper, unreasonable, or against local company law.
(4) Any instructions as to implementation are given by or on behalf of the Board.

Individual ownership

The risks of a finding of UK residence are clearly greater where the shares are directly owned by a UK individual than where the offshore subsidiary is part of a properly-run UK group. With individual ownership, the reality normally is that the shareholder's wishes determine how the company is run. Frequently offshore companies owned by individuals are passive investment vehicles, and, as a result, even a genuinely independent board would require only in-frequent meetings. In these circumstances, SP 1/90 suggests the Revenue will in appropriate cases contend that the company's residence is that of the share-holder.

In some cases, such as *R v Dimsey*, such a contention may succeed, for some individual owners do effectively control the company's business and assets, so that, as in *Unit Construction*, the directors are mere cyphers or must be regarded as having stood aside. But with reasonable care this need not be the position. There is no reason why the four steps outlined above cannot be followed.

If the directors are persons advising or involved with the shareholder, decisions may be taken and implemented in discussion with him. In these circumstances the meetings between directors and shareholder may be the decision-making forum, and so, if such meetings take place exclusively in an offshore jurisdiction, the company should be resident there. Such a conclusion is supported by a Northern Ireland case, *John Hood & Co Ltd v Magee* (1918) 7 TC 327. Here a company was run by a single director who was the dominant shareholder, and he argued that the company's residence had followed him to New York. This argument was rejected by the court, on the ground that the company meetings were in fact held in Ireland.

Trustee ownership

Where a company is owned by non-resident trustees, central management and control of its business may be alleged to be exercised not by its directors or shareholders but by the settlor of, or the beneficiaries under, the trust. But as Lindsay J pointed out in *Re Little Olympian Each Ways Ltd*, in a trust struc-ture, the only persons who have any form of constitutional control are the trustees as shareholders and the directors. For this reason it is suggested that difficulties over company residence are greatly reduced if the company shares are held in a non-resident trust. An allegation that the company's residence fol-lowed that of the settlor or the beneficiaries would, it may be suggested, only succeed if the trust was a sham or if the trustees and directors had expressly or impliedly authorised the settlor or the beneficiaries to run the company's business.

A point sometimes raised is whether, if the trust has a UK protector, that protector can affect the residence of the company. This point arises particularly where the protector has power both to dismiss and appoint the trustees. The pro-tector is, however, unlikely to be material to the company's residence, for as with the settlor and the beneficiaries, he does not have non-fiduciary control to exercise. But UK protectors with extensive powers are ill-advised to involve themselves in practice in the affairs of companies owned by the trust.

Practical considerations which should be kept in mind in ensuring that the company cannot be attacked as UK resident are discussed in Chapter 16.

UK registered companies

In 1988, a statutory rule was enacted to the effect that any company incorporated in the UK is conclusively presumed to be resident here (FA 1988, s 66). As a result, incorporation is the test of residence for UK companies and the case law on central management and control is of relevance only to foreign registered companies.

There is one exception to the incorporation rule. This exception operates if the company was carrying on business before 15 March 1988 and had become non-resident before then pursuant to a general or a specific Treasury consent obtained under what is now TA 1988, s 765. If the consent was a specific consent, the company can remain non-resident regardless of where it is based, and it only becomes UK resident if it in fact becomes resident under the central management and control test.

If the consent was a general consent, a further condition has to be satisfied. This condition is that the company was taxable in a foreign territory. By 'taxable' is meant being liable to tax on income by reason of domicile, residence, or place of management, but not simply being liable to a flat-rate sum or fee (see FA 1988, Sch 7, para 5 and SP 1/90, para 6). Provided a company which migrated before 15 March 1988 pursuant to a general consent was taxable in a foreign state it may remain non-resident, but only so long as it is so taxable. There was in fact only ever one general consent, which applied where the company was formed after 1951 to carry on new business and over half its share capital was owned by non-residents.

The exception for companies which became non-resident pursuant to a specific consent applies also to companies which migrated after 15 March 1988 pursuant to a specific consent applied for before then. Such a company does however have to have commenced business before then.

Dual resident companies

A company is generally referred to as dual resident if the following conditions are satisfied:

(1) It is resident in the UK under UK domestic law whether as a UK registered company or under the central management and control test.
(2) It is liable to tax in some other state by reason of residence, domicile, or place of management.
(3) There is a double tax treaty between the UK and the other state.
(4) Under the tie-breaker clause in the treaty it is treated as resident in the other state for the purposes of the treaty.

In the OECD Model Treaty, the test under the tie-breaker article is where the company's place of effective management is situated. In *Wensleydale's Settlement Trustees v IRC* [1996] STC (SCD) 241, a Special Commissioner considered that the place of effective management is where the shots are called, implying realistic positive management. The Revenue consider that the place of effective management may, in some cases, differ from the place of control (SP 1/90, para 22).

The normal case of a dual resident company is a UK registered company whose effective management is in the treaty state. But a foreign registered company can also be dual resident, assuming effective management is not the same as central management and control. According to the Revenue, an example of a dual resident foreign registered company would be where the company's business is run by executives abroad with the final directing power resting with a non-executive board in the UK.

A company which would otherwise be dual resident is deemed for all UK tax purposes to be non-resident (FA 1994, s 249). This rule applies whether or not the company has hitherto claimed relief under the treaty concerned. It is not of great relevance to offshore tax planning, for virtually no offshore jurisdictions have double tax treaties in the UK with tie-breaker clauses as to residence.

Part two

UK domiciliaries

Chapter 5

Offshore trusts

Introduction

This chapter defines the extent to which offshore trusts may now be used by UK domiciliaries to shelter income and gains. It focuses on whether there are tax advantages in setting up such a trust now. Planning strategies for existing trusts are reviewed in Chapters 8, 9 and 10.

As is explained in Chapter 3 a trust counts as non-resident for both income tax and CGT purposes if all the trustees are non-resident and the general administration of the trusts is carried on abroad. For CGT purposes all forms of trust other than nomineeship are separate entities and thus opaque (see p 8). Income tax is more difficult, but as explained on pp 7–8, the net income of a fixed-interest trust after expenses is that of the life tenant. Discretionary and accumulation trusts are however opaque, in that the income is not that of the beneficiaries unless distributed, distributions being taxed as a new source. For income sheltering therefore, a trust needs to be in this form.

Income and gains able to be sheltered

Gains

Being non-resident, an offshore trust is not subject to CGT, whether in respect of UK or foreign assets (TCGA 1992, s 2; cf p 4). Subject to anti-avoidance legislation, offshore trusts are, therefore, capable of sheltering both UK and foreign capital gains. The sole exception arises if the non-resident trust is trading in the UK through a branch or agency. In this event UK branch or agency assets are subject to CGT (TCGA 1992, s 10). This is not of great practical importance but can be material if, for example, the trust owns in-hand UK farmland.

Income

Non-residents are not subject to UK tax on foreign income (pp 3–4), and so in the absence of anti-avoidance legislation, offshore discretionary or accumulation trusts shelter such income. Non-residents are, however, subject to income tax if the source of the income is in the UK. The liability of discretionary or accumulation trusts is at the 34% rate applicable to trusts (TA 1988, s 686; *IRC v Regent Trust Co Ltd* [1980] STC 140). Lower or basic rate liability is in most cases enforced by deduction at source. Non-resident trusts with UK beneficiaries cannot have bank and building society interest paid gross and nor is their liability to tax on other UK dividends and interest restricted to tax withheld (FA 1995, s 128(5); TA 1988, s 481(5)(k); SI 1990/2231, reg 4(1)(b)). These latter points mean that offshore trusts only operate as an income shelter insofar as the trustees do not invest in the UK.

Gains deemed to be income

Certain UK tax legislation deems capital gains to be income, and, in contrast to CGT, this normally applies to non-residents if the gain arises in the UK. One example of such legislation is TA 1988, s 776, which applies if UK land is acquired or developed with a view to realisation at a gain. Section 776 should be kept in mind whenever an offshore trust is contemplating short-term investment in UK property. The Revenue have power to direct purchasers of land from a non-resident to withhold tax at source, but it appears that this power can only be exercised once the land is under contract (TA 1988, s 777(9); *Pardoe* v *Entergy Power Development Corpn* [2000] STC 286).

Inheritance tax

As explained more fully in Chapter 15, a trust is subject to IHT if the settlor was domiciled or deemed to be domiciled in the UK when he made the settlement. This is so regardless of the residence or the domicile of the individual trustees. Because it is subject to IHT, any offshore trust made by a UK non-domiciliary should be structured in such a manner as avoids unnecessary IHT liability.

Discretionary trusts

In the absence of IHT, the most attractive form of offshore trust would be an accumulation or discretionary trust where the income is not that of the beneficiaries unless the trustees choose to distribute it. Unfortunately an offshore discretionary trust normally carries unacceptable IHT cost. Since the settlor is UK domiciled, the making of the settlement is an immediately chargeable transfer, taxable at 20% once his nil-rate band is exhausted (IHTA 1984, ss 3A(1)(c) and 7(2)). Equally important, the settlement is thereafter subject to the regime of ten-yearly and exit charges (IHTA 1984, ss 64 and 65). It is true that the rate of tax on these occasions cannot exceed 6% (IHTA 1984, ss 66–69), but even at these levels the tax is an impost which should be avoided if possible. Furthermore, there is always the possibility that future legislation might increase it.

There are however two situations where a discretionary trust does not create IHT liabilities. The first is where the trust is within the settlor's nil-rate band when he makes it, and remains within the nil-rate band on subsequent anniversaries. As a long-term proposition such a trust is unattractive in an offshore context for by definition its value is restricted to the nil-rate band (£234,000 in 2000–01), which hardly makes the expense of offshore trusteeship worthwhile. But a trust of this kind can be used as a holding device if the value of the funds initially settled is low. It is a quirk of the IHT rules that the rate of tax when a trust ceases to be a discretionary trust before the first ten-yearly anniversary is governed by the value of the funds when settled (IHTA 1984, s 68). Accordingly, if the initial value of the funds settled is within the nil-rate band, the trust can, if it has increased in value, be converted at no cost to a more favourable IHT form provided such is done before the first ten-year anniversary.

The second situation where a discretionary trust is attractive is if the property settled qualifies for full business property relief (IHTA 1984, s 104(1)(a)). Currently any shares in an unquoted trading company qualify for this relief (IHTA 1984, s 105(1)(bb)). Where the relief applies, both the gift into settlement and the settlement thereafter are free of IHT provided the company has no excepted assets within IHTA 1984, s 112.

Accumulation and maintenance trusts

Assuming these favourable cases where a discretionary trust may be appropriate are not in point, the preferred vehicle from an IHT standpoint is the accumulation and maintenance trust. As its name suggests this kind of trust allows income to be accumulated but, unlike the ordinary discretionary trust, there are no ten-yearly charges and no exit charges when the interests of the beneficiaries vest (IHTA 1984, s 71). Perhaps more important, the making of the trust is a potentially exempt transfer which means IHT is avoided provided the settlor survives seven years (IHTA 1984, s 3A).

The principal drawback of an accumulation and maintenance trust is that the beneficiaries do have to take interests in possession at 25 years of age or younger (IHTA 1984, s 71(1)(a)). At this point income sheltering ceases insofar as the beneficiaries who have become entitled to such an interest are UK resident. But this cessation need only be temporary, for any well-drawn settlement should contain power to reappoint a beneficiary's share on new trusts once he has reached age 25. As and when he has children that power can be exercised to appoint new accumulation and maintenance trusts in favour of his children. This will allow tax-free accumulation of income to resume, and, since the exercise is a potentially exempt transfer, it will be without IHT consequences provided the original beneficiary survives seven years.

Long-term trusts

These IHT considerations mean that the form of trust generally to be recommended for offshore sheltering for UK domiciliaries is the long-term accumulation and maintenance trust. Such trusts, indeed, are more readily drafted in offshore jurisdictions, for the absence of restrictions on accumulation means income can always be accumulated until the beneficiary presumptively entitled is 25 years old.

An accumulation and maintenance trust does, of course, presuppose there are suitable beneficiaries under 25. If there are none it is dangerous to 'borrow' beneficiaries, for unless there is a common grandparent, the entire fund has to vest within 25 years (IHTA 1984, s 71(2)). A way round this difficulty is to let the borrowed beneficiaries take interests in possession, say on attaining 18, and then appoint the fund away on new accumulation and maintenance trusts in favour of those who really are intended to benefit. Another solution is to create one or more interests in possession in favour of older family members, and make these subject to overriding powers of appointment. The latter can then be exercised to appoint accumulation and maintenance trusts once suitable beneficiaries are born, such appointment again being free of IHT provided the original life tenant survives seven years.

The obstacles

There are two principal obstacles which UK domiciliaries have to circumvent to shelter income and gains through offshore trusts. They are:

(a)   Anti-avoidance legislation attributing income to the settlor.
(b)   Anti-avoidance legislation attributing gains to the settlor.

Attribution of income to the settlor

The income of an offshore trust is assessable as the settlor's if the actual or potential beneficiaries include him or his spouse or if either of them receives a benefit or loan. This is achieved by two sets of provisions, namely TA 1988, s 739 and TA 1988, Part XV. The first of these codes deals with the transfer of assets abroad, whether or not involving settlements, and the second is concerned with settlements, whether resident or non-resident.

The settlement code was recast in 1995. It comes into issue where there is a 'settlement'. That term obviously comprehends settlements in the true sense but, in this context, it is also given the well-known extended definition in s 660G(1). It includes any disposition, trust, covenant, agreement, or arrangement, but this is subject to the overriding requirement implied by the courts, namely that bounty must be involved (*IRC v Plummer* (1979) 54 TC 1; *Chinn v Collins* (1980) 54 TC 311).

TA 1988, s 660A attributes the income of the settlement to the settlor unless the income is from property in which he has no interest. A settlor has no interest in property only if neither the property nor its income are payable or applicable to or for his or his spouse's benefit in any circumstances whatsoever (TA 1988, s 660A(2)). Income can also be attributed to the settlor if he or his spouse receives a capital sum, which includes receiving a loan or being repaid a loan (TA 1988, s 677).

Section 739 is analysed in Chapter 21. Unlike the settlement code it extends to all types of offshore arrangement, whether or not involving settlements or bounty. It is, however, subject to a motive test. It applies if the person respons-ible for setting up the offshore arrangements, the transferor, has what is called power to enjoy, or if he receives a capital sum. Power to enjoy is exhaustively defined, but basically a transferor has power to enjoy if he or his spouse benefits or could in any circumstances benefit from the offshore arrangements or if they have non-fiduciary powers of control. If any of these conditions is satisfied, the entirety of the offshore income is taxed as that of the transferor.

As will be apparent, there is a wide area of overlap between the settlement code and s 739. In cases of overlap the Revenue tend to invoke the settlement code. In tax planning terms there are two important points to watch about s 739. First, the term 'transferor' may extend to persons associated with the setting up of the offshore arrangements as well as to the transferor proper (see pp 176–8). Second, power to enjoy is widely construed. A transferor *could* have power to enjoy if the offshore transferee meets his moral obligations or even purchases properties from him in adverse market conditions (cf p 170 and *IRC v Brackett* [1986] STC 521). So too a transferor has power to enjoy under a settlement from which he is excluded if the trust fund could be advanced to another settlement under which he might benefit (*IRC v Botnar* [1999] STC 711; see further p 169).

Attribution of gains to the settlor

The gains of a non-resident settlement are assessable as the settlor's in the tax year in which the gains arise if what is called a defined person is an actual or potential beneficiary or receives a benefit. The term 'defined person' means not only merely the settlor and his spouse, but also his children and grandchildren and their respective spouses and companies controlled by all or any of the individual defined persons. These rules are laid down by TCGA 1992, s 86 and Sch 5, and are considered in detail in Chapter 24.

The extended definition of defined person means TCGA 1992, s 86 is the most far-reaching anti-avoidance legislation directed at trusts, whether resident or non-resident. All other anti-avoidance legislation applies only if the settlor or his spouse can or do benefit. The result is that an offshore settlement can be attributed to the settlor in many cases where the income is not so attributable.

There are certain transitional provisions for settlements created before 17 March 1998. Those are discussed in Chapter 25, but they are not material to trusts created now.

Sheltering now possible

Despite the obstacles described above, an offshore trust created by a UK domiciliary can still operate as a shelter for income and gains. There are three main contexts where this is possible:

(a)   Settlements where the settlor is dead.
(b)   Settlements where all defined persons within the meaning of TCGA 1992, s 86 are excluded.
(c)   Children's and grandchildren's settlements designed as an income shelter.

Settlements where the settlor is dead

It is self evident that the rules attributing income and gains to the settlor cannot apply if he is dead. Indeed, gains realised at any time in the tax year of death cannot be attributed to him either (TCGA 1992, Sch 5 para 3).

A settlement is in the position of having a dead settlor if it is an inter vivos settlement whose settlor has died or if it is a testamentary settlement. One advantage of a testamentary settlement is that the assets secure a tax-free updated base cost by reason of the settlor's death (TCGA 1992, s 62). The CGT advantages of an offshore settlement do not obtain during administration, for personal representatives have the deceased's residence and domicile (TCGA

1992, s 62(3)), but the vesting of the property in the trustee is not a CGT disposal (ibid, s 62(4)).

To be effective for CGT and income tax purposes, a will trust needs to be constituted by the will rather than by any variation made by the beneficiaries. This is because for income tax and CGT purposes, the settlor under a variation is the person making the variation (*Marshall v Kerr* [1994] STC 638, HL).

A testamentary settlement is subject to any inheritance tax chargeable on the death. Thereafter IHT considerations govern the form of the settlement. Ten-yearly charges normally make a discretionary trust unattractive unless the property is eligible for 100% business property relief. The trust should be in accumulation and maintenance or fixed interest form, where IHT in the future can be avoided by timely PETs.

Trusts with all defined persons excluded

Settlements where defined persons are all excluded are difficult to achieve now that the gains of grandchildren's settlements can be attributed to the settlor. But settlements are sometimes made by remote relations or friends of the beneficiaries, and these still operate as a shelter of both income and gains.

An important context in which such a settlement may be considered is to hold shares in newly-formed private companies, or other growth assets. The sum required for the settlement may be modest and the promoter may be able to persuade a friend or distant relative to contribute the initial sum required. Because the sum involved may be small, the trust can be discretionary, with accumulation and maintenance or interest in possession trusts appointed shortly before the first ten-yearly anniversary if a charge is then in prospect. In appropriate cases the promoter himself may be a beneficiary.

Where the friend or relative genuinely makes the settlement out of his own resources, he is the sole settlor for income tax and CGT purposes and sole transferor for the purposes of TA 1988, s 739. However, it should be stressed that where this is not so, the promoter will normally fall to be treated as a settlor or transferor. Thus a person is treated as the transferor for the purposes of s 739 if he procured the transfer (*IRC v Pratt* [1982] STC 756). A person is deemed to be a settlor under the settlement code if he made or entered into the settlement directly or indirectly, if he directly or indirectly provided funds, or if he made reciprocal arrangements for another person to make the settlement (TA 1988, s 660G(2)).

The principal difficulty in this area is that the promoter is often working for the company and building it up, and it is often feared that this makes him settlor, as happened in *Butler v Wildin* [1989] STC 22. However, the promoter is unlikely to be a settlor if he is remunerated on a proper commercial basis, and the risk and cost of financing the company is borne by the company and the settlement. It must be remembered that it is not the provision of services but of funds which makes a person a settlor (*IRC v Mills* [1975] AC 38 per Viscount Dilhorne).

Settlements made by friends or distant relatives achieve the ultimate in sheltering if the friend or relative making the settlement has neither an actual nor a deemed domicile for IHT purposes (cf pp 119–20). In this event, the settlement is excluded property, and so free of IHT (see Chapters 12 and 15). But here too, whatever is settled must be genuinely provided out of the resources of the non-domiciliary, for if it is not, and there is some reciprocal or indirect arrangement with a UK domiciliary, the latter will be treated as settlor and the settlement will not be excluded property. This result follows because the IHT definition of settlor is similar to that in the income tax settlement code, and thus includes providers of funds and indirect settlors (IHTA 1984, s 44).

Children's settlements

A children's or grandchildren's offshore settlement is still a perfectly effective shelter of foreign income. For IHT reasons the trust normally needs to be an accumulation and maintenance trust. In some cases a trust of this sort may come to operate as a CGT shelter, notably should the settlor die or emigrate. It may also happen if at some stage the capital is appointed away from the children and grandchildren.

Pending such developments, such a trust could hold either shares in a non-resident trading company operating wholly abroad or a portfolio invested abroad for income. In the former event, the profits in the company need to be distributed to the trust as income so as to avoid the build up of capital gains.

Investment for income is not the only method for such a trust to avoid CGT exposure. Certain types of asset are exempt from CGT, UK government securities and qualifying corporate bonds – ie sterling bonds – being prime examples. Investment in those assets, therefore, enables children's or grandchildren's settlements to avoid CGT.

Much more important is the fact that certain forms of capital gain count as income. The prime examples are offshore income gains, ie gains on the disposal of non-distributor offshore funds (see Chapter 29). Section 86 does not apply to such gains and instead, where the settlor and his spouse are excluded, they are taxed only insofar as resident beneficiaries receive capital (cf pp 248–50). It is true that offshore income gains do not qualify for taper or indexation relief but this drawback is outweighed by avoidance of tax on an arising basis. A further point about offshore funds is that switches of investment within the fund's portfolio are not taxed. Were the trust to hold an equivalent portfolio otherwise than through the medium of the fund, all investment switches would be taxable under s 86. The effect of those various points is that offshore funds provide a means for children's and grandchildren's settlements with portfolio investments to wholly avoid attribution of gains to the settlor on an arising basis.

Another example of a capital gain treated as income is the discount on deep discount securities which is deemed to be income under FA 1996, Sch 13. This deemed income is not taxed on an arising basis if it is received by a settlement from which the settlor and his spouse are excluded (Sch 13 paras 6(3) and 12). Capital gains tax on the settlor is avoided because the security is deemed to be a qualifying corporate bond (TCGA 1992, s 117(2AA)).

The practical result of these points is that it is possible to construct a portfolio which avoids gains assessable under s 86. There therefore remains considerable sheltering potential for children's and grandchildren's settlements.

Benefiting from the trust

The above discussion has shown that an offshore accumulation and maintenance trust or, in certain circumstances, a discretionary trust can still be an effective shelter for income and gains. The question which then arises is how the beneficiaries will eventually enjoy the rolled-up funds. Many of the factors bearing on this issue are discussed in Chapter 18, but the main points are summarised here.

Non-resident beneficiary

The first and most important point to make is that if a recipient beneficiary is not resident or ordinarily resident in the UK at the time of receipt, anything he receives is free of income tax. It is also free of CGT unless the beneficiary subsequently takes up UK residence and the trust gains to match it do not accrue until he does so (cf p 224). Assuming the trust is an accumulation and maintenance trust or interests in possession have vested, any advance of funds is free of IHT as well. It follows from this that in general, offshore trusts should operate on the premise that substantial distributions will only be made to non-resident beneficiaries. Emigration to avoid tax is now more difficult, for under TCGA 1992, s 10A, a beneficiary must be non-resident for at least five complete tax years to avoid CGT (see Chapter 35). However, this does not apply to income tax, and so if the trust has accumulated income rather than capital gains, shorter-term emigration may be considered.

Income receipts

If a beneficiary is not going to go abroad, the best method of benefiting him is for him to receive income as it arises. Indeed with an accumulation and maintenance trust this necessarily happens once his interest in possession vests. In such a case, the beneficiary is liable to income tax as the income arises, and, since the income is treated as his, he can claim credit for any UK or foreign tax withheld in the country of source (ESC B18). Should he be paid income when he does not have an interest in possession, such will be in exercise of the trustees' discretion and the income will be a new source (cf p 8). In law the beneficiary will not be entitled to credit for any tax borne by the trust, but by concession he may claim such credit (ESC B18). The trustees do, however, have to file returns and pay the full trust rate of tax on any UK income.

Distributions to minor children of the settlor are taxed as the settlor's income (TA 1988, s 660B). The settlor may by concession be allowed credit for any UK tax suffered by the trust (ESC A93).

Capital receipts

Matters become altogether less satisfactory if a resident beneficiary receives capital. There are two overlapping codes, namely TA 1988, s 740 which treats the capital as income, and TCGA 1992, s 87 which taxes it as a capital gain. These codes are analysed in Chapters 22 and 26, and basically the position is this:

(1)   Section 740 applies if the motive defence described in Chapter 23 is not available and there is undistributed income in the trust of the current or

past years which has not previously been allocated to a payment. When it applies, the payment is taxed as income.

(2) To the extent that it is not so taxed it is taxed as income under s 87 as applied by TA 1988, s 762 to the extent that the trust has offshore income gains not allocated to capital payments in past years.

(3) To the extent that it is not taxed as income when made it is taxed as a capital gain if the trust has unallocated trust capital gains.

(4) To the extent that it is not so taxed under any of the above it is carried forward and taxed as income or gains as and when income or gains arise in future years. If both income and gains arise in one year, it is taxed as income insofar as there is income.

These rules mean that if resident beneficiaries benefit in capital form from an offshore trust, the trust operates only as a deferral. In fact there are three reasons why the overall effect is in general worse than a deferral. The first is that the rate of tax will normally be higher than if the trust had been resident, for it will normally be the 40% top-rate payable by individuals. This contrasts with the 34% rate payable by resident discretionary or accumulation and maintenance trusts and the 25% rate payable by such trusts in respect of foreign dividend income. Second, there will be no credit for withholding or other taxes suffered by the income or gains as they arose to the trust, for ESC B18 does not in these circumstances apply. Third and last, if the payment attracts CGT it may be subject to additional tax in respect of notional interest. This additional tax is described on pp 225–7 and can take the total rate of CGT on a payment to 64%.

For all these reasons capital distributions to resident beneficiaries tend to be expensive. On occasion the potential exposure can be limited by suitable planning (see Chapter 18) but the scope for this may be restricted. In general offshore trusts should only be contemplated as a shelter for income and gains on the following scenarios:

(1) Capital is unlikely to be distributed to UK residents, either because the likely recipients are already non-resident or because some at least are likely to become so. It should be remembered that if CGT is in issue five years non-residence is essential.

(2) As and when the beneficiaries are benefited, current income will be sufficient. Here the previous sheltering offshore will produce an enhanced fund to generate the income for it will have accumulated gross.

(3) In practice the trust will invest for income or in assets whose gain is treated as income. This ensures that any capital distribution is taxed at most at 40%, although here the contrast with a UK trust and the possible loss of double tax relief must be remembered.

Creating the settlement

Form of settlement

The form of any new offshore settlement is largely governed by the IHT and other considerations discussed above. It will normally be an accumulation and maintenance trust although a discretionary trust may sometimes be used. One point to watch with accumulation and maintenance trusts is that the beneficiaries should not take absolute interests whether on attaining the specified age or subsequently. If they do, such absolute entitlement will result in liability under TA 1988, s 740 and TCGA 1992, s 87 as respects any accumulated income or gains. The best form of settlement is as described above, namely one which confers life interests on the beneficiaries at the specified age, subject to overriding powers vested in the trustees which can be exercised with due regard to tax considerations.

Assets to be settled

The ideal asset to settle is cash, and the trustees being left to build up a portfolio of investments, which is outside the ambit of CGT from the outset. Another favourable situation is where the initial settlement is of assets not showing any gain, for example shares in a newly-formed private company. If these are put into a suitable form of non-resident trust when the company is formed, the whole gain on any sale or flotation may be deferred or avoided.

Problems arise where the assets which the settlor wishes to transfer to the trust are already pregnant with gain. Here a gift to a non-resident trust triggers an immediate charge to CGT, for no form of hold-over relief is available where the recipient is non-resident (TCGA 1992, ss 166 and 261). In these circumstances, therefore, a judgement has to be made on whether the tax advantages of the trust being offshore outweigh the immediate charge to CGT on the gain which has already accrued. For most taxpayers it does not.

At one time taxpayers could have their cake and eat it. This was possible if the circumstances were such that hold-over relief was available on a gift into a resident trust. Where this was so, the assets were transferred into what was called a 'freezer trust', a settlement which was initially resident and which qualified for hold-over relief. The gain was held over and then, in the year of assessment before the assets were sold, the trust migrated. The migration triggered a charge on the held-over gain (FA 1981, s 79), but the subsequent gain was relieved for, by the time it was realised, the trust was non-resident.

Unfortunately, proceeding in this way is no longer attractive for migration now occasions a deemed disposal of all the trust assets at market value. As is described in Chapter 36, any gain is taxed as the settlor's if he or his spouse are beneficiaries, and otherwise at the trust rate of 34%. The position now is that an offshore trust can only be a satisfactory shelter of gains accruing after it is created or, if initially resident, after it has migrated.

Trustee borrowing

Anybody creating or acting as trustee of an offshore settlement needs to be aware of the rules introduced by FA 2000 imposing a deemed disposal of all trust assets for CGT purposes in certain cases where there is outstanding trustee borrowing (TCGA 1992, Sch 4B). These rules are explained in Chapter 27. The best advice is that trustees should not borrow. Any settlement which is created on the premise that the trustees will borrow some of the funds should not be entered into unless the implications of TCGA 1992, Sch 4B have been given the most careful consideration.

Compliance

It is fundamental to offshore trusts that the settlor and beneficiaries disclose all relevant liabilities on their tax returns and that all reasonable information requested by the Revenue is supplied. It should not be forgotten that the Revenue have wide information gathering powers, notably TA 1988, s 745 (where liability under TA 1988, ss 739 and 740 is suspected) and TCGA 1992, s 98, and Sch 5 para 10 (which relate to CGT).

Compliance obligations arise when an offshore trust is set up. Thus a person making a non-resident settlement must, if he is resident and domiciled in the UK, make a return to the Revenue within three months giving details of the trustees and the date on which the settlement was made (TCGA 1992, Sch 5A para 3). If assets are settled, a CGT disposal may have to be notified, and if the value transferred to a discretionary settlement involves a chargeable transfer of more than £10,000 an account has to be delivered to the Capital Taxes Office (IHTA 1984, s 216; The CTT (Delivery of Accounts) (No 2) Regulations 1981 (SI 1981/1440)). Perhaps most important of all is the duty imposed on professional advisers by IHTA 1984, s 218. If a professional adviser is concerned with the making of a non-resident settlement by a UK domiciliary which has not otherwise been notified to the Capital Taxes Office, he must make a return, specifying the names and addresses of the settlor and the trustees.

Chapter 6

Offshore companies

Directly-owned companies

On the face of it, directly-owned offshore companies ought to be as effective as trusts in sheltering income and gains. As described in Chapter 1, all companies are separate fiscal entities, and accordingly foreign income and gains accruing to an offshore company should be free of UK tax. Indeed in one respect offshore companies have an advantage over offshore trusts, for, provided the UK individual owns the company, the transfer of assets to it normally has no IHT consequences, for there is no loss to his estate. In fact, however, directly-owned offshore companies have little or no role in offshore tax planning.

Company residence

One reason for this is company residence. As is explained in Chapter 4, the residence of foreign-registered companies is still determined by the central management and control test. Recent cases have indicated that if the board of the company do meet and give proper consideration to any transactions the company undertakes, such will constitute central management and control. But inevitably there is the risk that proper procedures will not be followed and in such cases the Revenue may argue that the company is run by the controlling shareholder in the UK. If they succeed in that contention the result is disastrous, for the company's gains and income are subject to corporation tax. That tax applies to all companies resident in the UK, whether UK or foreign registered. Furthermore, if the company is a pure investment company it is unlikely to qualify for the small companies rate of tax (TA 1988, s 13A).

The dangers in this area are emphasised by *R v Dimsey* [1999] STC 846. Here the Revenue brought a criminal prosecution inter alia on the basis that certain individuals had cheated the Crown of tax on the profits of directly-owned offshore companies which the Revenue claimed were resident in the UK. The case was an extreme one but the Revenue persuaded the jury that the companies were centrally controlled and managed here. The defendants were accordingly convicted.

Attribution of income

Even if the company is established as non-resident, TA 1988, s 739 applies to its income. As is described in Chapter 21, this section applies as much to companies as to trusts and indeed transfers of assets to offshore companies in return for shares or loan-stock were originally its prime target. The effect of the section applying is to deem the income accruing to the company to be that of the transferor shareholder.

Section 739 can be avoided if the UK individual buys the company replete with cash or if he gives all the shares away (see p 167). But the benefit of so avoiding s 739 is more apparent than real, for the income accruing to the company cannot reach any UK shareholders otherwise than by way of dividend or on a sale or liquidation. In the former event tax under Schedule D Case V is chargeable. In the latter event, any distribution in the liquidation is chargeable to income tax under TA 1988, s 740 to the extent that income has accrued to the company (cf Chapter 22) and otherwise CGT has to be considered. Indeed overall, tax may be increased for there will be no credit for withholding or other taxes suffered by the company as the income arose.

Apportionment of gains

A further issue with a directly-owned non-resident company is that gains are subject to apportionment under TCGA 1992, s 13. This section is analysed in Chapter 28. It was tightened up by FA 1996, s 174 and now requires the gains of any non-resident close company to be apportioned among the participators. CGT is charged on those who are resident and, in the case of individuals, domiciled in the UK.

The term 'participator' has the same meaning as for the purposes of the income tax close company legislation (TA 1988, s 417(1)). The apportionment is done by reference to the extent of the participator's interest in the company and is on a just and reasonable basis (s 13(13)). If the gain is distributed within two years, income tax or CGT on the distribution is offset by any CGT charged on the participator in respect of the apportioned gain (s 13(5A)).

Except where the distribution relief applies s 13 increases tax, for although the corporate gain is apportioned to the shareholders, its value remains reflected in the company's shares. Accordingly, it increases the potential gain on those shares, and while in computing that gain any tax paid under s 13 may be deducted (s 13(7)), this relief is far from complete. It is a deduction of tax from gain and not a deduction of gain from gain.

Techniques for avoiding the now strengthened s 13 are periodically bandied about. The most widely recognised is if the company is resident in a country with which the UK has concluded a double tax treaty giving the other country sole taxing rights over gains accruing to its residents. As is described on pp 242–3, the Revenue do accept this precludes a s 13 charge. However, for chargeable gains occurring after 21 March 2000, TCGA 1992, s 79B overrides this treaty protection insofar as trustees are the participants in the non-resident company (see further pp 242–3).

Benefits in kind

If the Revenue are able to establish that the shareholder is a shadow director of the company Schedule E tax will attach to any benefit in kind received by him or by his family (TA 1988, s 154). For these purposes his family includes his spouse and children (ibid, s 168(3), (4)). Many advisers took the view that the Schedule E charge could not apply unless the shadow director was in fact an employee of the company, but in *R v Dimsey* [1999] STC 846, the Court of Appeal held that it did. A recent case has given the term 'shadow director' a wider meaning than was once thought and there is now little doubt that if a controlling shareholder or his family in fact benefit from the company in a form which is not taxable, a Schedule E risk in inescapable. The subject is discussed further in Chapter 19.

Offshore companies owned by offshore trusts

If directly-owned offshore companies are rarely used in practice, offshore companies owned by offshore trusts are common. For the most part their popularity has nothing to do with tax. It is driven by the practical advantages of owning the trust investments through one or more wholly-owned offshore holding companies. The tax issues raised by the use of these holding companies are however of some complexity.

Company residence

As is explained on p 34, company residence is a lesser difficulty if the company is owned by a trust, for the only persons legally entitled to exercise shareholder control are the non-resident trustees. However, care needs to be taken to ensure that the company really is run by either the trustees or the directors, for if in fact they stand aside and let the settlor or beneficiaries give all the instructions, it could be contended that the company's residence is that of the settlor or beneficiaries. Such a contention is unlikely to be sustainable if the trust is being properly run but the Revenue would be entitled to advance it if the facts so warranted.

Attribution of income

If the settlor or his spouse are beneficiaries under the trust the question arises of whether the company's income can be attributed to him. Attribution is only possible under the settlement code in TA 1988, Part XV if the company's assets can be said to be 'property comprised in the settlement'. It is generally accepted that the company's assets are not so comprised on account of dicta by Lord Macmillan in *Chamberlain v IRC* (1943) 25 TC 317 at 331, which were approved in *Lord Vestey's Executors v IRC* (1949) 31 TC 1, HL. Lord Macmillan's words were as follows:

> 'the settlement or arrangement must be one whereby the settlor charges certain property of his with rights in favour of others. . . . it must comprise certain property which is the subject of the settlement; it must confer the income of the comprised property on others, for it is income so given to others that is to be treated as nevertheless the income of the settlor.'

But even if TA 1988, Part XV does not apply, s 739 does have to be addressed. As is described in Chapter 21, this section applies both where income becomes payable to a non-resident entity as a result of the transfer alone and where it becomes so payable as a result of the transfer and one or more associated operations (s 739(1)). As a result it can apply to holding company income, for the formation or vesting of assets in the settlement is the transfer and the incorporation and funding of the company are associated operations (cf *Corbett's Executrices v IRC* (1943) 25 TC 305).

Attribution of gains

If the trust gains are attributable to the settlor under TCGA 1992, s 86, the gains so attributable include any which would be apportioned to the trust under TCGA 1992, s 13 if the trust were resident (see pp 243–4). As a result, the company's gains are attributable to the settlor if trust gains are so attributable.

Benefits and capital payments

If the company's gains and income are not taxed as the settlor's on an arising basis, their taxability as and when UK resident beneficiaries receive benefits or capital payments from the trust has to be considered. In general, the position is the same as where income or gains arise directly to the trust, in that the company's income can be matched with benefits under TA 1988, s 740 and the company's gains with capital payments under TCGA 1992, s 87 (cf pp 183 and 244).

Benefits in kind

The risk of benefits in kind being taxed under Schedule E arises in the same way as with directly-owned companies, if either the settlor or a beneficiary can be said to be a shadow director. It used to be thought there was little risk in this area, for the most they can do is make requests to the trustees, it being up to the trustees to communicate with the directors if they think fit. Unfortunately, as is described in Chapter 19, a recent case has widened the definition of the term shadow director and on one view at least a settlor or beneficiary could be caught if the actual directors regularly take account of his views.

Tax disadvantages of a holding company

Company residence and benefits in kind

When trustees use a holding company it is necessary to worry about company residence and benefits in kind. If the trustees hold the investments directly, issues as to the central management and control of the company and shadow directors simply do not arise.

Tax credit

A holding company causes any credit for foreign tax on income arising to be lost. This is material only if the income is not attributed to the settlor and is being paid out as income to the beneficiaries. In such a case the beneficiary may be entitled to credit for foreign tax on income arising to the trust, either as life tenant because the income is deemed to be his or as a discretionary beneficiary under ESC B18. The advantage of this is lost if a company is interposed, for then the income paid to the beneficiary is simply the dividends paid by the company.

Double counting

Use of a company doubles up income and gains. This is a very serious problem in the context of the rules relating to benefits and capital payments. Income is relevant income in the company and can only reach the trust either as dividend, in which case it is again relevant income, or on the sale or liquidation of the company, in which case trust gains accrue. So too gains in the company which count as trust gains can only reach the trust as relevant income in the form of a dividend, or as further trust gains when the company is sold or liquidated. In practice the Revenue allow a measure of relief, but only in that they do not treat income paid up as dividend as relevant income more than once.

Double counting also has to be considered where the trust is within TCGA 1992, s 86. It does not arise if a gain realised by the company is distributed to the trust within two years, for TCGA 1992, s 13(5A) is wide enough to allow the settlor to set his CGT on the gain against CGT or income tax on the distribution (see p 244). But otherwise double-counting does exist. The limited relief in s 13(7) allowing the deduction of tax from subsequent gain does not apply to gains assessed on the settlor, for he is not deemed to make the disposal generating the subsequent gain.

Initially these problems of double-counting may be avoided by capitalising the company by loan. Money can accordingly reach the trust by loan repayment. But sooner or later the loan will be exhausted and then the tax implications of transferring the company's accumulated value to the trust have to be faced.

Loss of taper relief

For the purposes of s 13 the company's gains are computed with the benefit taper but without indexation (s 13(11A)). Now that inflation is low, indexation is less attractive than taper, particularly where the base cost of the asset is small or business taper applies. Gains accruing to the trustees, by contrast, are computed with the benefit of any applicable taper relief.

Unexpected capital payment

A somewhat technical problem to note is that a payment from the trustees to the company may count as a capital payment to UK resident individuals. The problem arises because a capital payment to a non-resident company counts as a capital payment to any UK resident individual who controls it (TCGA 1992, s 96). By concession, the problem does not arise if, as is normal, none of the shares in the company is owned by a UK individual (TCGA 1992, s 96(10); ESC D40). If, however, the settlor or a beneficiary owns some shares and the trust the rest, a non-arm's length payment from the trustees to the company does count as a capital payment to the settlor or beneficiary, for the trust holding is attributed to them in determining whether they control the company (TA 1988, s 417(3)(b), (c)).

Updated base cost on death

If the trust is an interest in possession trust, its assets receive a tax-free updated base cost for CGT purposes on the death of the life tenant (TCGA 1992, s 72), albeit often at the cost of an inheritance tax charge. Where investments are held through a holding company, the new base cost extends to the shares in the company but not to the underlying investments. This can be particularly unfortunate should the company vest in UK beneficiaries absolutely on the death of the life tenant, for then they will potentially be subject to tax on the historic gains of the company under TCGA 1992, s 13.

Trustee borrowing

Under TCGA 1992, Sch 4B, a loan from the company to the trust is trustee borrowing. If the trustees do not apply the loan for normal trust purposes, any subsequent distribution or loan by the trustees will trigger a complete or partial disposal of all the trust assets (see further Chapter 27).

A related risk arises if the trustees borrow money from another source and transfer it to the company. Here too there will be a deemed disposal unless the transfer is structured as a subscription for shares or securities in the company.

Tax advantages of a holding company

A holding company does bring one or two advantages, although in most cases it may be doubted whether these outweigh the drawbacks.

Section 739

One advantage of a holding company arises where the settlor is a beneficiary of the trust. Here the settlement code catches the trust income, but income in a company is only attributed to the settlor if s 739 applies. Section 739 can be avoided if the company is bought replete with investments and so here there is a structure in which the settlor can be a beneficiary without having income attributed to him on an arising basis. Value cannot, however, be passed to the settlor for otherwise liability under TA 1988, s 740 may arise (see Chapter 22).

UK assets

Where the trust has UK assets use of a company means that UK tax on dividends and interest is restricted to tax withheld rather than the rate for trusts which now stands at 34% (FA 1995, s 128). Exemption from UK tax obtains in respect of bank and building society interest in that such interest may be paid gross to an offshore company (TA 1988, s 481; Income Tax (Building Societies) (Dividends and Interest) Regulations 1990 (SI 1990/2231) reg 4(1)(g)).

In appropriate cases these may be real advantages, although it should be remembered that there are now plenty of offshore sterling bonds and deposits on which tax-free interest can be earned. A further point is that even if income is free of UK tax in the hands of the company, it is still taxable as the settlor's if s 739 applies, and otherwise is included in relevant income in the taxation of benefits.

Trustee borrowing

As explained in Chapter 27, borrowing by a holding company does not count as trustee borrowing for the purposes of TCGA 1992, Sch 4B. This means all the risks entailed in that schedule are avoided. As a result where borrowing is needed to pay for an investment, holding the investment through a company may be attractive. But this is subject to all the drawbacks of using a company noted above.

Chapter 7

Existing settlor – interested settlements

Introduction

Existing trusts created by UK domiciliaries are the subject of this and the next chapter. This chapter focuses on the classic offshore trust of the 1980s, namely the trust where the settlor is a beneficiary, often the life-tenant. These trusts were created during the period before 1991 when all gains realised by offshore trustees were free of tax on an arising basis. Mostly they were created as a CGT shelter and a great number still exist. Many have substantial realised or latent gains and this chapter discusses whether such settlements are worth retaining and, assuming they are, how UK tax may best be minimised. The next chapter considers the same issues in relation to settlements where the settlor is excluded but his children are not.

Tax treatment

Income tax and CGT

Settlements where the settlor or his spouse are actual or potential beneficiaries now confer no tax advantage. This is because income and gains in both the settlement and in any underlying holding company are assessed as the settlor's as they arise. Liability on income is under TA 1988, Part XV and s 739 (see p 42 and Chapter 21). Liability on offshore income gains is under s 739 as applied by TA 1988, s 762(5)(a) (see p 249). Liability on capital gains is under TCGA 1992, s 86 (see Chapter 24).

Inheritance Tax

Where the settlor is life tenant the trust assets are treated as his for IHT purposes (IHTA 1984, s 49). In the event of his death, the trust incurs liability to IHT at his estate rate save insofar as the trust assets are relieved from IHT by reliefs such as business property relief.

In the relatively rare cases where the settlor is only a discretionary beneficiary the settlement is liable to the IHT regime of ten-yearly and exit charges (IHTA 1984, ss 58–69). In addition the property is treated as comprised in the settlor's estate under the gift with reservation rules save insofar as it was settled before 18 March 1986 (FA 1986, s 102).

Accumulated gains

Settlor-interested trusts may have accumulated trust gains which become chargeable under TCGA 1992, s 87 insofar as capital is distributed to the settlor or to any other beneficiary who is resident and domiciled in the UK (see Chapter 26). Such is the position if the trust realised gains before 17 March 1998 and such gains have not previously been allocated to capital payments. In some cases the rate of tax may be as high as 64% (see pp 225–7). These trust gains include gains realised before 17 March 1998 in any underlying holding company (see p 219).

Terminating the settlement

Since settlor-interested trusts now confer no tax advantage, the primary tax planning issue for the trustees is whether the settlement should be wound up and the capital distributed to the settlor or another member of his family. On the face of it, this is an attractive course of action, for it enables the settlor or another member of his family to regain control of the assets and avoids the fees and costs chargeable by the trustee. But in reality there may be significant tax obstacles, specifically two:

(1) Unallocated gains realised before 17 March 1998 will be attributed to the recipient of the distribution insofar as he is resident and domiciled in the UK.
(2) There may be latent gains in the current assets, which will be charged on the settlor on an arising basis when the assets are sold or distributed in specie.

As a result of these two points, terminating the settlement only makes sense in the following situations:

(a) The settlement has neither unallocated trust gains realised before 17 March 1998 nor latent gains. In such a case there is no disadvantage in distributing the entire trust fund to the settlor or to other beneficiaries.
(b) There are no latent gains and the settlement is being terminated by distribution to one or more non-resident or non-domiciled beneficiaries. In such a case the unallocated trust gains are attributed to the distribution but not charged (pp 223–4). If the recipients have emigrated since 17 March 1998 they must remain non-resident for a least five complete tax years (see Chapter 35).
(c) There are no unallocated trust gains, and the latent gains are capital gains which can be held over on a distribution to a resident beneficiary. In the context of an offshore trust the principal contexts in which a hold-over claim may be made are if the trust is discretionary (IHTA 1984, s 260) or if the asset is shares in an unquoted trading company (ibid, s 165(2)(b). This is subject to the held-over gain coming into charge if the recipient emigrates within six years (Chapter 35).

It may also be possible to terminate the settlement without tax cost if there are no latent gains and the unallocated trust gains are less than the value of the trust fund. In that event an amount equal to the unallocated gains may be distributed to non-resident or non-domiciled beneficiaries in one tax year. This will wash out the gains, enabling a tax-free distribution of the balance of the capital in the next tax year. Such a strategy is not possible if there are latent gains, for terminating the trust will involve realising those gains, and the ensuing charge on the settlor.

In connection with these various strategies it should be remembered that if trust assets are held through a holding company, the latent gains to be considered include both those on the shares in the company and those on the company's investments (cf p 219). There is now no relief for gains distributed by the company within two years of being realised, although if the settlor is charged under TCGA 1992, s 85 on the corporate gains, such tax may be set against s 86 tax on any gain on the company shares if the latter are disposed of within the two year period (cf p 244).

Inheritance tax consequences

If the trust is wound up, any distribution to the settlor is without IHT consequences provided he is life tenant (IHTA 1984, s 49). IHT will also be avoided if, for example, the assets qualify for 100% business property relief (IHTA 1984, s 105(1)(bb)).

In cases where the settlor is life tenant and the distribution is to another beneficiary, the distribution will be a PET (IHTA 1984, s 3A), which means IHT will be avoided provided the settlor survives seven years. In general, a distribution to a beneficiary who is not the settlor is good IHT planning for it removes the property from his estate and avoids IHT provided he survives seven years.

Should the trust be discretionary, there could be an IHT charge of up to 6% on any distribution, depending on the value of the fund and how recent the last ten-year anniversary was (IHTA 1984, ss 65 and 69). If the recipient is not the settlor, there may also be a PET under the gift with reservation rules (FA 1986, s 102(4)).

Artificial schemes

In recent years, a number of aggressive schemes for avoiding the s 86 charge on latent gains have been marketed. None has been tested in the courts and all invite Revenue challenge and scrutiny. None should be undertaken without specialist and impartial advice.

In recent years, the best-known scheme was the flip-flop scheme. As is described in Chapter 27, this scheme was blocked by FA 2000, which inserted TCGA 1992, Sch 4B. However although Sch 4B is wide in its ambit (see Chapter 27) it is said not be comprehensive enough to block all such schemes.

Other tax planning possibilities

The likelihood is that existing trust gains or latent gains will make termination of the trust unattractive. In that event two other options may be considered:

(1) Immigration to the UK.
(2) Exclusion of the settlor.

Immigration

Immigration of the trust to the UK is achieved by the offshore trustees retiring in favour of UK trustees (cf Chapter 36). It brings little advantage, for the trust income and gains remain attributed to the settlor (TA 1988, s 660A; TCGA 1992, s 77). Indeed there is one drawback, namely that gains are locked into charge, for the trust cannot subsequently leave the UK without a deemed disposal of all its then assets at market value (TCGA 1992, s 80; see Chapter 36). If the trust remains offshore, CGT on an arising basis is avoided should the settlor die or emigrate.

Exclusion of the settlor

Exclusion of the settlor is more attractive from a tax standpoint, although it may not commend itself to the settlor. If the settlor and his spouse alone are excluded, the trust's foreign income ceases to be assessable as his, but not the gains. To avoid attribution of gains, the settlor's children and their spouses have to be excluded as well (see p 200) and unless the grandchildren are also excluded, tainting since 17 March 1998 must be avoided (see Chapter 25). If after the exclusion the trust is fixed-interest, any income tax advantage may be illusory as the trust income will be assessable on the new life tenant (see pp 7–8). If therefore the children are to remain as beneficiaries, real tax advantage can only be obtained if the trust in accumulation and maintenance or discretionary form.

Exclusion of the settlor should not be effected by the settlor realising or assigning his life interest, for such is a disposal of the interest on which any gain is chargeable (TCGA 1992, s 85). Market value will normally be substituted and while in most cases overriding powers by trustee will render this nominal, such will not always be so. The prudent course of action is for the exclusion to be effected by the trustees in exercise of powers conferred on them. If they have no such powers the chances are the settlor's interest does have value and the exercise should not be attempted at all.

Should exclusion of the settlor appear attractive, IHT must be considered. Assuming the settlor has a life interest, termination of the interest is a PET if the new trusts are fixed interest or accumulation and maintenance. But if the trust becomes discretionary there will be an immediate charge to IHT, save insofar as the value is within the settlor's nil-rate band or the assets qualify for relief such as 100% business property relief.

Inaction

When all is said and done, the decision will often be to leave the trust as it is. Although the trust has no tax advantages now, inaction does bring one useful result. Assuming the settlor is life tenant all gains then realised will be eliminated on his death for on the death of the life tenant the assets in the trust are rebased without charge to tax (TCGA 1992, s 72).

It is true that unless an IHT exemption applies the death of the settlor will result in a charge to that tax. But this is no different to the trust assets being owned by the settlor outright. The advantage of the trust being retained is that once the settlor is dead assessment of the income and gains on an arising basis ceases. This would not be the position if the settlor owned the assets personally and they passed to his family on death.

A point to remember if the settlement is retained is the new rules in TCGA 1992, s 4B relating to the trustee borrowing and transfers of value. Should these be breached there will be a deemed disposal of the trust assets with gains attributed to the settlor. The best way of avoiding risk is to avoid trustee borrowing, including borrowing from any underlying company. These issues are discussed in Chapter 27.

If the settlement is retained, there is no particular tax reason to invest for income as against gains or vice versa, for both income and gains are taxed on an arising basis. However investment in roll-up funds is best avoided for such can result in doubling up of tax (pp 248–50).

A final point is that as noted on p 55, holding investments through a holding company can double up tax. Holding companies should therefore only be used after careful consideration. It is a matter of judgement as to whether existing companies should be wound up, but in general commonsense indicates this should only be considered where such will not trigger liability on latent gains. There may be some case for making new investments outside the company, but only if such can be done without borrowing from the company or another source.

Chapter 8

Existing children's settlements

Introduction

This chapter considers tax planning strategies for existing settlements where the settlor and his spouse are wholly excluded or are dead, but their children are beneficiaries. Most such settlements were created before 1991, when the present rules as to the attribution of gains to the settlor where enacted (see Chapter 24). As with all chapters in this Part it is assumed the settlor is or was resident and domiciled in the UK.

Tax treatment

Capital gains tax

The gains of the settlement are assessable as the settlor's provided he and his spouse are completely excluded (see Chapter 24). An exception is made where the settlement is a protected settlement but this is of little significance in practice (see p 202).

Income tax and IHT

The settlement may be discretionary in which case it is subject to the IHT regime of 10-yearly and exit charges. Unrestricted accumulation of income is normally possible and, as the settlor is excluded, such income is free of UK tax save insofar as it has a UK source.

The more normal settlement (see p 41) is an accumulation and maintenance trust insofar as the beneficiaries are under 25 and otherwise the beneficiaries are likely to have interests in possession. Such settlements are free of IHT exposure save that the trust property is treated as comprised in the estate of any life tenant (IHTA 1984, s 49). Income sheltering is possible during the accumulation and maintenance phase, but thereafter it ceases for the income is treated as that of the life tenant.

Offshore income gains are not assessed as the settlor's on an arising basis, for such only occurs if the settlor or his spouse are beneficiaries (pp 247–8).

Distributions

Income distributions from a discretionary or an accumulation and maintenance trust to a UK resident beneficiary are taxed as income as a new source under

Schedule D Case V. The tax which distributions of capital attract is as follows:

(1)   A distribution attracts income tax under TA 1988, s 740 insofar as the motive defence described in Chapter 23 is not available and income has been accumulated in the trust or any underlying company (see Chapter 22).

(2)   If s 740 is not in point, a distribution is subject to income tax insofar as the settlement or any underlying company has offshore income gains which have not previously been allocated to capital payments (see pp 248–50). Offshore income gains are taken into account whether accruing pre or post 17 March 1998.

(3)   Once any offshore income gains have been accounted for, a distribution attracts CGT insofar as trust gains realised before 17 March 1998 have not been allocated to the capital payments (cf Chapter 26). Here notional interest means the rate of tax may be as high as 64%.

Reimbursement of the settlor

The assessment of capital gains on the settlor creates an important practical issue, namely that although he bears the tax, the benefit of the gain accrues to the trust, from which he and his spouse are excluded. There is a statutory right of reimbursement (TCGA 1992, Sch 5 para 6) but as this is merely a right conferred by an English statute, it is far from clear it is enforceable against a trust governed by foreign law. The issue is discussed in Chapter 24, and, if the statutory right is not enforceable, the trustees may simply be unable to reimburse the settlor. Some settlors may as a result face ruin.

Avoiding CGT exposure

The major issue for the trustees is how to avoid the assessment of the trust gains on the settlor. If the settlor can be reimbursed such tax is a burden on the trust, and if he cannot there is potential for acute family difficulty.

The possible solutions are the same as those canvassed for settlor-interested settlements, namely:

(1)   Terminate the settlement by distribution to beneficiaries.
(2)   Immigrate the settlement to the UK.
(3)   Exclude the children and their spouses so that TCGA 1992, s 86 no longer applies.

Winding up the settlement

Terminating the settlement raises the same difficulties as apply with settlor-interested settlements (see Chapter 8). The termination will trigger the realisation of latent capital gains in the trust and any underlying company, assessable on the settlor. The ensuing distributions will be taxable to the extent of any hitherto unallocated relevant income, offshore income gains, or pre 17 March 1998 capital gains. Terminating the settlement is unlikely to be appropriate save where the trust fund is distributed to non-residents, or where there are neither latent gains nor unallocated past gains or accumulated income.

Immigration

If the settlement moves to the UK the assessment of gains on the settlor on an arising basis is avoided for the gains of a resident settlement are not assessed on the settlor unless he or his spouse are beneficiaries or receive a benefit (TCGA 1992, s 77). The gains are still in charge, but assessed directly on the trustees at the 34% rate for trusts (TCGA 1992, s 4(1AA)).

Immigration does however have drawbacks:

(1)   Assessment of the gains on an offshore trust on the settlor on an arising basis ceases once the settlor is dead. If the trust is UK resident, the gains are locked into charge regardless of whether the settlor is dead or alive.
(2)   The ability to accumulate foreign income tax free is lost, for the retained income of UK trusts is fully taxable (TA 1988, s 686).

These drawbacks will, in general, render immigration unattractive. But a compromise could be as follows:

(1)   In year one, all the trust assets which are not showing a latent gain are transferred to a new offshore settlement.
(2)   In year two, the trustees of the original settlement are replaced by UK trustees, who then realise the latent gains.

The advantage of this solution is that assessment of the existing latent gains on the settlor is avoided, while leaving at least some assets offshore. Any pre-1998 trust gains or offshore income gains will be apportioned to the trusts pro rata (see pp 218–9 and 248–9). The treatment of accumulated income for the purposes of TA 1988, s 740 when some assets are transferred to another trust is of some complexity and is discussed in Chapter 22

Excluding the children

The attractiveness of excluding the children and their spouses turns largely on family considerations. Normally it is possible for the grandchildren to remain as beneficiaries. But this is not so if the settlement was made after 17 March 1998 and it is also precluded with settlements before then if they have since become tainted (cf Chapter 25).

As with immigration consideration may be given to splitting the trust. The following steps are involved:

(1)   In year one, those assets not showing a latent gain are transferred to a new trust of which the children are beneficiaries.
(2)   Thereafter, but also in year one, the children and their spouses are excluded from the original trust.
(3)   In year two or subsequent years, the gains in the original trust are realised, assessment on the settlor then being precluded.

Retaining the trust as it is

Should none of the above strategies prove appropriate the trustees will be faced with leaving the trust as it is. In this event they may take some comfort from the following points:

(1)   Assessment of gains on the settlor on an arising basis ceases if he emigrates or dies.
(2)   In the event that one or more beneficiaries has a life interest under the trust, tax-free rebasing on their death(s) will be available (TCGA 1992, s 72). In appropriates cases, and with due regard to IHT considerations, the appointment of life interests could be considered.

If the trust is left as it is, the potential impact of gains being assessed on the settlor on an arising basis may be able to be minimised by selecting appropriate investments. This topic is discussed on p 45, and appropriate investments include investments principally yielding income, investments such as gilts which are exempt from CGT and investments such as roll-up funds where the capital gain is deemed to be income. Switching to such investments is attractive where the existing assets are showing few or modest latent gains. But this option will not be so helpful if the bulk of the trust fund is already invested in assets showing a substantial latent gain.

   Another matter to consider if the trust is left as it is any underlying holding company. As is explained in Chapter 6, these can have significant tax drawbacks, and so consideration should be given to dispensing with any such company if this can be done without triggering undue liability on latent gains.

Distributions

A second and perhaps equally important issue faced by the trustees of a children's trust is how to make tax-efficient distributions. The relevant issues are discussed in Chapter 18. The one point of difference is that if in fact gains are assessed as the settlor's, such gains will not need to be considered as trust gains in relation to distributions.

Other tax points

At the end of Chapter 18, a number of tax traps for existing settlements are listed. Although listed in relation to settlements where neither income nor gains are assessed on the settlor most are relevant to children's settlements of the kind described here. All are relevant and indeed Chapter 18 as a whole is relevant if the settlement remains offshore and assessment of gains on the settlor on an arising basis is avoided by one or other of the means described above.

Chapter 9

Investment products

Two investment products offer scope for offshore sheltering, namely life assurance and offshore funds. Both are the subject of anti-avoidance legislation,
described in Chapters 29 and 30, and in general both are far from the bespoke
structuring described previously in this part. They are normally inappropriate for
shares in private companies, real estate, and other one-off assets. But they merit
consideration where what is desired is tax-efficient portfolio investment.

Offshore funds

Offshore funds are offshore collective investment vehicles. They take the form
either of a unit trust with a non-resident trustee or a non-resident open-ended
company. In practice many international investment institutions encourage
investment through their managed funds rather than on a bespoke basis and
mutual funds are therefore of great importance.

General tax position

For CGT purposes any offshore fund is deemed to be a company. This is because
if it is an open-ended company it is a company and if it is a unit trust it is
deemed to be a company, the rights of the unit holders being deemed to be
shares (TCGA 1992, s 99).

For income tax purposes an open-ended company is simply a non resident
company. A offshore fund in unit trust form is not, however, a company, for that
treatment is only accorded to authorised unit trusts (TA 1988, s 468). Nor does
TA 1988, s 469 deem the offshore unit trust to be a separate fiscal entry, for that
section applies only to resident unit trusts. Instead the income tax treatment of
an offshore unit trust is governed by common-law principles, and the key issue
is whether or not it is transparent, ie whether the income of the fund is treated as
the income of the unit holders on an arising basis, or whether it is the income of
the trustees as a separate entity, any distributions to beneficiaries being a new
source. This issue falls to be determined by the principles described on pp 7–8 in
relation to trust income, namely whether or not each unit holder has a specific
equitable interest in each underlying investment or at least in the income each
produces. But assuming the underlying investments are pooled, the unit holders
do not have such specific rights in each investment and if so, under the test in
the *Archer Shee* cases, the income of the fund is not that of the unit holders.

Anti-avoidance legislation

One anti avoidance code, and one only, is targeted at offshore mutual funds, namely the offshore fund legislation in TA 1988, ss 757–64. This legislation is described in Chapter 29. It was first enacted in 1984 when the top rate of income tax was 75% and capital gains were taxed at 30%. It applies to what are called non qualifying offshore funds and deems the gain realised on the disposal of an interest in such a fund to be income. What it does not do is deem an apportioned part of the income of the fund to be that of the investor on an arising basis.

A non-qualifying offshore fund is any mutual fund which is not certified by the Revenue as having distributor status. As is described in Chapter 29, a fund can have distributor status if it pays out at least 85% of its income as income or if its income is nil or less than 1% of the average value of its assets. If it has distributor status it is only subject to the anti-avoidance legislation described in Chapter 29 insofar as the proceeds of any sale include an equalisation element.

No CGT anti avoidance legislation is specifically targeted at offshore mutual funds. However if the fund would be a close company if it were resident in the UK it falls within TCGA 1992, s 13 (see Chapter 28). This follows because it is in fact a company or it is a unit trust which is deemed to be one. As such gains can be apportioned to participators. In practice this is not an issue with the quoted funds bought by portfolio investors which are the primary subject of this chapter. The point does however arise with certain types of small fund.

Distributor funds

Since it distributes its income, a distributor fund offers no income sheltering possibilities. However, assuming s 13 is not in point it does enable any gains in the fund to be deferred. But this advantage is more apparent than real, for gains in the onshore equivalent are similarly exempt. Under TCGA 1992, s 100, gains realised by authorised unit trusts and investment trusts are exempt, as are those in open-ended investment companies (SI 1997/1154, reg 5).

Non-qualifying offshore funds

Investment in a non-qualifying offshore fund brings two income tax advantages:

(1)   There is a deferral in that the income in the fund is rolled-up tax-free and is not charged on the investor unless and until he disposes of his interest.

(2)   The deferral is converted into avoidance if by the time of realisation the individual has become non-resident. As the gain is income, the CGT rule that the individual must be non-resident for at least five complete tax years does not apply.

A non-qualifying fund operates as a CGT deferral, in the same way as a distributor fund, thereby postponing any charge until realisation. But the deferral carries a price inter alia for two reasons:

(a)   The gain charged on realisation is an income gain, so is neither tapered nor indexed. Had the investor held the assets directly any gains would have enjoyed those reliefs.

(b) On death there is a deemed disposal, and the gain then accruing is charged (TA 1988, s 757(3)). There is no tax-free updated base cost.

The practical result of the above points is that if the growth in a non-qualifying fund is capital rather than income, the tax treatment can be unattractive. However, it should be noted that the tax on gains is still deferred until the investor sells out of the fund and may be avoided if he becomes non-resident before then.

Non-qualifying offshore funds can be a useful investment for offshore trusts. This is because, as described in previous chapters, the tax regime for income is less severe than that for gains and accordingly any regime which turns capital gains into income is attractive. This subject is discussed on pp 45 and 46 and the technical detail of how offshore income gains accruing to offshore trust are taxed is explained on pp 248–50.

Life assurance

To the uninitiated, it may appear surprising that life assurance is an investment vehicle and still more so that it offers a means of offshore sheltering. However, the fact remains that it does. The reason is that for many years the sum payable on the maturity or surrender of certain kinds of policy has been with profits or unit linked. Where a policy is with profits the policyholder shares in the profits of the life office, usually in the form of bonuses credited to the policy annually. Where the policy is unit-linked, the sum payable on maturity or surrender is linked to the performance of an underlying fund. Units in the fund are allocated to the policy and the value of those units determines the amount payable.

In substance, unit-linked policies resemble a managed portfolio of investments. Indeed it is possible for a policy to be linked solely to its own fund, and for that fund to be managed by the policyholder or his authorised investment adviser. Such policies are known as personal portfolio bonds. They proved provocative to the Revenue, in that they sought to tax the income of the fund under TA 1988, s 739 (see Chapter 21). They unsuccessfully took a case to the House of Lords (*IRC v Willoughby* [1997] STC 995) and then, having lost, introduced punitive anti-avoidance legislation (FA 1998, s 89; see Chapter 30). This legislation means that personal portfolio bonds should be avoided unless they fall within the exceptions to that legislation described on pp 256–7.

Whatever the apparent substance, the legal reality of insurance products is that the policyholder owns not a portfolio of investments but merely a right in contract against the life office. Should the life office become insolvent, the policyholder is simply an unsecured creditor. Failure to appreciate this was one of the reasons why the Revenue lost in *IRC v Willoughby*.

Offshore life policies are policies issued by an offshore life office which does not trade in the UK. Their tax advantage flows from the fact that, being non-resident, the life office is not subject to UK tax. This means that the profits backing the policy can potentially accrue tax free. The UK tax legislation counters these advantages by modifying the general rules applicable to life policies (TA 1988, ss 539–554). The relevant legislation is described in Chapter 30, but it does leave certain planning opportunities.

Deferral

The basic attraction of life policies which are not personal portfolio bonds is the same as with offshore funds, namely deferral. Under the anti-avoidance legislation described in Chapter 30, the policyholder pays tax only when the policy matures or he takes a surrender or assignment. The charge is to income tax, but there is no notional interest to counter the deferral, and the tax is avoided altogether if the policyholder has become non-resident.

As with offshore funds, life policies are not so attractive from a CGT stand-point, for the gain on the policy is an income gain with no taper, and there is no tax-free uplift on death. But it remains the case that the fund backing the policy is a gross fund, thereby securing deferral of gains.

Partial withdrawals

A unique feature of the tax regime for life policies is that a partial surrender equal to up to 5% of the premium may be taken tax-free each year (see pp 253–4). The ability to take such surrenders is often referred to as the ability to take tax-free 'income'. In fact it is a misnomer to say that the 5% sur-renders are tax-free because the amount of the surrender is deducted in comput-ing the base cost when the policy matures or is sold or surrendered. Strictly therefore, it is only another form of deferral, and it is also true that once the total of tax-free partial surrenders equals the premium, future partial surrenders are immediately chargeable to tax. But the deferral does become avoidance if by the time the policy matures or is surrendered, the holder is non-resident. For the pol-icyholder who is considering emigration, a life policy does in a sense offer tax-free 'income' before emigration and tax-free proceeds thereafter.

Death

Another important point about the life policy code is that if the policy matures on death, the gain charged is not the difference between the proceeds and the base cost, but between the base cost and the surrender value immediately prior to death. Accordingly, if the surrender value is modest, as it may be where there is a significant element of life cover, substantial tax-free gains can accrue. This may be particularly significant where the base cost has been eroded by 5% withdrawals.

At one time the gain on the maturity of a life policy was tax free if the policy was held in trust and the settlor was already dead. But now if the settlor is dead, the gain on a policy in trust is subject to tax at the rate for trusts if the trust is UK resident. If it is non-resident, the gain is treated as relevant income for the purposes of TA 1988, s 740 (see pp 254–5).

Comparison with offshore trusts

Investments in life policies or non-distributing offshore funds offer the following advantages over a private offshore trust:

(a) An offshore trust cannot achieve a tax-free roll-up of income and gains unless the creator of the trust is wholly excluded. An individual can achieve a tax-free roll-up through a fund or life policy and still be able to take the proceeds at the end.
(b) Even where an offshore trust does operate as a tax-free roll-up, tax on any eventual distribution can be increased by the CGT supplemental tax (pp 225–7). There is no equivalent with an offshore fund or life policy.
(c) The 5% withdrawals from life policies allow the tax deferral to extend to some proceeds in the hands of the investor.
(d) As standard commercial investments, offshore funds and life policies may be less provocative to the Revenue and carry lower compliance costs.

The drawbacks include the following:

(i) A trust enables assets to be tied up for several generations. A life policy ends when it matures and an interest in an offshore fund is simply an asset which has to be given away or bequeathed or otherwise dealt with.
(ii) With a life policy or offshore fund, normally the only income and gains able to be sheltered is that from portfolio investments. Private company shares, land, and other one-off assets cannot generally be used.
(iii) The funds backing a life policy or in an offshore fund are managed by or on behalf of the life office or manager. The investor normally cannot use his personal choice of investment adviser, although in the case of a life policy the life office may in practice appoint the policyholder's recommended manager.
(iv) The overall charges involved in life assurance and offshore funds are often high and may be opaque.

Part three

Non-domiciliaries

Chapter 10

Domicile

Introduction

Domicile is a legal status whose primary role is as a connecting factor. It determines whether English or some foreign law regulates personal relationships, eg marriage, legitimacy and succession. Domicile has been adopted by the UK tax system as a factor limiting the UK tax jurisdiction but it should be remembered that it is a general legal concept, and not one created merely for tax purposes.

An individual can have only one domicile at any time: a domicile of origin; a domicile of choice; or a domicile of dependency. The place in which an individual is domiciled is not necessarily a nation in a political sense, but any geographical area governed by a single system of law (*Re Fuld's Estate (No 3)* [1968] P 675 at 682–684). Thus an individual is domiciled in 'England' or 'Scotland', rather than in 'the United Kingdom' and in one of the several states which make up such federal countries as Australia or the United States.

The concept of domicile evolved in relation to individuals and for tax purposes is material only in relation to individuals. It has been held that a company has a domicile where it is registered, but no aspect of corporate tax liability turns on domicile (cf *Gasque v IRC* (1940) 23 TC 210).

Domicile of origin

An individual acquires a domicile of origin when he is born (*Henderson v Henderson* [1967] P 77, [1965] 1 All ER 179). Normally, this is his father's domicile at the date of his birth, but if his parents are unmarried, it is the mother's domicile. A domicile of origin continues unless and until the individual acquires either a domicile of dependency or a domicile of choice: upon his acquiring one or other, that will remain his domicile until abandoned. If it is abandoned without another domicile of choice or dependency being acquired, the domicile of origin revives (*Udny v Udny* (1869) LR 1 Sc & Div 441).

A person's domicile of origin is often described as having an adhesive quality, although the recent case of *Bheekhun v Williams* [1998/99] 1 ITELR 491 has raised doubt as to how far this is so. The reasons why the domicile of origin is said to be adhesive are twofold. First, the burden is on whoever alleges a person has acquired a domicile of choice to prove it. Second, although the standard of proof is the civil standard it is variously said either that the burden is heavy (*Winnans v AG* [1904] AC 287, 291) or that the acquisition of a domicile of choice is regarded as a serious matter, not to be lightly inferred from slight indications or casual words (*Re Fuld's Estate (No 3)* [1968] P 675 at 684; *Buswell v IRC* [1974] STC 266, [1974] 2 All ER 520). It is this second point that is called into question by *Bheekhun v Williams*, for while the Court of Appeal affirmed that the burden of proof is on the person who alleges a change of domicile it weighed the evidence in the case on the ordinary civil balance of probabilities.

Domicile of choice

An individual can only acquire a domicile of choice if he is over 16. The classic formulation of the test was given by the Court of Appeal in *IRC v Bullock* [1976] STC 409, [1976] 3 All ER 353). He must voluntarily fix his sole or chief residence in a new territory and intend to remain there for the rest of his days, unless and until something occurs to make him change his mind. As will be apparent, this formulation makes it hard for anyone to prove an individual has acquired a domicile of choice if he asserts to the contrary.

In *Fuld v IRC* [1968] P 675 Scarman J said, in a much-quoted passage, that the test is whether the individual intends to reside in the new country 'indefinitely' or for an 'unlimited time'. These are looser terms than the formulation in *Bullock*, but, as was recognised in *Bheekhun v Williams*, *Bullock* explicitly clarified them.

Once a domicile of choice is acquired, it is relatively difficult to abandon. It is only abandoned if the individual both ceases to reside in the country of choice and ceases to intend to reside there permanently or indefinitely (*Re Flynn, Flynn v Flynn* [1968] 1 All ER 49, [1968] 1 WLR 103; *IRC v Duchess of Portland* [1982] STC 149, [1982] Ch 314). Normally loss of one domicile of choice is the occasion of the acquisition of another. This is not necessarily so, and if not, the domicile of origin revives.

Residence

It is to be stressed that the acquisition or abandonment of a domicile of choice involves the fact of residence as well as an intention. For these purposes it is clear that a residence only counts if it is the person's sole or chief residence. Thus in *Plummer v IRC* [1987] STC 698, [1988] 1 All ER 97, a young lady who intended to reside permanently in Guernsey did not acquire a domicile of choice there because her chief residence was in England, her home in Guernsey being on the facts merely secondary. So too in *IRC v Duchess of Portland* [1982] STC 149, a lady failed to abandon an English domicile of choice because, although she did not intend to remain permanently in England, her chief residence was here.

Intention

A person only acquires a domicile of choice in the new country if his intention to remain there is firm and settled (*Re Clore (No 2)* [1984] STC 609). It is frequently difficult to tell whether he has the requisite intention. But in *IRC v Bullock* [1976] STC 409, the Court of Appeal stated that this test is not satisfied if the person would return to the country of his origin on the happening of a certain and definite contingency. Such contingencies include retirement, the attainment of a specified age, inheritance of a title, or the earlier death of a spouse. Such contingencies would also, it may be suggested, include a change in government if there is a realistic possibility of that happening. Acquisition of a domicile of choice is not, however, precluded if the person merely says he would return to his country of origin when he has made his fortune, when he has had enough of the new territory or when his health fails (*Re Furse* [1980] STC 596). If these are contingencies at all, they are too remote and doubtful.

In determining whether an individual has the requisite intention all that he has said and done must be looked at. The task which has to be undertaken was described in graphic terms by Megarry J in *Re Flynn* [1968] 1 WLR 103 at 107:

> 'In one sense there is no end to the evidence that may be adduced; for the whole of a man's life and all that he has said and done, however trivial, may be prayed in aid in determining what his intention was at any given moment in time. The state of a man's mind is as much a fact as the state of his digestion, but, as Harman LJ is reputed to have observed, "the doctors know precious little about the one and the judges know nothing about the other". The difficulty is as old as the Year Books and the celebrated dictum of Brian CJ in 1477, uttered in theological terms which have waned in fashion: "*Le diable n'ad conusance de l'entent de home*". All that the courts can do is to draw inferences from what has been said and done; and in doing this, too much detail may stultify.'

Statements the person has made are not necessarily conclusive in determining whether he has acquired a domicile of choice. Thus in *Wahl v A-G* (1932) 147 LT 382, HL, a German applied for British naturalisation and stated to the Home Secretary he intended to reside permanently in the UK and had no intention of leaving it. This, however, was held to be insufficient to displace other evidence that a domicile of choice had not been acquired. Statements to the Revenue that the individual intends to remain indefinitely in the UK are not conclusive as to domicile either. Nor even are statements in an Inland Revenue affidavit that the deceased was UK domiciled if there is no evidence the issue had been properly considered by the person swearing the affidavit (*Buswell v IRC* [1974] STC 266; *Re Furse* [1980] STC 596).

The acquisition of nationality and a passport in the new country can point to the acquisition of a domicile of choice there but is not conclusive evidence. Thus in *Bheekhun v Williams* [1998/99] 1 ITELR 491 the deceased was a Mauritian who had come to the UK in 1960, and chose to retain a British passport when Mauritius became independent in 1968. The trial judge and the Court of Appeal accepted evidence that the deceased was then considering staying here all the time and concluded he had acquired a UK domicile of choice. In *F v IRC* [2000] STC (SCD) 1 by contrast, an Iranian exile with long-standing UK connections, including a UK home, obtained indefinite leave to remain in the UK in 1980 and British citizenship and a passport in 1982. On the evidence he intended always to return to Iran when it was safe to do so, and had acquired a British passport merely for travel convenience. On these facts, a Special Commissioner found he retained his Iranian domicile.

Domicile of dependency

A domicile of dependency can be attributed only to a child under 16. A child's domicile of origin is displaced by a domicile of dependency if the domicile of the parent upon whom the child's domicile depends changes. If this happens the domicile of choice, which the parent thereby acquires, becomes the child's domicile of dependency. On attaining 16 a domicile of dependency is retained by the child as a domicile of choice. But if the child does not live in the territory and never intends to live there, this acquired domicile of choice is forthwith abandoned. Normally in these circumstances the child's domicile of origin revives but if he is living in a third territory with the intention of remaining there, that territory becomes his domicile of choice (*Re Scullard's Estate* [1956] 3 All ER 898).

The domicile on which a child under 16 normally depends is that of his father, but his mother's domicile is the relevant domicile if the child is illegitimate, the father is dead, or the parents are separated and the child has no home with the father (see Law Commission report on the Law of Domicile, Cmnd 200 (1987) pp 4–5).

Until 1974, a married woman did not enjoy an independent domicile but took her husband's domicile as a domicile of dependency. This rule was abolished in 1973 (Domicile and Matrimonial Proceedings Act 1973, s 1). A married woman's domicile is now determined independently in the same way as that of her husband. But a woman who on 1 January 1974 had her husband's domicile, as a domicile of dependency, retained that domicile as a domicile of choice and must abandon it before she can acquire, or reacquire, her own domicile (*IRC v Duchess of Portland* [1982] STC 149, [1982] Ch 314).

Establishing an individual's domicile

In practical terms it is frequently important for a taxpayer to establish with the Revenue what his domicile is. In many cases it is necessary to do this before entering into a particular transaction, for the domicile of the taxpayer will affect the form the transaction takes.

Retaining a foreign domicile of origin

If the issue is whether a UK resident with a foreign domicile of origin has acquired a UK domicile of choice, the matter may be tested by ensuring that the taxpayer has some unremitted foreign income. As is described in Chapter 13 such income is not taxable unless the taxpayer is UK domiciled. Claims for non-domiciliary treatment should be made on form DOM 1, form P86 or on the individual's tax return. If a claim is made prior to the submission of the return the Revenue will respond with a ruling (*Tax Bulletin* 29 (June 1997) 425). If a claim is made on an individual's tax return, it will be conclusive as respects the year of the return provided the information given is not misleading and the Revenue do not raise an enquiry within the year following the 31 January deadline for submission of the return. The taxpayer's domicile is of course at large in future years if the Revenue enquire into the returns for those years.

In practical terms, the best way of substantiating a claim that the taxpayer does not intend to remain in the UK indefinitely is if he keeps a home or other property in his country of origin. Property in the country of origin is not however conclusive if other evidence clearly points to the acquisition of a domicile of choice in the UK (*Bheekhun v Williams* [1998/99] 1 ITELR 491). Another important practical step is that the taxpayer makes a will under the law of the country of origin, for if that country is indeed his domicile, its law governs the devolution of his estate. It also helps if it is his wish to be buried there (*Anderson v IRC* [1998] STC (SCD) 43).

Acquiring a foreign domicile of choice

The contrary situation is where a UK domiciliary migrates and wishes to establish a foreign domicile of choice. In this situation the Revenue will not give a hypothetical ruling, and so the best solution is for the taxpayer to wait until three complete tax years have elapsed and then make a gift in excess of the IHT nil-rate band to a discretionary trust.

It is necessary to wait for three complete tax years because, for IHT purposes, a UK domicile is deemed to persist for three years after it is in fact lost and is retained if the taxpayer has been resident in the UK in 17 of the last 20 years of assessment (see pp 119–20). The gift has to be to a discretionary trust, for otherwise it will be a PET. Provided such a gift consists of foreign situs assets, IHT will be chargeable unless the taxpayer has lost both his actual and his deemed UK domicile. Accordingly, if in fact the Revenue do not seek to charge IHT, it will be clear that they accept he has acquired a foreign domicile.

In practical terms, the Revenue are prepared to accept that migrants from the UK have acquired a foreign domicile if the facts warrant this. One point, however, is vital. Once the three year period has elapsed, the foreign domicile of the taxpayer should be established immediately. This safeguards the position if, later, the taxpayer has to return to the UK for medical or other reasons, for, once he has returned, it will be very difficult to prove he intended to remain abroad indefinitely.

Proposals for change

In 1987, the Law Commission proposed changes to the law of domicile (Cmnd 200), but so far no action has been taken to implement these proposals. The proposals were enshrined in a draft bill, the main points of which were as follows:

(1) The domicile of origin should be abolished.
(2) A child's domicile should be that of the country with which he is most closely connected. In the absence of evidence to the contrary, this country would be presumed to be the country where his parents are domiciled.
(3) On attaining adulthood, a person should retain his childhood domicile unless and until he acquires another domicile.
(4) An adult should acquire a new domicile if he is present in a new country and intends to remain there for an indefinite period. He should keep that domicile unless and until he acquires another one.

In 1988 the Inland Revenue published a consultative paper containing proposals which would, if implemented, have removed domicile as a connecting factor for income tax and CGT (Inland Revenue 'Residence in the United Kingdom' July 1988). These proposals were withdrawn in 1989. At the time of writing, no proposals for change have been brought forward by the present government.

Chapter 11

Planning without trusts

Introduction

This Part is concerned with sheltering the investments of individuals who are resident in the UK but not domiciled here. The UK has a most favourable tax regime for such individuals, described in Chapters 13–15. This chapter and Chapter 12 analyse the planning techniques which enable full advantage to be taken of the rules.

Basic planning

The simplest strategy for the non-domiciliary who is resident in the UK is to keep the investments outside the relevant territorial limits of UK tax. As is explained in Chapter 15, a non-domiciliary is not subject to IHT provided his investments are not situated in the UK, and he has not acquired an actual or a deemed UK domicile. As is explained in Chapters 13 and 14, he escapes liability to income tax and CGT provided the investments are abroad and both the income and the proceeds of any sale are kept outside the UK. In short, the non-domiciliary avoids UK tax on his investments provided they, and the income and proceeds of sale they generate, remain abroad.

Drawbacks

Unfortunately, there are many non-domiciled residents for whom this simple strategy is not sufficient. It has five drawbacks, some or all of which may prove unacceptable in particular cases:

(1) The income from, or even the proceeds of sale of, foreign investments may be required to fund UK spending.
(2) The individual may wish to invest in the UK. Any directly held UK investments are subject to IHT, regardless of the owner's domicile, and income and gains are taxed on an arising basis.
(3) There may be a risk that the individual will acquire a deemed UK domicile for IHT purposes which will happen if he is resident in the UK in 17 out of 20 years of assessment. Should this happen his world assets will become subject to IHT.
(4) There may be a risk that he will acquire an actual UK domicile. As well as exposing him to IHT on his world assets, this will mean his world income and gains become taxed on an arising basis.

(5)   He may wish to give or bequeath assets to or for the benefit of members of his family who are or may become UK domiciled.

The non-domiciliary for whom some or all of these drawbacks prove un-acceptable is typically the individual who is living in the UK on a long-term basis. Under the present law, many such individuals exist, for, as is described in Chapter 10, a foreign domiciliary only acquires a UK domicile of choice if there is no definite contingency upon which he would return to live in his country of origin.

There is no single solution which enables such a person to overcome all five drawbacks. Furthermore, the third, fourth and fifth cannot be addressed without the use of trusts. However, a variety of planning techniques which do not require trusts can make inroads into the first two and these form the subject of this chapter. The role of trusts is reviewed in Chapter 12.

Funding UK spending

Separate bank accounts

Separate bank accounts enable foreign income to be enjoyed tax-free in the UK. As is described in Chapter 13, the leading case of *Kneen v Martin* (1934) 19 TC 33 established that if foreign income is credited to one foreign account, and cap-ital to another, remittance from the latter is not a remittance of the income and so is tax free. The accounts in *Kneen v Martin* were maintained at the same New York bank, and so it is clear, and accepted by the Revenue, that the accounts can be at the same branch. But if the capital account is itself interest-bearing, the interest must be credited directly to the income account so as to avoid tainting the capital.

The income in the income account may either be spent abroad or reinvested. If it is reinvested, the proceeds of such investments must be credited to the income account for, once income, they remain income. However, it appears that investments count as capital if bought with income which arose prior to the tax year in which the individual assumed UK residence (see further p 103).

Capital and income accounts do not, however, wholly avoid UK tax, for CGT has still to be considered. As is explained in Chapter 14, if the capital account includes the proceeds of assets realised at a gain, any remittance will be treated as part chargeable gain, the proportion being the proportion the aggregate chargeable gains credited to the account bear to the whole account. It is not pos-sible to overcome this difficulty by segregating gain and base cost, for gain and base cost are not divisible in the same way that income and principal are.

In many cases, the CGT is more expensive in compliance than in tax. This is certainly so if gains form a relatively modest proportion of the capital account, for then the gains in any given year's remittances may be covered, or nearly covered, by the CGT annual exemption. However, three factors, discussed in Chapter 14, do enhance the gains which may accrue:

(1)   Losses accruing to non-domiciliaries on the disposal of foreign situs assets are not allowable (TCGA 1992, s 16(4)).
(2)   Bank balances denominated in a foreign currency are assets for CGT purposes (TCGA 1992, s 21(1)(b)). Gains accrue whenever funds are withdrawn if the currency concerned has appreciated against sterling.

(3) For other assets, gains for CGT purposes are computed not in local currency but by comparing the sterling value of the acquisition cost at the time of acquisition with the sterling value of the sale proceeds at the time of disposal (*Capcount Trading v Evans* [1993] STC 11, CA). In appropriate cases, this adds a currency gain to the gain computed in the local currency.

One solution to the CGT difficulties is to invest the entire portfolio either in sterling bonds or in sterling bank accounts. This, however, is in most cases too restrictive in investment terms. A second solution is to have a second capital account, so that one capital account is for the proceeds of assets disposed of at a gain, and the second for the proceeds of other assets. If remittances are taken only from the second account, CGT complications are avoided. The third solution to the CGT difficulties is to use a trust, as discussed in the next chapter.

Cessation of source

It is a fundamental rule of income tax that tax can only be charged if the source of the income exists in the tax year in which the tax is charged (*Bray v Best* [1989] STC 159 HL). In most instances this rule has been abrogated by statute, but it continues to apply to the remittance basis. As is explained in Chapter 13, it is accepted by the Revenue, and almost certainly good in law, that 'source' for these purposes means any particular investment or bank account.

As a result, income from a particular bank account or investment can be remitted free of income tax if the account has been closed, or the investment sold, prior to the beginning of the tax year in which the remittance takes place. This technique may be combined with the separate bank account procedure noted above. At the end of one tax year all the portfolio may be sold, and all the accounts closed, and the proceeds transferred to a temporary offshore sterling current account. At the beginning of the new tax year the money in this sterling account is transferred to a new interest-bearing account from which it is reinvested. This account becomes the new capital account, and the income it and the new investments generate is credited to a new income account. Remittance from the new capital account does not attract income tax as all the investments which generated the income in it have been sold. For income tax purposes one new capital account suffices, but two are needed if the proceeds of assets disposed of at a gain need to be segregated. Some advisers feel that the new accounts should be at a separate bank or branch, but this is not thought to be essential if the sterling current account is non interest-bearing (cf *Cull v Cowcher* (1934) 18 TC 449 and p 105).

Gifts abroad

If a non-domiciliary makes a gift of income abroad, subsequent remittance of the proceeds by the donee counts as a remittance of capital by him, and is not treated as a remittance of the income by the donor. Accordingly the gift of a fund which includes income avoids tax even if the donee subsequently brings the money to the UK. These principles are explained in Chapter 13 and it is essential to ensure that the gift is perfected abroad (*Timpson's Executors v Yerbury* (1936) 20 TC 155). Thus any gift of cash should be effected by debiting a non-UK account of the donor and crediting a non-UK account of the donee.

As is explained on pp 113–14, the gift abroad procedure may also be regarded as effective to avoid capital gains tax.

A caveat to the procedure is represented by *Harmel v Wright* [1974] STC 88. This case is discussed on p 106 and concerned employment earnings, but the principle is of general application. A gift abroad by an individual to a member of his family would certainly not fall foul of it if the donee was going to spend the money on himself. Obvious examples are gifts to children to fund university expenses or buy a house. Gifts to spouses are also in order so long as the recipient spouse uses the money for his or her own expenditure and not for that of the donor.

Traps

The remittance basis is not without traps. The first is that once an asset has been acquired out of income or gains it is always income or gains. As is explained on p 102, if the proceeds of the asset are remitted to the UK, they will be taxed, unless all the sources which gave rise to the income have previously been sold. Should an asset acquired out of income or gains be brought to the UK in specie, remittance occurs if and when it is converted to cash.

Second, remittance occurs if foreign income or gains are used to settle a UK liability. The example given in the cases is that of the non-domiciliary who settles his butcher's bill in the UK out of foreign income. In reality this problem more commonly arises where investments are paid for in the UK, as where settlement of a stock exchange purchase is through a London broker (see p 102).

A third trap to note is that of credit cards. If a foreign credit card is used in the UK, the amount spent here may be regarded as a remittance and so will result in a tax liability if the money used to settle the credit card bill includes foreign income or gains. So, too, use of any credit card with settlement in the UK results in a remittance of all the money spent, whether in the UK or abroad, for settlement itself constitutes a remittance.

The next point concerns deemed income of the kinds described on p 109. Insurance bonds should be entirely avoided by non-domiciliaries as the remittance basis does not apply at all (see p 254). In the case of deep discount securities and non-qualifying offshore funds it is not possible to separate gain from base cost and so tax is only avoided if the entire proceeds are never remitted to the UK by the taxpayer (p 247). As a result a non-domiciliary may be better advised to hold undiscounted interest-bearing securities and interests in distributor funds. This is because the interest or dividend is actual income and so can be dealt with under the techniques described above.

A final trap is that income sourced in Ireland should be avoided. This is because Irish investment income does not attract the remittance basis (TA 1988, s 68).

Investing in the UK

As explained at the start of this chapter the tax penalties faced by a non-domiciliary investing directly in the UK are twofold:

(1) The investment is subject to IHT.
(2) Any income or gains derived from the investment are immediately charge-
    able, without the benefit of the remittance basis.

In the absence of a trust the principal method of mitigating these penalties is
to hold the investments through an offshore holding company. However, such
mitigation is limited in character and the purpose of this part of this chapter is to
detail what is possible.

Inheritance tax

There is no doubt that a non-domiciliary does avoid the IHT consequences of
investing in the UK if he holds the UK investments through a holding company
registered in a foreign jurisdiction. The reason why this is effective is that the
relevant asset is then the holding company shares. As is explained on p 120, provided title to those shares passes only on registration, their situs is that of the
share register. Since this is outside the UK, the shares are excluded property.

There is one circumstance where a foreign holding company holding UK
investments can give rise to IHT liability and this is where the company itself
makes a transfer of value (IHTA 1984, s 94). Insofar as such a company owns
UK investments, such a transfer can be apportioned to the non-domiciliary.

Capital gains tax

On the face of it, holding UK investments through a foreign holding company
ought also to protect them from CGT. So long as the company is not resident or
trading in the UK, it is not subject to UK tax on chargeable gains (TA 1988,
s 11). The rules in TCGA 1992, s 13 for the apportionment of gains to resident
shareholders do not apply to non-domiciliaries (see Chapter 28).

The apparent shelter may not, of course, of itself be a complete avoidance, for
the non-domiciliary can only enjoy the gains in the UK if the company pays a dividend or is liquidated, and the proceeds are remitted to the UK. In either event the
remittance will result in a charge to income tax or CGT. However, this result may
be avoided by paying a dividend abroad prior to liquidation, and remitting the dividend in the year of assessment following completion of the winding up. An alternative solution would be to give the proceeds away and leave the donee to effect the
remittance. This, however, is subject to the difficulties noted earlier in this chapter.

In reality, however, it is unwise to use a non-resident company as a CGT
shelter on account of company residence. As is explained in Chapter 4, it may be
difficult in practice to show that a company directly owned by UK resident
individuals is non-resident, and this is particularly so where the underlying
assets are in the UK. If UK residence has to be conceded, capital gains realised
by the company are subject to corporation tax.

Income tax

A directly-owned foreign holding company can at best achieve only restricted
sheltering of UK source income. This is because, in contrast to CGT, income tax
attaches to income whose source is in the UK regardless of where the taxpayer

resides (*Colquhoun v Brooks* (1889) 14 App Cas 493). In general the only saving which can be achieved is of higher rate tax, for non-resident companies are subject to lower or basic rate tax in respect of UK income. However, tax on interest and dividends is restricted to tax withheld (FA 1995, s 128) and so bank and building society interest may be received free of tax since no tax is withheld (TA 1988, s 481; SI 1990/2231, reg 4(1)(g)).

However, even the limited income tax savings theoretically achievable with a non-resident company are rarely attained in practice. There are two reasons. The first is company residence, where the position is the same as with CGT. If the company is UK resident it has to pay corporation tax on and return its profits. A related risk is that the individual may well on the facts be a shadow director. As such any benefits from the company to him or his family, including rent-free accommodation, are taxable (see Chapter 19). Such benefits include benefits received abroad unless all the duties of the hypothetical employment can be said to be performed abroad.

The second problem with non-resident companies is TA 1988, s 739. As explained in Chapter 21, this applies just as much where an individual forms a company as where he forms a trust, and non-domiciliaries enjoy no relief in respect of the company's UK income. Where s 739 applies, it deems the income of the company to be that of the transferor, providing of course he is still a shareholder. If s 739 is in point, it is not even necessary to consider whether the company is non-resident, for it applies to any foreign registered company (s 742(8)). Section 739 is subject to a motive defence, but as explained in Chapter 23, this test is failed if the intent is to avoid any form of UK taxation (s 741; *Sassoon v IRC* (1943) 25 TC 154).

There are two scenarios in which liability under s 739 is avoided. One is for the non-domiciliary to buy a company replete with cash or investments from a third party. In such a case, provided the non-domiciliary does not inject cash or other assets into the company, he has not made a transfer of assets as a result of which income accrues to the company. The other is where the non-domiciliary can take advantage of the motive defence in TA 1988, s 741. The scope of this is now wider than at one time thought (see Chapter 23), but it is unlikely to be material with a directly-owned company unless the company was formed before the non-domiciliary came to the UK.

The result is that the only scenario where a directly-owned company is even a partial shelter for UK income is if s 739 is avoided in one or other of these ways and the company is so operated that it is indeed non-resident. Even then, it may only be a deferral, for should the non-domiciliary require the income himself he has to obtain it by dividend or by liquidating the company. In either case, further UK tax is chargeable if the proceeds are remitted to the UK, and indeed, since no credit is given for tax borne by the company, overall tax may be increased beyond the level chargeable if the company is not used at all. However, consideration may be given to attempting to avoid this tax by the techniques described above in relation to gains.

Chapter 12

Excluded property settlements

This chapter deals with how trusts may be used in tax planning for non-domiciliaries. As is explained below, inheritance tax should not be an issue, so there is no reason for the trust not to be discretionary. Since a discretionary trust confers flexibility the trusts discussed in this chapter are assumed to be of that form. In this chapter it will be assumed that the settlor is alive, resident in the UK, and a beneficiary. Planning for trusts where this is not so is discussed in Chapter 18, and at the end of this chapter there is a discussion of how the settlor may benefit his family.

Inheritance tax

The primary reason why a non-domiciliary should make a settlement is to avoid the third and fourth problems described on pp 83–4, namely the IHT consequences of acquiring an actual or a deemed UK domicile. As is described in Chapter 15, settled property is excluded property if two conditions are satisfied:

(1) the settlor was neither domiciled nor deemed to be domiciled in the UK at the time he made the settlement;
(2) the property is not situate in the UK.

The important point about this definition is that once it is established that the settled property is non-UK situate, the only domicile or deemed domicile which matters is that of the settlor at the time the settlement is made. Since the property is excluded, property settlements of this kind are generally known as excluded property settlements. Foreign property in the settlement remains excluded throughout the duration of the settlement, even if the settlor subsequently acquires an actual or a deemed UK domicile, or if, after his death, the beneficiaries are all resident and domiciled in the UK.

Since the settlement is excluded property, the discretionary trust regime of ten-yearly and exit charges is only in point insofar as the trust directly owns UK investments. If it does own such investments, the rate of IHT may take account of the initial value of all foreign assets put into the settlement, rather than merely the value of the UK assets at the time of the charge (see p 119). In practice this difficulty can be avoided by ensuring any UK investments are held through a non-UK holding company.

*The settlor and his spouse should not be initial life tenants of an excluded property settlement, since otherwise the settlement is only treated as made when

89

the survivor's interest ends (IHTA 1984, s 80). The settlor can however be a discretionary beneficiary. If he is subsequently excluded inter vivos, the gift with reservation rules mean he is treated as making a potentially exempt transfer, with the consequences described on p 124. This problem is avoided if he remains a beneficiary until death, even if he has then acquired an actual or a deemed UK domicile.

The well advised non-domiciliary coming to the UK should settle his assets on excluded property trusts before or soon after moving to the UK. It is essential he does so before the beginning of his seventeenth tax year of residence, since otherwise the concept of deemed domicile (see p 119) means the opportunity is lost for good.

Capital gains tax

An excluded property settlement also confers significant CGT advantages. As with all offshore trusts the trustees are not subject to CGT provided they are not resident in the UK and the general administration of the trusts is carried on abroad. This exemption extends to UK as well as foreign assets, for the UK assets of non-residents are not subject to CGT unless they are used in a branch or agency trade carried on in the UK.

Of greater importance is the fact that the rules in TCGA 1992, s 86 attributing gains to the settlor do not apply so long as the settlor remains non-domiciled or non-resident (see Chapter 24). The capital payment rules do not apply either insofar as any payments are made to the settlor and he remains non-domiciled (see Chapter 26). The practical effect of this is that an excluded property settlement can be kept outside the ambit of CGT so long as the settlor remains non-domiciled. In contrast to IHT there is no concept of deemed domicile.

The above considerations mean that an excluded property settlement offers a most attractive solution to the CGT problems presented by the remittance basis. Indeed in the short term, CGT considerations may provide a more powerful incentive than IHT to make an excluded property settlement. Even if, as described in the previous chapter, other solutions do enable CGT on remittances to be avoided, the attraction of a settlement is that it avoids the costs of record-keeping, computation, and compliance.

Income tax

The remittance basis

The income of the trust is assessable on the settlor under the income tax settlement code in TA 1988, Part XV, which applies both where the settlor is UK domiciled and where he is not. But non-domiciled settlors enjoy a measure of relief, for TA 1988, s 660G(4) provides that in Part XV, the term 'income arising under a settlement' does not include 'income arising under the settlement in that year in respect of which the settlor, if he were actually entitled thereto, would not be chargeable to income tax . . . by reason of his not being domiciled . . .'. Such income does however become income arising under the settlement and thus assessable as the settlor's if it is remitted to the UK in circumstances 'such that, if the settlor were actually entitled to that income when remitted, he would be chargeable . . .'.

TA 1988, s 739 can also apply to income arising directly to an excluded property settlement (cf Chapter 21). However, under s 743(3) a non-domiciliary is not chargeable 'in respect of any income . . . if he would not, by reason of his being so domiciled, have been chargeable to tax in respect of it if it had in fact been his income'. In all material respects this provision is in the same terms as its counterpart in s 660G(4) and so the position is reached that s 739 cannot impose a charge on direct trust income not in any event caught by Part XV.

The overall result is that the UK income of the settlement is taxable as the settlor's as it arises. The foreign income is free of income tax if it is accumulated and kept abroad by the trustees. In many cases this will suffice, as where the intention is to build up a long-term family fund in the trust. In practice, however, the trustees often make distributions to the settlor. If the distribution is made abroad and the settlor does not bring the money to the UK, it is generally accepted that there are no UK tax consequences, for there is no remittance.

The position is more difficult if the settlor needs money in the UK, and the various techniques described in the previous chapter for avoiding remittance have to be used. The existence of the trust makes them more complicated.

Banking arrangements

It is open to the trustees to operate capital and income accounts in the same way as is recommended for individuals on pp 84–5. If the monies required by the settlor are then distributed by the trustees from their capital account abroad to his capital account abroad, and thence remitted by him to the UK, there will be no remittance of the income arising to the trustees and liability under Part XV and s 739 will remain avoided.

There are, however, two points to note. The first is that the distribution by the trustees must be in exercise of a power to appoint or advance capital. If the distribution is simply in exercise of a power to provide the settlor with income, it may fall to be treated as income in his hands. Such income is a new source (*IRC v Berrill* [1981] STC 784), which would be assessable under Case V when the remittance from the settlor's capital account occurs. Such assessment is unlikely to be avoided by the fact that Part XV and s 739 apply to the trust income, if only because the trust's banking arrangements would mean the settlor had not been paid the income and had not been charged to tax in respect of it (cf TA 1988, s 743(4)).

The second point is that deemed income of the kind mentioned on p 109 should be avoided. Such income is caught by s 739 and/or Part XV and either the remittance basis does not apply at all, or techniques such as segregation of income and cessation of source cannot be used (see particularly p 254 (insurance bonds), ibid p 247 (offshore funds), and FA 1996, Sch 13 para 12 (deep discount securities)).

Alienation abroad

The alienation abroad technique represents a second method of bringing income from the trust to the UK without tax charge. This technique is described on p 85, and it may be used with settlements if, after receiving funds from the trustees, the settlor makes a gift abroad, and the donee brings the money to the UK. This should not bring Part XV or s 739 into play in relation to the trust income, for, if the income had in fact arisen to the settlor, remittance would have been avoided by the alienation.

The effectiveness of this technique is, however, subject to the general points made on p 86, particularly the undesirability of the income being spent to the settlor's benefit in the UK. In addition, an understanding by the trustees that the settlor was going to pass the money to the donee must be avoided. Such could cause the appointment to the settlor to be treated as to the donee, with the result that liability on him would attach under TA 1988, s 740 (cf pp 187–8). There is, however, one advantage of the alienation abroad technique and this is that the income can be distributed to the settlor as income, for, if effective, alienation abroad prevents remittance in relation both to the distribution from the trust and to the income arising to the trustees.

Capital gains tax

Distribution of capital to the settlor under the banking procedures described above does not trigger a liability under TCGA 1992, s 87, for the settlor is non-domiciled. Should he acquire a UK domicile, gains arising will only trigger a CGT liability on past (or current) payments if he no longer has an interest in the settlement within the meaning of TCGA 1992, s 86. So long as he does have such an interest, the gains will be assessable as his on an arising basis (cf Chapter 24).

Offshore income gains

The banking procedures described above may trigger liability if the capital account includes offshore income gains. This is a very complex subject and is discussed on pp 248–51. There is a risk of double taxation and generally it is unwise for the trustees to invest in non-qualifying offshore funds.

Holding companies

The trustees may well hold the trust investments through a holding company. This has the advantage of sheltering the trust's UK investments from inheritance tax. However, use of a holding company does carry certain risks, most notably that if the trustees stand aside and let the settlor assume de facto control of the company, the Revenue may argue that it is resident in the UK. Chapter 16 explains the steps required to avoid this risk, most notably that decisions by the company must be taken by the directors in properly minuted board meetings.

Foreign income

Providing the holding company is genuinely non-resident it is not subject to UK tax on its foreign income. Nor, furthermore, is the settlement code in TA 1988,

Part XV in point. At one time, TA 1988, s 681(1)(b) provided that the term 'income arising under a settlement' included income of a non-resident company which could have been apportioned to the trustees had the company been resident. But this provision was repealed when apportionment was abolished in 1989, and it is now most unlikely that income in a holding company is caught by Part XV (see p 53).

But even if company income cannot be attributed to the settlor under Part XV, it can be so attributed under s 739. As with trust income, s 743(3) applies to prevent a charge where the settlor's foreign domicile means tax would not have been chargeable had the income in fact been his. But this means tax is only avoided if neither the company, nor the trustees, nor the settlor bring the income to the UK.

Bringing money to the UK

If resources are required by the settlor in the UK, the techniques described above in relation to trust income have to be invoked. In using them, however, the new stage at which income can arise has to be remembered, namely if the company pays dividends to the trustees. A dividend so paid by the company constitutes income arising to the trustees and so is assessable in its own right on the settlor under TA 1988, Part XV and thus is taxable if remitted.

In practice, concerns over dividends should prove academic, for few well advised trustees need extract profits from an underlying company by way of dividend. The most generally adopted method is for the company to be capitalised by way of loan, with the result that funds are passed to the trustees by way of loan repayment. If this is done, remittances may be avoided if the company maintains a separate bank account for capital and income. Any UK investments will be paid for out of the company's capital bank account as will loan repayments to the trustees. In the trustees' hands the receipts from loan repayments should be credited to their capital account at the bank and not mixed with income monies.

Position where s 739 does not apply

In two situations s 739 does not or may not apply to holding company income at all. These situations are referred to in Chapter 21 and are where the motive defence applies and where the company is bought by the trustees and no money is injected.

In the case of the second of these situations, any benefit from avoiding s 739 maybe lost if money is paid out to the settlor, for then s 740 can apply by reference to the company income. Section 740 is analysed in Chapter 22, but it applies here precisely because the settlor is not taxable in respect of the company's income under s 739. Section 740 can attribute foreign income to any benefit received in the UK and so if funds in the company are paid up to the trust and thence to the settlor, the payment to the settlor is taxable by reference to the company's income if the payment is brought by the settlor to the UK. There is no scope for capital and income account procedures, and so in these cases the settlor is worse off than if s 739 had applied.

The position is otherwise with the motive defence, for this precludes both ss 739 and 740 (see Chapter 23). Although the motive defence does not apply if the intention was to avoid any form of UK taxation it is available where the intention was to avoid foreign tax (*IRC v Herdman* (1969) 45 TC 394, HL). It is, therefore, in point if the trust and holding company were formed before the settlor was contemplating UK residence, even if such formation was designed to avoid tax where he was then living. However, where s 739 applies because of an associated operation as well as the transfer, the defence is lost if the associated operation is tainted by UK tax avoidance (*Congreve v IRC* [1948] 1 All ER 948). Accordingly, even if the settlement is formed for non-UK reasons, formation of a holding company with UK tax in mind may still mean the latter's income is caught by s 739 (see further p 196).

The motive defence does not altogether simplify planning, for although it confers protection from s 739, it does not prevent dividends paid by the company to the trust being subject to TA 1988, Part XV if remitted, or income distributions by the trust from being taxable under Case V. The best way round these difficulties is to ensure that all sums passed by the company to the trust, and by the trust to the settlor, are capital. Such may be achieved if the company funds are extracted by loan repayment and the settlor receives funds by capital advance.

UK income

As noted above, TA 1988, s 739 applies on an arising basis to the company's UK income. This is only avoided in the circumstances described above, ie if either the motive defence applies, or the company was bought without injecting money into it.

If one of these scenarios applies there is the possibility of some sheltering of UK income. However, even here two points have to be remembered. First, any saving of UK tax is only partial, for important categories of UK income are subject to withholding or other UK tax. Second, except where the motive defence applies, TA 1988, s 740 applies to any capital advances received by the settlor or indeed by any other UK resident beneficiary from the trust. As is explained in Chapter 22, to the extent that there is UK income, such advances are taxable regardless of whether remitted to the UK. Indeed overall tax is increased, for in computing liability under s 740 no credit is given for any tax borne by the company.

Shadow director

The chances are that the non-domiciliary will be a shadow director of the company (cf Chapter 19). This means liability under Schedule E will attach to benefits such as living accommodation received from the company. Such benefits include benefits received abroad unless all the duties of the hypothetical employment can be said to be performed abroad (cf pp 152–3).

Trustee borrowing

The rules in TCGA 1992, Sch 4B as to transfers of value linked with trustee borrowing should be kept in mind. As is explained in Chapter 27 trustees who fall foul of these rules suffer a complete or partial disposal of all the trust assets for CGT purposes. Provided the settlor is non-resident or non-domiciled there is no CGT liability on an arising basis. But the gains potentially attributable to capital payments will have been increased (see pp 235–6).

Two particular areas where a Sch 4B deemed disposal would be triggered are:

(a) Where there is outstanding trustee borrowing at the time of a loan to an underlying holding company.
(b) Where there is outstanding trustee borrowing when a distribution is made to the settlor or another beneficiary. For these purposes, borrowing includes any loan from an underlying company.

Settlor acquiring a UK domicile

As noted earlier in this chapter an excluded property settlement preserves its IHT advantages if the settlor acquires a UK domicile. Gains, however, become assessable on the settlor on an arising basis under TCGA 1992, s 86. The income tax position is the same as for CGT. Once the settlor loses his foreign domicile, TA 1988, Part XV and s 739 apply on an arising basis. Accordingly, the world income of the trust is taxable under Part XV on an arising basis and s 739 applies both to that income and that of any underlying holding company, save insofar as the motive defence applies, or (in the case of the company) the company was bought and funds have not been injected into it.

In practice it may be possible for the settlor to predict his domicile will change before the change in fact happens. Should this be so, consideration could be given in the tax year before the change happens to distributing sufficient cash from the trust to him to fund his foreseeable expenses. He and his spouse can then be excluded from the trust, thereby precluding liability under TA 1988, Part XV and s 739.

The distribution will not attract income tax provided the banking procedures outlined above have been followed. The distribution will not attract CGT so long as the settlor continues to have an interest in the settlement within the meaning of TCGA 1992, s 86, for then the trust's gains will be assessable as his on an arising basis once he acquires his UK domicile (cf Chapter 24). However, if he ceases to have an interest in the settlement within the meaning of s 86, gains arising once he is UK domiciled will be assessable on him under TCGA 1992, s 87 by reference to the distribution save insofar as it has already been wholly matched with prior trust gains (cf p 224).

The amount distributed should not exceed foreseeable spending needs, since otherwise it will create an IHT liability on his eventual death. Should the settlor receive a distribution after becoming resident and domiciled in the UK, such will be taxable under s 87 by reference to any unallocated trust gains realised prior to the change of status. Such applies whether those gains are actual gains or deemed gains arising under TCGA 1992, Sch 4B (see Chapter 27).

Provisions for the settlor's family

So far the discussion in this chapter has revolved around benefits to the settlor. In reality, the trustees or the settlor may wish to see provision made for other beneficiaries. This will necessarily be so after the settlor's death but could arise in his lifetime.

Strategies for trustees of trusts seeking to benefit a beneficiary who is not the settlor are discussed in Chapter 18. Here a few issues peculiar to non-domiciled beneficiaries are addressed.

Distributions of income to non-domiciled beneficiaries

Income distributions to a UK beneficiary who is not the settlor are taxable as a new source under Schedule D Case V and the remittance basis applies provided the recipient is non-domiciled. It follows that UK tax is avoided if the money is received and kept abroad.

Capital distributions to non-domiciliaries

Since the residence and domicile of the settlor is no longer material to liability under ss 740 and 87, techniques for minimising the tax on capital distributions are essentially as described in Chapter 18. There may be more scope for such techniques with non-domiciled settlors, for the motive defence to s 741 is more likely to be in point and there may be an ample supply of non-resident or non-domiciled beneficiaries.

A point to stress about the s 740 charge is that income which has arisen at any time since 6 April 1981 can count as relevant income. So too capital gains or offshore income gains realised at any time after 6 April 1998 are trust gains. This backdating applies regardless of whether at the time the settlor, the trustees, or the beneficiaries had any connection with the UK.

A particular problem is that while a distribution to a non-domiciled beneficiary escapes charge under s 87 it only does so under s 740 if it is not remitted and the trust has no UK income. It is to be noted that tax liability under s 740 attaches if the distribution is remitted, regardless of whether it was made out of the foreign income. Accordingly, and in contrast to s 739, unremitted foreign income can found liability under s 740.

In many cases s 740 may be precluded by the motive defence, and in that event as is described in Chapter 18, capital distributions do in general provide a means of providing tax-free funds in the UK for non-domiciliaries. But this is not so where the motive defence is not in point and here s 740 presents real difficulties.

One possible solution is for the trustees to distribute all income as current income. The distribution is either to non-residents, or to non-domiciliaries who keep the money abroad. With the income stripped out, capital may be advanced to a UK resident non-domiciliary without a s 740 charge. Any charge under TCGA 1992, s 87 is avoided because the recipient is non-domiciled.

This solution does, however, entail the following difficulties:

(1)   The trustees may not on the facts have paid all the past income out. If de facto accumulation has occurred, payment out now is not possible unless (perhaps) all the income has been segregated in a separate bank account (cf p 182).

(2) If income is undistributed in the future, it may trigger a charge on the distribution then, insofar as the income arises in the UK or the capital distributed has been brought to the UK.
(3) If offshore income gains have been or are in the future allocated to a capital payment to a non-resident they become relevant income for the purposes of s 740 and so able to be matched with the distribution to the UK resident if the latter is remitted.
(4) If there are no trust gains at the time of the distribution, a s 87 charge will arise in the future if when trustees realise gains the recipient beneficiary is resident and domiciled in the UK.

An alternative solution is to accept that the tax cost of distributing capital to a UK resident non-domiciliary is too high. Instead income is distributed to him abroad as it arises and he is left to avoid UK tax by such means as he considers appropriate. As described above, he could make gifts abroad to his wife or children and leave them to make any remittance.

On the whole it is difficult to recommend a gift abroad followed by remittance by the donee where the money gifted has been distributed as capital from the trust. This is for the following reasons:

(1) In certain cases there may be an argument that s 740 is wide enough to treat a benefit received by one beneficiary and passed to another as received by the second beneficiary (see p 187).
(2) Section 740 liability will in any event arise if there is or is in the future UK source income in the trust.
(3) Section 87 liability will arise if there are no trust gains when any capital distribution occurs, and the recipient is both resident and domiciled in the UK when the trustees do realise gains.

Should the family be provided for by a settlement at all?

The difficulties with ss 740 and 87 described above and in Chapter 18 raise a question as to whether a settlement is the best means for a non-domiciliary to provide for family members in the UK. In a sense it is not, for if the non-domiciled settlor had kept the assets he could have given or bequeathed them to the beneficiaries in the UK without liability under either s 740 or s 87. This is particularly so where the family members are, or become, domiciled as well as resident in the UK, for on this scenario few of the techniques for circumventing ss 740 and 87, discussed in Chapter 18, are available.

But despite these points the wider advantages of the trust should not be forgotten. By putting the assets in the trust the settlor keeps them free from IHT in the hands of the beneficiaries, provided at the time the assets are settled he is neither domiciled nor deemed to be domiciled in the UK. This is particularly valuable if the beneficiaries are UK domiciled. Further, a trust does allow deferment of income tax and CGT. Either a large fund can be built up from which enhanced income can in due course be drawn, or the beneficiaries can convert deferral into avoidance by long-term emigration.

The optimal solution is for the non-domiciliary to make outright gifts abroad of such capital as the resident beneficiaries are likely to need in the UK, eg to fund house purchases. The risk of inheritance tax exposure on this on the part of the recipients should be accepted and mitigated, for example by PETs. The balance of the funds – which essentially represent long-term investment – should go into or remain in the trust where they attract the IHT shelter and the deferral of income tax and CGT. This should be a long-term family fund from which the income might be paid out, but otherwise the fund is only distributed insofar as a beneficiary is, or becomes, permanently non-resident.

Where the bulk of the funds concerned are already in trust, this optimal strategy may require a distribution to the settlor to fund the outright gifts. Such a distribution should be free of tax consequences provided it is made abroad and the settlor then has neither an actual nor a deemed UK domicile. Indeed, in such cases a distribution of the whole trust fund may make sense, followed by a re-settlement of the part which it is intended to be in trust. Provided the resettlement is genuinely a new trust, such a strategy will wipe out prior relevant income and trust gains and rebase the assets.

A further step which may usefully be considered is for a life-interest to be appointed to the settlor. This will rebase the retained assets for CGT purposes on his death (TCGA 1992, s 72), and so reduce the long-term potential for trust gains. Provided the life-interest is not conferred when the settlement is made and the appointment was not then in contemplation the settlement's excluded property status will be unaffected and as a result there will be no IHT consequences (cf IHTA 1984, s 82 and p 118).

Chapter 13

The remittance basis

General

The remittance basis principally applies to income chargeable under Schedule D, Cases IV and V. Case IV charges income arising from foreign securities and Case V income arising from foreign possessions. The term 'foreign possessions' has the widest possible meaning, and it includes land, shares (*Singer v Williams* [1921] 1 AC 41), interests in foreign partnerships (*Colquhoun v Brooks* (1889) 14 App Cas 493) and interests under non-resident discretionary trusts (*Drummond v Collins* (1915) 6 TC 525). It is also capable of including foreign securities, and accordingly the Crown can assess income from foreign securities under either Case IV or Case V (*Butler v Mortgage Co of Egypt Ltd* (1928) 13 TC 803). The issue of whether income has a UK source or is taxable under Cases IV and V as being from foreign possessions can sometimes give rise to difficulty and is discussed on pp 9–11.

The remittance basis does not apply to investment income arising in the Republic of Ireland (TA 1988, s 68).

History

Originally all income taxable under Cases IV and V was charged on the remittance basis. This remains the position where the taxpayer is a non-domiciled individual, but for other taxpayers the remittance basis was progressively abolished. In 1914 it was withdrawn from Case IV, and from stocks, shares and rents within Case V (FA 1914, s 5). In 1940 it was confined to income immediately derived from a trade, profession, or vocation carried on by the taxpayer (FA 1940, s 19). In 1974 it was completely abolished for all taxpayers save non-domiciled individuals and Commonwealth and Irish citizens not ordinarily resident in the UK.

The amount charged

The charge under Case IV is on 'the full amount . . . of the sums received in the United Kingdom'. The charge under Case V is 'on the full amount of the actual sums received in the United Kingdom' from any of the following:

(1) remittances payable in the UK;
(2) property imported;
(3) money or value arising from property not imported; or

(4)   money or value so received on credit or on account in respect of any such remittances, property, money, or value brought or to be brought to the UK.

On the face of it, the charge under Case V should only arise if the facts come within one of (1)–(4) in this list. However, in the leading case of *Thomson v Moyse* [1961] AC 967, Lord Radcliffe said that they should only be treated as illustrations of the way in which, when foreign income is transmitted to this country, the transmission may be affected. Accordingly, the charge under Case V is on the same basis as that under Case IV, namely on the full amount of the actual sums of the income received in the UK.

Claim

The remittance basis applies only if the taxpayer claims he is non-domiciled (TA 1988, s 65(4)). The normal time limit applies to such claims, namely 31 January five years and ten months after the end of the year of assessment (TMA 1970, s 43A).

Rate of tax

Remittances form part of the taxpayer's total income and so are subject to higher or basic rate tax as appropriate. The lower rate and the Schedule F rates are not available as those rates do not apply to dividends and interest taxed on the remittance basis (TA 1988, ss 1A(4)(a) and 1B).

As remittances are included in total income, personal reliefs, the starting rate and other deductions from total income are available. Accordingly, a non-domiciliary with no UK income can make modest tax-free remittances of income by utilising his personal allowance (£4,335 in 1999–2000).

If the remitted income has suffered foreign tax, double tax relief is allowed, but on the basis that the dividend is grossed up by the foreign tax (TA 1988, s 795(1)). In some cases, the credit for foreign withholding tax can mean remittance of the income occasions little or no UK tax, particularly if the taxpayer is not thereby brought into the higher rate band.

Basis of assessment

The remittance basis is now wholly on a current year basis. In other words, the charge under Case IV or V is on the amounts remitted in the year concerned. The remaining vestiges of the transition from the old preceding year basis ceased to be in point on 6 April 1998 (FA 1994, Sch 20 para 6(2), 7, and 14(2)).

Meaning of 'received'

At one time a very technical view was taken of whether income had been received in the UK. In *Hall v Marians* (1935) 19 TC 582 and *IRC v Gordon* (1952) 33 TC 226 the taxpayer had had accounts with the National Bank of India both at its London branch and at its Colombo branch. The taxpayer overdrew at the London branch, and from time to time the overdraft was transferred to the Colombo branch where it was cleared out of the taxpayer's foreign income. The House of Lords held that there had been no remittance of that income.

Hall v Marians and *IRC v Gordon* were reversed by what is now TA 1988, s 65(6)–(9), but in *Thomson v Moyse* (1958) 39 TC 291 an even more technical analysis found favour in the Court of Appeal. In *Thomson v Moyse*, the taxpayer had drawn cheques on his New York bank in favour of his UK bank, and the UK bank had bought the cheques and immediately credited the taxpayer's account with the sterling proceeds. Its agents in New York then presented the cheques through their New York bank, and the UK bank was credited in New York with the proceeds in dollars, which it sold in New York to the Bank of England for sterling. The Court of Appeal held that the taxpayer's US dollar income had not been remitted to the UK, on the grounds that the dollars had been sold by him to the London bank in New York.

It was this decision which was reversed in the House of Lords. Lord Radcliffe stated that Cases IV and V are concerned simply with the turning of income which has arisen in a foreign country into the expendable resources of the taxpayer in the UK. He encapsulated the principles which should apply as follows:

> 'the computation ... depends simply on the question, what is the amount of sums which have been or will be received in the United Kingdom in the year of assessment. No doubt proper construction of those words requires that the sums computable must be "of" the income, by which I would understand "sums of money derived from the application of the income to achieving the necessary transfer". But that is all. If sterling sums are received, and are so attributable, that is enough for liability.'

Thomson v Moyse represents a practical approach to the remittance rules and undoubtedly ended certain highly technical avoidance schemes. However, apart from *Hall v Marians* and *IRC v Gordon*, earlier decisions in favour of the taxpayer were left standing and these form the basis of current planning techniques for non-domiciliaries. It is to these techniques that attention must now be turned.

Do not bring the income to the UK

It goes without saying that if income is not remitted the charge under Cases IV and V does not arise. Accordingly, no liability arises if income is spent abroad or simply reinvested. The foreign domiciliary who does not need to spend his foreign investment income in the UK is thus able to accumulate that income abroad wholly free of UK tax.

There is no concept of constructive remittance. At the turn of the century the Revenue argued that life assurance companies who made up accounts showing unremitted foreign income as an asset must be treated as having remitted it. This argument, however, was rejected by the House of Lords (*Gresham Life Assurance Society Ltd v Bishop* [1902] AC 287).

Where the Revenue were more successful was in establishing that if a remittance is made from a mixed fund, it is presumed to be income to the extent that income has been paid into the fund. This was established in *Scottish Provident Institution v Allan* (1903) 4 TC 591, where the taxpayer had sent money out to Australia for investment on mortgage. Substantial amounts of interest had accrued and both this and the repayments of principal had been intermixed. In remitting money back to England the company's Australian agents designated the remittances as repayment of principal but this was held to be ineffective in the House of Lords. In a memorable phrase, Lord Halsbury LC observed that 'the mere nicknaming the sum received' could not alter the taxability of what was in substance profit earned abroad.

In practice a non-domiciliary often uses a mixed account to fund both foreign and UK spending. An issue often raised is whether, if foreign spending precedes UK spending, it should be regarded as having drawn off income rather than capital in the account. Logical application of *Scottish Provident Institution v Allan* suggests this is the right analysis. But there is neither authority nor published Revenue practice on the point.

The law is unclear on what is remitted when remittance is from a mixed fund consisting of some income taxed on the arising basis and some on the remittance basis. In practice the Revenue treat the income taxed on the arising basis as remitted first (Inspector's Manual, para 1566).

A point which must be remembered is that income counts as remitted if it is received in the UK; it does not have to be received by the taxpayer personally. Thus, receipt by some third party on the taxpayer's instructions counts as remittance (*Timpson's Executors v Yerbury* (1936) 20 TC 155, CA). This means that a remittance occurs if the taxpayer draws a cheque on his foreign bank account in favour of a UK supplier of goods or services. So too settling a credit card debt by payment to a UK bank account is a remittance, as is the use of a foreign credit card in the UK (Inspector's Manual, para 1569).

Mere reinvestment of foreign income abroad does not amount to remittance, although if the investment is sold outside the UK, the income is remitted if and when the proceeds are received in the UK (*Patuck v Lloyd* (1944) 26 TC 284; *Walsh v Randall* (1940) 23 TC 55). If the investment is in bearer form or is a chattel and physically brought to the UK no remittance then occurs (*Scottish Widows v Farmer* (1909) 5 TC 502, CS). But the income does count as remitted when any asset brought to the UK is sold in the UK (*Scottish Provident Institution v Farmer* (1912) 6 TC 34).

It is sometimes suggested that if a large one-off remittance is made from a mixed fund to meet capital expenditure such is a remittance of the capital in the fund and so tax-free. Such a proposition lacks authority and is of doubtful validity for income is taxable even if capitalised prior to remittance. This is apparent from the cases noted above where the income has been invested and the proceeds of sale brought into the UK.

Capital and income accounts

The procedure of operating capital and income accounts circumvents the decision in *Scottish Provident Institution v Allan*, for it enables the taxpayer to demonstrate that what is remitted is not income. The procedure requires the taxpayer to have two bank accounts, one of which is credited with income receipts and the other only with capital. Remittances to the UK are made only from this second account.

The Revenue challenged the capital and income account procedure in *Kneen v Martin* (1934) 19 TC 33. Here the taxpayer was a UK citizen who commenced residence in the UK in 1925. She had two bank accounts at the New York office of the Bankers Trust Company of New York. One was credited with the income from her US investments, and the other, from which remittances to the UK were made, with the proceeds of capital realisations. The Special Commissioners found she had not remitted income and this finding was affirmed in the Court of Appeal. The key findings of the Special Commissioners were as follows:

> 'the proper inferences for us to draw were that the actual sums remitted to the [UK] were all derived from the proceeds of realisation of investments owned by [the taxpayer] before 1925 and not from income, or the proceeds of realisation of investments acquired out of income, arising since that date, and that she was not resident in the United Kingdom before 1925. We also thought it a reasonable inference that the investments sold had been largely replaced by other investments acquired out of income arising in America.'

House of Lords approval to capital and income account procedures may be inferred from Lord Radcliffe's remark in *Thomson v Moyse* that the sum remitted must be income. The findings in *Kneen v Martin* show that the capital and income accounts may be at the same branch of the foreign bank, and that it matters not that the accumulated foreign income is reinvested abroad. It is, however, important to remember that the capital account cannot contain the proceeds of all investments sold; it can only be credited with proceeds of investments not directly or indirectly acquired out of foreign income. This is an application of the principle in *Patuck v Lloyd*, noted above.

The obvious example of investments not acquired out of income is inherited investments or investments acquired out of inherited capital; as is noted below a gift is capital in the hands of the donee even if made out of the donor's income. The passage from the Commissioners' decision in *Kneen v Martin* cited above suggests that money also counts as capital if it represents or is derived from income which arose prior to UK residence.

In law this last proposition may not be entirely correct, for before self-assessment the measure of liability in the first year of residence was remittances in the previous year (*Carter v Sharon* (1936) 20 TC 229). By definition such remittances had to have arisen prior to the assumption of residence. More generally, it is plain from *Timpson's Executors v Yerbury*, and in particular from Greene LJ's judgment ((1936) 20 TC 155 at 185), that under the remittance basis the ground of liability is income arising, and the measure is income remitted in the preceding year. Accordingly, as is implicit in the cessation of source rules discussed below, there is no liability unless the source exists in the year of charge. Equally, it is well recognised that once a ground of liability exists, the measure may be income which arose in a period when the taxpayer was not liable to tax, whether by reason of non-residence or otherwise. Such was first recognised in relation to the arising basis in *Singer v Williams* (1920) 7 TC 419 and formed the basis of the decisions in *Fry v Burma Corpn Ltd* (1930) 15 TC 113 and *Back v Whitlock* (1932) 16 TC 723. Logically, therefore, it ought to follow that a taxpayer who migrates to the UK with a continuing source of foreign income should be taxable on the amount remitted from that source, regardless of the fact that such amount arose while he was non-resident.

In practice the Revenue do not subscribe to this analysis, although prior to self-assessment they did follow *Carter v Sharon*. Revenue practice is that a remittance is not taxable unless the income arose during a year in which the taxpayer was resident in the UK, or during the basis period for such a year (Inspector's Manual, para 1563). Presumably under self-assessment the reference to basis period is irrelevant, and so the position is reached that income arising prior to the tax year in which residence commenced effectively counts as capital and is tax-free if remitted. Income also escapes charge if the source ceases before the date of arrival (IR 20, para 7.20).

Cessation of source

It is a well-established principle that income cannot be taxed in a year of assessment unless the source from which it is derived exists during that year. This principle was established in the 1920s in *National Provident Institution v Brown* (1921) 8 TC 57, HL and *Whelan v Henning* (1926) 10 TC 263. In many instances, for example post cessation trading receipts, it has been abrogated by statute, but otherwise, as *Bray v Best* [1989] STC 159, HL affirmed, the principle remains good law.

Practice

On the basis of the cessation of source principle a well-established practice of avoiding tax on remittances has grown up, whereby an investment is sold or a bank account closed in one year of assessment, and the income it produced remitted in the following year. It is clear that in these circumstances the Revenue do not regard such a remittance as taxable. Indeed in para 4.17 of the 1988 Consultative Document 'Residence: the scope of UK Taxation for Individuals' it was stated that the following procedure prevents income being regarded as a 'remittance':

> 'closing an account or selling an income producing asset in one year, and remitting accumulated income in the next when there is no longer a source of income that can be charged to tax.'

This practice has been widely exploited as a tax-avoidance strategy. But two questions do have to be considered in relation to it. The first is whether the practice is soundly based in law, and thus whether the Revenue could, with due notice, change it. The second is when a new bank account is a separate source.

Legal basis

The first issue arises because of *Diggines v Forestal Land, Timber and Railways Co* (1930) 15 TC 630. At the time to which that case related, taxpayers other than non-domiciled individuals were taxed on the arising basis on the average of the preceding three years under Rule 1 of Case V on income from stocks, shares, and rents, and on a remittance basis under Rule 2 on income from other foreign possessions. The taxpayer company held shares in several foreign companies, and the Court of Appeal decided each holding was a separate source, with the result, following *Whelan v Henning*, that if a given holding yielded no dividends in a year of assessment no tax was exigible for that year in respect of the holding. The House of Lords reversed this decision, deciding that no further subdivision of Case V beyond Rules 1 and 2 was appropriate. Rule 1 referred to 'the full amount' of the income from stocks, shares and rents, and this the House of Lords decided meant tax under Rule 1 could be charged provided any stocks, shares, or rents produced income in the year concerned.

The division of Case V into Rules 1 and 2 was abolished in 1940, but under TA 1988, s 65(5)(b) the charge under the now unified Case V is still on 'the full amount' of sums received in the UK. On the face of it, it may be argued that the ratio of *Diggines* applies to the effect that all sources within Case V must cease before remittance in a subsequent year can be tax free.

In fact such a conclusion is almost certainly wrong. In 1926, FA 1926, ss 29–31 replaced the three-year average with the now abolished preceding-year basis. Section 30 enacted what became TA 1988, s 67 to the effect that where in a year of assessment the taxpayer ceased to possess all or any part of a particular source of income, that source or part was treated separately. These rules were considered obiter by the House of Lords in *Goodlass Wall and Lead Industries Ltd v Atkinson* (1950) 31 TC 447, HL, and in three out of the four reasoned speeches they were construed as precluding income arising from assets the tax-payer had ceased to possess in one year being included in the measure of Case V liability the following year. In other words, they impliedly overruled *Diggines*. They were expressed in terms of income arising, but s 67(6) applied them to the remittance basis as if references to income arising were references to income received. So applied and construed they were generally regarded as providing a sound legal basis for Revenue practice.

At one time it was suggested that this conclusion was not the end of the matter, for one result of the introduction of self-assessment was to abolish the preceding-year basis and the closing rules in s 67 that went with it. Section 67 was repealed for new sources from 6 April 1994 and for continuing sources from 6 April 1998 (FA 1994, ss 207(4), 218 and Sch 20, para 7). If, therefore, the closing rules no longer apply, the implied overruling of *Diggines* has gone, and accordingly it could be argued that the *Diggines* ratio is revived in full force.

It is, however, improbable that this is the correct construction of the 1994 legislation, for it is clear from the transitional rules in s 218 and Sch 20 that that legislation affirmed the proposition, implicit in s 67, that each investment or bank account is treated as a separate source. Accordingly, there is clear legis-lative intent that 'source' should continue to be construed in the same way as under s 67.

Even if there were technical arguments for supposing the *Diggines* ratio had been revived, it is clear the Revenue do not take such a view. The Inspector's Manual (para 1563) makes it clear that a remittance is not taxable if it is from a source which has ceased prior to the tax year concerned.

Bank accounts

The question is sometimes raised of whether there is a new source if a bank account is closed and the money is transferred to a new account at the same branch of the bank. In law, a bank account is a contract between banker and customer under which the bank borrows the money from the customer on terms to repay it (see eg *Hart v Sangster* (1957) 37 TC 231). The argument is therefore that nothing changes if one account is closed and another opened at the same branch.

This argument is almost certainly wrong if one account is a deposit account at interest and the other a current account producing no interest. In such a case there is authority that the deposit account is a separate source (*Cull v Cowcher* (1934) 18 TC 449). The true principle appears to be that the source in the case of bank accounts is the deposit of the money on the agreed contractual terms (*Hart v Sangster*, supra). There is therefore a new source if there is any difference between the terms of the old account and the new.

The cautious course if cessation of source is being relied on is undoubtedly to have the old and new accounts at separate banks or at separate subsidiaries of the same bank. If this is not done, the money should pass into a non-interest bearing current account between the closing of the original account at interest and the opening of a new one. It is better too if the terms of the two interest-bearing accounts differ.

In practice difficulties of this sort tend only to arise in the Channel Islands or the Isle of Man, where banks are within the UK system. Elsewhere money at interest tends to be deposited for fixed periods at the end of which it is repaid. In such cases, repayment is plainly the end of the source, for even if the money is redeposited, the rate of interest is refixed.

Alienation abroad

Income is not remitted if it is given away abroad and brought to the UK by the donee (*Carter v Sharon* (1936) 20 TC 229). However, it is essential that the gift is perfected abroad: if the property in the money does not pass until it is in the UK, the money is treated as a remittance of income by the donor (*Timpson's Executors v Yerbury* (1936) 20 TC 155).

Advantage can be taken of this if a non-domiciliary gives income abroad to his wife, and she brings it to the UK, or if he settles it in trust, and the trustees bring the income to the UK for investment. However, before such strategies are embarked on, two caveats need to be sounded. The first is to remember Lord Radcliffe's words in *Thomson v Moyse*, to the effect that remittance occurs when the taxpayer turns his foreign income into his expendable resources in the UK. The second is to note the case of *Harmel v Wright* [1974] STC 88. In this case the taxpayer had used his foreign income to subscribe for shares in one foreign company, which lent the money to a second foreign company, which in turn lent the money to the taxpayer who brought it to the UK. The Special Commissioners found that the taxpayer had received the income in the UK and this finding was upheld by Templeman J. He characterised the circumstances of the case as peculiar, but observed that emoluments had come in at one end of a conduit pipe and passed through certain traceable pipes until they came out the other end to the taxpayer. Although the case concerned Case III of Schedule E, Templeman J reached his decision on the basis of the general meaning of the word 'received', rather than by relying on the extended definition applicable to Schedule E which is described below.

It may be suggested that a taxpayer's income could be treated as received in the UK if he gave it to his wife or another individual and the donee then spent it in the UK to the order or for the benefit of the taxpayer. So, too, remittance to the UK could perhaps occur if income gifted to a trust was brought to the UK, but only if the individual benefitted from the income. In other cases, where the gift abroad is a genuine alienation, it is clear that the bringing of the income to the UK by the donee cannot amount to remittance by the donor.

In practice the Revenue challenge gifts abroad if the gift was not completed abroad or if financial consideration for the gift is received in the UK (Inspector's Manual, para 1565).

Overdrafts and loans

The cases of *Hall v Marians* and *IRC v Gordon* have been noted above, together with their reversal by what is now TA 1988, s 65(6)–(9). Section 65(6) provides that income is to be treated as received in the UK if the taxpayer applies it outside the UK in or towards the satisfaction of any of the following:

(a)   the principal or interest of any loan made to him in the UK;
(b)   the principal of any loan made to him outside the UK, the proceeds of which are brought to or received in the UK;
(c)   the principal of any loan made to satisfy any debt within (a) or (b) above; this covers the actual scheme in *Hall v Marians* and *IRC v Gordon*.

Section 67(7) applies s 67(6) in cases where a loan made outside the UK is satisfied before the money lent is brought to the UK; in such a case the remittance takes place not when the loan is paid off but when the money is received in the UK. Section 67(8) counteracts back-to-back arrangements. It deems income to be applied in satisfying a debt if:

> 'it is applied in such a way that the money or property representing it is held by the lender on behalf or to the account of [the taxpayer] in such circumstances as to be available to the lender for the purpose of satisfying or reducing the debt by set-off or otherwise.'

There is one noteworthy gap in the list of constructive remittances in s 65(6)–(9), namely, that the use of foreign income to pay *interest* on a loan made abroad does not count as a remittance even if the proceeds of the loan are brought to the UK. Accordingly, a widely used avoidance technique has grown up, whereby non-domiciliaries borrow money abroad, spend it in the UK, pay interest out of foreign income, and eventually clear the loan either out of capital, or when they have ceased to be UK resident. Such loans can be safely secured on foreign situs assets, provided the latter have not been purchased out of foreign income.

A point of difficulty can, however, arise with this technique, namely whether, when paying the interest the non-domiciliary is required to deduct tax at source under TA 1988, s 349(2)(c). That subsection requires deduction at source where yearly interest chargeable under Case III is paid to a person whose usual place of abode is outside the UK. Where a non-domiciliary has a foreign loan, the lender's place of abode will ipso facto be abroad and the interest will almost always be yearly interest. Accordingly, s 349(2) applies if the interest is chargeable under Case III. Given that the borrower is resident in the UK, it is likely that it will (cf pp 9–11).

Acquiring a UK domicile

It is self-evident that when an individual acquires a UK domicile he can no longer take the benefit of the remittance basis. A more interesting issue is whether previously unremitted foreign income can be remitted without charge to tax. The Revenue view is that it can be (see *Taxation Practitioner* (December 1992) p 541), and this, it may be suggested, is in accordance with law. TA 1988, s 65(4) and (5) apply only where the taxpayer 'satisfies the Board that he is not domiciled in the United Kingdom'. Section 65(5) includes the provisions charging sums received in the UK, and so, once the taxpayer acquires a UK domicile, those provisions are disapplied.

If the taxpayer's domicile changes during the year of assessment, Revenue practice is to split the year in two (*Taxation Practitioner* (December 1992)). As a result the remittance basis applies before the change but unremitted income can be remitted tax free after the change. However, this practice of splitting the year may not be in accordance with law, for income tax is an annual tax charged by years of assessment. The charge under Cases IV and V in any year is on the full amount arising in the year, or, if the taxpayer 'satisfies the Board that he is not domiciled in the United Kingdom', on 'the full amount . . . of the sums received' in the UK in the year. The legislation makes no provision for splitting a year, and so in the year of change either the remittance or the arising basis must apply throughout. It is suggested the remittance basis should apply, for, if the words 'in the year of assessment' are implied into the phrase 'satisfies the Board that he is not domiciled in the United Kingdom', it is the case that an individual who is not domiciled in the UK during part of a year satisfies the pre-condition of not being domiciled in the UK in that year, albeit for only some of the time.

Employment income subject to the remittance basis

Case III of Schedule E is also subject to the remittance basis. Case III is the case which charges emoluments accruing to a UK resident insofar as they are received in the UK. It applies only to foreign emoluments which are not subject to the arising basis under Case I. Foreign emoluments are emoluments received by a non-domiciliary from employment with a non-resident employer (TA 1988, s 192(1)). They are excluded from Case I if the duties of the employment are performed wholly abroad (TA 1988, s 192(2)).

The charge under Case III is on 'the full amount of the emoluments received in the year in respect of the office or employment concerned'. The charge there-fore arises in the year of receipt. In contrast to Cases IV and V, 'received' is given an extended definition. Under TA 1988, s 132(5) emoluments are treated as received in the UK if 'they are paid, used or enjoyed in, or in any manner or form transmitted or brought to the UK'. It is doubtful, however, whether these words add much to 'received'. The only decided case on Case III is *Harmel v Wright* [1974] STC 88, and here Templeman J opined merely that s 132(5) was not inconsistent with the result he achieved by construing 'received' in accor-dance with the Case IV and V authorities.

It is clear that remittance under Case III is avoided by separate bank accounts: if Case III emoluments and assets representing them are not intermixed with funds which are brought to the UK, liability does not arise. Equally, cessation of source does not apply to Case III, for since 1989 the charge under Case III has applied whether or not the employment is held at the time the emoluments are received in the UK (TA 1988, s 202A). The rules as to bank accounts in TA 1988, s 65(6)–(9) are specifically applied to Case III.

It is comparatively rare for a UK resident to perform all the duties of his employment outside the UK. However, where some duties are so performed, it is possible to create two employments, one for the UK duties with a UK company, and the other for the foreign duties with an associated foreign company. Split contracts of this kind are used in practice, but they are scrutinised by the Revenue and careful attention to detail is needed. The emoluments cannot be loaded onto the foreign employment, for the split of emoluments between associated employments has to be reasonable (TA 1988, Sch 12 as applied by ibid, s 192(5)).

Deemed income

The UK tax code contains many provisions deeming what would otherwise be capital to be income. In many cases this deeming extends to sums arising abroad. In such cases the application of the remittance basis can be a matter of difficulty.

The principal points to note are as follows:

(1) If a sum of deemed income is taxed under Case VI, the remittance basis does not, in the absence of special provision, apply at all. This is because the remittance basis is expressed as applying only to Cases IV and V of Schedule D, and Case III of Schedule E. The biggest trap here is non-resident life policies, the gain on which is assessable under Case VI (see Chapter 30). Such policies should therefore be avoided by non-domiciliaries. Accrued income is also assessed under Case VI, but here non-domiciliaries are excluded from charge (TA 1988 s 715(1)(j)).

(2) The remittance rules do apply when a non-domiciliary disposes of a material interest in a non-qualifying offshore fund (see Chapter 29). But the relevant rules are the CGT rather than the income tax rules (TA 1988 s 761(5)). This means that techniques such as segregation of income and cessation of source cannot be used.

(3) The discount on a foreign deep discount security is charged under Schedule D Case IV (FA 1996, Sch 13 para 1). On the face of it this allows the remittance basis, but as discount and principal are also inseparable here it is difficult to see how segregation of income and cessation of source can apply.

Chapter 14

Capital gains tax

Introduction

An individual is chargeable to CGT so long as he is resident or ordinarily resident in the UK. However, gains accruing to non-domiciliaries on the disposal of assets situated outside the UK are subject to the remittance basis, and losses accruing on the disposal of such assets are not allowable.

Gains: the remittance basis

Section 12(1) of TCGA 1992 is expressed as applying 'in the case of individuals resident or ordinarily resident but not domiciled in the United Kingdom'. It provides that CGT is not charged on the disposal of assets situated outside the UK, 'except that the tax shall be charged on the amounts (if any) received in the United Kingdom in respect of those chargeable gains, any such amount being treated as gains accruing when they are received in the United Kingdom'. Section 12(2) extends the meaning of 'received' by treating as received in the UK 'all amounts paid, used, or enjoyed in or in any manner or form transmitted or brought to the United Kingdom'. It also incorporates the provisions as to loans in TA 1988, s 65(6)–(9) (see pp 106–7).

Section 12 contrasts with the Schedule D remittance basis in TA 1988, s 65(4), (5), for whereas the latter effectively neither defines nor extends the concept of receipt, s 12(2) does. Section 12(2), however, in all material respects replicates TA 1988, s 132(5), which applies to remittances chargeable under Schedule E, Case III (see pp 108–9). It is, however, unclear whether ss 12(2) and 132(5) add anything to the basic meaning of receipt. As is noted on p 108, the only case decided on either subsection is *Harmel v Wright* [1974] STC 88, but here Templeman J implied they may not extend the concept of remittance. The Revenue, however, do consider it is open to them to argue that a given set of circumstances amounts to the remittance of a gain under s 12(2), even though it would not amount to a remittance for the purposes of Cases IV and V (CGT Manual, para 25362–3).

Computation of the gain

As with all gains on foreign assets, the gain accruing to a non-domiciliary is computed by comparing the proceeds of disposal converted into sterling at exchange rates prevailing at the date of disposal with the acquisition costs, these each being converted to sterling at the rate prevailing when incurred (*Bentley v Pike* [1981] STC 360; *Capcount Trading v Evans* [1993] STC 11). It is not possible to express the gain in foreign currency and simply convert that amount to sterling.

Until 5 April 1998, indexation was computed by reference to the month in which the disposal occurred and the gain taxed on remittance was the gain after allowing the indexation allowance. Where a gain which accrued before 5 April 1998 is remitted after that date, the full indexation allowance remains allowed. As with all non-corporate taxpayers, indexation on disposals after April 1998 is frozen as at April 1998 (TCGA 1992, ss 53(1A) and 54(1A)).

Taper relief is available to non-domiciliaries, as to other individuals. It is computed by reference to the time for which the asset has been held as at the date of the disposal (TCGA 1992, Sch A1 para 16(4)). It is not, however, allowed until the year in which the gain is remitted, for it is only at that point that the gain comes into the non-domiciliary's total of chargeable gains within TCGA 1992, s 2. It follows that if in that year the taxpayer's gains do not exceed his losses, any taper relief is lost. It is unclear what the position is if part only of the gain is remitted. On a strict reading of TCGA 1992, s 2A the whole taper relief on the disposal is allowed at that stage. TCGA 1992, Sch 20 para 21 does provide for apportionments, although if read literally only where the legislation otherwise directs an appointment to be made.

Mixed funds

It is easy enough to see that a gain has been remitted if the proceeds of disposal are paid into a separate account and eventually find their way to the UK. But what is the position if the taxpayer has one or more mixed accounts? Such accounts may receive income as well as asset realisations and may be used to fund reinvestment or foreign spending.

As is explained on p 101 remittances are presumed to be income insofar as income has been credited to the account. Thereafter the Revenue view is that remittances are gain in the proportion that the gains bear to the total amount in the account (CGT Manual, para 25401). For this purpose the Revenue view is that the gains as computed in sterling should be converted back to the currency of the account at the exchange rate prevailing at the date of remittance (ibid, para 25392).

This is all very complicated and a glance at the examples at paras 25421, 25430 and 25440 of the CGT Manual will confirm such is so. In complex cases the Revenue allow any method to be used which produces a reasonable approximation to the strict liability.

Gains: avoiding remittance

Segregating gains

As with the income tax remittance basis it is clear that the non-domiciliary who simply spends or reinvests gains abroad escapes tax on those gains. The use of the words 'amounts received' in s 12(1) leaves no room for any concept of constructive remittance. However, an issue which does arise is whether only the gain need not be remitted or whether the entire proceeds of disposal of the asset must be kept abroad. As is indicated above, the latter is the approach taken by the Revenue. It accords with common sense, for whereas income is distinguishable from the income-producing asset, gain and base cost are a single indivisible sum, separated only by the artificial CGT computation rules. This approach is widely understood to have been upheld in an unreported case by a Special Commissioner.

It is clear from this that there is no justification for using separate bank accounts to segregate gain and base cost, and purporting to avoid CGT by remitting only from the latter. However, where separate bank accounts can be used is to separate the proceeds of disposals realising a chargeable gain from the proceeds of exempt assets or assets realised at a loss. Remittances from the latter are, self-evidently, not remittances of the gain and so are free of CGT.

Gifts and remittance in specie

The use of the word 'amounts' in s 12(1) indicates that money must be brought to the UK. The equivalent word in TA 1988, s 65(5) is sums, and since under s 65(5) a sum is treated as received in the UK when an asset brought to the UK is sold, so too in such circumstances an amount should be treated as received in the UK.

The use of the word 'amounts' has a further significance: if on a disposal or deemed disposal there is no consideration, any gain accruing cannot be remitted for there is no amount in respect of the chargeable gain capable of being received in the UK. This applies particularly on gifts and is accepted by the Revenue (CGT Manual, para 25331).

Cessation of source

The cessation of source technique is plainly not available to CGT, because the concept of source has no application to CGT.

Alienation abroad

As with income tax, an interesting question arises whether remittance occurs if the non-domiciliary gives away the proceeds of an asset abroad, and the donee remits the proceeds. Since the charge under s 12(1) is, like that under s 65(5), on amounts 'received' in the UK, it can safely be said that any such strategy is only effective if the gift is completed abroad. Further, both the case of *Harmel v Wright* and Lord Radcliffe's dictum in *Thomson v Moyse* are applicable to CGT, for *Harmel v Wright* was a decision on the comparable Schedule E provisions, and *Thomson v Moyse* turned simply (in this respect) on the meaning of received.

However, the question still remains whether a remittance by the donee will, for CGT purposes, be treated as a remittance by the donor if the gift is complete abroad, and there is no understanding or obligation that the gifted money will be used to benefit the donor in the UK. This issue turns on whether the words in TCGA 1992, s 12(2) purportedly enlarging the concept of receipt in fact extend its meaning beyond that adopted by the courts in relation to s 65(5). There is no authority on this question, for Templeman J expressly did not decide it in

Harmel v Wright. However, it is clear that *Harmel v Wright* would have been decided differently had the facts been less provocative and it is inherently difficult to regard a remittance by one person of his own unfettered money as a remittance of another person's gain.

Changes of residence and domicile

It is clear that the charge under s 12 cannot arise if the non-domiciliary remits gains which have accrued prior to the tax year in which he becomes UK resident; this follows because s 12(1) applies only to amounts received in respect of gains accruing while the taxpayer is resident. It is also clear that a charge does not arise if the non-domiciliary has ceased to be resident at the time of remittance. This follows because the remittance is treated as a gain accruing at the time of remittance, and as such the basic rule in TCGA 1992, s 2 means the amount cannot be chargeable. However, it would appear that if the non-domiciliary is non-resident for less than five complete tax years, gains remitted in the intervening years will be taxable on his return under TCGA 1992, s 10A (see Chapter 35).

An interesting question is what happens if remittance occurs while the taxpayer is resident but after he has acquired a UK domicile. Here the Revenue view is that, in contrast to income tax, the gain is in charge (CGT Manual, para 25311). This view is understood to be supported by a decision of General Commissioners, and it turns on whether the opening words of s 12(1) 'in the case of individuals resident or ordinarily resident but not domiciled in the UK' qualify the latter part of the subsection. As a matter of construction, it is suggested the section could be read either way.

Losses

Losses are disallowed by TCGA 1992, s 16(4). This disallows a loss if the taxpayer is not domiciled in the UK and the asset disposed of is situated outside the UK.

This subsection does not admit much elaboration, but its harshness may be seen by postulating a non-domiciled taxpayer, Mr A, who realises a foreign-situs loss of £20,000 and a UK situs gain of £20,000. Because of s 16(4) the loss cannot be set against the gain, and so, in contrast to the situation of a UK domiciled taxpayer in the same position, Mr A has chargeable gains of £20,000.

A similar position would arise if both the gain and the loss accrued on foreign situs assets. Here no CGT liability would arise if the proceeds of the asset disposed of at a gain were not remitted. But if they were remitted, then chargeable gains of £20,000 would accrue, and this would be so whether or not the proceeds of the asset disposed of at a loss were remitted.

Foreign currency

The CGT legislation expressly provides that foreign currency is an asset (TCGA 1992, s 21(1)(b)), and the normal rule that simple debts are exempt in the hands of the original creditor does not apply to foreign currency bank accounts (TCGA 1992, s 252(1)). The result is that any withdrawal from a foreign currency account is a disposal, for there is a disposal of a debt by the creditor whenever a debt is wholly or partially satisfied (TCGA 1992, s 251(2)). The only exception to these rules arises where the account represents currency acquired for personal expenditure abroad, including expenditure on a residence abroad (TCGA 1992, s 252(2)). These rules are unaffected by the treatment of currency gains as income in FA 1993, for that treatment applies only to companies.

Since it is a cardinal principle of CGT that gains or losses are calculated in sterling, the gain or loss on a withdrawal from a foreign currency account is the difference between the sterling value of the currency when paid into the account, and its sterling value at the time of withdrawal (*Capcount Trading v Evans* [1993] STC 11, CA). Obvious computational difficulties arise with accounts such as current accounts where there are a series of credits and withdrawals.

The general CGT rule is that a simple debt and thus a bank account is situated in the UK if and only if the creditor is resident here (TCGA 1992, s 275(c)). This is an abrogation of the common law rule which, as noted on p 121, determines the situs of a debt by the residence of the debtor. In practice, under SP 10/84, taxpayers are allowed to treat all bank accounts containing a given foreign currency as a single asset; this means gains and losses only accrue when the money is spent or converted into sterling or some other currency.

Both the above rules as to the situs of bank accounts and SP 10/84 are disapplied in the case of non-domiciliaries. Under TCGA 1992, s 275(l) a foreign domiciliary's bank account is not situated in the UK unless the branch of the bank at which it is kept is in the UK. This enables the remittance basis to apply to the non-UK foreign currency bank account of non-domiciliaries. There are, however, two problems. The first is that the disapplication of SP 10/84 means gains build up in a time of sterling depreciation when funds in the same currency are switched between accounts. The second is that the normal rule is that the disallowance of losses applies. This is serious, for over a period currency fluctuations should mean currency gains are substantially offset by currency losses, and as a result in the medium to long term net gains should be avoided. However, because losses are not allowed for non-domiciliaries, this cannot happen, and the result is that foreign currency banking arrangements lead to the progressive accrual of gains. These are taxable if and when funds representing the bank accounts concerned are remitted to the UK.

Chapter 15

Inheritance tax

General

The territorial limits of inheritance tax are expressed in terms of excluded property. That term is defined by reference not to residence but to domicile.

Definition of excluded property

Free estate is excluded property if two conditions are satisfied (IHTA 1984, s 6):

(1)   The owner of the property is not domiciled in the UK.
(2)   The property is not situate in the UK.

Settled property is subject to a different rule in that its status turns on the domicile of the settlor. It is excluded property if (IHTA 1984, s 48(3)):

(1)   The settlor was not domiciled in the UK at the time he made the settlement.
(2)   The property is not situate in the UK.

Exemption of excluded property

The IHT legislation gives effect to the excluded property concept by three principal rules:

(1)   The estate of a person immediately before his death does not include excluded property (IHTA 1984, s 5(1)).
(2)   No account is taken of excluded property which leaves a person's estate in determining whether an inter vivos disposition is a transfer of value (IHTA 1984, s 3(2)).
(3)   Relevant property, ie property subject to the discretionary trust regime of ten-yearly and exit charges, does not include excluded property (IHTA 1984, s 58(4)(f)).

Exempt gilts

There is an additional category of excluded property, namely UK government securities. Each issue is or is deemed to be subject to a condition that the stock is exempt from taxation if in the beneficial ownership of a person of a description specified in the condition (F(No 2)A 1915, s 47; F(No 2)A 1931, s 22; FA 1996, s 154; FA 1998, s 161). For all gilt issues the condition is that the beneficial owner is not ordinarily resident in the UK, but for some issues there is the additional requirement that he is not domiciled here.

A government security is excluded property if in the beneficial ownership of an individual of a description specified in the condition applicable to its issue (IHTA 1984, s 6(2)). Where government securities are settled the rules are as follows (IHTA 1984, s 48(4)):

(1)   If the settlement is subject to an interest in possession, the securities are excluded if the person entitled to the interest in possession is of the requisite description.
(2)   If there is no interest in possession the gilts are only excluded if all the beneficiaries are neither resident nor domiciled in the UK.

It will be noted that government securities are not excluded property if the owner or (in the case of a trust) the life tenant or a beneficiary is not domiciled in the UK but resident here. This is because the determinant of exemption is ordinary residence not domicile.

Settlements: special rules

There is an important qualification to the rule that the settlor's domicile at the time a settlement was made is the determinant of its excluded property status. This arises where the settlor or his spouse takes an initial life interest, or where they have successive life interests. In such a case the settled property is only excluded property if the settlor is non-domiciled when the settlement is made and he, or, as the case may be, his spouse is non-domiciled when the life interest or the successive life interest ends (IHTA 1984, s 82). This rule, however, only applies if and at such time as the settled property is held on discretionary trusts; if the settlement is subject to an interest in possession the settlor's domicile when the settlement is made is the sole determinant.

There are no express rules dealing with the settlements made by two or more settlors. However, there is a general IHT rule that a settlement is treated as separate settlements if there are two or more settlors and circumstances so require (IHTA 1984, s 44(2)). It is generally accepted that circumstances would so require if one settlor was UK domiciled and one was not and both provided funds from their own independent resources. In such a case, the property attributed to the notional settlements is the property provided by the settlors concerned (*Hatton v IRC* [1992] STC 140 at 159, per Chadwick J; *Tax Bulletin* 27 (February 1997) p 398).

An interesting issue arises where an individual makes a settlement while non-domiciled, and then adds to it after having acquired an actual or deemed UK domicile. At least in relation to the discretionary trust regime, there is much to be said for the view that the whole settled fund is excluded, for the discretionary trust rules in IHTA 1984 clearly contemplate that such a settlement is one settlement commencing when property first became compromised in it. The Revenue, however, argue that a separate settlement is made each time property is transferred to the trustees to be held on the relevant trusts (*Tax*

Bulletin 27 (February 1997) p 398). In relation to excluded property this has the merit of commonsense, but its correctness may be questioned.

A trap arises if a discretionary settlement holds UK property at the time of a ten-yearly anniversary. The hypothetical transfer used in determining the rate is not just of that property, but also of:

(a) any property which was outside the UK when put into the settlement and has remained so since then; and

(b) any property put into another settlement made by the same settlor on the same day (IHTA 1984, s 67(4)).

In both cases the value taken is the value of the property when settled. The main effect of this rather bizarre rule is that a charge may arise on an anniversary even if the property then in the UK is within the nil-rate band.

Another possible trap arises where property is transferred between settlements, as on an advance or resettlement. Here the rule under the discretionary trust regime is that the property is treated as remaining comprised in the first settlement (IHTA 1984, s 81). But in determining its excluded property status it is necessary to look both at the settlor of the first settlement at the time it was made and at the settlor of the second settlement at the time that was made. Only if both settlors had neither an actual nor deemed UK domicile at the relevant time can the property be excluded property (IHTA 1984, s 82). Further, it may also be necessary to look at the first settlor's actual or deemed domicile at the time the transfer between settlements takes place. This will be so if the first settlor falls within the definition of settlor in relation to the second settlement and the Revenue are right in saying that each transfer to the trustees is a separate settlement.

Matters are simpler insofar as the property in the second settlement is held on fixed interest or accumulation and maintenance trusts. Here there is no rule deeming the property to have remained in the first settlement. It would appear therefore that the only domiciles or deemed domiciles which are relevant are that of the second settlor when the second settlement is made and, if the Revenue are right, that of the first settlor when the transfer between settlements takes place.

Domicile

In general, an individual's domicile for IHT purposes is the same as under the general law (as to which see Chapter 10). However, it is possible for an individual to be deemed to be domiciled in the UK for IHT purposes (IHTA 1984, s 267). Such arises in the following two circumstances:

(1) the individual was in fact domiciled in the UK at any time in the preceding three years;

(2) the individual has been resident in the UK in 17 out of the 20 years of assessment ending with and including the current year.

In practice the second of these rules is the one which gives rise to difficulties, and the important point to remember is that the 17 years include the current year. In years prior to 1993–94, available accommodation is disregarded in determining whether an individual was resident in the UK (IHTA 1984, s 267(4)). Until

1993–94 a person with available accommodation was UK resident regardless of how many days he spent in the UK (see Chapter 2).

Situs of assets

There are no specific IHT rules governing the situs of assets, and so the common law applies. The law as to situs is a large subject, and only those situations which commonly arise in practice can be covered here.

Tangible property

It is self-evident that tangible property such as land or chattels is situated where it is found. The same applies to interests in such property: thus a lease of land has the same situs as the land itself. In *IRC v Stype Investments (Jersey) Ltd* [1982] STC 625 the Court of Appeal held that the interest of the beneficial owner of land held under a bare trust had the same situs as the land.

Shares

A share is part of the capital of a company, to be distinguished from a security or loan stock, which is an obligation of the company (*Singer v Williams* [1921] 1 AC 41). The basic rule is that a share is situated where it can be effectively dealt with as between the owner and the company (*Brassard v Smith* [1925] AC 371). For these purposes a share only counts as effectively dealt with if and at such time as the transferee becomes legally entitled to all rights of a member (*R v Williams* [1942] AC 541). The question of where a share can be effectively dealt with has to be determined by the constitution of the company. However, where only registration on the register of members constitutes a person a member as against the company, the situs of the register is the situs of the shares (*Brassard v Smith* [1925] AC 371).

It may be that the company's constitution allows the maintenance of more than one registered office or the keeping of branch registers in two or more separate countries. In this event the choice between those countries is made on rational grounds, which in practice means selecting the country where the owner is more likely to deal in the shares (*Ontario Treasurer v Blonde* [1947] AC 24; *Standard Chartered Bank Ltd v IRC* [1978] STC 272). It is, however, important to distinguish multiple registry offices or branch registers from mere copy registers. This distinction was drawn in *Standard Chartered Bank Ltd v IRC*, where the company register was at its head office in South Africa, with a duplicate register listing UK members in the UK. The evidence was that a transferee only became a member as against the company when entered in the head office register and this meant the shares were situate in South Africa.

There is no English authority directly in point on bearer shares. These are shares where simple delivery of the share certificates or other documents of title gives the transferee all rights of membership as against the company. Title to the shares is not subject to registration. Application of the effective dealing test indicates such shares are situated where the certificates or other documents are found, for the shares can only be dealt in there. Such has been held to be the law in Canada (*Secretary of State of Canada v Alien Property Custodian for US* [1931] 1 DLR 890).

Bearer shares must be distinguished from registered shares whose certificates are endorsed with transfers executed by the shareholder in blank. In *R v Williams* [1942] AC 541, the testator had so endorsed his share certificates, and it was accepted that a delivery of the endorsed certificates was a good assignment of the shares, since it passed legal title to the assignee. The endorsed certificates were fully marketable in New York where they were kept by the testator. However, it is clear from the judgment of the Privy Council both in that case and in *Ontario Treasurer v Blonde* [1947] AC 24 that the situation of the certificates could not prevail over the location of the register, for delivery of the certificates merely conferred the right to registration. However, since in *R v Williams* there were two registers the situs of the endorsed certificates was material in deciding between registers on rational grounds, and resulted in the situs of the shares being in New York.

It is noteworthy that in *R v Williams* the registered owner of the shares was the person who held the certificates and signed the blank transfer. It is suggested in *Dicey and Morris, Conflict of Laws* (12th edn 1993, p 931) that the location of a certificate with an endorsed blank transfer may be decisive of situs where the holder of the certificate is not the registered holder of the shares. Wright and Kennedy JJ so decided in *Stern v R* [1896] 1 QB 211 where the endorsed certificates were in the UK. The basis of their decision was that such endorsed certificates were freely marketable in the UK and thus fell to be treated in the same way as other negotiable instruments in accordance with *A-G v Bouwens* which is discussed below.

Unless the distinction drawn in *Dicey and Morris* is a valid one, *Stern v R* is not consistent with *R v Williams*. The distinction, however, is not drawn in *R v Williams* or any of the other decided cases, and in the Canadian case of *Royal Trust Co v R* [1949] 2 DLR 153, *Stern* was not followed. *Stern* is inconsistent with *IRC v Stype Investments (Jersey) Ltd* [1982] STC 625 in that the latter case indicates that the beneficial owner's rights to nominee property have the same situs as the property itself. *Stern* was referred to without disapproval in *Winans v A-G* [1910] AC 27, but the latter case concerned bonds rather than shares. In all the circumstances, it may be questioned whether *Stern* is good law.

Debts and securities

A debt is a chose in action, and as such the basic rule is that it is situated where it can be enforced (*Kwok Chi Leung Karl v Comr of Estate Duty* [1988] STC 728, PC). In the case of an individual this means the debt is situate where the debtor resides (*AG v Bouwens* (1838) 4 M & W 171). This is so even if the debt is secured (*Payne v R* [1902] AC 552).

With companies the position is more complicated because, for the purposes of suit, a company resides wherever it carries on business in its own name. In this event the situs of any debt owed by the company is the place where, under the contract governing the debt, the obligation to pay falls to be performed. Thus the situs of a bank account is the branch at which the account is kept, for that is where the customer can withdraw his money (*R v Lovitt* [1912] AC 212). So, too, debts under an insurance policy are situate where the money is payable rather than at the company's head office (*New York Life Insurance Co v Public Trustee* [1924] 2 Ch 101, CA).

There are two exceptions to the basic rule. The first is that a negotiable instrument is situate in the country where it is found if its value can in practice be realised by sale. An example cited in *A-G v Bouwens* was a foreign bill of exchange of a kind which at the time that case was decided was usually sold on the Royal Exchange: if physically situate in the UK such a bill had a UK situs. The principle applies also to bearer bonds, whether of governments or companies, if these are freely marketable where found (*Winans v A-G* [1910] AC 27). It does not, however, extend to promissory notes, unless the note is negotiable and there is an available market (*Kwok Chi Leung Karl v Comr of Estate Duty* [1988] STC 728, PC). Nor does it extend to renounceable letters of allotment (*Young v Phillips* [1984] STC 520). As noted above it is unclear whether it extends to share certificates with endorsed blank transfers.

The second exception is that a specialty debt is situate where the deed is physically situate (*Stamps Comr v Hope* [1891] AC 476). The classic definition of a specialty debt is 'an obligation under seal securing a debt, or a debt due from the Crown or under statute' (*R v Williams* [1942] AC 541, 555). It is clear that a debt does not have to be secured to be a specialty: this is apparent from *Gurney v Rawlins* (1836) 2 M & W 87, where an unsecured obligation under seal to pay insurance monies was held to be a specialty and so situate where the policy was found. Equally it is also clear that a mortgage debt can be a specialty if the mortgage is by deed: see *Stamps Comr v Hope* [1891] AC 476. This latter case also shows that the execution of a deed containing an express covenant to repay the debt converts a simple debt into a specialty.

It is plain that in the case of a mortgage, the situs of the mortgagor's debt is determined by the nature of the debt rather than the situs of the land. Thus, in *Stamps Comr v Hope*, the debt was held situate in Victoria, where the deed was, rather than in New South Wales, where the land was. But where there are duplicate deeds securing the debt, the situs of the land, together with factors such as the residence of the debtor, may be taken into account in choosing which of the deeds determines situs: *Toronto General Trusts Corpn v R* [1919] AC 679.

It is widely thought that the physical location of the deed only determines the location of a specialty debt if that location is in a jurisdiction which recognises specialties. This view is referred to inter alia in *Dymond, Capital Taxes*, at para 30.352. It follows that if a specialty is being relied on to determine the location of debt, advice should be taken in the jurisdiction where it is kept that it is recognised there.

Gifts with reservation

The gift with reservation rules apply to non-domiciliaries, for they are expressed in terms of gifts rather than in terms of transfers of value (FA 1986, s 102(1)). A gift is a gift with reservation (GWR) if one of two conditions is satisfied (FA 1986, s 102(1)):

(a) the donee does not bona fide assume possession and enjoyment of the gifted property, or
(b) the property is not enjoyed to the exclusion, or virtually to the exclusion of:
      (i)   the donor, and
      (ii) any benefit to him by contract or otherwise.

A benefit the donor obtains by operations associated with the gift is treated as a benefit to him by contract (FA 1986, Sch 20 para 6(1)(c)). An outright gift of cash avoids the GWR rules (Sch 20 para 2(2)); this does not however apply to settled property, where the rules are applied in relation to the property for the time being comprised in the settlement (Sch 20 para 5).

A gift into settlement is a GWR if the settlor is a discretionary beneficiary (*Oakes v Comr of Stamp Duties of New South Wales* [1954] AC 57). But where he retains only a reversionary interest there is no GWR (*Stamp Duties Comr of New South Wales v Perpetual Trustee Co Ltd* [1943] AC 425). Special rules now apply to determine whether a gift of real property is to be treated as a gift with reservation (FA 1986, ss 102A–102C).

Where a GWR has been made and the property is still subject to the reservation at the donor's death, it is treated as being property to which he is then beneficially entitled (FA 1986, s 102(3)). This means it is included in the notional transfer which is treated for IHT purposes as taking place immediately before his death (IHTA 1984, s 4), and so is subject to IHT at the death rates. Where the reservation ends inter vivos, the donor is treated as having made a disposition of the property which is a potentially exempt transfer, or PET (FA 1986, s 102(4)).

GWR rules and excluded property: death

The interaction of the GWR rules with the excluded property concept is of some complexity. The first situation to take is that of the absolute gift where the reservation subsists until the donor's death. Here common sense indicates that the property concerned is excluded property in relation to the donor if, and only if, it is situated outside the UK and at the time of his death and the donor neither is nor is deemed to be domiciled in the UK. However, it does have to be observed that IHTA 1984, s 6(1) provides that property is excluded if the person beneficially entitled to it is non-domiciled; in the case of an absolute GWR the person in fact beneficially entitled is the donee. There is therefore an argument that foreign situs property comprised in a GWR is only excluded property if the donee has neither an actual or deemed UK domicile. This argument is almost certainly wrong, for the effect of the GWR legislation is that there are competing beneficial entitlements – the deemed one of the donor and the actual one of the donee. In such a case IHTA 1984, s 5(1) and 6(1) do, when read together, indicate that the status of property as excluded is determined by the domicile of the person whom it is sought to charge, ie that of the donee in the case of the donee's death, and that of donor in the case of the donor's death.

GWR rules and excluded property: gifts

The next situation is that of an absolute gift where the reservation ends inter vivos. Such would happen if, for example, the donor ceased to have the use of the gifted property. In such an event the rule in s 102(4) that the notional disposition is a PET in theory leaves no room for the excluded property concept. Before a disposition can be a PET it must be a transfer of value, and once it is a transfer of value it is by definition not a disposition of excluded property (IHTA 1984, s 3(2)). Accordingly, on a strict reading of the legislation, the inter vivos ending of a reservation is a PET, and so subject to IHT if the donor fails to survive seven years, regardless of where the donor is domiciled and indeed regardless of whether he has any connection whatever with the UK.

It is very unlikely that this reading of the legislation would find favour in the courts if the matter was litigated. As was affirmed in *Clark v Oceanic Contractors Inc* [1983] STC 35, UK tax legislation is subject to territorial limits (cf also p 4). However, as that case also demonstrated, it is a matter of some difficulty to identify what those limits are if they are not precisely defined by legislation. In the present context the obvious solution would be to say that the ending of a reservation would only be a PET if at that time the donor has an actual or deemed UK domicile or the property was UK situated. But it is not impossible that a looser connection with the UK would be held to be sufficient, for example simply residence in the UK.

A point which also arises is the same as that arising on the donor's death, namely whether, assuming excluded property is relevant at all, the relevant domicile is that of the donor or the donee. So far no guidance on these problems arising from the inter vivos termination of a reservation has been given in either decided cases or published Revenue practice. Pending such guidance the only safe course is to avoid a reservation at all, or, if unavoidable, ensure that it subsists until the donor's death.

Settled property

The third situation is where the gift is into settlement and the reservation subsists until the settlor's death. Here the position is clear, for the settled property rules as to excluded property apply. Once property is settled, those rules prevail over the free estate rules (IHTA 1984, s 48(3), (6)). Accordingly, provided the donor was non-domiciled when he made the settlement, the property to which he is treated as beneficially entitled under the GWR rules is excluded property regardless of whether he is still foreign domiciled. The correctness of this point has long been recognised by the Revenue.

The final situation is that of the settled gift where the reservation ends inter vivos. As with an absolute gift, the ending is deemed to be a PET, and so the same issue arises as to whether the excluded property concept has any place at all. Assuming it does, the issue would then arise of whether the test should be whether the property is excluded property under the settled property rules, or whether, in applying the excluded property concept, it should be treated as still in the donor's free estate. Parity of reasoning with the position on death suggests the former is correct. But the position is far from clear, and so the inter vivos termination of a reservation over settled property is definitely to be avoided.

Part four

Practical issues

Chapter 16

The integrity of offshore structures

Tax is not saved merely by setting up offshore trusts and companies. It is also necessary to ensure that the arrangements are properly operated in practice. On the one hand it is necessary to ensure that the trustees satisfactorily reflect the wishes and aspirations of the settlor and his family. On the other it is equally necessary to ensure that the arrangements cannot be characterised as a sham and that the entities concerned are genuinely non-resident.

The law on the doctrine of sham is considered in Chapter 17, and the residence of companies and trusts is discussed in Part one. This chapter outlines some practical steps which trustees, company directors, settlors and beneficiaries should take so as to avoid falling foul of the relevant rules and legal principles.

The importance of this subject is emphasised by two criminal cases, *R v Dimsey* and *R v Allen* [1999] STC 846. The defendants in the first case were a UK taxpayer called Chipping, together with his solicitor and a Jersey individual, Dimsey, who provided trust and company management services. The other prosecution was against a second UK taxpayer, Allen, who had no connection with Chipping but also used Dimsey's services. Chipping and Dimsey were convicted of conspiring to cheat the Revenue inter alia because they had caused offshore companies which were found to be UK resident not to make proper tax returns. Allen was convicted inter alia of failing to include offshore companies in a list of assets supplied to the Revenue during an investigation into his affairs. The companies concerned were held in two trusts which were found to be shams.

The two cases are extreme in that they involved misleading the Revenue during prior investigations. Further it appears from an earlier case, *R v IRC ex parte Allen* [1997] STC 1141, that Dimsey had been prosecuted in 1980 for fraud. Nonetheless, the cases emphasise the importance of ensuring that offshore trusts and companies are genuine and non-resident, and the consequences which follow if they are not.

Setting up the structure

As is explained on p 136, both the putative settlor and the potential trustees must be clear as to the nature of the legal relationship they are entering into when a settlement is created. If this issue is not clarified and the settlor expects the trust property to continue to be treated as his own, then if the trustees do comply the arrangement may be a sham and if they do not there may be conflict between them and the settlor.

The key point that the settlor must understand is that it will be the trustees who are in the driving seat. It is particularly important to make sure that this point is understood when the proposed settlor is non-domiciled, for the trust concept may be alien to his country of origin and thus more difficult for him to comprehend than would be the case with a UK settlor.

Ideally when a trust is created the settlor should be advised by his own legal advisor, who either draws up the settlement or vets a draft provided by the prospective trustee. Where this is not the position, there may be a real issue as to whether the settlor has understood the document, or even read it, for trust deeds are lengthy and expressed in technical language.

This problem too, is particularly acute if the settlor is a non-domiciliary whose first language is not English. A practical solution may be to provide a one page memorandum summarising the key terms – ie the beneficial class, whether the trusts are discretionary or fixed interest, the extent of the discretions vested in the trustee, remuneration and exoneration clauses, and powers to appoint or dismiss the trustees. The settlor should be asked to sign this memorandum, confirming he has read and understood it.

Operating the trust

A trust cannot be attacked as a sham if the trustees behave as trustees should. Thus trust accounts should be prepared on a regular basis, for, as is trite law, the first duty of a trustee is to be ready with his accounts. In many cases the accounts can be simple statements of assets, income and expenditure. But often more complex accounting may be needed for UK tax purposes if, for example it may be necessary to know whether a distribution is income or capital or, if capital whether it is taxable under TCGA 1992, s 87 or TA 1988, s 740.

Equally trite is the proposition that the trustees must obtain title to and control over the trust assets. Thus shares must be registered in their name (or that of their nominee) and it must be they who open and control bank accounts. If the settlor or any beneficiary has the use of trust property such should be in exercise of the trustee's discretion and formalised in writing.

A fundamental point is that the trustees must give genuine consideration to decisions taken by them. Strictly there is no need for trustee decisions to be recorded in minutes of meetings or written resolutions. But such documentation is undoubtedly to be recommended, both because it is prima facie evidence of due consideration and because in the case of complex matters, the reasoning behind the decision can and should be recorded.

Related to this is the proposition that any act of the trustees should comply with the necessary formalities. Thus the general rule is that unanimity is required in decisions of trustees, and so any written resolution should be signed by all the trustees unless the governing law or the trust instrument expressly provide to the contrary. So too certain decisions may require a third party consent, for example that of the settlor or of a protector. It is self evident that any such consent must be given in due form as prescribed by the trust instrument.

Often the Revenue request completion of Form 50(FS) which supplies details necessary for determining the tax liabilities of settlors and beneficiaries. If such liabilities are likely to be in issue there is no harm in completing this form and such is normally to be recommended. There is however no obligation to do so and the exercise can be time consuming and expensive.

Since the residence of trusts is not governed by any management and control test, trustee residence is not normally a difficult issue. However two practical points are worth mentioning.

The first is that a trust will be UK resident if some or all of the trustees are UK resident, the precise position depending on the factors enumerated in Chapter 3. A possible danger can arise if a trustee is an offshore subsidiary of a UK based group. Here inappropriate internal disciplines in the group could lead to the possibility of the offshore trustee being UK resident under the central management and control test (see Chapter 4). This is a point which should be watched although in practice there is little sign of the Revenue ever having taken it and certainly there is no reported case.

The second point is to reiterate that for CGT purposes an otherwise non-resident trust can become UK resident if the general administration of the trusts is carried on here. General administration is not defined, but an obvious danger is if the trust assets are a portfolio of investments managed on a discretionary basis by a fund manager in the UK. The manager's activities could perhaps amount to general administration, particularly if he operates the only bank account and his portfolio statements are the only accounting records. Here again there is little indication of the Revenue taking such points, but prudent trustees and advisers undoubtedly avoid arrangements of this sort.

The settlor's wishes

The above points do not mean the trustees should ignore the settlor's wishes and expectations in exercising the powers vested in them. The best guidance is generally felt to come from *Re Manisty* [1973] 2 All ER 1203:

> 'The reasonable trustees will endeavour, no doubt, to give effect to the intention of the settlor in making the settlement and will derive that intention not from the terms of the power necessarily or exclusively but from all the terms of the settlement the surrounding circumstances and their individual knowledge, acquired or inherited.'

This emphasis on the settlor's wishes is born out by a Bahamian case, *Private Trust Corporation v Grupo Torras SA (Butterworths Offshore Service, Cases Vol 2)*. Here Sheikh Fahad had transferred assets to a Bahamian discretionary trust of which the Sheikh was named as Primary Beneficiary. The key issue in the case issue was whether the Sheikh exercised effective control so as to justify extending a Mareva injunction to the trust assets. The Bahamian Court of Appeal held that he did on the grounds that the trustee would not in practice reject a request by the Sheikh for a distribution to himself. 'That', the Court said 'is perfectly lawful because of express provision in the trust contemplating it and permitting it'.

However what is plain is that the trustees must not follow the settlor's wishes without independent consideration. If they do such will undoubtedly provide evidence that the trust may be a sham (see Chapter 17). Even if this is not the case, their acts may fall to be treated as nullities. In the English case of *Re Turner* [1983] 2 All ER 745, the evidence was that the trustees executed documents placed before them by the settlor because he asked them to do so and because they believed all decisions in connection with the settlement were a matter for him. The trustees did not appreciate they had a discretion and did not 'consider' the documents they signed. On these facts Mervyn Davies J held the various deeds were ineffective.

In many cases, the settlor formalises the expression of his wishes in a letter or memorandum delivered to the trustees. An Australian case, *Hartigan Nominees Pty Ltd v Rydge* [1992] 29 NSWLR 405, is perhaps the leading case on letters of wishes. Here the settlement had been created by a dummy settlor, but the real settlor, or instigator as he was referred to, had supplied a memorandum of wishes. In due course a grandson applied for a distribution but the trustees refused on the grounds that 'there is no provision in the instigator's memorandum which would entitle the trustees to make any payment to you at his time'. The New South Wales Court of Appeal held the trustees were entitled to take account of the letter of wishes, provided they were satisfied it still represented the settlor's wishes

As with any expression of wishes, what must be stressed is that a letter of wishes is not binding on the trustee. This is best illustrated by another Bahamian case, *Bank of Nova Scotia Trust Co (Bahamas) Ltd v Barletta* (*Butterworths Offshore Service Cases Vol 1*, p 5). Here trustees had asked the Court to approve the sale of several family companies to one of the beneficiaries and the point was taken that this was not consistent with the settlor's letter of wishes. The Court did not accept this contention on the facts and observed that the influence of the wishes of a settlor on discretionary trustees is limited. Two trenchant observations of the judge are significant:

> 'It is beyond argument that the superior document is the trust instrument. A letter of wishes ranks beneath it. If it is the intention of the settlor to circumscribe the trustees' discretion in the matters to which the letter of wishes speaks, there is nothing to prevent a suitable provision from being incorporated in the terms of the trust instrument.'
>
> 'The whole point is that if a settlor wants to secure a legal power to influence the course of the administration of a discretionary trust, he should have himself named as a trustee in the settlement. If he omits to do so then, in relation to the exercise of the discretion by the trustees, his wishes though naturally deserving of respectful consultation, lack that compulsive quality of being enforceable on the trustees in the exercise of their powers'.

Companies

With companies the key practical issue is company residence. As is described in Chapter 4, an offshore company should avoid UK residence provided its directors do genuinely give consideration to matters put before them and it is clear they would not agree to any request put to them if such is improper unreasonable or against the relevant company law.

In practice matters requiring board decision should be properly considered by the board, and proper minute books and accounts should be kept. The law under which the company is incorporated may not require the accounts to be audited but they should be sufficient to comprise an adequate record of the company's activities over the period concerned. The board should ensure that it has control of and title to all the company's assets.

As with trusts, the board should comply with due formality. Thus if a given number of directors is required to form a quorum, that number should be present at any meeting. If there is a procedure for giving notice of meetings or waiving notice, that should be followed. Should these steps not be taken any decisions are likely to be nullities unless ratified and the bona fides of the whole structure could come into question if investigated by the Revenue.

The practicalities of convening meetings can be difficult if the board is widely scattered, but most offshore company laws allow telephonic meetings or written resolutions. The latter are particularly useful in practice, although it is desirable that the relevant reasons for the board decision are set out and any relevant documents annexed. One particular advantage of the written resolution is that it avoids argument over whether notice was given and who was present. It goes without saying that no director should participate in a telephonic meeting or sign a written resolution whilst in the UK.

As is described above, it is normal and proper for trustees to wish to give effect to the wishes of the settlor. Where the investments are held through a company, there is inevitably temptation for the settlor to express such wishes direct to the directors. Such should be avoided insofar as the settlor is resident in the UK or otherwise present there when communicating with the directors. Any expression of the settlor's wishes should be to the trustees who should then consider them and communicate any ensuing decision to the board. The board should then itself give the matter such consideration as it would any request from a controlling shareholder.

The residence of a company is not jeopardised if it uses UK professional advisers. However two points should be watched. The first is that there are dangers where all the company's funds are managed on a discretionary basis by a UK fund manager. Should the directors take no interest in the manager's performance, there may be risk that central management and control may be held to have passed to the manager. This will be particularly so if the manager is in periodic contact with the settlor or beneficiaries in the UK. The correct procedure is that the board should genuinely review the manager's reports and consider and if thought fit, approve his strategy. Any input of a UK based settlor or beneficiary should come via the trustees.

The second point is that UK advisers may be tempted to draft board minutes or resolutions, particularly for complex transactions. Such is not per se a bad thing but there are obvious dangers if, for example, the UK adviser acts for a UK settlor or beneficiaries and the minute is implementing a request by them. It is also wrong if directors simply sign a written resolution without considering it or, worse still, sign minutes of a meeting without convening it. If tax liability is at issue such slackness will be fraud and a criminal offence.

In general, the sham issue does not arise with companies in the same way as it does with trusts. However in the case of a company wholly owned by trustees, it is necessary to be clear as to whether the company holds as nominee or beneficially. A nomineeship is attractive if it is desired to avoid arguments over company residence or shadow directors, whereas beneficial ownership can be essential for IHT reasons with excluded property settlements. Whichever is desired, clarity should be achieved by properly drawn resolutions and accounts and this is yet another reason why proper company secretarial procedures are as essential offshore as onshore.

Chapter 17

Sham trusts

If a trust is characterised as a sham, the legal analysis is that the trustee holds the assets not on the trusts laid down in the trust instrument, but as nominee of the settlor. A finding that a trust is a sham is often the result of family litigation and in that context can be serious for the trustee for he may end up being found to have misapplied money that was not his, particularly where the settlor is dead. But the importance of the sham concept in a fiscal context has been emphasised by the recent criminal case, *R v Allen* [1999] STC 846.

What is a sham?

In English law the generally accepted definition of what constitutes a sham was given by Diplock LJ in *Snook v London and West Riding Investments Ltd* [1967] 2 QB 786, 802. His words are as follows:

'As regards the contention of the plaintiff that the transactions between himself, Auto Finance and the defendants were a "sham", it is, I think, necessary to consider what, if any, legal concept is involved in the use of this popular and pejorative word. I apprehend that, if it has any meaning in law, it means acts done or documents executed by the parties to the "sham" which are intended by them to give to third parties or to the court the appearance of creating between the parties legal rights and obligations different from the actual legal rights and obligations (if any) which the parties intend to create. One thing I think, however, is clear in legal principle, morality and the authorities (see *Yorkshire Railway Wagon Co v Maclure* [1882] 21 Ch D 309 and *Stoneleigh Finance Ltd v Phillips* [1965] 2 QB 537), that for acts or documents to be a "sham", with whatever legal consequences follow from this, all the parties thereto must have a common intention that the acts or documents are not to create the legal rights and obligations which they give the appearance of creating'.

The important point about this definition is that all parties to a transaction must intend the real transaction to be different from that represented by the documentation. In a trust context, that means both settlor and trustee(s) must be parties to the sham.

A trio of cases have established the relevance of the sham concept in offshore contexts. The message of these cases is that in determining whether a trust is a sham, it is not simply a question of looking at what happened when the trust was created. It is also necessary to look at the subsequent conduct of the parties to see whether their conduct signifies a true trust or whether in reality they are behaving as nominee and absolute owner.

Rahman

The leading case, *Abdel Rahman v Chase Bank (CI) Trust Co Ltd* [1991] (*Butterworths Offshore Service Vol 1*, p 433) concerned a Middle Eastern settlor who wished to protect his assets from forced heirship claims. On English legal advice, a trust was formed, which inter alia gave the settlor right to revoke the trust as respects one-third of the assets in any one year. The income was payable to the settlor, he had power of appointment over what was to happen after his death, and the trustee had power to appoint all the capital back to him, exercisable solely in his interest.

The dispossessed heirs duly attacked the trust after the settlor's death, and their principal line of argument was that the trust fell foul of an old Jersey maxim '*donner et reteinr ne vaut*'. This maxim applies where a donor retains power to dispose of what he has given or where what is given remains in his possession. The Royal Court in Jersey held that the maxim applied to trusts, and that the Rahman trust did indeed fall foul of it. This aspect of the decision has been reversed in relation to offshore trusts by the Trust Law (Jersey) Article 8A.

What is of significance in the present context is that the Royal Court went on to consider how the Settlor and the trustee in fact conducted themselves. After a lengthy review of the facts the Court concluded the trust was a sham in the following terms:

> 'Therefore, having taken into consideration the whole of the evidence and documentation, we were able to reach but a single and unanimous conclusion. KAR retained dominion and control over the trust fund throughout his lifetime. The settlement was a sham in the sense that it was made to appear to be what it was not. The *don* was a *don* to an agent or nominee. The trustee was never made the master of the assets. KAR intended to and in fact retained control of the capital and income of the trust fund throughout his lifetime and used the trust and the deed of appointment made under the trust to make testamentary dispositions. In our opinion, KAR's advisers and the trustee lent their services to the attainment of his wishes'.

The factual findings which led the Royal Court to this conclusion included the following:

(1)   Chase Bank in Switzerland opened the trust account on terms requiring it to make or change investments on the direction of the settlor.
(2)   The settlor negotiated and gave instructions for the replacement of Chase by Advicorp as investment manager in May 1978.
(3) $1m was diverted from money due to the trust in February 1978 on the orders of the settlor. Similar diversions were made subsequently.
(4)   Chase Bank took investment instructions from the settlor.
(5)   The settlor orally stated the trust fund was his own money to use as he wanted.
(6)   Reversionary beneficiaries were not told about the trust.
(7)   All distributions were made on the settlor's orders, without the trustee considering which power was being exercised or executing proper documentation.
(8)   The settlor regularly took money from the trust bank without consulting the trustee.
(9)   On the evidence there was no circumstance in which the trustee would have refused a request from the settlor.

(10) The trustees made loans to settlor's wife on the instructions of the settlor on terms that only the settlor could call in the loans.

(11) The trustees acted in relation to a Liechtenstein Establishment to the order of the settlor.

(12) Advicorp managed the investment on the instructions of the settlor and in practice regarded themselves as answerable to him.

Wyatt

The second case is an English bankruptcy case, *Midland Bank plc v Wyatt* [1995] 3 FLR 11, (also referred to in [1994] Private Client Business, 410). Here a husband and wife owned their house in equal shares. On 17 June 1987 they executed a properly drawn Declaration of Trust declaring they held the house on trust as to half for the wife and as to the other half for their two daughters. The Declaration was then put away and forgotten about until 1991 when it was produced when one of the husband's bank creditors sought security over his share of the house.

The wife could not remember executing the Declaration and the evidence was that the husband never referred to it in business dealings and indeed behaved towards third parties as if he was still part-owner of the house. The judge found that the husband had not in fact intended to give his daughters any immediate beneficial interest but intended the document for production only if the business he was then setting up failed.

A point arose as to whether the wife could be said to be a party to the sham given she did not remember executing the document. As to this the judge said:

'I consider a sham transaction will still remain a sham even if one of the parties to it merely went along with the "the shammer" not either knowing or caring about what he or she was signing'

Allen and Dimsey

The third case is *R v Allen* [1999] STC 846, which concerns a failed tax avoidance scheme. Here, as part of a tax investigation, the accused had been asked to list his assets and he had omitted any reference to assets held in two offshore trusts. Subsequently those trusts came to the attention of the Revenue, and they prosecuted the taxpayer, inter alia claiming that the trust assets should have been included in the list of his assets. The basis of this claim was that the trusts were shams, so that the accused was indeed beneficial owner of the assets held by the trustees.

The accused was convicted in a jury trial in London, and appealed to the Court of Appeal on the grounds that the jury had been misdirected by the trial judge. This appeal was rejected on the grounds that there was overwhelming evidence that the assets were the accuser's 'to dispose of as he would'. The accused treated the assets as his and there was 'no question of the trustees possessing any real power or discretion in the matter'. The evidence is not set out in the report of the case, but once again, the key point is what in practice happened after the alleged trusts were created.

Consequences

Quite apart from demonstrating how a trust may be found to be a sham, these three cases also illustrate the severity of the consequences. In *Rahman* and *Wyatt*, the result was that the assets were at the disposal of the heirs or, as the case may be, the creditors. A question of particular difficulty for any trustee would be if after the death or bankruptcy of the settlor he had incurred fees or even made distributions in accordance with the fictitious trust. In all probability the trustee would have to make these good, for he would have been dealing with the property without the authority of the beneficial owner.

Allen was a tax case and it illustrates the obvious point that if a trust is a sham any hoped-for fiscal advantages are not achieved. Perhaps more seriously, it demonstrates that criminal liability can arise as well.

Minimising risk

Examination of the facts of these three cases shows the risk areas to avoid. The classic danger is where the settlor is a non-domiciliary from a civil law country who thus has little familiarity with trusts. The trustee is a bank who manages his assets, and submits a standard form trust document. The bank says that although this document confers wide discretion on the trustee, in practice nothing will change and the settlor's wishes will continue to be followed. The only difference will be that on the settlor's death the assets will devolve in accordance with the trust and not in accordance with the heirship rules of the settlor's home country or his will. Once the trust is set up, the reality is that in fact nothing changes, and the trustee in practice regards itself as bound by settlor's instructions. Indeed he may often be referred to as 'the client' and his wishes as 'instructions'.

There is no doubt that such a trust is vulnerable to a sham attack. The best way of avoiding such risk is to follow guidelines of the kind set out in the previous chapter and in particular ensure:

(a)   The settlor fully understands what a trust is and, in particular, that it is the trustee who is in the driving seat.

(b)   A trust is in fact the kind of legal relationship the settlor wishes to enter into.

(c)   Once set up, the trustee behaves as a trustee, in the manner described. That is not to say he cannot have regard to and indeed normally follow the settlor's wishes, but it must be clear that the settlor can do no more than make requests, to which the trustee must give genuine consideration.

Chapter 18

Distributions and existing settlements

Some or all of the beneficiaries of many offshore trusts are resident in the UK. Where neither the income nor the gains are assessable on the settlor on an arising basis the key UK tax issue for the trustees is whether and if so how to make tax-efficient distributions to those UK beneficiaries.

Trusts where neither the income nor the gains are assessable on the settlor include the following:

(1) Settlements where the settlor is dead.
(2) Settlements where the settlor, his children and grandchildren, and their respective spouses are totally excluded.
(3) Settlements where the settlor and his children, and their respective spouses are totally excluded but his grandchildren are not. These settlements must have been made before 17 March 1998 and be untainted (see Chapter 25).
(4) Settlements where the settlor is non-resident.
(5) Settlements where the settlor is resident but not domiciled in the UK and he and his spouse are wholly excluded.

A fundamental point about all these settlements is that the tax treatment of distributions is largely unaffected by the residence or domicile of the settlor. For this reason planning strategies for these trusts and in particular distributions are considered here, rather than separately according to the residence or domicile of the settlor. Where however residence and domicile remain important are in relation to the beneficiaries.

Tax treatment of distributions in summary

The tax treatment of distributions to UK beneficiaries may be summarised as follows:

(1) If the distribution is income, it is subject to income tax, the income being treated as a new source. The remittance basis applies if the beneficiary is non-domiciled (see Chapter 13).
(2) If the distribution is a capital distribution and there is relevant – ie accumulated – income in the trust or any underlying company, it is taxed as income under TA 1988, s 740. This is subject to the motive test in TA 1988, s 741 (see chapter 23). It is also subject to a form of remittance basis if the beneficiary is non domiciled and there is no UK income in the structure (see pp 186–7).

(3)   If and to the extent that there is no relevant income, or the motive defence applies, the capital distribution is subject to income tax to the extent that the trust has offshore income gains not previously allocated to a distribution (see pp 248–51). This charge is imposed by TCGA 1992, s 87 as applied by TA 1988, s 762 and does not apply to the extent that the recipient is non domiciled

(4)   Insofar as the distribution is not taxed under any of the above it is subject to CGT under TCGA 1992, s 87 or Sch 4B to the extent of unallocated capital gains in the settlement. This liability does not arise where the recipient is non domiciled, but where liability does arise the rate of tax may be as high as 64%.

Income distributions

Many offshore trustees distribute trust income as income. This happens automatically with fixed-interest trusts and otherwise is a matter of discretion. Such a strategy has the following specific advantages:

(1)   Any withholding tax borne by the income is set against any UK tax charged on the beneficiary (*Singer v Williams* [1921] 1 AC 41; ESC B18).

(2)   Particularly with discretionary and accumulation trusts, the income may be directed at low or nil income beneficiaries such as children.

(3)   UK tax is avoided if the recipient beneficiary is non-resident or non-domiciled. As just noted, in the case of non-domiciled beneficiaries, avoidance of tax is subject to the income not being remitted to the UK (see further Chapter 13).

If income is distributed as income it cannot be taken into account as relevant income under TA 1988, s 740 in relation to a subsequent capital distribution. This is of advantage if the income is paid to a non-resident or non-domiciled beneficiary and the s 740 recipient is resident and domiciled in the UK. But it should be noted that removing the s 740 liability from the distribution may result in a rather higher liability to CGT under TCGA 1992, s 87 and that where this is not so, liability under s 740 will arise if income is accumulated in the future (cf Chapter 22).

Should a beneficiary be non-domiciled an income distribution may be more attractive than a capital distribution. This is because an income distribution attracts the remittance basis under general rules whereas a s 740 distribution is subject to the more restrictive rules in s 740(3) (cf pp 186–7).

Should the trust income consist of or include foreign dividends it is more attractive for a UK resident and domiciled beneficiary to hold an interest in possession rather than receive income in exercise of the trustee's discretion. This is because in the former event he pays tax at the Schedule F rates of 10% and 32.5% (TA 1988, s1B).

Should s 740 apply?

If the distribution is not income, TA 1988, s 740 is the first head of charge to consider. As noted above, this section is subject to the motive test in TA 1988, s 741. That test is analysed in Chapter 23, and if it is satisfied, a capital distribution cannot be taxed under s 740.

Obviously the question of whether the test is satisfied is one of fact. But s 741 does not apply unless evidence sufficient to satisfy the Revenue is supplied and so it is effectively open to the trustees to decide whether or not to supply such evidence and so invoke the test.

At a superficial level invoking the motive test is attractive in that it avoids one potential liability to tax. But as noted above, if a capital distribution is not taxed under s 740 it may be taxed by reference to offshore income gains or capital gains. Since in the latter event the rate of tax is as high as 64%, invoking the motive test can be an expensive mistake.

As a general rule, securing the motive defence is attractive where the likely recipients of any current or future distribution are non domiciled. This is because a non domiciliary is or may be subject to tax under s 740 but is not taxed in respect of offshore income gains or capital gains. Accordingly precluding s 740 by the motive defence renders any capital distribution to him tax-free.

The converse proposition is that as a general rule invoking the motive defence is unlikely to be attractive where the likely recipients of any distribution are both resident and domiciled in the UK, but this will not always be true. Specifically if the likely distributions exceed both the relevant income and the offshore income gains and the capital gains, securing the motive defence will avoid tax on at least part of the distribution while not affecting the fact that part is exposed to CGT at rates of up to 64%.

Section 740 does not apply

No trust gains

If at the date of any capital distribution there are no unallocated offshore income gains or capital gains, the distribution is tax free when made. Tax will however be payable under s 87 insofar as the trustees realise offshore income gains or capital gains in years to come. This result will ensue if the recipient beneficiary is resident and domiciled in the UK when the gains are realised (cf pp 223–4).

This future liability is avoided if the distribution is of all the trust fund for then there is no subsisting trust in which future trust gains can accrue. The liability may also be avoided if any remaining trust fund is resettled in the tax year after the distribution, for then the capital payment will not carry forward. But this technique is subject to the resettlement not itself triggering gains for if it does the capital payment will be taxed by reference to those gains. It is also subject to the two settlements not being viewed as one for the purposes of s 87, an issue discussed on p 200.

Utilising the CGT annual exemption

Modest planning may be achieved by distributing to each UK beneficiary each tax year an amount equal to the basic annual CGT exemption (£7,200 in 2000–01). But this is not effective to the extent that the beneficiary otherwise uses his exemption. It is also unwise if in the year of the distribution there are no trust gains, for then the distribution will not be treated as a gain in the beneficiary's hands until the trustees do realise gains. In that year his exemption may not be available.

Trustees implementing this strategy need to remember that offshore income gains are allocated to any distribution first. There is no annual exemption for offshore income gains so this strategy will not work unless and until all offshore income gains have been washed out.

Distributions to non-residents or non-domiciliaries

Assuming the above strategies are not appropriate, the best solution to the problems posed by s 87 is to confine capital distributions to non-resident or non-domiciled beneficiaries. As noted above, such distributions are not taxed by reference to either offshore income or capital gains. If the distribution to the non-resident or non-domiciliary is of the entire trust fund, the tax problems are at an end. It is however important to ensure that any non-resident recipient satisfies the five year absence rule (see Chapter 35).

The trust's tax problems may also be solved if the trustees distribute to non-resident or non-domiciled beneficiaries an amount equal to the net trust gains to date. In such a case, the trustees may then distribute the balance of the trust fund tax free to UK beneficiaries. The distribution must be in the next year, since otherwise the trust gains will be allocated pro rata between the distribution to the non-residents and distribution to the residents (TCGA 1992, s 87(5)). A further and obvious point is that the distribution to the UK residents must not itself occasion further gains.

It may be that the trust is kept in being after the capital gains and any offshore income gains have been washed out by distributions to non-residents or non-domiciliaries. In such a case it should be remembered that the trust will case to be clean once gains are realised in the future. Here there is a particular trap. This arises if in one tax year the gains are washed out and in the next year hopefully tax-free distributions are made to UK residents. If after this, part of the fund stays in trust, the distribution to the UK residents will be taxed under s 87 as and when the trustees realise future gains in this rump.

A further trap arises if the capital payments in year one to the non-residents or the non-domiciliaries exceed the then total of trust gains. Should the settlement remain in being, gains corresponding to the excess are not treated as accruing until the trustees realise further gains. If by then a recipient of the prior capital payments is UK resident and domiciled, tax liability ensues (see pp 223–4).

IHT implications

Any distribution or resettlement of the kind discussed above should take account of the IHT implications. If the trust is an accumulation and maintenance trust, what can be done may be circumscribed by the terms of the trust itself, given that it has to satisfy the conditions of IHT 1984, s 71. Should a beneficiary enjoy an interest in possession, IHT will not be chargeable on an outright distribution to him or on a resettlement on new trusts under which he is life tenant (IHTA 1984, s 53(2)). But if these conditions are not met the exercise is likely to be a PET. In the event that the original settlement is discretionary, IHT exposure (if any) will be under the discretionary trust regime.

A particular point to note is that even distributions to utilise the annual CGT exemption can have IHT consequences. If the trust is discretionary, there will be a small IHT exit charge, and otherwise there may be a PET unless the trust is an accumulation and maintenance trust or the recipient is life tenant.

These IHT considerations do not apply if the settlor was non-domiciled, save insofar as the property concerned is UK situs (see Chapter 15).

Other strategies

If distributions to non-resident or non-domiciled beneficiaries are impractical or undesirable, there is little that can be done if the trust gains are large relative to the trust fund, apart perhaps from considering avoidance schemes which may from time to time be marketed. When the gains are relatively modest, two possibilities may be considered:

(1) Wash the gains out by distribution to a charity. The Revenue have confirmed that s 87 does not apply on distributions to a charity provided the distribution is applied for charitable purposes (*Tax Bulletin* 36 (August 1998) p 573)).

(2) Split the trust fund, transferring funds equal to the proposed distribution to another trust, and then in the next tax year distributing from that trust. In such a case only a proportionate part of the trust gains will be transferred to the new trust (pp 218–19) and so only that proportion will be capable of attribution to the recipient beneficiaries. The effectiveness of this technique presupposes the two settlements cannot be treated as one, an issue discussed on p 220.

Latent gains

Hitherto, it has been assumed that trust gains have been realised gains. Different strategies are possible where there are few or no realised gains but there are substantial latent gains.

Should a life interest subsist in the assets concerned, any capital gains will be wiped out on the death of the life tenant (TCGA 1992, s 72). Retaining the life interest may have IHT implications however, in that IHT will be charged on the life tenant's death at the estate rate if the settlor was UK domiciled or reliefs such as business property relief do not apply. In appropriate cases, life interests may be appointed where not previously subsisting, but only with due consideration of the income tax and IHT implications. It should also be noted that gains on interests in non qualifying offshore funds are not wiped out on the death of a life tenant.

A more aggressive strategy for latent gains, applicable to any form of settlement, is to split the trust fund as follows:

(1) In one tax year, assets in the trust fund not showing latent gains are transferred to a new trust.

(2) In the next year the asset with the latent gain is sold.

(3) Distributions are made from the new trust. The gain realised in year two in the original trust cannot be attributed to the distributions, as they are made from a different settlement (cf p 221).

Trustees should not implement this scheme by borrowing the funds to advance to the new trust for then they will suffer a deemed disposal of the retained assets under TCGA 1992, Sch 4B (see Chapter 27). Trustees should also ensure that the transfer to the new trust cannot be treated as a capital payment to one of the beneficiaries under that trust and consider whether there is any risk of the two trusts being treated as one. These issues are discussed on pp 220–1 and mean this strategy is not without risk.

Section 740 applies

Should the motive defence not apply to the settlement, TA 1988, s 740 has to be considered as well as s 87. Where it applies, s 740 may be more difficult to avoid for its wording is vague and general.

Dry trusts

Many trusts are often regarded as outside s 740 in practice, for either they have no income or all such income is distributed as income or used in expenses. Such trusts are sometimes known as dry trusts.

It is commonly believed that s 740 does not have to be considered in relation to a dry trust. Such a belief is incorrect, for, if any capital distribution to a UK resident is not matched with capital gains or offshore income gains when made, it becomes taxable under s 740 if and when income is retained in the future. As is explained on p 182, the better view is that future income is not relevant income unless accumulated, but even this is not completely certain. Future liability under s 740 is only avoided in the following scenarios:

(1)   The trust is wound up by outright distributions to beneficiaries.
(2)   The beneficiary who received the benefit is wholly and irreversibly excluded from the trust before the income arises (cf p 182). If before his exclusion part of the trust fund is transferred to another trust he may remain a beneficiary of that trust, although then any income received in that trust from the transferred fund will be relevant income triggering tax liability on the original distributions. The CGT implications of any such transfer should also be considered (see above and p 220).

Distribution to non-residents

Distributions to non-residents avoid the charge under s 740 as well as those under s 87. If at the time of the distribution the structure has only relevant income and not capital gains, the CGT five year absence rule is not in point and so a much shorter absence will suffice. However tax will be charged if offshore income gains or capital gains are realised in the future and the beneficiary is then domiciled in the UK and is or (in the case of capital gains) is deemed to be resident.

Distributions to non-residents do not, in contrast to capital gains, wash out relevant income. Accordingly a subsequent distribution to a UK resident beneficiary is caught by s 740 even if the prior distribution to the non-resident exceeded the relevant income.

A further and rather curious point is that distributions to non-residents do not if s 740 applies, wash out offshore income gains. As is explained on pp 248–51, offshore income gains are treated as relevant income for the purposes of s 740 if not allocated to a capital payment to a resident beneficiary. In practical terms this means they become relevant income for the purposes of s 740.

Distributions to non domiciliaries

As described in Chapter 22, s 740 contrasts with s 87 in charging distributions to non domiciliaries. Only a limited form of the remittance basis applies and even where it is secured the foreign source relevant income otherwise attributable to the distribution is not washed out unless and until remittance takes place.

Distributions to utilise the CGT annual exemption

Self-evidently distributions to UK beneficiaries designed to utilise their annual CGT exemptions will not have that result if the trust has relevant income. This is because the relevant income is allocated to the distributions in priority to the gains and so results in the distributions being taxed as income.

Tax may however be avoided if the recipient beneficiary's personal income tax allowance (£4,385 in 2000–01) is otherwise unutilised. In this event a distribution equal to the allowance absorbs relevant income but is tax-free. However what cannot be done is to make a distribution equal to the personal allowance plus the CGT exemption for then (assuming there is sufficient relevant income) the part of the distribution equal to the CGT exemption is subject to income tax.

Choice of investment

It is a truism that investment decisions should in general be made on commercial rather than tax grounds. But insofar as tax is a factor, income is preferable to capital growth if capital is likely at some stage to be distributed to beneficiaries resident and domiciled in the UK. This is because income will result in such distributions being taxed at 40%, whereas capital gains could result in tax at a rate as high as 64%.

As explained on p 45, certain kinds of investment convert capital gains into income on account of UK deeming legislation, notably deep discount securities (FA 1996, Sch 13) and roll-up funds resulting in offshore income gains (see Chapters 9 and 29). Such investments may therefore be considered. However it should be noted that where a gain is income no taper relief is available. Tax at 64% on a fully tapered gain is much the same as tax at 40% on an untapered gain.

If the distributions are likely to be made to non-domiciliaries resident in the UK, investments whose return is wholly or mainly taxed as capital gain may be preferable. This is because distributions to non-domiciliaries are only taxable to the extent of trust income. However the risk of certain beneficiaries acquiring a UK domicile before the distribution is made should not be forgotten.

With most trusts, capital distributions are unlikely to be made save to non-residents. In this event UK tax is not chargeable whether the trust has realised income or gains. The one caveat is that if the recipient of any distribution is non resident for less than five years, distributions will attract tax by reference to trust capital gains, but not by reference to income or offshore income gains.

Underlying companies

Where the trustees hold the trust investments through an underlying holding company, trust gains and relevant income are likely to be increased. This is because of the potential doubling-up of income and gains (see p 55), and also because there cannot be any credit on distributions by the trust for withholding tax suffered by the company (see p 54). Holding companies are frequently capitalised by loan from the trust with only a nominal share capital. Where this is so, the gain on the shares may far exceed the gain on the underlying investments, particularly if income has been accumulated.

As explained in Chapter 6, holding companies should in general be avoided. Difficult issues arise where the bulk of a trust's investments are already in a company and here the first step is to consider whether the company can be eliminated without tax cost. This is possible if there is no net latent gain on either company's shares or its investments. It is also possible if commercially the company can be sold as a going concern and its shares are free of gain. In all such cases serious consideration should be given to dispensing with the company.

Assuming the shares in the company do show a gain, it is normally worth keeping the company in being, for eventually 40% of the latent gain on its shares will drop out of charge under taper relief. But it is prudent to avoid future growth in the company. In this regard it will help if new investments are effected outside the company in the direct name of the trustees. This however may be difficult if all the trust assets are in the company. Consideration may be given to making loans from the company to the trust but such will be trustee borrowing within TCGA 1992, Sch 4B and so give rise to the risks noted in Chapter 27.

Assuming the company is kept in being, issues will arise as to whether the trustees should receive its income by way of dividend or leave it in the company, thereby increasing the potential gain on its shares. It is difficult to generalise but some relevant considerations are as follows:

(1)   In general distribution of the company's income as income is prudent, for at worst it is relevant income for the purposes of s 740. This means it does not attract notional interest if later distributed to beneficiaries. There is an informal and unpublished Revenue practice not to double count company income paid up to the trust as dividend for the purposes of s 740.

(2)   An exception to this rule is where the trust has a UK life tenant, for then dividends will be assessable on him as they arise.

(3)   Dividends may also be less attractive if capital is likely to be distributed to non-domiciled residents, for such distributions may be taxed by reference to relevant income but not by reference to gains.

Free use of property

This chapter has not considered the free use of property or interest-free loans as a tax planning technique. This is because the Revenue consider that such arrangements amount to an annual benefit under s 740 or a capital payment under s 87 equal to the rent or interest forgone (see pp 184 and 221). The High Court has held the Revenue to be right in relation to s 87. Assuming the judgement is upheld on appeal, the cumulative annual charge is expensive, especially when it is considered that there may be a further benefit or capital payment should the capital eventually be distributed outright.

Traps

The UK tax code now sets many traps for offshore trusts and their UK beneficiaries. It is important to keep these in mind.

The long tail of relevant income and trust gains

It should be remembered that the income taken into account as relevant income, and the gains constituting trust gains, go back as far as 6 April 1981. The practical effect of this is that much research may be needed to confirm that a distribution really will be tax-free and there is clearly a danger old income or gains may be overlooked.

There are two exceptions to the long tail. One is that if the settlor was non-resident or non-domiciled the cut-off date for offshore income gains and capital gains is 6 April 1998 (see p 224). The second is that any gains or income assessed on the settlor on an arising basis are excluded. It should be noted that gains are unlikely to have been so assessed before 17 March 1998 on account of the transitional provisions for pre 1991 settlements (see Chapter 25) and that income within s 739 but not remitted can be relevant income for the purposes of s 740 if the settlor is non domiciled (cf p 183).

Trustee borrowing

The new rules relating to trustee borrowing and transfers of value present real difficulties for offshore trustees. The best practical advice is that trustees should not borrow. If they do borrow any proposed course of action thereafter needs to be reviewed to check it is not a transfer of value under TCGA 1992, Schs 4B and 4C (see Chapter 27).

Tainting

Of much less significant now are the rules as to tainting, (see Chapter 25). However if breached they could bring a pre-1998 grandchildren's' settlement within TCGA 1992, s 86 and so result in gains being attributed to the settlor on an arising basis. If therefore the settlor is alive and is or may become resident and domiciled tainting should be avoided unless in any event the grandchildren and their spouses are all wholly excluded.

Benefits to the settlor

It must be remembered that if the settlor is alive and resident in the UK, inadvertence can cause gains or even income to be assessed as his. This is so in relation to gains if any tax year he or his immediate family receives a benefit (cf TCGA 1992, Sch 5 para 2(i)(c)). In relation to income the same result can follow if he or his spouse receives a benefit (TA 1988, ss 729 and 742(2)(c)). More seriously the receipt of a capital sum or loan can cause the whole income in the structure to be assessed as his for ever or at least until the loan is repaid (TA1988, ss 677 and 739(3)). Great care is therefore required in all dealings as between the settlor and the trust.

Beneficial interests

No UK resident beneficiary should effect a disposal of a beneficial interest in an offshore trust. Should he do so, the transaction is subject to CGT, for the exemption for beneficial interests does not apply unless the trust is UK resident (TCGA 1992, s 85). A particular sting is that normally the beneficiary has a nil acquisition cost, for the creation of an interest under the terms of a settlement does not involve a corresponding disposal and so market value is not substituted (TCGA 1992, s 17(2)). An exception to this is where the trust has emigrated from the UK without previously having been non-resident, for then beneficial interests are rebased (TCGA 1992, s 85(3)).

A beneficiary disposes of his beneficial interest if he sells it, gives it away, or releases it. Save in the case of a sale, market value is substituted, for the transaction is not at arms length (TCGA1992, s 17(1)). In many instances where an interest is released, market value will be nil, for the interest is either discretionary or subject to overriding powers. But save where this is clearly so transactions in beneficial interests should be avoided.

Schemes to avoid the charge on beneficial interests have in the past involved repatriating the trust to the UK prior to the sale of the beneficial interest, or repatriating the trust and then emigrating it again. These schemes are now blocked, the former completely (TCGA 1992, s 76(IB)) and the latter wherever there are unallocated trust gains outstanding at the time of the emigration (ibid s 85(10)).

Transfer to new trusts

As previously discussed, the transfer of all or part of the trust fund to a new trust gives rise to CGT difficulties, particularly the possibility that the transfer is a capital payment to a beneficiary if made in exercise of a power to benefit that beneficiary. This and related issues are discussed on pp 220–1.

Involuntary vesting

Some offshore settlements, particularly older ones, provide for one or more beneficiaries to become absolutely entitled on attaining a specified age or on a specified event. Common examples are accumulation and maintenance settlements which confer absolute interests, or fixed-interest settlements where the remainderman takes absolutely.

Such settlements can be a disaster in tax terms. In the case of the death of the life-tenant, the settled fund may suffer IHT at 40% and then the net proceeds received by the beneficiary may be taxed at 40% under TA1988, s 740 or 64% under 1992, s 87. In the case of vesting under an accumulation and maintenance trust there will be the latter charges and, unless a hold-over election is possible, the total of trust gains will be inflated by any gains on the deemed disposal occasioned by the absolute entitlement (TCGA 1992, s 71). A further misfortune arises if the settlor was non domiciled but the recipient beneficiary is not, for then the assets are propelled straight into the IHT net.

These difficulties may be avoided if the funds are able to be and are appointed on new trusts prior to absolute vesting. Where there is not an overriding power, recourse has to be had to express or statutory powers of advancement. Normally these can be used, for avoidance of the tax penalties can be viewed as sufficient benefit to the beneficiary. But if the exercise amounts to an advance to a new trust, the Revenue are likely to contend it is a capital payment (see pp 220–1) and generally it is essential to take specialist advice, both as to local trust law and as to UK tax.

Chapter 19

Shadow directors

Whether an offshore company is directly owned or owned in a trust, the issue arises of whether there is anybody who can be said to be a shadow director. This issue is relevant because of the code for taxing benefits in kind under Schedule E. That code deals with living accommodation in TA 1988, ss 145–6 and with other benefits in ss 154–168F. It treats any such benefit provided by an employer for an employee as taxable emoluments and there are elaborate computational rules determining the quantum of the benefit. The most relevant in the present context is living accommodation, where the annual benefit is the annual value of the property plus interest at the official rate on such of the purchase price as exceeds £75,000 (see further Chapter 20).

Extended definition of director

On the face of it the benefits in kind code has nothing whatever to do with offshore companies save in the unlikely event that a UK resident is an actual employee or director. In fact this is not so, for TA 1988, s 168(8) gives the term 'director' an extended meaning for the purposes of the code.

Who is caught by this definition turns on how the company is managed. If the company is managed by a director or board of directors, the term 'director' not surprisingly includes any actual director. Should the company be managed by a person similar to a director or by a body similar to a board, the term includes that person or any member of the body concerned. Where the company is managed by the members, the terms includes any member. Last and most important the term 'director' includes any person 'in accordance with whose directions or instructions' any of the persons listed above 'are accustomed to act'.

Strictly only the last of these categories may be a shadow director in the true sense, but in practice the term may be used to describe everybody in the above list who is not an actual director. There is an exclusion for professional advisers (s 168(9)).

For a long time the better view was that the definition in s 168(8) did not bring any shadow director who was not an actual employee into the benefits in kind code. The basis for this view was that the code applies to employees and employment and, while s 168(8) treats certain non directors as directors it does not also deem them to have an employment. This view was however rejected by the Court of Appeal in *R v Dimsey* [1999] STC 846 and so the position now is that if a person falls within the definition of shadow director in s 168(8) he is caught by the code.

That of itself is not quite the end of the matter for, in the present context the putative employer is an offshore company and so non resident. However, as was affirmed in *R v Dimsey* the only territorial limit to the benefits in kind charge is the general Schedule E territorial limit, ie the charge applies if the putative employee is resident in the UK or, if he is non resident, insofar as he performs duties here (TA 1988, s 19).

Who is a shadow director?

Ensuring a person is not a shadow director has been rendered difficult by another recent Court of Appeal decision, *Secretary of State for Trade and Industry v Deverell* [2000] 2 All ER 365. This is not a tax case but turned on the company law definition of shadow director in the Company Directors Disqualification Act 1986, s 22(5). This defines a shadow director as follows:

'a person in accordance with whose directions or instructions the directors of the company are accustomed to act'.

This definition is essentially in the same terms as the final limb of s 168(8), and like s 168(8) it excludes professional advisers.

In *Deverell*, the trial judge asserted two important limitations to the definition, as follows:

'. . . advice on its own will not do. Only if such advice is so given and so accepted as to amount to a direction of instruction (coupled with a pattern of the board being accustomed to act on it) is it relevant'

'Directions or instructions are both words with a mandatory effect. Coupled with the word "accustomed" they . . . contemplate a situation where the board has cast itself in a subservient role to the "shadow", i.e. it does what it is told or to borrow an expression from trust law it "surrenders its discretion" to the shadow. Being accustomed to follow what somebody says does not of itself make what is said a direction/instruction . . . what the court has to find, whether on direct evidence or inference is that the board does what [the shadow] tells it and exercises no (or at least no substantial) independent judgement'.

These limitations were based on obita dicta in earlier cases and widely regarded as correct by advisers. However they were rejected by the Court of Appeal who in substance accepted the Secretary of State's formulation as follows:

'It is suggested that the definition is concerned to identify those with real influence in the corporate affairs of the company whatever the label given to the communications from the shadow to the board. Thus, it is argued, all that is required is that what is said by the shadow to the board is not by way of professional advice but is usually followed over a wide enough area and for long enough. In other words frequent non-professional advice usually acted on is sufficient'.

The Court also held that the shadow director's influence did not have to be over the whole field of the company's activities. Instead it adopted the words of an Australian judge (Finn J) in *Australia Securities Commission v AS Nominees Ltd* [1995] 133 ALR 1:

'The reference in the section to a person in accordance with whose directions or instructions the directors are "accustomed to act" does not in my opinion require that there be directions or instructions embracing all matters involving the board. Rather it only requires that, as and when the directors are directed or instructed, they are accustomed to act as the section requires'.

The Court in *Deverell* held that the two individuals under attack were shadow directors. The facts were complex and are not altogether easy to follow in the reported case. However the following words effectively summarise the factual basis for the decision:

'[The judge's findings] make it plain that Mr Deverell was concerned at the most senior level and with most aspects of the direction of the company's affairs. This could only be achieved by an ostensible consultant if those who were directors acted upon his directions or instructions conveyed by words or conduct. The judge held in terms that Mr Deverell "bossed everyone around from the directors downwards". It is immaterial that, as the judge observed, he was the sort of man who would boss anyone around. The facts, as found, show that he bossed the directors around and, because what he achieved was within the province of the directors, the directors were accustomed to submit to his requirements'.

Implications of Deverell

Prior to *Deverell*, most advisers in an offshore context approached the question of whether a person was a shadow director on the lines taken by the trial judge. In other words danger was avoided provided the board gave genuine consideration to matters put before it, and the alleged shadow gave what could fairly be said to be advice. This approach is clearly no longer valid and the position now appears to be that if the board of an offshore company consistently comply with a non board member's wishes, that individual is at least at risk of being categorised as a shadow director, save insofar as his advice is given in a professional capacity.

Prior to *Deverell*, the view generally taken was that an offshore company was unlikely to have a shadow director resident in the UK unless the involvement of the alleged shadow was such that the company was in any event resident in the UK under the central management and control test. This follows from the fact that genuine consideration by the board negatives residence in the UK (pp 32–3) and was thought to negative shadow directorship. Comparison between *Deverell* and the cases on company residence referred to in Chapter 4 indicate this is no longer so, for it is clear that regularly followed advice may make a person a shadow director under *Deverell*.

Also prior to *Deverell* a commonly-held view was that an individual was much more likely to be a shadow director if he directly owned the company as distinct from being settlor of or beneficiary under a trust which owned it. The rationale of this view was first that a direct controlling shareholder is legally able to remove the board and so in practice can give instructions and second that in any event the shareholder could count as a shadow director as being a member managing the company. These points are still good in relation to directly owned companies and, especially after *Deverell* make it difficult for a controlling shareholder in an offshore company who is not a director to avoid being a shadow director.

But what may have changed as a result of *Deverell* is the position where the offshore company is owned by the offshore trust. Here as is explained in Chapter 16, the trustees are entitled to and indeed bound to take account of the wishes of the settlor, and may after due consideration in practice follow them. So too even after the settlor is dead the trustees may at the behest of the settlor be entitled to and in fact follow the wishes of someone designated by him, normally the beneficiary or a protector.

Of itself the fact that the trustees follow the wishes of such a person does not make him a shadow director of any company they might own. But three factors may lead to a contrary conclusion. The first is that the person's wishes may be communicated directly to the directors of the company. Second, the trustees may so conduct themselves that they are effectively members managing the company, with the result that the settlor or other person becomes shadow director because of wishes he communicates to them. Third and last, the same individuals acting on behalf of the trustee in relation to the trust may also be directors of the company. In such a case it may be unclear to whom the settlor is in reality addressing his wishes or advice.

Practical steps

For the above reasons, the practical impact of *Deverell* on trust structures is that where trustees regularly take account of and follow the wishes of the settlor or a protector or beneficiary, such person is at least at risk of being characterised as a shadow director of any underlying company. What can be done?

First and obvious, the parties can so conduct themselves as to avoid the settlor or other person being a shadow director. But as the discussion above has indicated, such a strategy may not be certain of success if the parties in fact want to give effect to the wishes of the settlor or other person insofar as is possible.

Second and perhaps less obvious if the alleged shadow director is a beneficiary it may not matter that he is caught under the Schedule E benefits in kind code. This is because, as beneficiary, he is likely to be taxable on any benefit, whether under Schedule D Case V or under TA 1988, s 740 or TCGA 1992, s 87. However in many if not most cases such a solution will not be attractive, partly because the benefit in kind code has different computational rules to Case V and ss 740 and 87, and partly because in many cases a benefit within the code will not be within Case V or ss 740 and 87. Examples of the latter are benefits in kind to a non domiciled beneficiary where either the beneficiary is the settlor or the structure has no income (cf Chapters 22 and 26).

Third it should be remembered that if the settlor or other person whose wishes are followed is non resident, the benefit in kind code should not bite. This is because, as described above, it is subject to the Schedule E territorial limitations. However it is essential to avoid any acts which can be described as 'duties' in the UK, for non residents are subject to Schedule E as respects UK duties (Schedule E Case II). This point means that provided the shadow avoids anything which can be construed as duties in the UK, a benefits in kind charge is avoided even if members of his family resident in the UK are in enjoyment of such benefits. It is however of course important that those family members cannot themselves be characterised as shadows.

It may be the benefits in kind code can also be avoided if the putative shadow director is resident but not domiciled. As described on p 108, the emoluments of such a person are subject to the remittance basis provided the employer is foreign and the duties are performed wholly abroad. A tentative suggestion would be that a benefits in kind charge could be avoided if all acts alleged to constitute the individual a shadow director are performed abroad and the benefit is enjoyed exclusively abroad.

In many cases none of these solutions is practical in which case only a fourth is left. This is to ensure that the alleged shadow director does not in fact benefit from the company at all, or, that if he does, such is in any event subject in charge to income tax. In many cases this may be easy to achieve. The biggest difficulty is undoubtedly where the benefit is living accommodation, and here possible solutions are described in relation to non-domiciliaries in Chapter 20.

Chapter 20

Non-domiciliaries and UK homes

Introduction

Non-domiciliaries frequently wish to own a UK home. This chapter analyses the tax problems which arise. It principally addresses the problems faced by non-domiciliaries who are resident in the UK, but at the end consideration is given to non-domiciliaries who are non-resident.

Direct ownership

The natural way for a non-domiciliary who is resident in the UK to acquire a UK or indeed any other home is in his direct ownership. From a tax standpoint this has the advantage that it can be protected from CGT by the private residence exemption (TCGA 1992, s 222). However, it must be remembered that where the UK residence is not on the facts the non-domiciliary's main residence, an election is required if the exemption is to apply (TCGA 1992, s 222(5)). This election must be made within two years of the time when the individual first has two or more residences (*Griffin v Craig-Harvey* [1994] STC 54). An individual is treated as having two or more residences even if one of them is let, or one of them is abroad.

But although protection can be obtained from CGT, direct ownership poses two problems, one major and one minor. The minor problem is that the residence constitutes a UK asset of the non-domiciliary which means UK probate is required on his death. This is tiresome, particularly if he has no other assets.

Inheritance tax

The major problem is inheritance tax. As the home is UK situate it is subject to IHT regardless of the fact that the non-domiciliary has a foreign domicile. If the non-domiciliary dies while still owning it, tax is due at the rate of 40% insofar as it and any other UK assets he has exceed the nil-rate band, which currently (2000–01) stands at £234,000. Since non-domiciliaries tend to own quite valuable homes, this prospective tax burden can be considerable.

There are a number of solutions. One is to acquire the home in multiple ownership, for example the non-domiciliary, his wife, and his children as tenants in common. Provided they have no other assets, the multiplicity of nil-rate bands should be sufficient to avoid IHT, and there will be no gift with reservation difficulties provided the children's shares are funded by cash gifts abroad before the acquisition rather than gifts of interests in the house afterwards (FA 1986, Sch 20 para 2(2)).

Another simple solution is to plan on the basis that the non-domiciliary will sell the house before he dies and remit the proceeds abroad, thereby converting them back into excluded property. Life assurance can be used as protection against untimely death. The disadvantages of this are that life assurance can be expensive and that selling and remitting the proceeds abroad does not secure excluded property status if the non-domiciliary has by then acquired an actual or deemed UK domicile. A variant of this approach is for the non-domiciliary to leave the house to his spouse with her selling or remitting the proceeds abroad. But if this approach is taken it should be remembered that if at the time of his death he has on actual or deemed UK domicile and she does not, only £55,000 of the spouse exemption is available (IHTA 1984, s 18(2)).

A third solution is for the non-domiciliary to give the house to younger members of his family while still relatively young. The gift will be a PET and so provided he survives seven years it will escape IHT. However, there is a snag and this is the gift with reservation (GWR) rules. If after the gift the non-domiciliary goes on living in the house, the gift will be ineffective for IHT purposes, and, if the non-domiciliary is still living in the house when he dies, IHT will be chargeable on his death. This difficulty can be avoided by effecting the gift in cash before the house is acquired, so that the donee makes the acquisition. If this is done, the donor's subsequent occupation of the house does not make the gift a GWR (FA 1986, Sch 20 para 2(2)). However, it should be remembered that the house will then be in the donee's UK estate, which will give rise to an IHT liability in the event of his untimely death.

Mortgages

A more complex solution to the IHT problem is to rely on the IHT rule whereby liabilities charged on a particular asset are taken to reduce the value of that asset (IHTA 1984, s 162(4)). This rule means that if the house is subject to a mortgage which reduces the value of the net equity to below the nil-rate band, IHT is avoided provided the donor has no other UK assets.

A substantial mortgage against the property is probably the best method of overcoming the IHT problems posed by direct ownership, coupled with joint ownership by husband and wife so as to increase the tax-free net equity to a level which provides adequate security. The loss of income resulting from the payment of the interest can be compensated by investment abroad of the funds which would otherwise have gone into the house.

There can, however, be a problem with a substantial mortgage, and this arises from the mechanics of making interest payments. The simple method is to take the borrowing from a UK bank or building society, and meet the interest out of UK income. If this is done the interest may be paid gross without deduction of tax at source (TA 1988, s 349(3)). Many non-domiciliaries, however, have insufficient UK income for this purpose, and the issue which then arises is that the bringing of foreign income to the UK to meet the interest is a remittance of such income, thereby bringing it into charge.

There are three possible ways round this difficulty. One is to use the capital and income account procedures described in Chapter 11 to ensure that what is brought to the UK is not a remittance of income. This is to be recommended as it is straightforward. The next possibility is to make a back-to-back deposit with a foreign branch of the bank and offset the interest on that deposit against the interest chargeable on the loan. The difficulty here is that the existence of the deposit could perhaps give the Revenue grounds for arguing that the loan is not in truth an incumbrance on the property. A further point is that the deposit should not be made out of foreign income, for otherwise the whole exercise could amount to a constructive remittance (TA 1988, s 65(8); see pp 106–7).

The third possible solution is for the borrowing to be from a foreign bank with the interest payments made directly to that bank abroad. The difficulty here is that the non-domiciliary may then be required to deduct lower rate tax at source under TA 1988, s 349(2), for the lender's usual place of abode is outside the UK. The question of whether deduction is required turns on whether the interest has a UK source and so is chargeable under Case III. This issue is discussed on pp 9–11 and the conclusion reached is that an interest has a UK source if the lender is UK resident. The assumption should therefore be that deduction at source is required if interest is paid by a resident individual to a foreign lender.

A way round the problem which is sometimes suggested is for the borrowing to be from a bank in a country with which the UK has made a double tax treaty giving the country of residence sole taxing rights over interest. In such a case, application may be made to the Revenue for a direction to pay the interest gross (the Double Taxation Relief (Taxes on Income) (General) Regulations 1970 (SI 1970/488)).

Direct trust ownership

As explained in Chapter 12, non-domiciliaries frequently own their investments through offshore discretionary trusts. During his lifetime the settlor is normally a discretionary beneficiary. A question which often arises is whether a UK residence can be owned directly by the trust.

Such ownership overcomes one of the problems with direct ownership, namely the need to obtain UK probate in the event of the non-domiciliary's death, for the trust does not die. It is true that offshore trustees are often reluctant to take title to UK properties, but this problem can be overcome by use of a nominee company.

Capital gains tax

Since the trustees own the house directly, all CGT difficulties can be avoided by a private residence election (TCGA 1992, s 225). Even if an election is not made, the trustees are not subject to CGT for they are non-resident. Any chargeable gain is only attributable to the settlor under TCGA 1992, s 86 in the unlikely event that he is both resident and domiciled in the UK when the house is sold. So too, capital payments are not taxable under s 87 by reference to any chargeable gain provided the recipient is non-resident or non-domiciled (cf pp 223–4).

There is one CGT trap. As described on pp 221–2, the Revenue contend that any rent-free occupation by a beneficiary is a capital payment each year equal to the rent forgone. The High Court has held the Revenue to be right, and assuming the judgment is upheld on appeal, capital payment is allocated to trust gains each year and is tax-free so long as the occupying beneficiary remains non-UK domiciled (TCGA 1992, s 87(7)). But if there are no trust gains, the payment is carried forward and allocated to gains as and when they are realised, for example when the house is sold if no private residence election is in force. If by then the occupying beneficiary is UK resident and domiciled, he will be taxable (see further pp 223–4). This trap is only material insofar as the occupying beneficiary is not the settlor, for if he is the settlor and is resident and domiciled when the house is sold he will then be assessable on an arising basis.

Inheritance tax

Strictly the non-domiciliary occupies the house only by licence of the trustees pursuant to express powers conferred by the settlement. As such the Revenue are likely to contend that his occupation of the house is such as to give him an interest in possession in it for IHT purposes (SP 10/79). This means the house is subject to an exit charge, when he first goes into occupation. This charge cannot exceed 6%, and is nominal if the house has just been purchased, for then the house will only have been relevant property for one or two years (IHTA 1984, ss 68(3) and 69(4)).

A more serious consequence of an interest in possession arising is that IHT will be chargeable on the occupier's death at the death rates by reference to the house if he is then still living in it. If he moves out, or the house is sold, the effect will be that his interest in possession terminates and the true discretionary trusts will resume. As such he will make a transfer of value, immediately chargeable at the rate of 20% once the nil-rate band is exceeded.

This difficulty with the notional interest in possession can be avoided if the trustees grant the non-domiciliary a licence or tenancy at will, at a nominal rent of say £100 per year. It appears from SP 10/79 that the Revenue accept that such an arrangement is sufficient to prevent the notional interest in possession arising. However, if the licence or tenancy depreciates the value of the property at all, for example because the trustees would require a court order if the non-domiciliary refused to give up possession, the extent of the depreciation will be subject to an exit charge under the discretionary trust regime. For this reason it is essential that the licence or tenancy really is terminable at will. A further point is that any rental payment is subject to UK income tax under Schedule A, and the non-domiciliary may be required to deduct tax at source if he makes payment direct to the trustees (TA 1988, s 42A).

Assuming the interest in possession point is overcome, the house is a UK asset owned by a discretionary trust and the IHT regime of ten-yearly and exit charges applies. The rate of tax is determined not simply by the value of the house and other UK assets alone, but by their value plus that of the rest of the settled property when it went into settlement (see p 119). However, under current law, the maximum rate is 6% every ten years, and in appropriate cases this may be regarded as acceptable.

If it is not, the taxable value of the house can be reduced by charging a loan against the house. The trustees can take the borrowing abroad and pay the interest out of trust income. If they do the issues as to deductibility of UK tax should not arise, for the key element present when an individual borrows, namely residence in the UK, will be absent. But borrowing abroad is not a complete solution, for whereas with an individual tax is avoided if his UK assets are below the nil-rate band, with a trust the nil-rate band is taken into account in computing the average rate to which all the trust assets are subject. As just noted the foreign assets of the trust are included in this exercise at their value when settled.

One IHT advantage trust ownership brings over direct ownership arises if the non-domiciliary acquires an actual or deemed domicile. Trust ownership means that selling the property and remitting the proceeds abroad still means they are converted back into excluded property. The change of domicile means such opportunities are lost in the case of direct ownership.

Benefits

A final matter to address with direct trust ownership is TA 1988, s 740, under which benefits from offshore trusts received by UK resident beneficiaries are charged to income tax. As is explained in Chapter 22, the Revenue contend that the rent-free occupation of a house is a benefit equal to the rent forgone. This will not matter if the settlor is occupying the house, for, as is explained on p 186, the settlor is not subject to s 740. But in the case of any other beneficiary it does have to be addressed. The neatest way of avoiding difficulty is to hold the house in a separate trust with no income-producing assets, but this creates problems in funding outgoings, and also interest payments in the event of borrowing.

Ownership through a company

The simplest way of overcoming the IHT difficulties with direct or trust ownership is for the house to be owned by a foreign-registered holding company in which the non-domiciliary owns all the shares. If this is done, the shares are the relevant asset for IHT purposes, and, being foreign situs, are excluded property. Unfortunately such a strategy cannot be recommended.

Company residence

The first difficulty is that as with all directly-owned companies it may be difficult to prevent the company from being UK resident. As is described in Chapter 4, it is necessary to show that central management and control is exercised by the board of directors abroad, and this may be difficult, particularly where the sole asset is a UK house lived in by the controlling shareholder. If the company is found to be UK resident, the main practical consequence is that it is subject to corporation tax if a gain is realised on the sale of the house. The corporate ownership means the private residence exemption is not available.

The Schedule E risk

A more compelling danger in using a company is that the non-domiciliary's occupation of the house may be a benefit in kind under Schedule E. Under TA 1988, ss 145–146 an annual charge is imposed where 'living accommodation is provided for a person . . . by reason of his employment'. The amount charged is the annual value of the accommodation plus notional rent equal to a percentage of the amount by which the cost of providing the accommodation exceeds £75,000. The percentage used is the same as the official rate of interest used in taxing free loans and varies with commercial interest rates. The rate for 2000–01 is 6.25% (IR Press Release, 25 January 2000). This represents a very substantial tax charge, the assessable benefit being £57,812 annually on a house costing £1m.

There is no doubt that occupation of a UK residence can be charged under ss 145–146 if the non-domiciliary is an actual director or is an employee of the foreign holding company. This follows because any accommodation provided by the employer for an employee or his family is treated as provided by reason of his employment (s 145(7)). But non-domiciliaries are not normally directors or employees of foreign holding companies, if only because a UK resident director or employee would jeopardise the non-resident status of the company. However, even where the non-domiciliary is not a director or employee, the occupation of the house may still be taxable under ss 145–146. This is because TA 1988, s 168(8) defines the term 'director' as including any shadow director (*R v Dimsey* [1999] STC 846). The meaning of the term 'shadow director' is considered in Chapter 19, and as is concluded there it may be difficult for a non-domiciliary in occupation of the house to avoid being characterised as a shadow director.

Avoiding the risks

One way to avoid the risks entailed in using a company is for the non-domiciliary to buy the house and then give it to the company. This does not occasion IHT, for he owns the shares. There is still liability on the annual value under s 145, but a charge under s 146 is avoided, for the interest factor is applied only to the cost of the house (s 146(4)). Since in the hands of the company that cost is nil, there is no charge. However there are difficulties in taking this route, one of which is company residence, and another Stamp Duty which is chargeable ad valorem at a rate of up to 4% on the gift (FA 2000, s 119).

An alternative solution is to demonstrate that the non-domiciliary is not on the facts a shadow director. This is most likely achieved if the shares in the company are owned in trust, with the evidence demonstrating that if anyone tells the directors what to do it is the trustees. But as is explained on p 152 the recent case of *Secretary of State for Trade and Industry v Deverell* [2000] 2 All ER 365 makes it far from certain this strategy will work.

Using a trust also brings additional problems, namely that if the occupier of the house is not the settlor, his occupation may be taxable as a benefit under TA 1988, s 740 or as a capital payment under s 87 if he acquires a UK domicile. These problems are as discussed earlier in this chapter in relation to direct trust ownership.

Transfer pricing

The new transfer pricing rules are described in Chapter 33 and have applied for income tax purposes since 6 April 1999. There is an argument that a market rent can be imputed to a non-resident company if it owns a house occupied by a shareholder or by a beneficiary under a shareholding trust. As the company is non-resident, any such imputed rent would be chargeable to basic rate income tax. If this argument succeeded its effect would be almost as draconian as a benefit in kind charge. The Revenue have, however, made it known that it will not be their practice to take the point.

Conclusion

The only clear conclusion is that there is no one method which is always right for structuring the ownership of UK houses. Each case has to be considered on its own facts. However, direct ownership gives rise to the fewest problems, the IHT risk either being accepted or countered by one of the methods described above. There is much to be said for the view that his UK home is the one asset a non-domiciliary resident in the UK should own directly.

Non-residents

Many individuals who own residential property in the UK are both non-resident and non-domiciled. At one time any accommodation available in the UK ipso facto made such an individual resident here, but this is no longer so (see Chapter 2).

Direct ownership of the property results in IHT exposure in the same way and to the same extent as if the individual is UK resident. The techniques for avoiding the exposure while still retaining direct ownership are as described on pp 155–7. One technique which has rather more potential, is the mortgage solution, for since the individual is non-resident, deduction at source should not be required on any interest on a foreign loan. Further foreign income can be used to meet interest on a UK loan and indeed other expenses, for, since the individual is non resident, remittances are not taxable.

Trust ownership of the property entails broadly the same considerations as are discussed on p 157. However, as the individual is non-resident, occupation cannot result in a taxable benefit for the purposes of TA 1988, s 740 and it only constitutes a capital gain if the occupation is not matched with trust gains as it happens and by the time there are trust gains the occupier is both resident and domiciled in the UK (cf pp 223–4).

In practice non-resident individuals normally own UK residential property through offshore companies, owned either directly or in trust. For the reasons given above, there may be an individual who on the facts is a shadow director of the company. But as is explained on p 152 providing on the facts no duties of the hypothetical employment can be said to be performed in the UK, there is no Schedule E charge.

Avoidance of duties may be easy if the shadow director is not the occupier, for example where the occupier is a member of his family. But if the shadow director is the person who uses the house, the Revenue could perhaps argue that such matters as organising repairs and insurance are duties, by definition performed in the UK. This danger, if such it be, may be avoided if the company appoints a managing agent to discharge those duties, so that the only obligations imposed on the occupier are negative ones such as avoiding damage to the property or annoyance to neighbours.

Since the individual is non-resident, company residence in a corporate owner-ship structure is unlikely to be an issue. Such risk as there is should be avoided if the director of the company and the trustees conduct themselves properly (cf Chapter 16).

Part five

Anti-avoidance legislation

Chapter 21

Section 739

Introduction

Section 739 was originally enacted in 1936 (FA 1936, s 18). It passed into the 1970 consolidation legislation as TA 1970, s 478. It has long been the Revenue's principal weapon for countering offshore avoidance by individuals.

In 1996 the then government instituted a working party of Revenue officials and practitioners to review s 739 and the other legislation relating to the transfer of assets abroad. This group reported at the end of 1997 but its work did not result in legislation. However, the Revenue published key areas of their established practice in *Tax Bulletin* 40 pp 651–653 (April 1999; RI 201).

Conditions for liability

The conditions for liability under s 739 are as follows:

(1) The taxpayer must be ordinarily resident in the UK in the year of charge.
(2) He must have made a transfer of assets.
(3) Income must be payable to a person resident or domiciled outside the UK.
(4) The income must be so payable by virtue or in consequence of the transfer, either alone or in conjunction with associated operations.
(5) The motive defence in TA 1988, s 741 must not apply.
(6) The taxpayer or his spouse must have power to enjoy the income or receive a capital sum.

The motive defence is discussed in Chapter 23. The remaining conditions for the application of s 739 are discussed in this chapter.

The transfer of assets

The most obvious example of a transfer of assets is the transfer of cash or investments to a foreign company in exchange for an issue of shares or debentures: this class of transaction was the original target of s 739. But the term 'assets' includes property or rights of any kind and, in relation to rights, 'transfer' includes the creation of rights (TA 1988, s 742(9)). Accordingly, 'transfer of assets' includes:

(1)   A transfer of property.
(2)   A transfer of rights.
(3)   The creation of rights.

It is rarely worth contending that a transfer of assets has not taken place. In particular, the inclusion of the creation of rights embraces the making of a settlement or a declaration of trust. The phrase has been held to include the grant of a lease, and extends to the formation of a partnership (*Vestey's Executors v IRC* [1949] 1 All ER 1108, 31 TC 1). A taxpayer also creates rights if he enters into a contract of employment and so a taxpayer who agrees to work for an offshore company is effecting a transfer of assets (*IRC v Brackett* [1986] STC 521). A transfer of assets also occurs where a person takes out a life policy with an offshore life assurance company (cf *IRC v Willoughby* [1997] STC 995).

Whatever form the transfer takes, the recipient need not be resident or domiciled outside the UK when it is made. Thus s 739 can apply if the original transfer is made to a resident company provided the company subsequently migrates (*Congreve v IRC* [1948] 1 All ER 948). So too the creation of a resident settlement which subsequently becomes non-resident is clearly caught.

The view is sometimes expressed that s 739 does not apply if the assets transferred are already abroad when the transfer is made. Section 739 is contained in TA 1988, Part XVII, Chapter III, which is headed 'Transfer of assets abroad' and s 739(1) predicates income becoming payable to non-residents. Semantically it is difficult for assets to be transferred abroad if they are already abroad, and for income to become payable to non-residents if it is already so payable. However, commonsense indicates that such an interpretation of s 739 is unlikely to be right, and a Special Commissioner so held in *IRC v Willoughby* [1995] STC 143, 161.

Associated operations

An operation is an associated operation even if it is effected by someone other than the person who made the original transfer. Associated operations can be operations of any kind effected in relation to any of the following (TA 1988, s 742(1)):

(1)   any of the assets transferred;
(2)   any assets representing those assets, whether directly or indirectly;
(3)   any income arising from assets transferred or assets representing them;
(4)   any assets directly or indirectly representing accumulations of income.

If an operation is not effected in relation to any of the above, it cannot be an associated operation. Thus where the transferor exchanges shares in a UK company for shares in an offshore holding company, the assets transferred are the shares exchanged and the assets representing them are the holding company shares. If the holding company subsequently buys in its shares from other shareholders or enters into contracts with third parties such would not be associated operations, at least insofar as not funded by dividends from the original UK shares (*Carvill v IRC* [2000] STC (SCD) 143, 164–5).

The term 'operation' does not include omission, and so associated operations do not extend to omissions. It is, however, plain that the operations need not have been contemplated as part of a single scheme at the time of the transfer. Thus in *Corbett Executrices v IRC* [1943] 2 All ER 218, the formation and sale of investments to a Canadian subsidiary were quite unconnected with the original transfer to the UK parent.

In decided cases, the inclusion of operations relating to income of the assets transferred has proved significant. Thus the accumulation of income by a transferee company and the management of the transferred assets have been held to be operations associated with original transfer to the company (*IRC v Herdman* (1967) 45 TC 394). So too the activities of the partnership in which the transferee was partner were held to be associated with the transfer of the partnership share to the transferee (*Latilla v IRC* [1943] AC 377, [1943] 1 All ER 265).

Associated operations can bring an otherwise innocent transfer within s 739. Thus in *Congreve v IRC* [1948] 1 All ER 948, the original transfer did not offend, for the transferee company was then registered and resident in the UK. But the company was subsequently exported and this was held to be an operation associated with the transfer, thereby enabling s 739 to be invoked. Similarly, where an original transfer to a UK company was not caught, the subsequent sales of investments by that company to its Canadian subsidiary brought s 739 into operation (*Corbett Executrices v IRC* (supra)).

Almost the only occurrence which has not been regarded as an associated operation is death (*Bambridge v IRC* [1955] 3 All ER 812). Since it was held that making a will was an associated operation, exclusion of death is of little practical significance.

In the Revenue view, a transaction effected before the transfer can count as an associated operation (*Tax Bulletin* 40 (April 1999) p 652).

Income payable

It is fundamental that income be payable to a person resident or domiciled out of the UK. The person to whom the income is so payable need not be or include the original transferee (*Corbett Executrices v IRC* [1943] 2 All ER 218). But the income must become payable to the non-resident or non-domiciliary by virtue or in consequence either of the transfer alone or of the transfer in conjunction with associated operations. This prevents s 739 from applying to income of a non-resident company if the transferee buys the company as a going concern and does not put any cash into it. Such was conceded in *Vestey v IRC* [1980] AC 1148, [1979] 3 All ER 976 in relation to the income of an insurance company purchased by the transferee trustees.

It is sufficient if the entity to whom the income is payable is domiciled outside the UK, even if it is resident here (cf *Gasque v IRC* [1940] 2 KB 80, 23 TC 210). All foreign registered companies are deemed to be resident outside the UK (TA 1988, s 742(8)). This deeming, however, applies only for the purposes of s 739, and so the income of a foreign registered company resident in the UK is potentially assessable either to corporation tax on that company or to income tax under s 739 on any person who is transferor (*R v Dimsey* [1999] STC 846).

There is no doubt that s 739 applies if income is payable to non-resident discretionary trustees. This is so even if the proper law of the settlement is that of one of the constituent countries of the UK (*Vestey v IRC* [1980] AC 1148, [1979] 3 All ER 976). The position is less clear with fixed-interest trusts and the application may depend on the proper law of the settlement. If that law is

English then the life tenant's residence or domicile should determine whether s 739 applies. This result follows because English law deems the life tenant to be specifically entitled to each item of trust income (*Baker v Archer-Shee* [1927] AC 844 at 866 per Lord Wrenbury; see further p 7). The position will be the same if the trust's proper law is that of any other jurisdiction which in this respect follows English law. If, on the other hand, the proper law does not attribute rights in specific income to the income beneficiary, the income is that of the trustees and their residence or domicile may well be the decisive factor (*Archer-Shee v Garland* [1931] AC 212; *Astor v Perry* [1935] AC 398).

In *IRC v McGuckian* [1997] STC 908 the taxpayer had created an offshore trust of which his wife was life tenant. The offshore trustee then sold the right to a dividend for a substantial capital sum. The assignment fell to be disregarded under the *Ramsay* principle, and the House of Lords held that this meant that the dividend was income received by the trustee for the purposes of s 739. The point that it was the life tenant's income if the sale was disregarded appears not to have been considered.

At one time uncertainty arose with mixed-residence trusts, in that income could not properly be said to be payable to persons resident outside the UK if one or more of them was resident in the UK (cf *Dawson v IRC* [1989] STC 473, [1990] 1 AC 1). Now, however, this difficulty no longer exists, for all trustees of a mixed residence trust are deemed to be UK resident unless the settlor was non-resident and domiciled when he put funds in the settlement (TA 1988, s 110).

Power to enjoy

An individual is chargeable under s 739 if he made the original transfer and he or his spouse has power to enjoy the income of the non-resident entity (s 739(2)). The taxpayer is treated as having power to enjoy in five situations specified in paras (a)–(e) of TA 1988, s 742(2).

These definitions are so wide that it is difficult to conceive of actual enjoyment which is not also deemed enjoyment. Furthermore, the normal rules of construction have to be waived in two respects (s 742(3)). First, attention is directed to the substantial result of the transfer and any associated operations; and second, benefits which may accrue to the taxpayer have to be taken into account, even if he has no right in law or equity to them.

In the majority of cases the sole question worth asking in relation to power to enjoy is whether the taxpayer or his spouse is an actual or potential beneficiary or has non-fiduciary powers of control. If the answer is affirmative, the taxpayer almost certainly has 'power to enjoy'; if negative, he probably does not.

Para (a)

The first situation in which a taxpayer has power to enjoy is where the income concerned is in fact so dealt with as to be calculated to enure for the benefit of the taxpayer. The application of this paragraph has been held to be a question of fact. In *Vestey's Executors v IRC* [1949] 1 All ER 1108 at 1116 Lord Simonds said the paragraph required precise findings of fact and in *Vestey v IRC (No 2)* [1978] STC 567 at 579 Walton J considered that 'calculated' meant 'reckoned' or 'estimated' rather than 'likely'.

IRC v Botnar [1999] STC 711 is the leading case on para (a). Here the taxpayer had created a Liechtenstein settlement under which the only named beneficiaries were persons in the legal profession connected with the protector. The taxpayer was named as an excluded person and as such clause 23 of the settlement prevented him from taking 'any benefit in accordance with the terms of this Settlement'. Clause 3 of the settlement included wide overriding powers including power, by clause 3(c), to transfer the trust fund to another trust, freed and discharged from the trusts of the original settlement, and notwithstanding that persons who were not beneficiaries of the original settlement might be beneficiaries of the transferee settlement. Clause 3(c) did not contain any express provision preventing the taxpayer from benefiting under any such transferee settlement. A memorandum made when the original settlement was created indicated that it was envisaged that the power in clause 3(c) could at some stage be exercised to transfer the trust fund to a new trust, whose trustees would in due course add the taxpayer as a beneficiary. There was also evidence that leading English counsel had advised that this would be a proper course to take. During the years 1974–1990, no income accrued to the trustees but well in excess of £100m was received by underlying holding companies in dividends from a UK company run by the taxpayer.

The Court of Appeal held that the retention of the income by the holding companies amounted to dealing with the income and that the Commissioners were entitled to find, as they had, that it had been so dealt with as to be calculated as to enure at some point in time for the benefit of the taxpayer, as para (a) requires. However, a more fundamental point arose because it was accepted by the Revenue that para (a) could only be invoked if the trustees' purpose in so dealing with the income was proper – in other words if their intention to transfer the trust fund to a new trust from which the taxpayer could benefit was proper. Two members of the Court of Appeal held that as a matter of construction it was and the third held that while as a matter of construction it was not, the scheme could still have been effected lawfully, for the settlement gave the trustees power to take and act on the opinion of suitably qualified counsel.

IRC v Botnar is an important decision, not least because it confirms that if there is any possibility of benefit being lawfully conferred on the taxpayer, s 739 is likely to be in point. An interesting point is the acceptance by the Revenue that para (a) does not apply if income is dealt with unlawfully or in breach of trust.

A question raised by para (a) is whether it extends to income accumulated and beneficially owned by a natural person. This question would arise if the taxpayer had given the assets to a natural person on the understanding, albeit not the obligation, that the donee would deal with them as the taxpayer directed. Such arrangements may be vulnerable, if in reality the income will at some stage be paid over to the taxpayer. Similarly, devices to route payments out of trusts or companies through natural persons to the taxpayer could be caught, for, as noted, potential benefits can be taken into account, even if the taxpayer has no legal entitlement to them (s 742(3)).

Para (b)

Paragraph (b) operates where the income increases the value to the taxpayer of assets held by him or for his benefit. It catches the classic operation at which s 739 was originally aimed: sale of income-producing assets to a foreign company in consideration of the issue of shares or debentures. It extends to situations where the purchase price is simply left outstanding or is secured by promissory notes. Here para (b) applies because the income increases the company's assets, thereby enhancing the security, and hence the value of the loan notes (*Howard de Walden v IRC* [1942] 1 KB 389, [1942] 1 All ER 287; *Ramsden v IRC* (1957) 37 TC 619).

Since para (b) refers to assets held for benefit of the taxpayer, its ambit includes cases where he has settled shares in the transferee company and retains a life interest under the settlement. It probably also extends to settlements of shares where the taxpayer is only a discretionary beneficiary, for then it can be said that he may benefit from any enhancement in the value of the shares (cf s 742(3)).

Para (c)

Paragraph (c) applies if the taxpayer in fact receives a benefit, or is entitled to receive one. The benefit must come from either the income or monies available because of the effect of associated operations on the income. The term 'benefit' includes any payment (s 742(9)(c)), so there is an overlap with s 739(3), which, as described below (p 171) deems the income of the transferee to be that of the transferor if he receives or is entitled to receive a capital sum.

The application of para (c) to companies is substantially covered by that of para (b). But one instance where the former would apply and the latter not, would be where the taxpayer has divested himself of the company's shares and the company was empowered to (and did) make a donation to the taxpayer.

Paragraph (c) catches benefits conferred by trustees in breach of trust. Thus in *IRC v Botnar* [1999] STC 711, trustees had funded the acquisition of a flat for the settlor, who was not a beneficiary. It was accepted that the funding had been a misapplication, but nonetheless the settlor's use of the flat was an actual benefit within para (c).

Para (c) has been held to apply in certain rather surprising contexts. Thus in *IRC v Brackett* [1986] STC 521, a taxpayer was held to receive benefits where an offshore company (i) bought properties from the taxpayer in an illiquid market; (ii) provided money for repairs; and (iii) paid a salary to the taxpayer and provided for his moral obligations.

Para (d)

Paragraph (d) applies if the taxpayer may become entitled to beneficial enjoyment of the income concerned, and the events which will cause him to become so entitled are the exercise of one or more powers. It does not matter in whom the powers are vested, or that consent may be required to their exercise. This paragraph is directed at fiduciary powers and accordingly is principally applicable where income is payable to trustees. It catches the classic device of the revocable settlement, and also settlements where trustees have power to appoint absolute or income interests back to the settlor.

The powers must be so as to confer entitlement to income. Discretionary powers to pay or apply income to the taxpayer after it has arisen are not caught. Thus in *Vestey v IRC* [1980] AC 1148, [1979] 3 All ER 976, potential discretionary income beneficiaries were ignored. Whether a power to appoint accumulations of income is caught was discussed but not resolved in that case.

In *IRC v Botnar* [1999] STC 711 the income had been paid to and retained by offshore companies. The taxpayer was excluded from the settlement which owned those companies, but as noted above, he could have been added as a beneficiary of a settlement to which the trust fund had been transferred. The Court of Appeal held on these facts that the reference to the successive exercise of powers included power to procure a dividend and powers by potentially exercisable by the transferee trustees.

Para (e)

This paragraph applies where the taxpayer is able in any manner to control the application of the income. The Revenue successfully invoked this paragraph where the transferee was a split-level company in which the taxpayer had retained the voting shares (*Lee v IRC* (1941) 24 TC 207).

The Revenue have been less successful with trusts. Situations where a taxpayer is a protector, or where he can hire and fire trustees or otherwise direct how the trust income is dealt with, might seem vulnerable. But the paragraph has not been so applied (*Vestey's Executors v IRC* [1949] 1 All ER 1108, 31 TC 1 and *IRC v Schroder* [1983] STC 480). Apparently, control within para (e) does not extend to fiduciary powers vested in the taxpayer as trustee or protector of a settlement.

Capital sums

Section 739 also applies if the taxpayer or his spouse receives a capital sum, either before or after the original transfer (s 739(3)). The payment of the sum must be connected with the transfer or an associated operation. The term 'capital sum' includes the making or repayment of a loan. Otherwise the term 'capital sum' includes any capital sum not paid for full consideration, and a sum is treated as paid to the taxpayer if it is paid to a third party at his direction, or as the result of an assignment by him of his right to receive it (s 739(4) and (5)).

The courts have tended to construe this head of charge restrictively. Where the purchase price of assets is left outstanding, the debt is not a loan and thus the eventual payment by the transferee to the transferor is not caught. However, it should be noted that the existence of the debt gives the taxpayer power to enjoy within s 742(2)(b) (*Ramsden v IRC* (1957) 37 TC 619). It has been held that a short-term loan to reduce the transferee's pre-existing indebtedness to a bank was not caught on the grounds that it was not connected with either the transfer or with any associated operation (*Fynn v IRC* [1958] 1 All ER 270, 37 TC 629).

The quantum of the taxpayer's liability

Power to enjoy

Under s 739(2), the taxpayer is liable if by virtue or in consequence of the transfer and associated operations he has power to enjoy any income of a non-resident or non-domiciled person. If he is so liable, all that income is to be treated as his for all tax purposes, regardless of the size of the actual or potential benefit he does or could enjoy. This was established in *Howard de Walden v IRC* [1942] 1 KB 389, 25 TC 121, where all the transferee's assets had come from the taxpayer.

The question which the court left open in *Howard de Walden* was what the taxpayer's position would be if he had provided some only of the transferee's assets; if, for example, he had exchanged assets for shares in a pre-existing foreign investment company. In *Congreve v IRC* [1948] 1 All ER 948, the court held, obiter, that all the income would be taxed as the transferee's if he had the requisite power to enjoy. It now appears this is not the law, for it is quite clear that in *Vestey v IRC* [1980] AC 1148, [1979] 3 All ER 976 the House of Lords regarded a taxpayer as assessable only on income from assets he had himself transferred. This is accepted by the Revenue (*Tax Bulletin* 40 (April 1999) p 651). It was followed by a Special Commissioner in *Carvill v IRC* [2000] STC (SCD) 143, 169.

It is plain from the wording of s 739(2) that liability only arises if the taxpayer has power to enjoy in the tax year concerned. He is not caught merely because he had such power in a previous year.

Capital sum

As regards capital sums, it is clear that the charge is on the transferee's income which has become his by virtue of the transfer and associated operations. Receipt of a single small capital sum can accordingly cause the transferor to be taxed on the entirety of the income concerned for ever (*Vestey v IRC* [1980] AC 1148, [1979] 3 All ER 976). But the charge is restricted to income derived from assets the taxpayer himself transferred. It is to be stressed that once the transferor has been in receipt of a capital sum within s 739(3), liability under s 739 remains forever even if in subsequent years the transferor does not and cannot benefit. In many respects this is a trap, particularly where, for example the transferor might be paid a capital sum out of a settlor-interested settlement and then excluded. An exception is made if the s 739(3) charge was occasioned by a loan to the taxpayer and that loan has been repaid for then liability under s 739(3) ceases in the tax year following repayment (s 739(6)).

Trading profits

It is often argued that s 739 does not extend to trading profits, on the grounds that what a trading transferee receives are gross receipts rather than income payable to him. Such arguments cannot be supported (*Latilla v IRC* [1943] AC 377, 25 TC 107; *Chetwode v IRC* [1977] STC 64, [1977] 1 All ER 638; *IRC v Brackett* [1986] STC 521). In many cases, however, trading profits are protected from s 739 by the motive defence. The Revenue allow trading profits to be offset by past trading losses, but only insofar as losses and profits accrue to the same company (*Tax Bulletin* 40 (April 1999) p 652).

Actual benefit

Section 743(5) imposes a special rule where the transferor has power to enjoy by virtue of s 742(2)(c), and that sub-paragraph applies solely by reason of the transferor having received an actual benefit. It charges the full amount of the benefit to income tax in the year of receipt, save insofar as the transferor has already been taxed on the income from which it is derived. This subsection is expressed as applying notwithstanding the rule that the transferor is not subject to basic-rate tax on income which has borne basic-rate tax in the hands of the transferee. In *IRC v Botnar* [1999] STC 711, the Court of Appeal decided that where para (c) applies solely by reason of actual receipt of benefit, s 743(5) restricts the charge to the amount or value of the benefit. This decision, it should be noted, will only be of advantage to the transferor where the benefit is not a capital sum within s 739(3), for if it is, the latter subsection will, as noted above, attach to all the transferee's income.

The Court of Appeal in *IRC v Botnar* did not have to consider how the benefit should be valued, but the Special Commissioner did ([1998] STC 38). The benefit in question consisted of the rent-free occupation of a flat under licence and the Special Commissioner held that the value of the benefit for each of the two years in question was the rent the taxpayer would have had to pay on an arm's length letting.

The charge to tax

Income deemed to be the transferor's under s 739 is charged under Schedule D Case VI. An exception is made for UK and foreign dividends where the charge is under Schedule F (TA 1988, s 743(1)). This means the rate of tax is 32.5% rather than 40% (or 10% rather than basic rate if the transferor is not a higher-rate taxpayer) (TA 1988, ss 1A and 1B).

Tax at the basic rate, lower rate or the Schedule F ordinary rate is not charged insofar as the income has already born such tax whether by deduction at source or otherwise (s 743(1)).

Deductions

TA 1988, s 743(2) allows the taxpayer the same deductions and reliefs as if the income had been his, but no more. Accordingly the management expenses of a transferee investment company are not allowed (*Chetwode v IRC* (supra)).

An important issue is whether, in computing s 739 liability, the transferor should be allowed deductions for such matters as trading losses and interest payments incurred by the transferee. The logic of s 739 deeming the transferee's income to be that of the transferor suggests that they could, the transferee's deemed s 739 income being the transferee's total income as computed for UK tax purposes. Dicta in *Carvill v IRC* [2000] STC (SCD) 143, 169, however indicate this is not the correct analysis, each item of the transferee's income being separately attributed to the transferor with no credit for general deductions. This approach is also that adopted by the Revenue, in that they do not allow the transferor to credit the transferee's trading losses against the transferee's other income (*Tax Bulletin 40* (April 1999) p 652).

There seems to be no reason why the transferor's actual deductions and reliefs should not be set against his deemed s 739 income. The wording of s 743(2) suggests that this can be done and such is consistent with the deeming tenor of s 739.

Double tax treaties

Non-resident entities potentially caught by s 739 are frequently resident in jurisdictions with which the UK has concluded a double tax treaty. Normally the treaty exempts certain categories of income accruing to the non-resident from UK tax and the issue which arises is whether such exemption confers protection from s 739. Dicta in the Court of Appeal in *Bricom Holdings v IRC* [1997] STC 1179 at 1195 suggest it does, for s 739 simply deems the transferee's income to be that of the transferor. In *IRC v Willoughby*, however, the Special Commissioner took a different view on a point not considered by the Court of Appeal ([1995] STC 143 at 168–169). In that case, the income in question accrued to a Manx enterprise, and as such formed part of the commercial profits of the enterprise exempted from UK tax by Article 3(2) of the Double Taxation Relief (Taxes on Income) (Isle of Man) Order 1955. The Special Commissioner decided that this exemption applied only to the actual person to whom the profits accrued, not to a person whose income they might be deemed to be under s 739.

Deemed income

Income taxable under s 739 includes offshore income gains under the offshore fund legislation (TA 1988, s 762(5); see p 249) and deep discount (FA 1996, Sch 13 para 12). It also includes sums which would be treated as income under the accrued income scheme if the offshore entity was UK resident (TA 1988, s 742(4)). The accrued income scheme applies when securities are sold and its effect is to treat the accrued income element in the sale proceeds as income (TA 1988, ss 713–14). It applies to foreign corporate and governmental bonds as well to UK bonds and so is material whenever an offshore entity holds fixed interest investments (cf TA 1988, s 710(2) and (12)).

Multiple structures

It is common for offshore trusts to hold assets through one or more holding companies. Strictly, the s 739 liability can be doubled up, as where the company receives income and then distributes the income as dividend to the trust. In practice the Revenue seek to avoid such double charging, although such practice has not been formalised in any published statement. A problem can occur if the company does not pay a dividend but is liquidated or wound up. In that event the gains attributed to the settlor under TCGA 1992, s 86, are not reduced by the income taxed under s 739.

Overlap with settlement code

In law, income arising to an offshore trust is taxable under both the income tax settlor code and under s 739 if the settlor is a beneficiary. In practice the Revenue do not regard themselves as entitled to tax the settlor twice (*Tax Bulletin* 40 (April 1999) p 652). Normally the settlement code is invoked rather than s 739. It appears that this practice is also applied where the income arises to an underlying company, but only if it is paid up immediately to the trust.

Overlap with other charging provisions

Section 739 applies even if the income is in fact otherwise chargeable to tax (*IRC v McGuckian* [1997] STC 908). It is unclear whether the effect of s 739 is to deem the income not to be that of the transferee, so precluding the Revenue from charging him as an alternative. It appears from *R v Dimsey* [1999] STC 846 that if the Revenue sought to tax both the transferor and the transferee, such could be prohibited as an abuse of power.

Non-domiciliaries

Until 1981, non-domiciled transferors were potentially liable in respect of foreign-source income under s 739 for the section predicates that the income is received in the UK (*Congreve v IRC* [1946] 2 All ER 170, 30 TC 163, 190, per Wrottesley J). But a relaxation was introduced in 1981 and now a non-domiciliary is relieved from tax on such income as would not be chargeable had it in fact accrued to him (TA 1988, s 743(3)). This is discussed further in Chapter 12 and effectively it introduces the remittance basis, applying if neither the taxpayer nor the transferee makes a remittance.

As noted above, a transferor who has power to enjoy because he receives a benefit within s 742(2)(c) is taxable on the amount or value of the benefit (unless the benefit is also a capital sum in which case s 739(3) deems all the transferee's income to be his). This rule is contained in s 743(5), which is expressed to apply insofar as the benefit is not derived from income already charged under s 739.

Section 743(5) is not expressed to be subject to the remittance basis and so on one view could be said to catch distributions of income to non-domiciliaries made and kept abroad. The Revenue have, however, given no sign of reading it this way and indeed have confirmed that TA 1988, s 740 cannot apply to distributions to the transferor where the remittance basis has prevented s 739 applying. As noted above, *IRC v Botnar* [1999] STC 711, 732 established that s 743(5) is a separate charging provision. But this was in the context of cutting down rather than enlarging liability where there is power to enjoy only by virtue of an actual receipt. In all the circumstances, s 743(5) must be read as subject to the remittance basis.

Subsequent receipts

Relief is given where the taxpayer subsequently receives income taxed under s 739. This relief applies if (a) the transferor has been charged to tax on income which has been deemed to be his under s 739 and (b) it is subsequently received by him. If this occurs the income received is deemed not to form part of his income again for income tax purposes (TA 1988, s 743(4)).

Strictly, this relief applies only if the transferor has actually been charged under s 739 rather than being merely chargeable. In theory this rule could cause hardship in cases where s 739 is invoked only after some part of the relevant income has been paid to the transferor as income, for, strictly, such income would be chargeable both at that time and under s 739. In practice the Revenue are not thought to take this point. A more serious issue is that relief is not conferred from any tax save income tax. Accordingly, if income is payable to a non-resident company in which the taxpayer holds shares directly, and that company is liquidated, the transferor will be liable to CGT in respect of the shares, and the gain will reflect all the income already taxed as his under s 739. Such a charge is avoided, and s 743(4) applies, if the accrued income is paid out as dividend, for then it is income in the hands of the transferor.

The relief for subsequent receipts applies notwithstanding the fact that the receipt is a new source of income, for if the receipt was not a new source, there would be no separate entity to which the income was originally payable, and thus no s 739 charge at all. Accordingly, the relief exempts distributions from a transferee company or trust. It should also exempt distributions which have had to go through both a company and a trust, although in practice there may be evidential difficulties in identifying the company income charged under s 739 with the payments eventually made from the trust.

The transferor

The landmark case of *Vestey v IRC* [1980] AC 1148 established that s 739 only applies if the taxpayer himself was transferor in relation to the original transfer and he or his spouse has power to enjoy or receive a capital sum. Obviously a person counts as a transferor if he effects the original transfer. But the *Vestey* case left open a number of questions concerning the transferor.

Multiple transferors

In *Vestey*, Lord Wilberforce helpfully observed that no difficulty arose with multiple transferors, and in *IRC v Pratt* [1982] STC 756 Walton J explored the matter further. Here a private company had effected the offending transfer and the Revenue sought to treat as transferors three directors who together only owned a minority of the shares. Walton J was clearly of the view that if more than one person transferred assets to an offshore entity each would be liable under s 739 on an appropriate proportion of the income and this is accepted by the Revenue in practice (*Tax Bulletin* 40 (April 1999) p 651). The same is the position if there is a single transfer and each owns an identifiable part of the asset transferred, as where they are tenants in common.

Where the Revenue may be in difficulty is if it is impossible to separate out what each multiple transferor has transferred. Such is the position if two transferors are joint tenants in equity of the asset transferred or if they are the beneficiaries of a discretionary trust who together direct the trustees to make the transfer. The implications of Walton J's remarks is that assessment under s 739 would not be possible. It may be doubted whether the Revenue would accept this.

Quasi transferors

The problem of quasi transferors stems from a subsidiary ratio in the case over-ruled in *Vestey*, *Congreve v IRC* [1946] 2 All ER 170, 30 TC 163. The central dramatis personae of *Congreve* were the taxpayer, her father, and a successful trading company the father had built up and ran. Initially, in 1928, the father transferred 60% of the shares in the trading company to a Canadian holding company and in 1932 he transferred all the shares in that company to the tax-payer. The next stage, also in 1932, was the interposition of a second holding company between the original holding company and the trading company shares. The original holding company was then liquidated, leaving the second holding company directly owned by the taxpayer.

At the same time as these events were taking place, both the taxpayer and the trading company transferred foreign portfolio investments they held to further Canadian holding companies. The final transaction in this series, which was the first of only two at issue in *Congreve*, was the sale by the taxpayer's father of another 28% of the trading company to the second holding company, raising its holding from 60% to 88%, or 93% if an earlier direct transfer by the taxpayer is included.

The result of all these transactions was that the foreign income of the tax-payer and of the trading company, and the dividends paid by the trading company, were payable free of income tax to assorted holding companies abroad. The taxpayer had power to enjoy this income because the consideration for the transfers consisted mainly of debentures repayable on demand.

The Commissioners accepted that everything done in relation to the transactions was brought about by the taxpayer's father, the taxpayer merely signing as she had been instructed. The issue was whether the taxpayer could escape liability under s 739 in respect of the trading company dividends or its transferred portfolio investments, on the grounds that the investments were transferred by the trading company, and the shares in the trading company by the original holding company and the taxpayer's father.

Lawrence J considered that s 739 extended to transfers effected by an agent of the taxpayer or by her wholly-owned company, and this brought the transfer by the original holding company into the section. But he held that the father's transfer was not caught with the result that the dividends attributable to the 28% of the shares transferred by him to the second holding company escaped. He appears also to have considered that the trading company's transfer escaped, for at the time of the transfer the taxpayer only controlled 65% of the company.

In the Court of Appeal and the House of Lords, all the difficulties were brushed aside, for, in the ratio overruled by *Vestey*, it was held that the taxpayer was liable under s 739 regardless of whether she had been the original transferor. But in the Court of Appeal, Cohen LJ formulated a subsidiary ratio, to the effect that even if s 739 were restricted to the original transferor, it applied if he or she had procured the transfer. For these purposes Lawrence J's identification of wholly-owned companies with the taxpayer was rejected, but on the facts, the Court of Appeal held that the taxpayer had, through her father as agent, procured all the transfers concerned.

Close reading of the speeches in *Vestey* makes it clear that only the principal ratio of *Congreve* was in terms overruled. The survival or otherwise of Cohen LJ's subsidiary ratio is a matter of difficulty, for while Lords Dilhorne and Keith affirmed it, the other three law lords did not as such endorse it. Instead Lord Wilberforce merely contemplated, as an aside, that s 739 'may be' extended to persons 'associated' with the transfer. The better view must be that Lord Wilberforce's aside, in conjunction with the affirmation by Lords Dilhorne and Keith, does preserve the subsidiary ratio and such was accepted by Walton J in *IRC v Pratt* [1982] STC 756. Accordingly the issue is what exactly Cohen LJ meant in the subsidiary ratio. Undoubtedly the best, perhaps the only, guide to this is to look at the father's role in *Congreve*. Effectively he was the person who devised and set up the schemes, and accordingly it is such persons, the promoters, who are best regarded as quasi transferors.

Such a conclusion is confirmed by *IRC v Pratt* [1982] STC 756, for here Walton J accepted the proposition that the subsidiary ratio could render a person who procured the transfer taxable under s 739. Indeed the term 'quasi transferor' comes from *Pratt*. However, Walton J rejected the proposition that the three directors who were minority shareholders were quasi transferors. He held that the subsidiary ratio applied only to persons who procured the transfer, and that procurement could only take place if the alleged transferor had the power to procure. In a company context this means he has to have control of the company, as in *Congreve* itself.

Walton J's approach in *Pratt* indicates a person cannot be a quasi-transferor if the party who in fact effected the transfer is an individual and the alleged quasi-transferor merely used persuasion. In *Carvill v IRC* [2000] STC (SCD) 143, 163, a Special Commissioner accepted that to treat such a person as quasi-transferor would be a considerable extension of the principle. However, he contemplated there might be exceptional cases where the alleged quasi-transferor's influence over the actual transferor is so strong as to make him a quasi-transferor.

The Revenue, in addressing the issue of quasi transferors, follow the decided cases. Their view, following Lord Wilberforce's words in *Vestey*, is that s 739 can potentially apply to someone who was associated with the transfer, and that such would include a person who procured the transfer (*Tax Bulletin* 40 (April 1999) p 651).

Non-resident transferor

Income arising before 26 November 1996 was not caught by s 739 unless the transferor was ordinarily resident in the UK at the time he made the original transfer (*IRC v Willoughby* [1997] STC 995). Now s 739 applies provided the transferor is ordinarily resident in the year in which the income arises (s 739 (1A)).

The Revenue indicated (IR Press Release, 18 December 1997) that they would apply *IRC v Willoughby* to income arising before 26 November 1996 if:

(a) it was not subject to an assessment which had become final; or
(b) any such assessment became final after 16 December 1994; or
(c) the assessment related to a personal portfolio bond.

Compliance

Taxes Act 1988, s 739, and the other provisions dealing with transfers of assets abroad are dealt with by Special Compliance Office and Financial Intermediaries and Claims Office. The Revenue expect taxpayers to draw the Revenue's attention to the implications of the legislation when submitting details of transactions to which it may potentially apply. Disclosure must be made even if the taxpayer is relying on the motive defence. See *Tax Bulletin* 40 (April 1999) p 652 and p 197 below.

Chapter 22

Benefits: section 740

Introduction

Until 1979, s 739 applied to anybody who had power to enjoy or received a capital sum, regardless of whether such person had made or been associated with the transfer. When the landmark case of *Vestey v IRC* [1980] AC 1148 established that s 739 applied only to transferors and quasi transferors it opened a potential gap in the legislation, for it meant capital received by non-transferors was free of income tax. This gap was filled in 1981 by what is now TA 1988, s 740.

Section 740 was first enacted at the same time as TCGA 1992, s 87, the section attributing gains to capital payments (see Chapter 26). But despite the two sections addressing an essentially similar problem each uses completely different language and terminology. The language of s 740 follows that of s 739 and indeed the two sections form part of the single code dealing with transfers of assets abroad (TA 1988, Pt XVII Chapter III). Most importantly this means that, like s 739, s 740 is subject to the motive defence (see Chapter 23).

Preconditions

The preconditions for the operation of TA 1988, s 740 are as follows:

(1) There has been a transfer of assets.
(2) Income has become payable to a person resident or domiciled outside the UK.
(3) The income has become so payable by virtue or in consequence of the transfer, either alone or in conjunction with associated operations.
(4) An individual ordinarily resident in the UK receives a benefit.
(5) The benefit is provided out of assets which are available for the purpose by virtue or in consequence of the transfer or any associated operations.
(6) The individual is not liable to tax under s 739 by reference to the transfer.

Where these conditions are satisfied the amount or value of the benefit is taxable as the recipient's income. However, it is only so taxable in the year in which it is received if it equals or is less than what is called the relevant income for that and previous years. If it exceeds this relevant income it is carried forward and taxed as and when there is relevant income in the future.

As noted above, s 740 is subject to the motive test in TA 1988, s 741. It does not apply if avoiding liability to taxation was not one of the purposes of the original transfer or the associated operations. Nor does it apply if those operations were bona fide commercial transactions not designed to avoid taxation. The motive defence is a very important limitation on s 740 and is discussed in Chapter 23.

Transfer and associated operations

The terms 'transfer' and 'associated operations' have the same meanings as for the purposes of s 739 (TA 1988, s 742). Thus the term 'transfer of assets' comprehends the creation of rights and includes the formation of a trust or company as well as the transfer of assets to it. As is explained on p 166 an operation is associated if effected in relation to the assets transferred, assets representing those assets or income arising from the assets.

An important point to note is that the transfer can be effected by anyone, for in contrast to s 739, s 740 is not concerned with the taxation of transferors. There is no reason why the transferor cannot be a company or even, it may be suggested, the trustees of a trust.

A point which arises with associated operations is whether an operation is only associated if it takes place after the transfer. The s 739 cases on associated operations have all concerned subsequent operations (cf pp 166–7) and s 741(1) does refer to operations effected in relation to any of the assets 'transferred'. The use of the past tense suggests that at the time of the operations the transfer must already have taken place. The Revenue view, however, is that a transaction which precedes the transfer can be an associated operation if it is undertaken in relation to the transfer (*Tax Bulletin* 40 (April 1999) p 652).

Identifying the transfer

In view of the broad definition of 'transfer' and 'associated operation' it is often unclear whether a transaction is a transfer or whether it is an operation associated with another transaction which is the transfer. To take the typical case of trustees who incorporate a holding company to hold investments, is the income payable to the holding company so payable because of the transfer represented by the transfer of cash or investments to the holding company? Or is it so payable because of the transfer of assets to the settlement together with an associated operation represented by the transfer to the holding company?

The latter represents the commonsense view but there are arguments in favour of the former. In *IRC v Herdman* (1967) 45 TC 394, the House of Lords held that a transfer and associated operations were only together treated as satisfying the preconditions for s 739 where the transfer alone did not satisfy them. Parity of reasoning suggests that where there is a transfer which on its own causes income to become payable to a non-resident, that alone is the relevant transfer for s 740. If this view were right it would only rarely be necessary to resort to associated operations to determine whether precondition (3) above is satisfied. However, one instance where it would be is where the transfer is to a resident trust and the trust then migrates. Migration is not a transfer but it is an associated operation (*Congreve v IRC* [1948] 1 All ER 948).

If the above were to be correct a further issue is whether, in the fifth pre-condition listed above on p 179, associated operations can only be taken into account if they were taken into account in relation to the third precondition. In other words, if the transfer alone caused income to become payable to the non-resident, must the assets out of which the benefit is provided be available by virtue of only that transfer. In the example given above, this would mean the assets would have to be available solely by virtue of the transfer to the holding company. It may be suggested, however, that this is not the correct construction, for the legislation (s 740(1)(b)) refers to *any* associated operations. Accordingly, in a trust and holding company structure, distributions from the trust would be within the fifth precondition, for any payment from the company to the trust would be an operation associated with the original transfer of funds from the trust to the company.

The problem of identifying the transfer also arises in other contexts. Take the following two examples:

(1)   Trust A makes an outright advance to Trust B.
(2)   Trust A sells an asset to Trust B.

Common sense would indicate that in the first of these examples, the transfer is the creation of Trust A, with the advance to Trust B being an associated operation. If right this means relevant income in Trust A could be used to bring a distribution from Trust B into tax, or vice versa. Such is the approach one might expect the Revenue to adopt, but it is at variance with the analysis above. A further point may be that if it is right, a distribution from the advanced funds in Trust B could not be taxed by reference to income arising from any funds which were in Trust B prior to the advance.

The second example is more straightforward, and most people would accept that the transfer once the asset is in Trust B is the creation of that trust. But the difficulty in spelling this out from the legislation indicates just how much ambiguity there is in s 740.

Relevant income

Relevant income is income arising to a non-resident entity, which by virtue of the transfer or associated operations can directly or indirectly be used to provide a benefit for the beneficiary concerned (TA 1988, s 740(3)). However, income cannot be taken into account more than once, and so once it has been allocated to one benefit it drops out of the cumulative total attributable to future benefits (TA 1988, s 744).

The associated operations which may be taken into account in determining whether income can be used to benefit the beneficiary are stated simply to those referred to in s 740(1). As such they comprehend both associated operations by virtue of which income is payable to the non-resident entity (precondition (3) on p 179) and operations taken into account in determining whether the assets out of which the benefit is provided are available for the purposes (precondition (5)).

Timing issues

A difficult issue is fixing the point in time at which it is determined whether income is relevant income – ie when is the moment at which it has to be asked whether the income is capable of being used to benefit the individual. In relation to income which has arisen prior to the benefit, it may be suggested the relevant time is when the benefit is conferred, for otherwise income which arises in a trust prior to the beneficiary in receipt of the benefit being a beneficiary could be excluded. Such income would include income arising before the beneficiary was born, or, in the case of a person who becomes a beneficiary by marriage, before the marriage.

In the case of income arising in the same tax year as the benefit is conferred or in a subsequent year, a strict reading of s 740(3) indicates the question as to whether income is relevant income has to be asked as the income arises. Thus if the income could be used to benefit the beneficiary the income is relevant income, regardless of what is in fact done with it. It may however be doubted whether this is right, for if it were, distributed income would be relevant income, even if the income was in fact paid to the individual who received the benefit. Double taxation would then result These considerations indicate that future income is only relevant income if it is retained by the non resident entity, and assuming that is the correct analysis, the issue of whether it is relevant income is determined at the time the decision is taken to retain it.

The Revenue's view on these difficult issues is not wholly clarified, but in *Tax Bulletin* 40 (p 651), it is stated that relevant income "is treated as not including such part of the income as has already been genuinely paid away to a beneficiary or to a bona fide charity". This broadly supports the above conclusion as to future income. In practice the Revenue also accept that income paid in expenses is not relevant income, and, although this is not explicitly stated in *Tax Bulletin* 40, it must be right as income used in expenses cannot be used to benefit any-body. *Tax Bulletin* 40 does however make it clear that once income is relevant income it continues to be relevant income until extinguished by a benefit, even if capitalised. This is clearly right.

A point that does seem reasonably clear is that at least in a trust context subsequent income cannot be relevant income if by the time it arises the beneficiary who received the benefit has been wholly and irreversibly excluded. This is because when the income arises it cannot be used to benefit him.

Less clear is the position if income is segregated, accumulated, and then distributed as capital to a non-resident beneficiary who is not charged under s 740. Logically at that point it should cease to count as relevant income even though it was not then taken into account in charging tax under s 740. This result follows because once it is distributed, it can no longer be used to benefit any of the other persons. *Tax Bulletin* 40 does not, however, deal with this point.

An important point to remember is that income can count as relevant income even if it arose while the beneficiary was non-resident. If the motive defence is not in point, an immigrant may find himself taxed under s 740 by reference to income which, had he received it himself, would have been received by him while non-resident and so been free of UK tax.

Which income is relevant income?

Where income arises directly to an offshore trust it is relevant income because, by virtue of the transfer of the settled property to the trust, the income can be used directly to benefit the beneficiaries. Where the income arises to an under-lying holding company, the income is relevant income because it can be used indirectly to benefit the beneficiaries by virtue of the transfer of the investments to the holding company. It can be so used because it can be distributed to the trust, and then distributed or advanced by the trustees to the beneficiaries.

A point which arises with all trust and holding company structures is that the same money can amount to relevant income on more than one occasion, as where the income arises from investments held by the holding company and then is paid by way of dividend to the trust. In law this would mean overall receipts by beneficiaries could be taxed as income to a far greater extent than income received by the offshore structure as a whole. In practice the Revenue are not thought to treat holding company dividends as relevant income where the com-pany's income is relevant income. But this practice is not formally published. Further there is no avoidance of duplication if one receipt is income and the other capital gain, as where income accrues to a company which is then liquidated.

Transfers between settlements

On p 181 it was suggested that if settled property is transferred from one trust to another, ie from Trust A to Trust B, income in one trust can constitute relevant income in relation to a benefit conferred from the other trust. The question which now arises is whether there is any situation in which this result is avoided.

The answer it may be suggested is that there are two. These arise where the benefit is conferred from Trust A before the advance and at that time, and until the benefit, there is no or insufficient income in Trust A. In this scenario, income arising in Trust A after the advance is not relevant income in relation to the advance if before the income arises the recipient beneficiary has been excluded, for at the time it arises the income could not be used to benefit him. So too income arising in Trust B cannot be relevant income if the recipient beneficiary has never been a beneficiary under that trust, or is excluded before the income arises.

A more interesting scenario is if income arises in Trust A prior to the advance and the benefit is conferred from Trust B after the advance. If before then the recipient beneficiary is wholly excluded from Trust A, is the former income in Trust A still relevant income in relation to the advance from Trust B. This turns on the question of when it has to be determined whether income is relevant income (p 182).

Overlap with s 739

Income cannot be taken into account more than once in charging tax under ss 739 and 740. But if it can be taken into account under both sections it is so taken into account on a just and reasonable basis (s 744).

In the normal case of a trust under which the settlor is a beneficiary, the income is taxed under s 739 in the year in which it arises, thereby preventing it from being relevant income in relation to other beneficiaries. Questions of apportionment only arise if another beneficiary receives a benefit in the same tax year, or had received one previously which is hitherto untaxed. A trap exists if the settlor is non-domiciled and there is unremitted foreign income, for then that income can be treated as relevant income in relation to a benefit received by another UK resident beneficiary. A tax charge arises if he is UK domiciled or, if non-domiciled, if he remits the benefit.

Another case where s 740 can apply even where the settlor is a beneficiary is if the trustees purchase a fully capitalised company. Here s 739 is precluded in relation to the company's income (p 167), but s 740 applies if the settlor or indeed any other beneficiary receives a benefit from the trust.

Deemed income

Relevant income includes sums treated as income under the accrued income scheme (TA 1988, s 742(4)). It should be remembered that that scheme extends both to UK and to foreign securities (TA 1988, s 710(2)). Relevant income includes gains on life policies under the chargeable event legislation (p 255) and deep discount (FA 1996, Sch 13 para 12). In certain limited circumstances it can also include offshore income gains (see pp 248–51).

What is a benefit?

The term 'benefit' is not defined, save only that it includes a payment of any kind (TA 1988, s 742(9)). It is plain that the term includes a cash advance to the beneficiary or the transfer of an asset in specie. Since it is the amount or value which is taxed, the charge is on the amount if the benefit is in cash and on its value if it is in kind.

Free use of property

Great difficulty is occasioned where trustees allow a beneficiary free use of trust property or make him interest-free demand loans. Such are certainly benefits in the broad sense of the term but it is far from clear whether they are caught by s 740. The Revenue view is that they are (*Tax Bulletin* 40 (April 1999) p 651) but there are powerful arguments against this view.

An initial point is that s 740 requires the benefit to be provided 'out of assets'. In the case of a loan of money, this condition may be met, for the cash is passed from the trust to the beneficiary. With a licence to use property the position is different, for the property remains unimpaired in the ownership of the trust. Can the licence then be said to be provided 'out of' the property?

In certain cases the borrower or licensee has an interest in possession in the money or property when the benefit is conferred. In such a case it is difficult to see what benefit there is, for the beneficiary is merely enjoying the property in specie in lieu of taking the income.

The central issue, however, is whether, assuming the loan or licence is a benefit, it has a value. In the case of a loan or licence for a fixed term it plainly does – the benefit is conferred at the outset and is equal to the value of the right to use the money or asset for the fixed period. But normally the loan or licence is terminable at will, and in such a case the Revenue view is that there is an annual benefit equal to the rent or interest foregone.

The compelling argument against the Revenue view is that s 740 lacks any rules as to how such rent or interest should be determined. In this it contrasts with other provisions in TA 1988, which do provide how loans and rent-free benefits should be valued. The prime example is the Schedule E benefits in kind legislation (TA 1988, ss 153–168G). That this is a relevant consideration is confirmed by Vinelott J's judgment in *O'Leary v McKinlay* [1991] STC 42. Here an employer made an interest-free loan to a trust benefiting an employee, which was outside the benefit-in-kind charge on free loans because the recipient was a trust (TA 1988, s 160). In the course of his judgment Vinelott J observed that the benefit of an interest-free loan was not an emolument within the general meaning of the term, for the benefit could be quantified.

Two decisions bear on the point. In *IRC v Botnar* [1998] STC 38 the Special Commissioner decided that the value of the benefit for the purposes of TA 1988, s 743(5) was the market rent of the flat (see p 173). But this may not be applicable to s 740, because the expansionary words of s 742(3) do not apply to s 740. In *Cooper v Billingham* Lloyd J decided that an interest-free loan was a benefit for the purposes of TCGA 1992, s 87 (see p 222), the benefit being the trustee's successive acts in not calling in the loan, to be valued retrospectively as equal to the interest which would have been charged had the loan been at a commercial rate. This case, however, is under appeal. It may in any event be distinguishable because:

(a)   Section 87 requires the valuation of 'the benefit conferred' by the capital payment, whereas s 740 speaks merely of 'the amount or value' of the benefit.
(b)   Section 87 refers to the 'conferring of any . . . benefit' whereas s 740 only applies if the benefit is 'provided out of assets'.

For the present the issue must be regarded as open. The only sensible advice to taxpayers is to make full disclosure to the Revenue but not concede the point until it is settled in the courts.

Life interests

The Revenue consider that a benefit does not arise when a life interest is appointed to a beneficiary or when a beneficiary sells a life interest (*Tax Bulletin* 40 (April 1999) p 651).

Double taxation

It may be that the relevant income taken into account in taxing a benefit has suffered UK or foreign tax as it arose. Indeed the benefit may be paid out of accumulated income which has itself been subject to withholding or other taxes. In these circumstances the question arises whether tax on the benefit may be relieved by double tax relief. The answer is that it cannot, and so the position is reached that if taxed offshore income is accumulated and paid out as a benefit overall tax may be increased.

Income benefits

A benefit is only taxable under s 740 if it is not otherwise taxable as income (s 740(1)). This means s 740 does not apply to dividends from an offshore company or income distributions from an offshore trust. It is often more advantageous for a payment from a trust to be income, for that may attract relief for any foreign tax on the underlying income arising directly to the trustees (ESC B18).

Benefits to the transferor

As noted on p 95, s 740 only applies if the benefit is received by someone who is not liable to tax under s 739 by reference to the transfer. As such the transferor is excluded from liability under s 740 should he receive capital. It is sometimes suggested this exclusion may not extend to a non-domiciled transferor who escapes liability under s 739 because all the income is unremitted foreign income (cf Chapter 12). This concern is almost certainly ill-founded in law for such a transferor is still liable to tax under s 739, and in practice the Revenue do not take the point (*Tax Bulletin* 40 (April 1999) p 651).

Foreign element

A benefit is taxable if the recipient is ordinarily resident in the UK in the year of assessment in which the benefit is received (TA 1988, s 740(1)). The benefit is fully taxable even if it is received and kept abroad: thus on the Revenue view a benefit is received if offshore trustees allow a beneficiary the use of a holiday home in, say, Spain.

A factor which is also immaterial to the benefits code is the residence and domicile of the settlor or transferor who set up the offshore arrangements. Section 740 can apply even if he has never been resident and domiciled in the UK, although in such circumstances a beneficiary in receipt of benefits may be able to invoke the motive defence (see Chapter 23). A point to stress in such cases is that the relevant income by reference to which any benefit is taxed includes income which arose before the recipient was resident in the UK. Perhaps more important in the case of a settlor-interested trust where the settlor has died, it also includes foreign income which arose in the settlor's life but escaped tax under s 739 because of the remittance basis. This result is only avoided if all such income was distributed (cf p 182).

The only concession to territoriality s 740 makes is in s 741(5): an individual is not taxable in respect of a 'benefit not received in the UK' by reference to relevant income which is such that if 'he had in fact received it he would not, by reason of his being [foreign] domiciled have been chargeable to income tax in respect of it'. The effect of this provision is that a benefit paid to a non-domiciliary escapes tax if it is received abroad, but only to the extent that the relevant income does not include any UK income.

Interesting issues arise with s 741(5). First, when is a benefit not received in the UK? Does that phrase simply mean not paid over by the trustees in the UK or does it require the beneficiary who receives the benefit abroad not to bring it to the UK? If the latter, is receipt in the UK avoided if the original beneficiary alienates the benefit abroad and the recipient brings it to the UK? It is fairly clear that a benefit is caught if the recipient subsequently brings it to the UK, for s 741(5) incorporates the rules as to deemed remittance in TA 1988, s 65(6)–(9) (see pp 106–7). This only makes sense on the presupposition that a subsequent remittance triggers the liability to tax. Otherwise common sense indicates that the income tax rules as to remittances apply, with the result that the recipient is caught if he brings the benefit to the UK but not if he effects a genuine alienation.

A second issue is the reference to income which would not in fact have been chargeable by reason of the recipient's domicile had it in fact arisen to him. The better view is that this has the same effect in relation to s 740 as TA 1988, s 743(3) has in relation to s 739: in other words foreign income is caught if it is brought to the UK either by the trustees, by any holding company if it arises to such a company, or by the recipient of the benefit himself. If this is right, trustees desiring to invest in the UK should operate capital and income accounts so that they can demonstrate that funds brought to the UK for investment do not represent foreign income.

A final point to note about s 740(5) is a trap. It may be in the year in which the benefits paid there is no relevant UK income. Accordingly, if kept abroad, the benefit is then tax-free. But if in a subsequent year there is UK income, it would seem the benefit can be carried forward to it and thereby rendered taxable if the recipient beneficiary is then still UK resident.

Onward gifts

Since non-residents are not taxable under s 740, it is normally good tax planning for trustees to make capital distributions to them (cf Chapter 18). In some cases, the non-resident may pass some or all of the money on to another family member who is resident in the UK. The issue which then arises is whether the Revenue could argue s 740 imposes liability on the UK resident by reference to income in the trust.

On this issue, the first question is whether the distribution is a valid distribution to the non-resident as a matter of trust law. If the distribution is not validly made to the non-resident, and the UK resident is also a beneficiary under the trust, the correct analysis would probably be that the distribution had been made to him and so was caught by s 740. If the UK resident is not a beneficiary of the trust, and if the original distribution is invalid, it will be a fraud on the power and should thus be a nullity. This ought to mean the money could be returned to the trust without fiscal consequences.

The test of whether the distribution to the non-resident is a valid distribution to him is likely to be the same in both cases (cf *Re Dick* [1953] 1 All ER 559, CA). It may be suggested it will not be such a valid distribution if:

(a) the gift to the UK resident is a condition of the distribution;
(b) the purpose of the trustees in making the distribution was to benefit the UK resident; or
(c) on receiving the distribution the non-resident was under 'irresistible moral suasion' to make the onward gift.

Once it is established that as a matter of trust law the distribution was validly made to the non-resident, it could in theory still be argued that the UK resident is taxable under s 740. All that s 740(1)(b) requires is that the benefit received by an individual be provided out of assets which are available for the purpose by virtue inter alia of associated operations. Read literally, the distribution to the non-resident is an operation associated with the setting up of the settlement, and as a result of the distribution the money distributed is available to the non-resident to make the onward gift.

But it may be suggested the wider context of s 740 makes this construction untenable. If the UK resident was taxable under s 740, logically the same principle would apply where a UK resident recipient of the distribution makes an onward gift. In such a case, both the original beneficiary and the onward donee could on this construction be assessed under s 740 or the Revenue would have to make a choice between them. In *Vestey v IRC* [1980] STC 10, the House of Lords recoiled from such duplication and discretion and it was one of the reasons which led to the restriction of s 739 to transferors. A similar approach should be taken to s 740, to the effect that it bites only on the individual who as a matter of general law has received the benefit from the offshore structure.

It is clear that such risks as these are minimised if the non-resident has a reasonable period of unfettered use of the money. It may also be material if he mixes it with his other assets, and there is no obvious correlation between the amount he gives to the UK resident and the amount received from the trust. If these precautions are taken it is not thought the Revenue would have any basis for attack and, although there is no published practice, there are no indications they would in fact do so.

Benefits and capital payments compared

Differences between TA 1988, s 740 and TCGA 1992, s 87

TCGA 1992, s 87 is analysed in Chapter 26, and, as explained Chapter 26, ss 87 and 740 can potentially apply to the same benefit or payment. The main differences between the two codes may be summarised as follows:

(1)   Section 740 applies if there has been a transfer of assets, and s 87 only if there is a settlement.
(2)   Section 740 is subject to a motive test but applies whether or not the transfer involved bounty. Section 87 is not subject to a motive test, but the use of the term 'settlement' connotes bounty.
(3)   Section 740 can apply to a non-domiciled recipient but s 87 cannot.
(4)   Section 740 does not allow income to be washed out by payments to non-resident or non-domiciled recipients but s 87 does allow gains to be so washed out.
(5)   If tax is charged under s 87 it can be increased by notional interest. Tax under s 740 cannot be so increased.

Both sections apply regardless of the residence or domicile of the settlor or transferor.

Avoidance of double tax

The same payment cannot be taxed under s 87 as a capital payment and to income tax as a benefit within the meaning of TA 1988, s 740. This is for the following reasons:

(1) If the payment is taxed under s 740 in the year in which it arises it is not a capital payment since the definition of capital payment excludes payments liable to income tax.

(2) If a payment is not taxed under s 740 in the year it arises, it constitutes a capital payment (TCGA 1992, s 97(1)).

(3) Such a capital payment is nonetheless taxable under s 740 unless in any prior year it has caused trust gains to be attributed to beneficiaries (TCGA 1992, s 97(3)(a)).

(4) Once the payment has caused trust gains to be attributed to beneficiaries it cannot subsequently be taxed under s 740 (TA 1988, s 740(6)). This applies whether the trust gains are so attributed under s 87 or under the provisions in TCGA 1992, Sch 4C relating to trustee borrowing (see s 740(6)).

(5) If the capital payment is taxed under s 740, it does not count as a capital payment in the year in which it is so taxed and in any subsequent year (TCGA 1992, s 97(3)(b)).

Chapter 23

The motive defence: section 741

Sections 739 and 740 of TA 1988 are both subject to the motive defence enacted by TA 1988, s 741. The onus is on the taxpayer, but if he discharges it, the income of the transferee cannot be assessed on an arising basis under s 739 and benefits cannot be taxed under s 740.

The motive test does not, it should be stressed, mean tax is necessarily avoided altogether. Income arising directly to the trustees of a settlement can be assessed under TA 1988, Part XV if the settlor is a beneficiary, regardless of motive (see p 42). So too a capital distribution from a trust may be subject to CGT under TCGA 1992, s 87 even if the motive test displaces s 740 (see Chapter 26).

The statutory conditions

Under s 741, the taxpayer has to show to the satisfaction of the Board that one of two conditions is met. There is a right of appeal to the Special Commissioners, but their decision is likely to be final as the question is one of fact.

The first condition is that the purpose of avoiding liability to taxation was not either (a) the purpose, or (b) one of the purposes for which either (i) the transfer, or (ii) any associated operation was effected.

The second condition is that the transfer and any associated operations were:

(a)   bona fide commercial transactions; and
(b)   not designed for the purposes of avoiding liability to taxation.

It will be noted that s 741 refers to 'taxation' rather than tax. This means the defence is lost if the intention is to avoid any form of UK tax, including taxes on capital (*Sassoon v IRC* (1943) 25 TC 154). But the term 'taxation' does not extend to foreign taxes, and so foreign tax planning does not jeopardise s 741. This is so even if the foreign tax avoided is as close to home as the Republic of Ireland (*IRC v Herdman* [1969] 1 All ER 495, HL).

It will also be noted that the first condition is failed if one of the purposes of the transfer or associated operation is tax avoidance, whereas the second condition asks simply whether they were designed for tax avoidance purposes. It is implicit in this distinction that the second condition is met provided the *main* purpose is not tax avoidance (*Carvill v IRC* [2000] STC (SCD) 143, 166). On the face of it this suggests that the second condition is looser than the first, but the correct approach is to regard it as different, for unlike the first, it requires the transactions to be bona fide commercial.

Transfer and associated operations

It is to be stressed that the motive defence is lost if either the transfer or an associated operation fails the test. In view of the breadth of the term 'associated operation' (p 166) this is a significant restriction. The result is that a wholly innocent transfer may be tainted by a subsequent tax-driven operation.

In relation to s 739, an important limitation was imposed in *IRC v Herdman* [1969] 1 All ER 495, HL. In that case the House of Lords decided that a distinction must be drawn between cases where the transfer alone causes income to be payable to a non-resident entity and gives the transferor power to enjoy, and cases where these conditions are satisfied only with inclusion of associated operations as well. In the latter event, it is necessary to show that neither the transfer nor any of the associated operations was tainted by tax avoidance. But in the former event only the transfer need be free of tax avoidance; it is irrelevant if subsequent operations were undertaken to avoid tax.

It appears that the Revenue intended by amendment enacted in 1969 to reverse *IRC v Herdman* (see *Tax Bulletin* 40 (April 1999) p 652). There is no doubt that as a matter of construction this intention was not achieved, and the Revenue now accept this. Revenue practice on the point is stated in the following terms in *Tax Bulletin* 40 (April 1999) p 652.

> '[It] has been the Revenue's practice in considering whether a defence under Section 741 is available to consider only the transfer and any associated operations which directly establish a power to enjoy the income of the overseas person under any particular sub-head in Section 742(2).'

It may be argued that the principle in *IRC v Herdman* also applies to s 740. But it is unclear whether such arguments mean that only the transfer has to satisfy the motive test if it alone causes income to be payable to the non-resident. The alternative view is that other operations in such a case must satisfy the test if they are taken into account in determining whether assets are available for the purpose of providing benefits as per s 740(1)(b). The former would be more in accordance with the scheme of the legislation but the latter represents the common sense view.

Purpose

Although the defence in s 741 is generally referred to as the motive defence, the section in fact refers to the purpose of the transactions rather than their motive. The Revenue take the purpose to be the end it is sought to achieve by the transaction.

The Revenue consider the test is objective (*Tax Bulletin* 40 (April 1999) p 651). In other words if a transaction in fact involves tax avoidance, such is considered to be one of its purposes even if subjectively such was not the intention of the transferor. This view gains support from a passage in Lord Nolan's speech in *IRC v Willoughby* cited below (pp 108–09). However, in *Beneficiary v IRC* [1999] STC (SCD) 134, the Special Commissioners distinguished the question of whether a transaction amounts to tax avoidance from its purpose. In their view, Lord Nolan's words were directed at the former question, and the latter requires a subjective test. So too in *Carvill v IRC* [2000] STC(SCD) 143, 148, another Special Commissioner took the view that the relevant words of Lord

Nolan were doing no more than summarise the Revenue argument and that there was clear authority that the test is subjective. It follows that on this point the Special Commissioners have twice found the Revenue view to be wrong and taxpayers should not therefore accept it until the position is clarified in the courts.

The onus is on the taxpayer to show that none of the relevant transactions had a tax avoidance purpose. In practice the Revenue allow the onus to shift in certain circumstances. This practice is explained in the following terms in *Tax Bulletin* 40 (April 1999) p 651.

> 'Where the taxpayer has been able to establish that at least one of the purposes for undertaking the transactions did not entail tax avoidance, the Revenue will regard it as incumbent on them to indicate why in their view tax avoidance may also have been involved. They will explain their reasons to the taxpayer, after considering fully all the arguments he or she have advanced and all the documents submitted in support of his or her contentions, and will do so prior to any Special Commissioners' hearing.'

Meaning of tax avoidance

The term 'avoiding liability to taxation' is used in both heads of s 741. There is now a plethora of authority on what constitutes tax avoidance. The basic definition is that given by Lord Templeman in the Privy Council in *IRC v Challenge Corpn Ltd* [1986] STC 548. This definition was approved by the House of Lords in *Ensign Tankers (Leasing) Ltd v Stokes* [1992] STC 226 and adopted in relation to s 741 by the House of Lords in *IRC v Willoughby* [1997] STC 995. Lord Templeman's definition draws a contrast between tax mitigation and tax avoidance and is as follows:

> 'Income tax is avoided and a tax advantage is derived from an arrangement when the taxpayer reduces his liability to tax without involving him in the loss or expenditure which entitled him to that reduction. The taxpayer engaged in tax avoidance does not reduce his income or suffer a loss or incur expenditure but nevertheless obtains a reduction in his liability to tax as if he had.'

The practical implications of the definition are indicated by examples of tax mitigation which Lord Templeman gave in the following terms:

> 'When a taxpayer executes a covenant and makes a payment under the covenant he reduces his income. If the covenant exceeds six years and satisfies certain other conditions the reduction in income reduces the assessable income of the taxpayer. The tax advantage results from the payment under the covenant.
>
> When a taxpayer makes a settlement, he deprives himself of the capital which is a source of income and thereby reduces his income. If the settlement is irrevocable and satisfies certain other conditions the reduction in income reduces the assessable income of the taxpayer. The tax advantage results from the reduction of income.
>
> Where the taxpayer pays a premium on a qualifying insurance policy, he incurs expenditure. The tax statute entitles the taxpayer to reduction of tax liability. The tax advantage results from the expenditure on the premium.'

In *IRC v Willoughby* [1997] STC 995 at 1003 Counsel for the Revenue formulated the following propositions specifically in relation to s 741:

'The hallmark of tax avoidance is that the taxpayer reduces his liability to tax without incurring the economic consequences that Parliament intended to be suffered by any taxpayer qualifying for such reduction in his tax liability. The hallmark of tax mitigation, on the other hand, is that the taxpayer takes advantage of a fiscally attractive option afforded to him by the tax legislation, and genuinely suffers the economic consequences that Parliament intended to be suffered by those taking advantage of the option. Where the taxpayer's chosen course is seen upon examination to involve tax avoidance (as opposed to tax mitigation), it follows that tax avoidance must be at least one of the taxpayer's purposes in adopting that course, whether or not the taxpayer has formed the subjective motive of avoiding tax.'

Lord Nolan described the formulation as generally helpful and said he accepted the essence of the Revenue's submissions. Later he encapsulated in his own words what was meant by tax avoidance:

'Tax avoidance within the meaning on s 741 is a course of action designed to conflict with or defeat the evident intention of Parliament'

This sentence was adopted by the Special Commissioner in *Carvill v IRC* [2000] STC (SCD) 143.

The s 703 cases

Like ss 739 and 740, TA 1988, s 703 is subject to a motive defence. Its terms are not identical to those of s 741, in that the taxpayer has to show that the obtaining of tax advantages was not one of the main objects of the transactions under attack and that the transactions were either carried out for bona fide commercial reasons or in the ordinary course of making or managing investments (s 703(1)).

The Courts have held that the existence of a legitimate commercial use for monies extracted from a company is capable of bringing transactions within the defence (*IRC v Brebner* [1967] 2 AC 18; *Clark v IRC* [1978] STC 614). In a much quoted passage in the former case Lord Upjohn said:

'My Lords, I would only conclude my speech by saying, when the question of carrying out a genuine commercial transaction, as this was, is reviewed, the fact that there are two ways of carrying it out – one by paying the maximum amount of tax, the other by paying no, or much less, tax – it would be quite wrong, as a necessary consequence, to draw the inference that, in adopting the latter course, one of the main objects is, for the purposes of this section, avoidance of tax. No commercial man in his senses is going to carry out a commercial transaction except upon the footing of paying the smallest amount of tax that he can. The question whether in fact one of the main objects was to avoid tax is one for the Special Commissioners to decide upon a consideration of all the relevant evidence before them and the proper inferences to be drawn from that evidence.'

This passage was cited by the Court of Appeal in *IRC v Willoughby* [1995] STC 143 at 183 in the context of s 741. The principle is clearly relevant, particularly where s 741 is being relied on to protect commercial structures.

IRC v Willoughby

IRC v Willoughby [1997] STC 995 is now the leading case on s 741. It concerned offshore personal portfolio bonds, which are life policies where the return on maturity is linked to a portfolio of investments selected by the policy-holder (cf Chapter 30). They constituted about 2% of the offshore bonds issued by life offices, the return on remainder being linked to general funds of the life office concerned. Since 1984, the proceeds of offshore life policies have been subject to basic and higher rate tax under TA 1988, ss 539–554. Personal port-folio bonds are now subject to a punitive tax regime imposed by FA 1998, s 89, as described on pp 255–7.

The Revenue always accepted that policies linked to general funds were not caught by s 739. However, in *IRC v Willoughby* they sought to bring personal portfolio bonds within s 739, on the grounds that in substance the position is no different from where the policyholder owns the investments directly. This contention was rejected by the House of Lords, on the simple ground that a policy-holder merely has a right in contract against the Life Office, and not a right in rem against the assets held by the Life Office to which his policy is linked.

The underlying reasoning which led the House of Lords to apply s 741 was that offshore bonds are a means of saving, with a tax regime specifically pro-vided by Parliament. On the facts Professor Willoughby had genuinely incurred the expenditure involved in buying the bonds and had in fact bought them to provide for his retirement. As such the bonds fell within the category of tax mitigation rather than tax avoidance.

Application

Commercial structures

Section 741 is clearly in point where a taxpayer carries on business abroad. Absent s 741, the incorporation of a local company by a sole trader or partner-ship would bring s 739 into play. So too could such an incorporation by a privately-owned UK company. With s 741, such transactions are kept outside s 739 provided the reasons are commercial, as they normally are. It is to be stressed that s 739 has no exempt activities test such as is found in the CFC legislation; the motive defence in s 741 is the sole protection commercial structures have against s 739.

IRC v Carvill represents a useful illustration of this principle. Here the tax-payer was an Irish domiciliary whose UK company placed reinsurance at Lloyd's on behalf of US brokers. He decided it was commercially advantageous to deal directly with the US primary insurers, using US personnel, but that to do this his group needed to have its ultimate management in a neutral territory. To that end he incorporated a Bermudian holding company. Initially the Revenue were successful before the Special Commissioners in resisting the motive defence but on a fuller examination of the facts before different Special Commissioners the taxpayer prevailed ([2000] STC (SCD) 143).

Settlements

Section 741 should plainly be in point where structures are designed and put in place by an individual who is not resident in the UK and is not at the time con-cerned with UK tax. Such structures may well be designed to avoid foreign taxes, but as noted above, this does not prevent s 741 from applying. In these cases the motive defence will be of value if the individual concerned subsequently comes to the UK, for then, if he is able to benefit, it will confer protection from s 739. The motive defence will also protect members of his family from attack under s 740 if they receive benefit whilst resident in the UK.

A more difficult area is where a settlement is created with the benefit of UK tax advice, but where it is claimed the real reason is not UK tax at all. A typical example would be a settlement made by a resident foreign domiciliary to avoid foreign tax or for family or succession reasons. In *Beneficiary v IRC* [1999] STC (SCD) 134 the Special Commissioners held that such a settlement made by a Japanese gentleman for the benefit of his UK resident daughter was indeed protected by s 741. On the face of it any such settlement should be protected by s 741, even if the precise form or location of the settlement takes account of UK tax considerations.

It may be argued that any offshore settlement from which the settlor is wholly excluded is protected by s 741. Such a settlement is tax mitigation in the same way that any similar UK settlement would be, for the settlor suffers the real economic consequence of losing all possibility of benefiting from the assets settled. If this is right, capital distributions from any children's or grandchildren's settlement are capable of being kept out of s 740. But it is difficult to see either the Revenue or the courts accepting the logic of this if it is clear on the facts that tax led to the settlement being located offshore rather than onshore. The taxpayer's argument would of course be much stronger if non-tax factors, such as more flexible trust law, led to the settlement being offshore.

Associated operations

It is to be stressed that in all the above cases a structure protected by s 741 can subsequently be tainted by a tax driven associated operation. It is true that under s 739 only limited associated operations are relevant, but the better view is that this is not so as regards s 740 (see p 192). Care is therefore needed over such simple steps as, for example, accumulating income or paying it to one beneficiary rather than another.

An important area where associated operations come into issue is where the trustees of a settlement made by a non-domiciliary incorporate an offshore holding company to hold UK investments. On the face of it, use of the holding company is tax driven, for it confers protection from inheritance tax (see p 92). However, in *Beneficiary v IRC*, UK investments were held through a holding company and, while the benefit provided to the beneficiary was not funded by the company, it is difficult to see why its income was not relevant income. As such it can perhaps be inferred that it too was protected by the motive defence.

Such a conclusion may gain support from an earlier point in the case, in that the Special Commissioners had decided that the non-domiciled settlor was protected by s 741 when he transferred funds to Jersey from a UK sterling account, such transfer being effected specifically to protect the money from IHT. The Commissioners considered such a transfer was no different from switching the UK account to a foreign currency account at the same bank, which would have been protected from IHT by IHTA 1984, s 157. As such, the switch would plainly be tax mitigation, for it simply takes advantage of an express relief. It may be that the same reasoning would extend to holding UK investments through an offshore holding company.

Practice

As already noted, the availability of the motive defence only applies if the tax-payer can show to the satisfaction of the Board that one of the two tests in s 741 is met. As a matter of law, the onus is on the taxpayer to bring the facts to the attention of the Board and prove s 741 applies. If the Board do not accept the taxpayer's case, the taxpayer can appeal to the Special Commissioners, who then hear the matter de novo (*Beneficiary v IRC* [1999] STC (SCD) 134).

Taxpayers and their advisers have sometimes taken a view on the motive defence, decided it applies, and accordingly made no returns under ss 739 and 740. Such a strategy was never to be recommended, partly because it was wrong in law, and partly because the more time that elapses, the harder it is to adduce the necessary proof. Furthermore, the interest and penalties payable if s 741 is not in point will be growing. ·

The self-assessment return now requires transfers of assets or benefits received to be disclosed in answers to question 6, and the amount taxable under ss 739 or 740 to be entered on the foreign pages. Taxpayers who rely on the motive defence to omit income or benefits should so state in box 6.5A. On the face of it, this disapplies the law, for it appears to allow taxpayers to rely on the motive defence without satisfying the Board first. However, this practice is to the advantage of taxpayers, for the Revenue can only investigate the matter by enquiring into the return. If the time for enquiries elapses without an enquiry being initiated, the Revenue accept that they are bound by the defence for the year in question unless it was claimed fraudulently or negligently (TMA 1970, s 29; *Tax Bulletin* 40 (April 1999) p 652). Provided the return is filed before 31 January the time for enquiries expires on the following 31 January (TMA 1970, s 9A(2)).

Chapter 24

Attribution of gains to the settlor

Introduction

From 1981 until 1991 gains arising to a non-resident settlement were not in any circumstances charged to UK CGT as they arose. The sole respect in which they were exposed to UK taxation was under the capital payments code, described in Chapter 26. In 1990 and early 1991 there was widespread press comment on the tax avoidance possibilities of offshore settlements. Although in many respects this comment was misinformed, it led to legislation in the 1991 Finance Act attributing the gains of certain offshore settlements to the settlor. In 1998 further misinformed comment, and embarrassment on the part of a government minister, led to an enlargement of the categories of settlement caught by the 1991 legislation.

Perhaps because the legislation was prompted by press criticism it is badly thought out and unduly severe. Until 1991, no anti-avoidance legislation had attributed either income or gains of any settlement to the settlor unless he or his spouse were actual or potential beneficiaries or enjoyed a benefit. The 1991 legislation breached this sensible principle, for attribution is possible even if the settlor and his spouse are wholly excluded. In this respect the gains of offshore settlements are more severely taxed than their income, and indeed more severely taxed than income and gains realised in onshore settlements.

The present legislation is TCGA 1992, s 86 and Sch 5. It applies if at any time during the tax year in which the gains arise two principal conditions are satisfied:

(1)   The settlor has what is called an interest in the settlement.
(2)   The settlement is a qualifying settlement.

The settlor

The gains of a qualifying settlement can only be attributed to the settlor if in the year in which the gains arise he is both resident and domiciled in the UK (TCGA 1992, s 86(1)(c)). Self-evidently they can only be attributed to him if he is alive during the year, and, in a curious relieving provision, they cannot be attributed in the year of his death (TCGA 1992, Sch 5 para 3).

A person is a settlor in relation to a settlement if the settled property consists of or includes property originating from him (ibid, Sch 5 para 6). The term 'originating' is further defined as property provided by the settlor and property representing property so provided. The term 'provided by' figures in the income tax settlement code and connotes bounteous provision (see *IRC v Leiner* (1964)

41 TC 589 and *Tax Bulletin* 16 (April 1995) p 204). As in the income tax code, the provision can be direct or indirect and reciprocal arrangements are countered.

The settlement

The term 'settlement' is not given its extended income tax definition. Accordingly, s 86 applies only to settlements in the true sense of the term. However, bounty must have been involved in the making of the settlement for, as noted above, a person is only settlor if he has made bounteous provision in some form. It follows that a settlement made to attract and motivate staff is outside s 86 (*Tax Bulletin* 16 (April 1995) p 204).

Interest in the settlement

Gains can only be attributed to the settlor if he has what is called an interest in settlement at some time in the year in which the gains accrue. The settlor is treated as having an interest in the settlement if one of two conditions is satisfied (TCGA 1992, Sch 5 para 2(3)):

(1)   property or income in the settlement is or will or may become applicable for the benefit of a defined person or payable to him in any circumstances whatsoever; or

(2)   a defined person enjoys a direct or indirect benefit from any property or income in the settlement.

The following individuals are defined persons (ibid, Sch 5 para 2(3)):

(a)   the settlor;
(b)   the settlor's spouse;
(c)   any child of the settlor or of his spouse;
(d)   the spouse of any child;
(e)   any grandchild of the settlor or of his spouse; and
(f)   any spouse of such grandchild.

For these purposes step relationships are treated as natural (ibid, Sch 5 para 2(7).

Subject to the exceptions described below, the principal effect of the rules is that the settlor has an interest in the settlement if he, his children, his grandchildren or any of their spouses is an actual or potential beneficiary. But it should be remembered that the settlor can have an interest in a settlement even where the class of beneficiaries wholly excludes such persons. Under head (2) above, the settlor has an interest in the settlement in any year in which a defined person receives a benefit.

Exceptions

There are important exceptions to these rules. The first is that the settlor does not have an interest in the settlement if a defined person can only benefit in the event of:

(a)   the bankruptcy of a beneficiary;
(b)   an assignment or charge by a beneficiary of his interest;
(c)   in the case of a marriage settlement, the death of both parties to and any children of the marriage; or
(d)   the death of a beneficiary under 25.

The next exception is that gains are not attributed to the settlor if only one defined person has an interest in the settlement in a year of assessment and that person dies during the year or if two or more persons have interests and they all die during the year (TCGA 1992, Sch 5 paras 4 and 5). Gains are not attributed either if the only defined person with an interest in the settlement is the spouse of the settlor, or the spouse of one of his children or grandchildren, and the marriage ends during the year concerned (ibid, Sch 5 para 4).

A third and very important exception concerns the inclusion of grandchildren and their spouses in the class of defined person. This exception applies if two conditions are satisfied:

(a)   the settlement was created before 17 March 1998; and
(b)   all individual defined persons apart from grandchildren and their spouses are completely excluded from actual or potential benefit.

Where these conditions are satisfied, the settlor is not treated as having an interest in the settlement unless and until one of four conditions specified in Sch 5 para 2A are met (para 2A(1)). The most important of those conditions is the addition of property to the settlement; all four conditions are discussed in Chapter 25 below.

Effectively this exception prevents gains from being attributed to the settlor if the settlement was made before 1998 and it is a grandchildren's settlement from which the settlor, his children and their respective spouses are totally excluded. It should be noted that it is not necessary for them to have been excluded on or before 17 March 1998; provided the four conditions have not been breached since 6 April 1998, all that is necessary is that the settlor, his children, and their respective spouses are excluded throughout the tax year in which the gains are realised.

Collateral arrangements

Head (1) in the definition on p 200 above does not in terms require the settled property to be applicable for the benefit of, or payable to, the defined person under the terms of the settlement. It has been held in relation to similar wording in the former TA 1988, s 673(2) that the property or income can be payable or applicable under some collateral arrangement having legal force (*Muir v IRC* (1966) 43 TC 367 at 381 per Pennycuik J).

Thus in *Jenkins v IRC* (1944) 26 TC 265, the trustees were expressly empowered to apply income in repaying any loan they had incurred and they borrowed money interest-free from the settlor. The Court of Appeal held that in these circumstances the settlement income was applicable for the benefit of the settlor. *Jenkins v IRC* was followed in *IRC v Wachtel* (1970) 46 TC 543, where the settlor made an interest-free deposit with the bank to support a borrowing by the trustees at a nominal rate of interest. Trust income was applied in reducing the borrowing and corresponding reductions were made in the settlor's deposit.

The principle which emerges from these cases is that if a defined person enters into some bounteous arrangement in favour of the trust, the settlor will have an interest if there are circumstances in which the defined person could be recouped out of trust income or capital. Such arises in the case of interest-free loans, or if the defined person guarantees some obligation of the trust and has a right to be indemnified out of the trust assets.

It might be thought that the settlor could have an interest if the trustees enter into a commercial transaction with a defined person. For example a purchase by the trustees from the defined person would render the purchase price payable to him. It is however clear that the words 'payable to' in para 2(3) connote an out-and-out parting with the trust property (*Lord Vestey's Executors v IRC* (1949) 31 TC 1 at 83, HL). Accordingly, transactions with a defined person only give the settlor an interest in the settlement if they involve some benefit to the defined person. The case of *Lord Vestey's Executors v IRC* is authority for the proposition that a loan on commercial terms to a defined person is not an application for his benefit.

Qualifying Settlement

When TCGA 1992, s 86 and Sch 5 were first enacted a settlement was only a qualifying settlement if either:

(a) it was made on or after 19 March 1991; or
(b) it was made before that date but one of the four conditions in Sch 5 para 9 had been breached since then. Those conditions are in all material respects the same as those which apply to grandchildren's settlements under para 2A (supra) and are thus as described in Chapter 25.

As a result of the amendments introduced by FA 1998, s 132, all settlements are now qualifying settlements, regardless of when made. There is one exception, namely protected settlements. Under Sch 5 para 9(10A), a settlement is a protected settlement in any tax year if the beneficiaries are confined to children of the settlor who are under 18, unborn children of the settlor, and persons who are not defined persons at all. A child counts as under 18 if he is under 18 at the beginning of the tax year concerned. Future spouses of the settlor or his children are also allowed to be included as beneficiaries.

A protected settlement is not a qualifying settlement provided

(a) it was created before 19 March 1991,
(b) it was a protected settlement on 6 April 1999, and
(c) none of the five conditions set out in Sch 5 para 9 has been breached since 19 March 1991 (Sch 5 para 9 (1B)).

The five conditions are the four described in Chapter 25 which applied to all pre-1991 settlements until 17 March 1998 plus one additional one. This is that the settlement has not ceased to be a protected settlement at any time after 5 April 1999 (Sch 5 para 9 (6A)). The main circumstance in which a protected settlement would cease to be a protected settlement is if a child of the settlor attained the age of 18 and was not excluded before the beginning of the following tax year.

On a strict construction of para (10A), a settlement is not protected if the settlor's grandchildren are beneficiaries. In practice, however, the Revenue allow the beneficiaries to include grandchildren (*Tax Bulletin* 38 (December 1998) p 620).

Computation of the gains attributed

Where the conditions for the operation of s 86 are satisfied, a computation is made of the amount on which the trustees would have been chargeable to CGT for the tax year concerned if they were UK resident (TCGA 1992, s 86(1)(e)). Certain rules apply in determining this amount (TCGA 1992, Sch 5 para 1):

(1) It is assumed no annual exemption is available.
(2) The fact that gains would be attributed to the settlor under TCGA 1992, s 77 if the settlement were resident is ignored.
(3) Current year losses are allowed. Losses carried forward from previous years are also allowed, but only if in the year concerned any gains would have been attributable to the settlor under s 86.
(4) No account may be taken of either losses or gains which accrued before 19 March 1991.
(5) Where the trustees are participators in a non-resident close company, gains in the company may be taken into account if two conditions are satisfied. First, the gains must be such as would be apportioned under TCGA 1992, s 13 if the trustees were resident, and second, the trust's interest in the company must have originated from the settlor. Section 13 is considered in Chapter 28, and, as there noted, tax assessed on the settlor by virtue of s 13 may be credited against any tax due from him in respect of distributions from the company made within two years of the s 13 gain accruing.

In carrying out the computation taper relief is allowed. This is not stated explicitly in the legislation but follows implicitly for the computation is on the amount upon which the trustees would have been chargeable under TCGA 1992, s 2(2). Taper relief operates as a reduction in the amount so chargeable (TCGA 1992, s 2A).

The charge on the settlor

The amount computed as above is charged under s 86 as the top slice of chargeable gains accruing to the settlor for the year concerned (ibid, s 86(4)). It is not in his hands eligible for taper relief as that relief has been given in computing the amount attributed (TCGA 1992, s 86(4A)).

Until 1997–98, the amount charged on the settlor could be offset by his personal losses. This is no longer possible (ibid, s 2(4)). The annual exemption is and has always been available and where the settlor's personal gains are absorbed by carry forward losses, the exemption is set against amounts charged under s 86 (TCGA 1992, s 3(5B)).

Reimbursement by the trustees

The settlor has a statutory right to recover the tax he pays from the trustees (ibid, Sch 5 para 6). The Revenue do not regard this right, or any provision in the trust deed recognising it, as causing the trust income to be assessable on him under TA 1988, Part XV or s 739 or as a reserved benefit for IHT purposes (SP 5/92 paras 8–10).

In practice few offshore trusts expressly recognise the right of reimbursement, if only because most predate the enactment of s 86. In many cases the settlor is a beneficiary, and so the trustees can reimburse him in exercise of their fiduciary powers. But where this is not so, it is widely believed that the settlor is in difficulty in enforcing reimbursement. This is because the right to reimbursement is conferred by an English statute, and so, unless the proper law of the settlement is English, it is not part of the trust's governing law. As such it is generally believed that a court outside the UK would not recognise it.

A possible solution for the settlor may be to bring proceedings in the English courts and then serve the trustees out of the jurisdiction. Assuming this is possible and that he then obtains judgment, one of two courses is likely to be open to him.

(1) If the trust has English assets he could enforce against those.
(2) If the trust is based in a jurisdiction with which the UK has a convention for the mutual recognition of judgments, he could enforce the judgment against the trustees in their home jurisdiction.

At present such routes are largely untested. However, in *Prestwich v Royal Bank of Canada Trust Co (Jersey) Ltd* (1998) 1 ITLR 565, Judge Howarth held that the settlor was entitled as of right to serve the trustees out of the jurisdiction under RSC Ord 11 r 1(2)(b) or, that failing, was entitled to leave under Ord 11 r 1(1)(n).

Should the trustees end up reimbursing the settlor by one means or another, the Revenue do not regard such reimbursement as a capital payment within TCGA 1992, s 87 (SP 5/92 paras 8–10).

Temporary non-residence of the settlor

If the settlor is non-resident for less than five complete tax years, all gains which would have been attributed to him under s 86 had he not emigrated are treated as accruing to him in the year of his return. This is the same as with gains accruing to him directly (see p 301) and is expressly provided for by TCGA 1992, s 10A(2)(b).

TCGA 1992, s 86A addresses a problem this poses. This problem is that until the settlor returns, gains in the trust realised in the intervening years are trust gains within TCGA 1992, s 87 because, as the settlor is then non-resident, s 86 does not apply. Should capital payments be made to resident beneficiaries, they are taxed by reference to the trust gains and yet, when the settlor returns, he is then assessable on those gains under a combination of ss 10A and 86.

Section 86A addresses this problem by defining two sums (sub-s (1)(b)). These are:

(a) The pool of trust gains carried forward for the purposes of s 87 as at the end of the year of the settlor's departure.

(b)   Distributions during the intervening years actually charged to CGT as gains accruing to resident beneficiaries under the capital payment rules.

If the distributions at (b) exceed the pool carried forward at (a) there is an 'excess'. Where there is such an excess, gains realised by the trust in the intervening years cannot be assessed on the settlor save insofar as they exceed the excess. If after application of this rule, trust gains are still assessable on the settlor, they drop out of the pool of trust gains carried forward to the year of return for the purposes of s 87.

The general rule is that a capital distribution to a UK resident beneficiary from an offshore trust is assessable to income tax under TA 1988, s 740 to the extent of relevant income (see Chapter 22). Only if relevant income is exhausted is it taxable as a capital payment (p 189). Section 86A does *not* allow capital distributions assessed to income tax under s 740 to be deducted from the gains assessed as the settlor's in the year of return.

Multiple settlors

Since the definition of settlor includes any person who has provided property it is perfectly possible for a settlement to have more than one settlor. In this event any given settlor only has an interest in the settlement if property originating from him could be used to benefit a person who is a defined person in relation to him, or if such a person receives a benefit from such property (TCGA 1992, Sch 5 para 2(2)). A particular settlor is only chargeable on gains accruing on disposals of property originating from him (s 86(1)(e)). So too he is only credited with losses on property originating from him. Gains in an underlying company are attributed to him if the shares in the company originated from him (Sch 5 para 1(2)).

Corporate settlors and beneficiaries

Unlike other anti-avoidance legislation, TCGA 1992, s 86 and Sch 5 make express provision for the position where a company is settlor or where one or more companies are beneficiaries.

Corporate settlor

An individual, for the purposes of the settlement, can be treated as providing property, and thus as settlor, if a company provides the property (TCGA 1992, Sch 5 para 8(4)). An individual is treated as providing all the property provided by the company if he is the only person who controls it. If two or more persons each control the company separately, each is taken to provide the property in equal shares. If two or more persons only control the company by taking them together, they are each treated as providing an apportioned part of the property, subject to a de minimis limit of 5%. For these purposes provision by a company is taken into account whether the company is resident or non-resident, but the company must be close.

The applicable definition of control is that in TA 1988, s 416, the income tax close company definition. In broad terms an individual has control if he has voting control, if he owns over half the company's shares, or if he is entitled to over half any dividend or distribution in a winding up. In determining whether an individual has such control the rights and powers of his associates are attributed to him. An individual's associates are defined in s 417(3) as:

(a)   his relatives, ie his ancestors, descendants, siblings and spouse;
(b)   the trustees of any settlement of which he is settlor;
(c)   the trustees or personal representatives of any trust or estate under which he is interested in the shares.

The last head in this definition of associates is unclear in its meaning. However, it has been held that a personal representative is himself interested in shares in a deceased's estate and so even if an individual is a personal representative with no entitlement under the will or intestacy, any shares held by the estate are treated as his in determining whether he has control (*Willingale v Islington Green Investment Co* (1972) 48 TC 547, CA). A question of some difficulty is whether beneficiaries under a trust or an estate are interested in shares held by the trust. Fixed-interest beneficiaries must be, and the better view is that discretionary beneficiaries are as well, for there is no requirement that those interested should have a quantifiable interest (cf *Leedale v Lewis* [1982] STC 835). The effect of this is that a beneficiary controls a company if the trust controls it, or if he and the trust, or he, the trust and members of his family, control it.

If the income tax definition of control stood alone in determining who is settlor, an individual could be settlor in relation to a settlement even if he personally owned no shares in the providing company. The legislation attempts to remove this possibility by providing that a person is not for these purposes treated as controlling a company unless he is himself a participator (TCGA 1992, Sch 5 para 8(8)). Unfortunately this provision does not fully hit its target, for the term participator includes actual shareholders and loan creditors, and anybody having a share or interest in the capital or income of the company (TA 1988, s 417(1)). The word 'interest' in this definition certainly brings in fixed-interest beneficiaries in relation to trust shareholdings, and very possibly discretionary beneficiaries as well. The result is that it is still possible for a beneficiary under a settlement to be treated as controlling a company, and thus as a settlor in relation to funds provided by the company, even if he personally owns no shares in it. Fortunately this defect has been recognised by the Revenue, and ESC D40 provides that for these purposes a beneficiary under a trust is not by concession to be treated as a participator solely because of his status as a beneficiary.

Corporate beneficiary

The term 'defined person' includes any company controlled by any one or more of the individual defined persons listed on p 200 above and any other company associated with such a company. The rules for determining whether a company is controlled by one or more individual defined persons are the same as those applicable in determining who is settlor, save that ESC D40 does not apply. As under those rules the term 'associated' is also defined with reference to the income tax close company legislation (ibid, Sch 5 para 5(9)). Two companies are associated if one controls the other or both are under common control (TA 1988, s 416(1)).

In determining whether a pre-1998 grandchildren's settlement attracts the transitional exemption described on p 201, the companies which must be excluded from benefit are restricted to those controlled by the settlor, his spouse, or their children and companies associated with any such company. However, this is of little practical significance, for as described above, under TA 1988, s 417, a person's associates include his descendants.

The practical importance of defined persons including companies is that even if all individual defined persons are excluded, the settlor will still have an interest in the settlement if companies are, or are being capable of being added as, beneficiaries under the settlement and such companies do not exclude those which fall within the definition of defined person. The problem may be more widespread than at first appears, for most powers of addition are expressed in terms of persons and the term 'person' normally includes companies. In English law, such is implied by Interpretation Act 1978, Sch 1.

Chapter 25

Tainting

Introduction

As explained in the previous chapter, when the rules in TCGA 1992, s 86 attributing gains to the settlor were first enacted they did not in general apply to settlements made before 19 March 1991. This was achieved by TCGA 1992, Sch 5 para 9, which provided that a pre-1991 settlement was only qualifying, and thus within s 86, if it fell foul of four specified conditions. Falling foul of one of those conditions became colloquially known as becoming 'tainted'.

These rules now apply in determining whether a protected settlement as described on pp 202–3 continues to remain non-qualifying. Almost identical rules to those in para 9 are enacted in Sch 5 para 2A and apply to settlements made before 17 March 1998. They govern whether account can be taken of grandchildren and their spouses in determining whether the settlor has an interest in such a settlement and thus effectively determine whether a pre-1998 grandchildren's settlement remains outside s 86 (see p 201).

The original conditions

As originally enacted, para 9 provided that a settlement made before 19 March 1991 became a qualifying settlement if one of the following conditions had become satisfied since 19 March 1991:

A Property or income was provided directly or indirectly for the purposes of the settlement otherwise than under a transaction entered into at arm's length.

B The settlement, having previously been resident, became neither resident nor ordinarily resident in the UK.

C The terms of the settlement were varied so that a person within para 9(7) became for the first time a person who would or might benefit from the settlement.

D A person within para 9(7) who was not capable of benefiting from the settlement before 19 March 1991 enjoyed a benefit for the first time.

In conditions (C) and (D), the persons within para 9(7) were as follows:

(i)   any settlor;
(ii) any spouse of any settlor;
(iii) any child or stepchild of any settlor;
(iv) any spouse of such child;

(v) any company controlled by all or any of the above, and any company associated with such a company.

An exception to condition (A) was made in the following circumstances:

(1)   the settlement's expenses relating to administration and taxation for a year of assessment exceeded its income for that year; and
(2)   the added property did not exceed the shortfall.

Protected settlements

Conditions (A)–(D) above and the exception for expenses now apply in determining whether a protected settlement becomes qualifying. A fifth condition, however, is added, namely the settlement ceasing to be protected.

Grandchildren's settlements

The conditions relating to pre-1998 grandchildren's settlements follow the original (A)–(D) above save as follows:

(a)   The settlement is only tainted if one of the conditions has been breached since 17 March 1998, and that is the relevant date for seeing whether a person was capable of benefiting within condition (D).
(b)   The class of persons within para 9(7) who thus cause conditions (C) and (D) to be breached is restricted to grandchildren and their spouses, together with companies (and associated companies) controlled by either grandchildren and their spouses alone or by such persons and other defined persons.

Significance of tainting

The four conditions, and in particular condition (A), were until 17 March 1998 of immense importance, for almost all offshore settlements made by a UK settlor before 19 March 1991 were within s 86 if one of the conditions was breached. In many cases substantial amounts of tax were at stake. In 1992 the Revenue issued one of the longest ever statements of practice, SP 5/92. SP 5/92 was subsequently amplified by articles in *Tax Bulletins 8* (August 1993) and *16* (April 1995). Unfortunately it raised more problems than it solved, and much of the discussion of tainting revolves around assertions it makes. Because the conditions have been retained in relation to protected settlements and grandchildren's settlements this discussion is of continuing relevance, although its importance is thankfully much reduced.

Added property: the law

The first condition, condition (A), is only infringed if the added property is 'provided'. The provision can be by anybody, and thus condition (A) is infringed not merely if the settlor makes the addition but if the addition is received from a third party, for example the trustees of another settlement. The word 'provided' was used in the former income tax multiple settlor rules in TA 1988, s 679 and in that context it was held that the provision must be bounteous (*IRC v Leiner* (1964) 41 TC 589 at 596). An interest-free loan represents the provision of the property lent (*IRC v Wachtel* (1970) 46 TC 543).

The provision of the property must be for the purposes of the settlement. This is a matter of evidence. Thus in *IRC v Mills* [1974] STC 130 at 135, HL, Viscount Dilhorne said:

'Where it is shown that funds have been provided for a settlement, a very strong inference is to be drawn that they were provided for that purpose, an inference which will be rebutted if it is established that they were provided for another purpose. In this case there is not a shred of evidence that the funds were provided for any other purpose.'

Property is provided whether it is provided directly or indirectly. Cases on other statutory provisions give guidance as to the meaning of 'indirectly'. In *Potts' Executors v IRC* (1950) 32 TC 211, the House of Lords held that sums paid to the settlor's creditors were not loans made directly or indirectly to him within the meaning of what is now TA 1988, s 677. Lord Simmonds stated that 'indirectly' does not cover payment to a third party for his own use or benefit, and Lords Normand and Oaksey observed that indirect payments include only payment to a third party accountable to the settlor. In *Yuill v Wilson* [1979] STC 486 at 494, Buckley LJ said in the Court of Appeal that if A transmits an opportunity to B with the knowledge or assurance or expectation that he will pass it to C, he is providing C with the opportunity indirectly, and the same may apply if he merely persuades B. It may be concluded from these cases that indirect provision within condition (A) requires the third party to be accountable to the settlement or there to be an expectation that the third party will pass any such provision on to the settlement.

If it is right that the term 'provided' connotes bounty, the exception in condition (A) for arm's length transactions may be otiose. The term 'transaction' rather than 'bargain' is used, which means that the exception does apply where the other party to the transaction is connected with the settlement (cf TCGA 1992, s 18(2)). In an IHT case, *IRC v Spencer-Nairn* [1991] STC 60, certain factors were identified as potentially pointing to a transaction having been at arm's length, notably professional representation for the parties and evidence of genuine negotiation and marketing. However, none of these factors were in fact present in the case. A sale thought by the parties to be between unconnected parties at a market value had in fact been between connected parties at a massive discount on account of a misunderstanding of the law. It was still held that such a transaction was capable of being at arm's length. The conclusion which may be drawn is that it is highly desirable to have separate representation and genuine negotiation but that this is not necessary if the parties believe that they are transacting at arm's length.

Added property: particular transactions

Outright transactions with the trustees

Clearly condition (A) is infringed if somebody transfers assets or income to the settlement with bounteous intent. Equally it is not infringed when there is no bounteous intent and the transaction is at full value. In practice the difficulty which arises is when the settlor or somebody connected with him wants to enter into a transaction with the trustees at full value, but, because of his relationship with the trust, is concerned as to whether the Revenue will accept that the transaction is in fact at market value. The problem is particularly acute where the asset is difficult to value, for example private company shares, or where the asset is likely to see a dramatic increase in value.

In practice, common sense indicates that it ought to be sufficient for the transaction to take place at a genuine third party valuation, for such would negative there being bounteous intent. Prudence would perhaps dictate going slightly further and arranging for each side to instruct professional advisers to conduct a genuine independent negotiation. Given the comments in *Spencer Nairn*, it is difficult to see how the Revenue could contend such a transaction was anything other than at arm's length.

For some reason the Revenue did not in SP 5/92 confirm that transactions with independent representation are outside condition (A). Instead they provided another route for avoiding condition (A), namely for the contract of sale to include an adjuster clause, ie to provide for an adjustment of price with compensating interest if the Revenue do not accept the price as market value (SP 5/92, paras 12–15). This route has the advantage of obviating the necessity for two lots of advisers although it does appear one independent valuation is required. The adjustment can be either up or down or (if appropriate) one way (*Tax Bulletin* 16 (April 1995) p 204).

Loans

In SP 5/92, para 22, the Revenue confirmed that a loan to the settlement at a low or nil rate of interest is regarded as a provision of property infringing condition (A). The practical difficulty is determining what rate of interest needs to be charged to avoid this difficulty. Loans are often made to a settlement precisely because bank finance is not available or is prohibitively expensive, and this in turn often reflects a lack of realisable security. However, it would be difficult to regard the loan as bounteous provision provided a normal rate of interest is charged, ie something approximating to bank base rates.

The experience of practitioners is that the Revenue do not regard condition (A) as infringed if the official rate of interest is charged, ie the rate fixed for the purposes of taxing loans to employees in TA 1988, s 160. This broadly follows mortgage rates but there is no statutory authority for using it in the present context.

Despite the fact that the practice of allowing a subsequent adjustment is expressed in terms of sales, it is thought the Revenue would accept an adjuster clause.

Guarantees and indemnities

In SP 5/92, paras 34 and 35, the Revenue stated that the giving of a guarantee is a provision of funds and that the giving of an indemnity can be so regarded depending on the facts of the case. One type of indemnity which is not treated as the provision of funds is that given by new trustees to retiring trustees. In practice, the Revenue are likely to regard the giving of a guarantee as the provision of funds if the guarantee is given on a sale and it increases the price or it prevents the trust from being exposed to the same degree of risk as other vendors accept (*Tax Bulletin* 16 (April 1995) p 204).

It may be suggested that the Revenue are wrong in stating that the mere giving of a guarantee or indemnity represents the provision of funds. No property is provided until the guarantee is called or the indemnity enforced. When a guarantee is called, condition (A) would be infringed unless the contract under which the guarantee was given was at arm's length. With indemnities, however, even enforcement of the indemnity may not infringe condition (A). This, it may be suggested, is the position with indemnities given to trustees against possible breaches of trust, for, when enforced, such indemnities provide funds for the trustees personally rather than for the settlement. The trustee has to make good the loss to the trust fund whether or not he has a guarantee or enforces his indemnity.

Underlying companies

In SP 5/92, para 16, the Revenue state that provision to a company owned by the settlement can amount to indirect provision of property for the purposes of the settlement. The Revenue recognise an exception where funds are left in the company for the company's purposes, for example waived dividends or remuneration. But this exception is only likely to apply where the trust owns a relatively small proportion of the company (*Tax Bulletin* 16 (April 1995) p 204).

It may be suggested that the Revenue view is wrong, on the basis of the case law on the meaning of 'indirect' referred to above. Strictly, property provided to a company should only count as provided indirectly for the purposes of the settlement if the company is going to pass the property to the settlement by way of dividend or otherwise, or if it is accountable to the settlement. It follows that cheap loans from the settlor or other family members to the company should not infringe condition (A), although it is unlikely the Revenue would accept this.

Services

The Revenue regard both the gratuitous provision of services and the gratuitous improvement of trust property by a tenant as the provision of property (*Tax Bulletin* 16 (April 1995) p 204). As regards services their view is at variance with *IRC v Mills* [1974] STC 130 at 135, where Viscount Dilhorne distinguished the provision of services from the provision of funds.

Receipts from companies

Should a fixed-interest trust receive an enhanced scrip dividend, it may be unclear whether it is income or capital or whether some compensating payment to the life tenant is required (cf SP 4/94). If the trustees take and follow professional advice, the Revenue do not contend there has been any addition if the dividend is treated as capital (*Tax Bulletin* 16 (April 1995) p 205).

When a UK company purchases its own shares, the proceeds are capital in trust law, but income for tax purposes unless the relief in TA 1988, s 219 applies.

Should the settlor be a beneficiary, the proceeds will be taxable as his income and he will make an addition unless he claims reimbursement from the trust of the tax he has to pay (*Tax Bulletin* 16 (April 1995) p 205).

Expenses

The exception for expenses relating to administration and taxation is important in practice but circumscribed. In SP 5/92, paras 25–32, the Revenue made the following comments:

(1) Expenses count for these purposes whether charged to income or capital.
(2) 'Administration' excludes loan interest and the costs of acquiring or selling assets.
(3) 'Taxation' encompasses UK tax, foreign tax, and interest and penalties.
(4) The expenses of an underlying holding company are not included.
(5) The measure of trust income is the total arising to the trustees rather than income which would be subject to UK tax if they were resident.
(6) The expenses relating to administration do not include expenditure in connection with a particular asset if that expenditure can be offset by the income of the asset. In such a case the income from the asset brought into account is the net income.
(7) An addition to meet excess expenses need not be made in the year of the shortfall, but should be made as soon as the relevant figures are available.

Far and away the most significant of these points is the exclusion of the expenses of an underlying holding company. This is particularly serious where the sole trust asset is a UK company held through an intermediate offshore holding company. In such a case the only way to fund the offshore company's expenses may be a dividend from the UK company.

A particular problem arises where the trust is a fixed-interest trust and the trustees incur expenses properly chargeable to capital. If in fact a capital expense is taken out of income and the life tenant does not object, that is a provision of property by him.

Statement of Practice SP 5/92 suggests two ways of overcoming this difficulty. One is where the settlement confers express power on the trustee to decide whether expenses should be debited to capital or income. In such a case, the Revenue accept that the debiting of a capital expense to income in exercise of such powers is not the provision of income. The other suggestion is for the trustees to borrow their charges from the income account and restore the money out of capital as and when they have capital funds, together with interest over the period of the loan. The appropriate rate of interest is considered to be that payable on the basic account administered by the Court Office of the Supreme Courts of Justice (*Tax Bulletin* 16 (April 1995) p 204). Borrowing from income and charging interest in this way is inconvenient in practice and will no doubt lead to tiresome computations. But if annual charges are indeed capital, it is what trustees have to do unless they have power to debit capital expenses to income.

Expenses chargeable to capital should include a corporate trustee's annual fee for this is for the benefit of the trust fund as a whole (*Carver v Duncan* [1985] STC 356, HL). In practice, the Revenue raise no objection if the annual fee is charged to income if this practice has been consistently followed and no part of the fee relates to duties specifically of a capital nature (*Tax Bulletin* 16 (April 1995) 204).

Condition (C): new beneficiaries

Condition (C) is infringed where the terms of the settlement are varied so as to make a person within para 9(7) a beneficiary. It may be suggested that it is infringed even if other such persons already are beneficiaries. The use of the word 'varied' signifies condition (C) is only in point where the trust is varied by court order or by all the beneficiaries when sui juris, and this is accepted by the Revenue (SP 5/92, para 36). The Revenue specifically state that the addition of a beneficiary under a power to add within a specified range of persons does not amount to a variation, and this, it may be suggested, applies even where the power to add is a power to add anyone except, say, the settlor and the trustees for the time being.

Condition (D): ultra vires payments

This condition is only infringed where a person within para 9(7) enjoys a benefit and would not have been capable of enjoying a benefit under the terms of the settlement as those terms stood on 19 March 1991 (or 17 March 1998 in the case of grandchildren's settlements). As the Revenue accept, it thus applies to ultra vires benefits and could catch a case where a person benefits in exercise of the trustees' investment powers.

Where the settlement confers power to add anybody except say the settlor and the trustees to be beneficiaries, this condition will not be in point unless the settlor or the trustees are benefited, for anybody else could have been added as a beneficiary before the relevant date. If the trustees have wide overriding powers to resettle or reappoint the trust fund, it may well be non-beneficiaries can incidentally be benefited by such powers. In this case, too, exercise of the power does not infringe condition (D), for the relevant power could have been used to benefit such persons at any time.

Chapter 26

Capital payments: section 87

Introduction

A capital payment from a non-resident trust is treated as a gain realised by the recipient beneficiary to the extent that the trust has realised gains which have been neither assessed on the settlor on an arising basis under TCGA 1992, s 86 nor allocated to prior capital payments. These rules were first enacted in 1981 and have since been elaborated in 1991 and 1998. The principal section is TCGA 1992, s 87. In broad terms s 87 catches gains realised by the trustees which are not assessed as the settlor's on an arising basis under TCGA 1992, s 86. Despite the expansion of s 86 in 1998, there are still many trusts it does not catch which therefore fall within s 87. Such trusts include:

(a) Trusts were the settlor is dead.
(b) Trusts where he is non-resident or non-domiciled.
(c) Trusts where all defined persons are excluded.

Originally trusts where the settlor was non-resident or non-domiciled were not within s 87 at all, but this limitation was removed in 1998. Section 87 therefore requires consideration whenever offshore trustees distribute capital. A unique feature of this code is that any tax charged can be increased by what is called supplemental tax, which is essentially a form of notional interest. In some cases this takes the rate of tax to the highest rate in the UK tax code, namely 64%.

The basic computation

In each year of assessment during which a trust is non-resident, a computation is made under TCGA 1992, s 87 of what are called the trust gains for the year. These are treated under s 87(3) as gains accruing to beneficiaries who receive capital payments in that year. They may also be treated as accruing to beneficiaries who have received capital payments in an earlier year, but only insofar as those payments have not already been taxed by reference to earlier trust gains. If the trust gains exceed the available current and past capital payments they are carried forward and form part of the trust gains of subsequent years.

The overall effect of the capital payments code is to treat trust gains as the gains of beneficiaries, but only on the remittance basis. Since the gains are those of the beneficiary, the rate of tax is governed by his marginal rate of income tax and his basic annual exemption. Until 5 April 1998 the gains could be offset by losses accruing to him in his personal capacity but this is no longer so (TCGA 1992, s 2(5)).

For the purposes of these rules 'settlement' and 'settlor' have the wide anti-avoidance meaning given to them in the income tax rules attributing income to settlor (TCGA 1992, s 97(7), incorporating the definitions in TA 1988, s 660G). Any provider of funds is thus a settlor. The provisions as to variations of a will or intestacy in TCGA 1992, s 62(6) do not prevent a person making such a variation from being a settlor (*Marshall v Kerr* [1994] STC 638, HL).

Trust gains

Under s 87, the trust gains for a year of assessment are the net gains on which the trustees would have been chargeable under TCGA 1992, s 2(2) had they been resident in the UK. As such, taper relief applies, for that relief operates as a reduction in the amount charged under s 2(2) (ibid, s 2A). An annual exemption is not allowed, as that exemption operates on the amount otherwise chargeable under s 2(2) (ibid s 3(5)).

As just noted, trust gains also include any gains carried forward from a previous year as a result of an insufficiency of capital payments (TCGA 1992, s 87(2)). Credit may be taken for any allowable losses which have accrued to the trust (s 97(6)). No account is taken of gains accruing to the trust before 6 April 1981 (s 97(10)), but losses accruing before then could be brought forward (s 97(6)).

Trust gains include both gains realised on selling investments and gains occasioned by the deemed disposal which occurs when a beneficiary or another trust becomes absolutely entitled to the trust property under TCGA 1992, s 71. On such a deemed disposal the amount otherwise included in the trust gains may be reduced by a hold-over claim. But such a claim is only possible if the person becoming absolutely entitled is resident in the United Kingdom and the facts come within one of the limited circumstances in which hold-over relief is available (see TCGA 1992, ss 165 and 260).

Since the trust gains are the gains on which the trustees would have been chargeable if resident, the death of the life tenant under a fixed-interest trust enables the trust assets to be rebased without generating trust gains (TCGA 1992, s 72). This is so even if the deceased life tenant was the settlor.

Gains attributed to the settlor under TCGA 1992, s 86 are excluded from being trust gains for the purposes of s 87 (TCGA 1992, s 87(3)). Gains accruing in the year of the settlor's death are, however, trust gains, for s 86 does not apply in the year in which the settlor dies.

Trust gains do not include any gain on a deemed disposal resulting from the rules as trustees borrowing in TCGA 1992, Sch 4B (see Chapter 27). Such gains are pooled separately and allocated to such capital payments as are left after the application of s 87 (TCGA 1992, Sch 4C para 8(2); see pp 235–6).

Transfer between settlements

Where one settlement becomes absolutely entitled as against another, any trust gains of the transferor settlement which are outstanding at the end of the year of assessment when the deemed disposal occurs are carried forward to the transferee settlement and form part of its trust gains (TCGA 1992, s 90). If only a part of the settled property has been transferred to the transferee settlement, then the outstanding trust gains are apportioned between it and the transferor settlement. This rule does not apply on a transfer between settlements to the extent that it is treated as linked with trustee borrowing under TCGA 1992, Sch 4B (s 90(5)(a)). As is explained in chapter 27, a transfer between settlements is treated as so linked if at the time of the transfer there is outstanding trustee borrowing. Schedule 4B does not in terms state how the extent of the linkage is measured, but presumably a transfer is wholly linked with trustee borrowing if it is equalled or exceeded by the borrowing and otherwise it is linked to the extent of the borrowing. The practical result is that the rules carrying trust gains forward to transferee settlements do not operate if at the time of the transfer there is outstanding trustee borrowing in excess of the amount transferred.

Gains in an underlying company

Under TCGA 1992, s 13(10) gains apportionable under s 13 can be apportioned to non-resident trustees who are participators in the company concerned. Section 13 is discussed in Chapter 28 and the result of s 13(10) is that if the trust holds its investments through a holding company, the latter's gains count as trust gains.

The inclusion of the corporate gains results in a doubling up of trust gains, for it means the trust gains include both the gains realised by the company on its investments and any gains realised by the trustees when the company is sold or liquidated. The credit which is otherwise available under s 13(7) on a sale or liquidation of the company does not apply to non-resident trusts, for the trustees do not themselves pay the s 13 tax. This subject is discussed further on pp 243–4.

Capital payments

For the purposes of s 87, the term 'payment' is not restricted to simple payments of money. It includes the transfer of assets *in specie*, the conferring of any benefit, and any occasion on which a person becomes absolutely entitled to trust property (TCGA 1992, s 97(2)). A payment is not a capital payment if made under a transaction at arm's length (s 97(1)(b)).

A payment is a capital payment if it is not subject to income tax or, if it is received by a non-resident beneficiary, if it is received otherwise than as income (s 97(1)(a)). Because payments subject to income tax are excluded, a payment which as a benefit under TA 1988, s 740 is excluded (see further p 189). So too are payments taxed as offshore income gains (see TA 1988, s 762 (4) and p 249). A payment which is taxed under the rules as to trustee borrowing in TCGA 1992, Sch 4B and 4C cannot subsequently be taxed under s 87 (Sch 4B para 9(1)(b)). A payment is only so taxed if in the tax year concerned there are no or insufficient s 87 gains.

The amount of a capital payment which is money is simply the money concerned. If the payment is not an outright payment of money its amount is the value of the benefit conferred (s 97(4)). This valuation rule is applied specifically to loans.

A capital payment is treated as received by a beneficiary if he receives it directly or indirectly. It is also caught if a third person receives it by direction of the beneficiary or if it is applied for his benefit (s 97(5)). If a person who is not a beneficiary receives a capital payment he is treated as if he were a beneficiary and so is liable to tax (s 97(8)). This does not apply if a beneficiary proper is treated as receiving the payment. It does not apply either if the recipient is another settlement (s 97(10)).

Transfers to another settlement

Difficult issues arise when the trustees transfer all or part of the settled property to another settlement or resettle it. As is explained above, TCGA 1992, s 90 provides that all or a proportion of the outstanding trust gains are carried forward to the transferee settlement.

The question which s 90 does not address is whether the transfer can constitute a capital payment to any beneficiary under the transferee settlement. On one view it cannot, for s 90 clearly envisages that transfers between settlements will occasion the carry forward of gains rather than a capital payment. Further even if the benefit a beneficiary takes under the transferee settlement were a capital payment the amount would be nil if the beneficiary's interest is discretionary or terminable by the trustees, for then it is valueless.

A contrary argument focuses on the wording of TCGA 1992, ss 97(2) and 97(5)(b). As noted above s 97(2) proves that the term payment includes the conferring of any benefit, and s 97(5)(b) states that a payment is received by the beneficiary if it is paid or applied for his benefit. Reference is then made to the fact that a resettlement or a transfer to a new settlement can be made in exercise of the statutory power of advancement in s 32 of the Trustee Act 1925, and the fact that that power only authorises the exercise if it is for the benefit of the particular beneficiary being advanced. In those circumstances it can be said that the resettlement falls squarely within the words of s 97(5)(b) and so is a capital payment to the beneficiary. Further, given that the resettlement is the application for his benefit, the value of his interest under new settlement is immaterial, for the amount resettled is the amount applied for his benefit and thus is the amount of the capital payment.

The Revenue is understood to adopt this analysis both in relation to advances under s 32 and in relation to similar powers exercisable for the benefit of a specific beneficiary. Whether the analysis is right given the s 90 regime for the transfer of trust gains is debatable. If it is right, the capital payment represented by the advance reduces and in practice would normally eliminate the outstanding trust gains carried forward to the new settlement.

In practice most transfers to a new settlement are effected not in exercise of the statutory power of advancement or some similar power, but in exercise of an express power authorising the trustees to transfer all or part of the trust fund to another trust. Such powers require some at least of the beneficiaries of the transferor trust to be benefits of the transferee trust, but the trustees in exercising the power are benefiting those beneficiaries collectively rather than any particular beneficiary. In these circumstances it is difficult to see the exercise as a payment or application for the benefit of a particular beneficiary within s 97(5)(b), and even if it was it would be such a payment or application for the benefit of all the beneficiaries common to the two settlements. On that scenario the value of the benefit to each, and thus the amount of any capital payment, would be impossible to determine.

The Revenue is understood to agree that where the power exercised is a power to benefit beneficiaries generally there is no capital payment and s 90 applies. Obviously there will be cases where it is difficult to tell which side of the line a power falls and here attention to detail is important.

Assuming the transfer to the new settlement is not a capital payment then, as already noted, outstanding trust gains carry forward. But outstanding capital payments do not, and further, capital payments from the transferee settlement cannot be taxed by reference to gains realised in future tax years in the transferor settlement. In theory at least this offers scope for divorcing payments from gains.

But in reality such divorce may not be simple to achieve. There are two possible difficulties. The first arises out of the case of *Eilbeck v Rawling* [1980] STC 192 where in the Court of Appeal Buckley LJ regarded funds transferred from one settlement to another as still subject to the trusts of the original settlement, the trusts of the transferee settlement being treated as if they were written out in the original settlement. *Eilbeck v Rawling* was a circular avoidance scheme, but Buckley LJ's reasoning was approved in the House of Lords ([1981] STC 174).

The second point is that as described above, the income tax definition of settlement applies to s 87, with the result that the term "settlement" includes any arrangement. In *Chinn v Collins* [1981] STC 1 a contingent appointment followed by the sale and vesting of the interest appointed was seen as a single arrangement with the original settlement. It is possible to see a similar argument being mounted if the transfer to the new settlement and the realisation of gains or the making of capital payments are all part of a pre-planned scheme. The result would be that the transferor and the transferee settlements would be a single arrangement, and thus settlement, with the result that gains in one would be able to be allocated to capital payments from another.

It is difficult to quantify the extent of these risks. However they are clearly less if the transferee settlement is a long-standing separate settlement rather than one created specifically for the purpose of effecting the transfer.

Free use of property

Trustees frequently allow beneficiaries to borrow from the trust at a low or nil rate of interest. So too, a beneficiary may be given a licence to occupy trust property at a low or nil rent. The question of whether such transactions occasion a capital payment, and if so when and in what amount, have occasioned controversy and difficulty.

In the case of a fixed term loan or licence, the matter is, as noted above, covered by s 97(4). There is a benefit, conferred when the loan is made or licence granted, and equal to the then value of the loan or licence.

If this approach were applied to demand loans and revocable licences, there would be a benefit, but its value would be nil, for at any time after the loan was made or licence granted it could be called in or revoked. On this basis there would be nothing to tax.

In *Billingham v Cooper* [2000] STC 122, however, Lloyd J decided that this is not the correct approach. The right answer is to focus on the trustees continuing decision to not call in the loan or revoke the licence. This is a benefit which falls to be valued and it is valued retrospectively according as to how long the loan or licence remains outstanding. If it needs to be determined when the benefit is conferred (as for the purposes of matching, pp 225–6 below), the period can be split as necessary. *Billingham v Cooper*, which was a case on demand loans, does not deal with the question of how the valuation should be done, but the taxpayer and the Revenue had agreed the benefit was a commercial rate of interest for the period in question.

In *Billingham v Cooper*, the trust was a fixed-interest trust where the demand loan had been made to the life-tenant. As a subsidiary argument, the taxpayer contended there was no benefit, for the taxpayer would have been entitled to the interest had it been charged. Lloyd J rejected this argument also. One wonders if the taxpayer was worse off through interest not being charged, for had it been charged, the interest would, under the principle in cases such as *Singer v Williams* [1921] 1 AC 41 have been a payment by the taxpayer to himself. It is an interesting question as to whether it would then be taxable.

Billingham v Cooper reversed a decision at Special Commissioner level in favour of the taxpayer and is itself under appeal to the Court of Appeal. Taxpayers who have so far resisted the Revenue argument as upheld in *Billingham v Cooper* should not concede the point until the case is finally determined. The difference in treatment as between fixed-term loans and licences on the one hand and demand loans and revocable licences on the other which is implicit in Lloyd J's judgment is curious. So too is the fundamental point that there is no proper valuation formulation for such transactions, as there is in the Schedule E benefit in kind rules dealing with free loans and the free use of property. These points, which weighed before the Special Commissioner, will give the taxpayer cogent arguments in the Court of Appeal.

A subsidiary point in some licence cases arises where occupying beneficiary himself owns a share in the property personally, he and the trustees thus being tenants in common. This was the position in *Carter v Hunt* [2000] STC (SCD) 17, where the taxpayer's share was 20% and the trustees 80%. Here the taxpayer's argument is that there is no benefit and thus no capital payment, for the taxpayer is in occupation by virtue of his rights as co-owner. The Revenue position is that there is a benefit, equal to the percentage of the market value represented by the trustees share. The point was not decided in *Carter v Hunt* and so is still at large.

A final and perhaps essential observation is that even if the principle of an annual benefit is conceded its value may on the facts be low or nil. Thus in *Carter v Hunt*, the taxpayer was obliged under the terms of the agreement between him and the trustees to insure and repair the property. During the years 1984–5 to 1997–8, the costs of those items exceeded the notional rent and, on the eve of a Commissioners hearing, the Revenue conceded there was no benefit and thus no capital payment for any of the years in question.

Payments by companies

Before 1991 it was an interesting issue as to whether a payment or benefit counted as a capital payment if it was made by a company controlled by the trust rather than by the trustees themselves. This issue arose because trust gains were only allocated to a payment if it was directly or indirectly received by the beneficiary from the trustees (TCGA 1992, ss 87(3), 97(5)). The issue turned on whether such a corporate payment could be regarded as received by the beneficiary from the trustees indirectly. The better view was that it could not. Indirect receipt connotes payment by the trustees through an intermediate third party, rather than payment by that third party itself out of its own resources (*Potts Executors v IRC* [1951] AC 443).

This issue is now academic, for TCGA 1992, s 96 provides that a payment received from a qualifying company controlled by the trustees counts as received from the trustees. 'Control' bears its income tax close company definition (TA 1988, s 416), save that no rights or powers of an associate are attributed to a person unless he is himself a participator in the company concerned (TCGA 1992, s 96(10)). A company counts as controlled by the trustees if they control it or if they and the settlor or a person connected with him control it (s 96(7), (8)). A company is a qualifying company if it is close or would be close were it United Kingdom resident (s 96(6)).

Payments to companies

A payment is also a capital payment if it is received by a non-resident company which would be close if UK resident (TCGA 1992, s 96(2)). Where such a company is controlled by a single UK resident it counts as received by him. If two or more persons each control the company separately, it counts as received by such of them as are UK resident, divided equally between them if more than one. If it is controlled by two or more persons only if they are taken together, the payment is apportioned among the participators, but excluding any to whom 5% or less would be apportioned (s 96(3)–(5)). Until 21 March 2000 this last provision only applied if the two or more persons were UK residents (cf FA 2000, s 96).

For these purposes control has the same meaning as in the income tax close company provisions (ie TA 1988, s 416), although rights and powers are not attributed to a person unless he is himself a participator (TCGA 1992, s 96(10)). A point overlooked in the legislation is that a beneficiary counts as a participator by virtue of trust holdings in a company (TA 1988, s 417(1)(d)), and this means, in law, that a capital payment by trustees to an offshore company they own, or between two such companies, counts as a capital payment to the beneficiaries of the trust. The absurdity of this is, however, relieved by concession, in that a beneficiary is not in practice treated as a participator solely by virtue of his status as a beneficiary (ESC D40).

Real difficulties, however, arise if the settlor or a beneficiary own a personal stake in a non-resident company in which the offshore trust, or an intermediate holding company, also own shares. In this event the trustees are associates of the settlor and the beneficiaries, and so, if the combined holdings give control, any capital payment made by the trustees to the company or between the companies, may be treated as a capital payment to the settlor or beneficiaries.

In practice the Revenue accept a payment between companies is not a capital payment if it is made under a transaction at arm's length, is subject to income tax, or is a repayment of capital in a winding up (SP 5/92, paras 38–40).

Foreign element

The beneficiary

A beneficiary is not taxable on a capital payment received by him if he is non-resident or non-domiciled (TCGA 1992, s 2 (non-resident) and s 87(7) (non-domiciled)). But trust gains are still allocated to the payment, and so the total of trust gains able to be carried forward is thereby reduced. Effectively, therefore, capital payments to non-resident or non-domiciled beneficiaries enable trust gains to be washed out.

There are, however, two traps in this. The first arises if at the time of the capital payment there are no trust gains. In such a case the payment is taxable if the beneficiary has become resident and domiciled by the time trust gains do accrue (s 87(4)).

The second trap arises out of the rules as to deemed residence. As described on p 301 below an individual remains in charge to CGT if he emigrated after 17 March 1998 and is non-resident for less than five complete tax years (TCGA 1992, s 10A). In such a case gains accruing during his absence are assessed in the year of return. This applies to capital payments made to him during his absence as much as to gains resulting from actual disposals, for capital payments to which trust gains are allocated are deemed to be chargeable gains. It can strongly be argued that a beneficiary is protected from his charge if during his absence he resides in a country with which the UK has concluded a Treaty giving that country sole rights over capital gains. The Revenue, however, are not thought to accept this.

Residence and domicile of the settlor

Until 17 March 1998 trust gains could not accrue unless the settlor was both resident and domiciled in the UK, either when the settlement was made, or in the year in which the gains accrued. Where the settlor had died it was only his residence and domicile at the time the settlement was made which counted. In the case of multiple settlements, it was sufficient for trust gains to accrue if just one of the settlors satisfied the residence and domicile tests. The effect was that a trust was wholly outside s 87 provided the settlor was and had remained non-resident or non-domiciled.

Finance Act 1998, s 130 changed the law with effect from 17 March 1998 and as a result, trust gains are taxable on beneficiaries in receipt of capital payments regardless of the settlor's residence or domicile. The following points may be noted about this:

(1) It does not apply to gains realised by the trustees before 17 March 1998.
(2) Before 17 March 1998 a capital payment could result in tax even if when the payment was made the settlor was non-resident and non-domiciled. This came about if the payment was made in anticipation of the settlor becoming resident and domiciled (TCGA 1992, s 89(1)). It is unclear whether a capital payment made before 17 March 1998 in anticipation of the settlor becoming resident and domiciled resulted in tax if the gains are not realised in the trust until after 17 March 1998.
(3) Apart from any such cases, capital payments made before 17 March 1998 are not brought into charge by s 130. This is provided for by FA 1998, s 130(4). Without such provision a capital payment before 17 March 1998 from a trust with insufficient trust gains could have been rendered taxable by gains realised after that date.
(4) The extension of the capital payments code by s 130 means that in some cases a capital payment is taxable even if received from a settlement which has no connection with the UK and may never have kept appropriate records.
(5) Where a trust has been brought within s 87 by s 130, losses realised before 17 March 1998 are not allowed.

Onward gifts

Since it remains the position that capital payments to non-residents or non-domiciliaries are tax-free, the question arises of whether liability arises under s 87 if such a person subsequently passes the money on to a beneficiary who is resident and domiciled in the UK. In other words can the payment be characterised as a capital payment to the latter beneficiary? The relevant issues are discussed in relation to s 740 on pp 187–8. It is thought no issue can arise under s 87 provided as a matter of trust law the payment is a valid distribution to the original recipient. TCGA 1992, s 97(5) requires the payment to be received from the trustees, and provided the distribution is validly made to the original recipient, it is difficult to see how anyone other than him receives it, even indirectly, from the trustees.

Migrating settlements

If a UK resident settlement migrates, capital payments made in anticipation of the migration count as capital payments for the purposes of TCGA 1992, s 87 (TCGA 1992, s 89(1)). Other capital payments made while the settlement was resident are ignored.

Where a non-resident settlement becomes UK resident and the trust gains for the last year of the non-resident period are not (or not wholly) attributed to the beneficiaries in that year, they are treated as chargeable gains accruing in the first year of the resident period to beneficiaries who receive capital payments in that year, and so on for the second and subsequent years until the amount treated as accruing to the beneficiaries is equal to the amount of the trust gains for the last year of the non-resident period (s 89(2)). As in the case of non-resident settlements, the attribution must be in proportion to but may not exceed the capital payments and the beneficiary.

Notional interest

The tax charged on capital payments may in certain circumstances be increased by supplemental tax representing notional interest. The rules are laid down in TCGA 1992, ss 91–95. The most important point to realise is that these rules cannot come into operation unless CGT is charged in respect of the payment, and only impose notional interest on whatever tax is in fact charged. Sections 91–95 do not therefore extend the basic territorial scope of the capital payment rules, so capital payments are free of both CGT and the supplemental tax if the recipient beneficiary is non-resident or non-domiciled.

Matching

The supplemental tax can only be charged if a capital payment is matched with a qualifying amount of the settlement for the last but one or an earlier year of assessment (TCGA 1992, s 91(1)(c)). For years up to and including 1989–90 there was no qualifying amount (FA 1991, Sch 17 para 2 passim).

In 1990–91 the qualifying amount was the trust gains for that year, less capital payments made to beneficiaries during the year (FA 1991, Sch 17 para 2(2); TCGA 1992, s 92(2)). For 1991–92 and subsequent years the qualifying amount is the amount computed for the year under TCGA 1992, s 87(2), ie the net gains realised by the trustees in that year, excluding any trust gains carried forward from previous years (TCGA 1992, s 92(1), (2); FA 1991, Sch 17 para 2(3)). Where a non-resident settlement became resident before 1990–91, the qualifying amount was the trust gains outstanding at the end of 1990–91 (FA 1991, Sch 17 para 2(4), (5); TCGA 1992, s 92(2).

The basic rule is that capital payments are matched with qualifying amounts on a first-in first-out basis, ie earlier payments are matched with earlier amounts (TCGA 1992, s 92(4)(a)). Thus a capital payment can never be able to be matched with a qualifying amount of 1991–92 or a subsequent year until the entire qualifying amount of 1990–91 is exhausted. If a payment cannot be matched with a past amount (because there is none) it is carried forward (TCGA 1992, s 92(4)(b)). Where the capital payments in a year exceed the trust gains, the part of each payment treated as a chargeable gain is matched before any part of any payment not so treated (TCGA 1992, s 92(5)).

Supplemental tax

The supplemental tax does not apply unless the capital payment is matched with the qualifying amount for the last but one year of assessment or an earlier year (TCGA 1992, s 91(1)). If the recipient beneficiary is taxable on the payment under s 87, the CGT otherwise due is increased by an amount equal to interest at 10% on the tax (TCGA 1992, s 91(2), (3)). The tax is computed on the basis that the capital payment is the first slice of the beneficiary's gains for the year (*Tax Bulletin* 16 (April 1995) p 205).

This notional interest runs for the chargeable period. That period ends on 30 November following the year of assessment in which the payment is made. It begins six years earlier or (if later) on 1 December following the year of assessment in which the qualifying amount matched with the capital payment accrued (TCGA 1992, s 91(4), (5)). The rate of interest may be varied by the Treasury but the total supplemental tax cannot exceed the CGT otherwise chargeable (TCGA 1992, s 91(2), (6)). At current rates of interest the maximum supplemental tax on a higher-rate taxpayer is 24%, which gives total tax of 64%.

Where a capital payment is matched with the qualifying amounts of two or more years of assessment, each earlier than that preceding the making of the capital payment, the capital payment is treated as being as many payments as there are qualifying amounts (TCGA 1992, s 93(1), (2)). The CGT is divided up and attributed to the notional payments on a just and reasonable basis and the supplemental tax computed accordingly. Where part of a capital payment is matched with the qualifying amount or amounts of the last but one or an earlier year of assessment and part is not, the capital payment is divided up and the supplemental tax is only added to tax on the part or parts of the payment matched with the last but one or earlier years of assessment (TCGA 1992, s 93(1), (3)). Necessary apportionments are also directed where a capital payment is matched with part only of a qualifying amount, ie where it is less (TCGA 1992, s 93(4)).

Transfer between settlements

Special rules apply where the trustees of one settlement advance or appoint all or part of the settled property into or on the trusts of another settlement (TCGA 1992, s 94). If all the settled property is so treated, any unmatched qualifying amounts of the transferor settlement are treated as qualifying amounts of the recipient settlement. They are treated as qualifying amounts of the recipient settlement for the same year as they were in fact qualifying amounts of the transferor settlement. The recipient settlement is assumed to have existed and been non-resident in the years concerned if not in fact so. If part only of the settled property is advanced or appointed, any unmatched qualifying amounts are apportioned between the two settlements. It would appear that capital payments made from the recipient settlement have to be first matched with the recipient settlement's own qualifying amounts prior to the year of the transfer (if any), and then with those inherited from the transferor settlement (TCGA 1992, s 95).

These rules appear not to be precluded where the transfer between the settlements is linked with outstanding trustee borrowing and so results in a deemed disposal under TCGA 1992, Sch 4B (see Chapter 27). The consequence would therefore seem to be that in such a case part of the trust gains are syphoned off into the transferee settlement for the purposes of computing notional interest, but not for the purposes of determining whether that settlement has trust gains (cf p 219 above).

Chapter 27

Trustee borrowing

Finance Act 2000 inserted important new rules into the CGT treatment of off-shore trusts, namely TCGA 1992, Schs 4B and 4C. These schedules impose a complete or partial disposal of all the trust assets in certain circumstances where the trustees have outstanding borrowings. Schedule 4B is the principal schedule, Sch 4C containing supplemental provisions charging beneficiaries where the trust is not one whose gains are attributed to the settlor on an arising basis under TCGA 1992, s 86 (see Chapter 24).

Revenue press releases at the time of the 2000 Budget stated that Schs 4B and 4C were being introduced to counteract a scheme known as the 'flip flop' scheme. This scheme has not been tested in the courts, but if it worked it avoided both the charge on the settlor under TCGA 1992, s 86 and the liability of beneficiaries on capital payments under TCGA 1992, s 87.

In essence the scheme involved the following steps:

(a) in year 1 the trustees borrowed money against the security of the trust assets and advanced the cash to a new settlement;
(b) in year 2 the trustees realised gains;
(c) distributions to the beneficiaries were made from the new settlement.

In the case of TCGA 1992, s 86, the scheme was thought to work because the settlor and his children and grandchildren and their respective spouses were all excluded from the original settlement before the start of year 2 when the gains were realised. In the case of TCGA 1992, s 87, capital distributions from the new trust were thought not to be taxable by reference to gains realised in the old trust in year 2, because capital gains only carry forward from one trust to another if realised in the same year as the transfer between the trusts or an earlier year (TCGA 1992, s 90; on pp 220–1).

But even if the reason for enacting Schs 4B and 4C was as stated in the Budget press releases their impact is far, far, wider than flip flop schemes. They undoubtedly impose a deemed disposal in many entirely innocent and unexpected contexts and, even worse, the language of the schedules is riddled with uncertainty. The best advice which can now be given to trustees is never borrow.

Preconditions

Schedule 4B para 1 sets out three conditions for the operation of the new rules:

(1) The trustees make what is termed a transfer of value.

(2)   In the tax year of the transfer the trust is within TCGA 1992, s 86 or s 87. By this is meant either that any net gains in that year are assessable on the settlor on an arising basis or that if there were trust gains and capital payments in that year, a chargeable gain would be treated as accruing to the beneficiary in receipt of the capital payment (Sch 4B para 3). As will be apparent from Chapters 24 and 26 this language comprehends any trust which is not resident in the UK, regardless of whether it has any connection with the UK.

(3)   The transfer of value is linked with trustee borrowing. By linked is meant simply that at the time of the transfer there is what is called outstanding trustee borrowing (Sch 4B para 5(1)). This is the key concept in the schedule and requires consideration first.

Outstanding trustee borrowing

Determination of whether there is outstanding trustee borrowing requires two questions to be asked:

(a)   has there been trustee borrowing?
(b)   is it still outstanding?

Trustee borrowing

Trustees are treated as borrowing if money or any other asset is lent to them, or if an asset is transferred to them on terms that it or another asset must be transferred back to the transferor or another person (para 4). Trustee borrowing thus includes loans in the normal sense of the word and the extension of the term to transfers with the obligation to transfer back is anti-avoidance.

The amount of a loan is the amount or value lent (para 4(2)(a)). The amount of a transfer is the value of the asset received on the transfer, less any consideration received by the transferor (para 4(2)(b)). This latter formulation means no account is taken of the obligation of the trustees to make the retransfer, but does allow a deduction for consideration passing from the trustees when the transfer is made.

It is to be noted that the trustee borrowing can be from anybody. Loans from underlying companies, other trusts, or beneficiaries are caught, just as much as commercial borrowing such as bank loans. The language would seem wide enough to cover drawing down on an informal overdraft as well as structured borrowing.

When is trustee borrowing outstanding?

The basic rule is that borrowing is outstanding until it is repaid. However, borrowing which has been applied for what are called normal trust purposes may be disregarded (Sch 4B para 5(2)). Normal trust purposes do not mean any legitimate purpose of the trustees but instead only expenditure falling within three tightly defined heads. These are as follows (Sch 4B para 6):

(a) payments in respect of ordinary trust assets. This does not connote any proper expenditure on any legitimate asset but instead it too is closely defined, (see below),
(b) discharging a pre-existing loan applied for normal trust purposes (Sch 4B para 6(3),
(c) bona fide current expenses incurred by the trustees in administering the settlement or any of the settled property (Sch 4B para 6(4)).

Ordinary trust assets

The following, and only the following, are ordinary trust assets (Sch 4B para 7):

(a) shares or securities, securities bearing the standard CGT definition in TCGA 1992, s 132;
(b) tangible property, whether moveable or immovable;
(c) property used in a business carried on by the trustees or by a beneficiary who has an interest in possession;
(d) rights in or interests over such tangible or business property.

Expenditure on one of these assets does not qualify as normal trust purposes unless the asset is held by the trustees immediately after the transfer of value. If the asset is not so held the expenditure can only qualify if (para 8):

(a) the asset is then represented by other ordinary trust assets; or
(b) the asset was destroyed or became of negligible value so that TCGA 1992, s 24 applied.

A further point is that expenditure on such assets does not count unless it is on arms length terms and would constitute allowable expenditure within TCGA 1992, s 38 on the disposal of the asset (Sch 4B Sch 6(2)). Expenditure which is disallowed for CGT purposes solely because it is an income tax deduction also counts.

This definition of ordinary trust assets if fraught with problems. The first and most obvious is that not all assets are included, specifically intangibles. Obvious exclusions are insurance policies and intellectual property. But potentially more serious is simple debts. A debt is an asset of the creditor for CGT purposes (TCGA 1992, s 21(1)(a)) and perhaps the most common category of simple debt is a bank deposit. The practical result is that trustees who borrow money and pay it into the bank are not making an application for normal trust purposes.

This leads on to a second problem, namely when must the expenditure on ordinary trust assets occur. Must it occur when the borrowing is incurred, as a direct application of the proceeds, or are the proceeds allowed to be represented by another asset first. To take a specific example, can the trustees put borrowed money in the bank, thereby acquiring a debt, and then spend it on ordinary trust assets, or must the money move directly from the lender to the assets. Common sense indicates that the borrowing need not be spent on ordinary trust assets when incurred, but the fact that this issue arises at all shows how ill thought-out Sch 4B is.

A third problem is that particular items of expenditure on ordinary trust assets may not qualify. Thus under TCGA 1992, s 38, enhancement expenditure has to be reflected in the state or nature of the asset at the time of the disposal. Much expenditure, for example routine maintenance or improvements subsequently obviated, is not so reflected. It would seem such does not count as normal trust purposes under Sch 4B.

Fourth and last, the fact that simple debts are not ordinary trust assets means any simple loan or capital contribution to any company owned by the trustees is not normal trust purposes. The only way such expenditure can count is if the trustees subscribe for shares or securities in the company. As House of Lords decision have affirmed, the term security means something akin to loan stock and should involve an appropriate document (cf *Aberdeen Construction Group Ltd v IRC* [1978] STC 127; *W.T. Ramsay Ltd v IRC* [1981] STC 174).

Bona fide current expenses

There is no definition of this term, but two points are to be noted. The first is that the expenses must be current. The term current, it may be suggested, is wider than just 'income' and would for example include trustee and fund management fees. But one-off capital expenditure is not included, and so, unless incurred on ordinary trust assets, such is not for normal trust purposes. An example of expenditure so excluded would be the often substantial expenditure incurred in fees when a trust is reorganised.

The second point is that the expenditure must be incurred by the trustees in administering the settlement or on the settled property. This plainly excludes expenditure incurred in administering any underlying holding company. It is for consideration as to whether it excludes the one-off annual fees charged by offshore jurisdictions in respect of exempt companies or IBCs.

Regulations

As will be apparent the rules defining normal trust purposes are a mess and give every impression of being drafted by people with little knowledge of how trusts operate in practice. The one redeeming feature is that the Treasury has taken power to amend the rules by regulation (Sch 4B para 9). It is to be hoped this power will be used to rewrite them, hopefully following appropriate consultation.

The transfer of value

The term 'transfer of value' does not bear the IHT meaning with which practitioners are familiar. Instead trustees are treated as making a transfer of value in any of the following circumstances (Sch 4B para 2):

(1) they transfer an asset to any person gratuitously or at an undervalue;
(2) they lend money or any other asset to a person;
(3) they issue a security gratuitously or at an undervalue to another person.

The term 'asset' includes sterling (para 13(1)) and the term 'transfer' includes any act which constitutes a disposal for CGT purposes other than a part disposal which constitutes the creation of an asset (para 13).

This definition plainly covers the ostensible target of Sch 4B, namely flip flop schemes, for those schemes involved the gratuitous transfer of cash to another trust. But as with Sch 4B generally the ambit of the definition is far wider. In particular it includes any distribution to a beneficiary and it would appear that all distributions are included whether capital and substantial or income and small and recurrent. Bizarre though it may seem, even a modest income distribution triggers a deemed disposal under Sch 4B if there is outstanding trustee borrowing.

Further issues are raised by the inclusion of loans. The first issue is that a loan can be made in one instance where the expenditure is for normal trust purposes. This is when the trustees subscribe for a security, and the issue which arises is whether that transaction is a transfer of value, attracting a deemed disposal under Sch 4B, or expenditure for normal trust purposes. Common sense indicates the latter.

The second point is more basic and is at least unless the loan is a subscription for a security, any loan to a beneficiary, another trust, or an underlying company is caught. Informal loans to underlying companies are particularly common in practice, but now if one is made when there is outstanding trustee borrowing the result is a deemed disposal, inter alia of the trust's shares in the company.

Third, as noted above, the technical legal analysis of a bank deposit is that it is a loan by the depositor to the bank. Accordingly on a literal reading, whenever the trustees place money in the bank they are making a transfer of value. If this is right it will often render the question of whether expenditure for normal trust purposes need be immediate academic, for there will be a supervening transfer of value represented by the deposit of the proceeds of the loan in the bank.

The deemed disposal

The transfer of value occasions a deemed disposal under Sch 4B if the trustee borrowing is outstanding at the material time. The term 'material time' is defined by reference to the transfer of value as follows (Sch 4B para 2 (2)):

(1) if the transfer of value is a loan or security, when the trustees make the loan or issue the security;
(2) if the transfer of value is the transfer of an asset when the transfer is 'effectively completed'.

The term 'effectively completed' is new to the CGT legislation and means the point at which the transferee becomes for practical purposes unconditionally entitled to the whole of the subject matter of the transfer (para 2 (2)).

The deemed disposal is of all the chargeable assets which are retained in the trust immediately after the material time. Either there is a complete disposal of all those assets, or each asset suffers a proportionate disposal. For these purposes the term 'chargeable asset' means any asset on which a gain would be chargeable (para 10 (3)). The term thus includes foreign currency but excludes, for example, sterling and qualifying corporate bonds. The deemed disposal is deemed to be on arm's length terms at market value (para 10 (2)).

The deemed disposal is of the whole of each retained chargeable asset if the value transferred is more than both the effective value of the retained chargeable assets and the outstanding trustee borrowing (para 11 (4)). In other cases, a proportion of each asset is deemed to be disposed of. The proportion is determined by a fraction of which the denominator is the effective value of the retained chargeable assets and the numerator is the lesser of the value transferred and the amount of the outstanding trustee borrowing (para 11 (2), (3)).

For these purposes the effective value of a chargeable asset is its value net of any trustee borrowing attributable to it (para 11 (5)). Trustee borrowing is attributable to an asset if either (Sch 4B para 12)

(a)   the asset itself was borrowed and has not been applied for normal trust purposes. This will normally be in point where the asset borrowed was foreign currency;

(b)   the proceeds of the trustee borrowing were applied in acquiring or enhancing the value of the asset, or another asset which it represents. This only applies to the extent that the borrowing is still outstanding at the material time.

The value of the transfer

Schedule 4B includes express rules valuing determining the amount of the transfer. In the case of a loan the amount is equal to the amount lent (para 2 (3)). The amount represented by a security is the value of the security less any amount received by the trustees for it (para 2 (5)). The Revenue are understood to consider that the amount received excludes the promise to pay of the other party to the security and in the context of Sch 4B this is surely right. In the case of a transfer, the basic rule is that the amount transferred is equal to the value of the cash or other asset transferred (para 2 (4)). But if the trustees receive consideration for the transfer, the amount of the transfer is reduced by such consideration unless any part of the value of the asset is attributable to trustee borrowing (para 2 (4)).

Linkage with trustee borrowing

A point to stress is that the deemed disposal is triggered regardless of whether the transfer of value is funded by or in any way related to the trustee borrowing. All that is necessary is that at the material time there is trustee borrowing which is outstanding. Further even if the borrowing has ceased to be outstanding because the proceeds have been expended on an ordinary trust asset, if that asset is comprised in the transfer of value, the borrowing reverts to being outstanding in relation to that and subsequent transfers of value. This is because expenditure on an ordinary trust asset is not an application for normal trust purposes unless the asset or an asset representing it is in the trust immediately after the material time (Sch 4B paras 6 (2) (b) and 8)

Proportion of the chargeable assets deemed to be disposed of

As should be apparent from the above, if the transfer of value is small, only a small proportion of each chargeable asset is deemed to be disposed of. This is because the value of the transfer is the numerator of the fraction referred to above unless it is more than the outstanding trustee borrowing. This point means that on a series of small distributions only modest proportions of each chargeable asset are disposed of. But even if the ensuing gains are small there may still be formidable computation and compliance costs.

In one scenario, the proportion of the chargeable assets disposed of will be greater than might be expected. This will be the position where the value of any such asset is attributed to trustee borrowing for then that part of the value is excluded in determining the denominator in the above fraction. Accordingly proportion disposed of is correspondingly greater. Thus in an extreme case where the sole retained asset was borrowed by the trustees by way of outstanding trustee borrowing (eg foreign currency or an insurance product), the whole of that asset would be deemed to be disposed of regardless of how small the transfer of value is.

Exclusion of trustee borrowing on future transfers

Once trustee borrowing has been taken into account in relation to one transfer of value it ceases to be outstanding for the future (Sch 4B para 5(2)(b)(ii)). The amount which so drops out is the amount of the value transferred or, if less, the total borrowing then outstanding (Sch 4B para 5(3)).

The charge to tax

The effect of the deemed disposal if the trust is within s 86 is that the net gain or loss is brought into account in determining whether for the year as a whole the trust has net gains. If it has such net gains, they are attributed to the settlor. Where s 86 does not apply, Sch 4C contains special rules for attributing the gain to capital payments. Sch 4C applies in place of TCGA 1992, s 87.

The gains which are subject to Sch 4C are referred to as 'Sch 4B trust gains'. Such gains must be computed in relation to each transfer of value within the meaning of Sch 4B. The following may be deducted:

(a) such of the net gain on the transfer of value as is treated as accruing to any settlor of the settlement under s 86 (para 6);
(b) any net loss treated as accruing under Sch 4B by reference to any other transfer of value in the same tax year (para 7(1));
(c) any Sch 4B losses from a previous year which have not already been set against Sch 4B trust gains (para 7(3)).

The Schedule 4B trust gains after making these deductions are attributed to a beneficiary if the following conditions are met (para 8):

(1) The beneficiary is a beneficiary of either the transferor or any transferee settlement. The transferor settlement is the settlement suffering the deemed disposal. The term transferee settlement does not mean any settlement whose funds are derived from the transferor settlement. Instead it is defined by reference to the transfer of value and means any settlement which is the recipient of the transfer of value (para 14).
(2) The beneficiary has received a capital payment from either trust in the year in which the Sch 4B trust gains accrue or in the immediately preceding year (para 9(3)(b)).

(3)   The capital payment has not been taxed by reference to actual trust gains under TCGA 1992, s 87 in either the current or a previous year or by reference to Sch 4B trust gains in a previous year.
(4)   The capital payment was made on or after 21 March 2000 (Sch 26 para 9(3)).

The gains attributed to the beneficiary if these conditions are met are all the Sch 4B gains, or, if the available capital payment is less than the gains, an amount of the gains equal to the available payment. Any Sch 4B trust gains in excess of the available capital payment are carried forward. They are treated as accruing on a transfer of value in the following year and so on until set against capital payments (para 8(3). The effect of these rules is that brought forward Sch 4B trust gains are only set against a capital payment after both current and brought forward ordinary trust gains.

Once Sch 4B trust gains are attributed to a beneficiary then, as with s 87, they are taxed as his gains. No tax is therefore chargeable if he is non-resident (subject to the rules for absences of less than five years) or if his annual exemption is available. As with s 87, the attributed gains do not attract taper relief in the beneficiary's hands (para 11) and non domiciled beneficiaries are not charged to tax on gains attributed to them (para 9(2)). The rules in s 96 treating capital payments by and to companies apply as do the definitions in s 97 (TCGA 1992, ss 96 and 97 as amended by FA 2000, Sch 26, paras 3 and 4).

Rules increasing the tax charge by notional interest apply to tax charged under Sch 4C. These are similar to the rules applicable to s 87 (pp 225–7) but they are not the same and are separately enacted by Sch 4C para 13. In contrast to s 87, these rules are not disapplied where the capital payment is made in the year following the year of the gain and so a small amount of interest would accrue if the capital payment is made after 1 December in that year. As with s 87 notional interest cannot run for more than six years (para 13(5)(b)).

The effect of Sch 4C is that a separate pool of trust gains is created, namely gains accruing under Sch 4B. It is expressly provided that this pool is ringfenced so that:

(i)   ordinary s 87 losses cannot be set against Sch 4B gains;
(ii)   Schedule 4B losses cannot be set against ordinary s 87 gains (paras 1 and 2).

Such ring-fencing is unfair and unsatisfactory and applies harshly if at the time of the Sch 4B deemed disposal the trust assets are showing a loss, but at the time of their subsequent actual disposal they are showing a gain. The gain would not be relieved by the loss and so an artificial gain would have been manufactured.

Practical steps

As noted above, the best practical advice to trustees in the light of Sch 4B is to avoid borrowing. If borrowing cannot be avoided it should be repaid as soon as possible and immense care should be taken as regards any investment or disposition of the trust funds in the meantime. Pending clarification of Sch 4B by regulation or otherwise, it is difficult to identify any course of action which is completely free of risk, particularly in view of the apparent difficulties over bank accounts.

One point which may be made is that borrowing in an underlying holding company does not count as trustee borrowing. Accordingly if the trust is borrowing for investment such may safely be done in a company. However the money must not then be lent up to the trust. The reality is that the company may have to make the investment, a course which normally has drawbacks from other tax standpoints, as described in Chapter 6.

Trustees with subsisting borrowing face particular difficulties for Sch 4B applies if the transfer of value (or more correctly the material time) is on or after 21 March 2000 (FA 2000, s 92(5)). In such cases the best advice is to clear the borrowing as soon as possible, but there will undoubtedly be many instances where trustees inadvertently trigger a deemed disposal under Sch 4B before they or their advisers fully understand the ramifications of the new legislation.

A similar problem may be faced by trusts with no existing connection with the UK if they find themselves with a UK resident and domiciled beneficiary in the future. Here Sch 4B will be material in computing trust gains if a payment is made to him, but the trustees may have no idea whether they have triggered a Sch 4B disposal since 21 March 2000, and no means of ascertaining whether such has in fact happened.

The overall verdict on Sch 4B is that it is an ill-thought piece of legislation going far beyond the mischief it is intended to counter. Conversely some advisers have already suggested that it does not catch all variants of the flip flop scheme and it may well turn out to have opened new loopholes. If that is indeed so, it is difficult to feel sympathy for those who drafted it.

Chapter 28

Attribution of corporate gains

Non-resident close companies are subject to special rules under TCGA 1992, s 13 to prevent their use as devices for avoiding CGT. Section 13 formed part of the original CGT legislation in 1965 and was loosely drawn. It was circumvented by a number of avoidance schemes, and as a result it was tightened up by FA 1996, s 174. The changes made by s 174 have applied since 28 November 1995 (FA 1996, s 174(11)).

The apportionment

Section 13 applies wherever a gain accrues to a non-resident company which would come within the income tax definition of close company if it were UK resident (TCGA 1992, ss 13(1) and 288(1)). It requires all or a proportionate part of the gain to be apportioned to persons resident in the UK (TCGA 1992, s 13(2)). The person to whom an apportionment can be made are resident individuals, resident trusts, or resident companies, but a resident individual is excluded if he is not domiciled in the UK. The term 'close company' bears its normal income tax definition (TCGA 1992, s 288(1)).

Until 28 November 1995, the apportionment could only be to UK residents who were shareholders. Now the apportionment is to any UK resident who is a participator.

The term 'participator' has the same meaning as in the income tax close company legislation (s 13(12)) and thus includes any person having a share or interest in the capital or income of the non-resident company (TA 1988, s 417(1)). It includes loan creditors other than banks (s 417(1)(b) and (9)). The logic of including loan creditors is difficult to follow for, as a general rule, a person who lends money to a company does not benefit from appreciation in its capital assets. It is regrettable that simple loan creditors are not excluded.

A beneficiary under a trust cannot be treated as a participator if and to the extent he would otherwise be a participator by virtue of his beneficial interest (TCGA 1992, s 13(14)). A gain apportioned to a UK resident company cannot be apportioned to shareholders in the company save in the limited circumstances described below where the gain is treaty protected and the shareholder in the UK company is a trust.

Amount apportioned

Until 28 November 1995, the proportion of the company's gains attributed to the shareholder was determined by the proportion of the company's assets he would have been entitled to on a liquidation. Now the proportion attributed is determined by the extent of his interest as a participator (TCGA 1992, s 13(3)). His interest refers to all the factors by which he is treated as a participator, and its extent involves comparing his interest with those of all the other participators (s 13(13)). An apportionment between his interest and those of the other participators is then made on a just and reasonable basis.

These apportionment rules are much less certain than the old ones and as a result may be criticised. Any appeal has to be brought to the Special Commissioners (s 13(15)). A particular point of uncertainty is how the apportionment should be made between holders of shares and holders of loan capital. Is it to be by the value of their respective assets or by the extent to which the value of their asset is increased by the company's gain? The Revenue view is thought to be that the apportionment should be made to those participators who have the real economic interest in the company and will derive the benefit from the gain.

Subsidiaries

In practice, the participators in a non-resident close company frequently consist of or include another non-resident close company. Where this happens, a proportionate part of any gain accruing to the first company is apportioned to the second company and thence to its participators (TCGA 1992, s 13(9)). This process can be continued through any number of non-resident close companies.

Motive test

Section 13 is not subject to a motive test. The result is that the innocent investor is just as much caught by s 13 as the tax avoider. Under self-assessment the compliance burden on taxpayers with non-controlling holdings in private overseas companies is considerable.

Exemptions and reliefs

Exempt assets

Gains on the following assets are excepted from apportionment under s 13:

(1) Tangible property, whether movable or immovable, used only for the purposes of a trade carried on by the company wholly outside the United Kingdom (TCGA 1992, s 13(5)(b)).
(2) Currency or a debt representing money in use for the purpose of a trade carried on by the company wholly outside the United Kingdom (TCGA 1992, s 13(5)(c)).
(3) Assets used in a branch or agency trade in the UK, in respect of which gains are in any event chargeable under TCGA 1992, s 10 (TCGA 1992, s 13(5)(d)).

Losses

A participator may set gains apportioned to him under s 13 against personal losses. Such is not precluded by TCGA 1992, s 2.

A loss accruing to a non-resident company may be used by a participator only to reduce or extinguish chargeable gains on which he is chargeable under TCGA 1992, s 13. This applies only to the participator and not to the company, so that each gain and each loss is separately apportioned to the resident participator. A gain reduced or extinguished under this provision must be one accruing in the same year of assessment in which the loss accrues (s 13(8); see also *Ritchie v McKay* [1984] STC 422). This right of set-off is not restricted to gains and losses made by the same company but applies to all gains and losses chargeable under s 13. Thus losses apportioned to the taxpayer from one company to which s 13 applies may be set-off against gains apportioned to him in the same year from other companies. But the set-off only extends to gains otherwise charged under s 13; it does not extend to the participator's other gains.

Indexation and taper relief

Section 13(11A) provides that gains and losses are computed for the purposes of s 13 in the same way as they would be if the company was resident in the UK. This means that neither taper relief nor the freezing of indexation as at April 1998 applies. Instead indexation continues to apply in full in computing s 13 gains.

Section 13(10A) provides that gains apportioned under s 13 are not eligible for taper relief in the hands of the participator. This is logical in view of the fact that such gains are fully indexed.

De minimis limit

Until 28 November 1995, a shareholder was not charged under s 13 if 5% or less of the gain was apportioned to him, No account was taken of connected persons, so avoidance was possible by spreading shares round family members or trusts.

This 5% de minimis exemption remains, but connected persons can now be taken into account in applying the 5% limit (TCGA 1992, s 13(4)). 'Connected' bears its normal CGT meaning (TCGA 1992, s 286). The result is that a participator is free of tax under s 13 if his participation, and those of persons connected with him, attract apportionment of 5% or less of the gain.

Non-resident groups

Where there is a non-resident group of companies liable to apportionment under s 13, transfers of assets within the group are governed by the CGT group rules which are specifically applicable to non-resident groups (TCGA 1992, s 14(2)). Such transfers are therefore no gain/no loss disposals, and they are so treated in apportioning gains to both corporate and individual participators (see *Tax Bulletin* 7 (May 1993) p 74). The de-grouping charge (TCGA 1992, s 179), which applies where companies cease to be members of a group, also applies to non-resident companies under this provision.

'Non-resident group of companies' is defined as:

(1) In the case of a group with no members resident in the United Kingdom, that group (TCGA 1992, s 14(4)(a)(i)).

(2)   In the case of a group two or more members of which are not resident in the United Kingdom, the members which are not resident in the United Kingdom (s 14(4)(a)(ii)).

Relief from double charge

Until 28 November 1995, s 13 did not apply if the gain was distributed less than two years after it accrued (TCGA 1992, s 13(5)(a)). The distribution could either be by dividend or in the liquidation of the company.

This relief is now replaced by a credit relief under s 13(5A). The credit relief applies if the following conditions are satisfied:

(a)   a person pays tax in respect of the company's gain under s 13;
(b)   the company does not reimburse the participator;
(c)   the company distributes an amount in respect of the gain by dividend or in liquidation; and
(d)   the distribution takes place within two years of the gain accruing.

Where these conditions are satisfied the person who paid the s 13 tax may deduct that tax from any CGT or income tax chargeable on him in respect of the distribution. The distribution is treated for these purposes as the top slice of his income (TCGA 1992, s 13(7A)). This credit relief is much less attractive than the exemption relief it has replaced. One obvious point is that credit relief is of no use if the distribution is not taxable, as where loss relief applies or the participator has a high base cost.

A further relief, without time limit, is conferred by s 13(7). Any CGT paid by the participator on the apportioned gain is allowable as a deduction in computing any gain when he disposes of whatever interest caused him to be a participator. This is far from being a complete relief from double tax, for it is a deduction of tax from gain, rather than of tax from tax and it is not available insofar as the company reimburses the tax. This relief is capable of applying within the two-year limit under s 13(5A), and indeed is the only relief from double charge available where the person sells his interest in the company. Strictly s 13(7) relief only applies if the s 13 tax has been paid, but in practice the Revenue are thought not to insist on this (CGT Manual, para 57362).

Double tax treaties

As a matter of practice, the Revenue allow a participator to credit an appropriate proportion of any overseas tax borne by the company against the UK CGT. Alternatively, he may deduct the overseas tax from the apportioned gain (SP D23).

Where the company is resident in a country with which the UK has concluded a Double Tax Treaty, the treaty normally gives the other country sole taxing rights over the company's gains, for the latter are realised by a resident of that country. The Revenue accept that such a provision precludes the gains from being taxed under s 13.

Section 79B prevents this disapplication of s 13 in two specific circumstances. The first is where the participators in the non-resident company are or include trustees. Here s 79B(2) provides that double tax relief cannot operate to prevent gains apportioned to the trustees under TCGA 1992, s 13 from being charged to tax.

The second circumstance is where a UK close company is a participator in the non-resident company and a double tax treaty prevents gains apportioned to the UK company from being charged under s 13. Here s 79B(3) operates insofar as the participators in the UK company are or include trustees. It provides that s 13 has effect as if the UK company were not resident. This means the gain in the actual non-resident company can be apportioned through the UK company to the trustees. It is then able to be charged, for s 79B(2) prevents the double tax treaty from relieving it. It is further provided (in s 79B(3)(3)) that if the participators in the UK close company are or include another UK close company that company also is deemed to be non-resident, and so on. The effect is that the treaty-protected gain can be apportioned through any number of UK close companies and, if at the end of the chain there are trustee shareholders, they are charged on the treaty gain. It might be thought that this provision only applies if the relevant UK company(s) are dual resident. But this cannot be right for dual resident companies are in any event deemed to be non-resident for all tax purposes (FA 1994, s 249).

The new s 79B is a disgraceful piece of legislation. Although there may be cases where trustees have deliberately caused non-resident companies to reside in treaty jurisdictions so as to avoid CGT, there are also cases where trustees own companies in treaty jurisdictions for genuine trading or investment reasons. In such cases it is wrong for trustee participators to be penalised by anti-avoidance legislation of this sort.

Equally irrational is the way in which s 79B targets trustee shareholders rather than individual or company participators. In particular, this means that trustees holding only a minority interest in a company could be penalised if controlling individual or corporate shareholders cause an offshore company to move to a treaty jurisdiction, although the controlling shareholders will not themselves be within s 13.

SP D23 has not been abrogated or qualified in connection with s 79B. It follows that trustees caught by s 79B should claim credit for the appropriate part of any foreign tax born by the non-resident company on the apportioned gain.

Reimbursement

The shareholders or participators have no statutory right to require the company to reimburse any tax assessed on them. But if in fact the company pays the tax, such is not treated for any tax purpose as a distribution to the participator (TCGA 1992, s 13(11)).

Non-resident trusts

As well as being apportionable to UK resident participators, gains in a non-resident close company are also apportionable to any participator which is a non-resident trust (TCGA 1992, s 13(10)). The apportionment does not, of course, result in the trustees being charged to tax for, being non-resident, they are exempt. But if the trust is within TCGA 1992, s 86, any apportioned gains are assessed as the settlor's and, if it is subject to the capital payment rules in TCGA 1992, s 87, the apportioned gains are included in the total of trust gains. These rules are described in Chapters 24 and 26.

Application of reliefs

In one respect s 13 bears more heavily on non-resident trusts than on UK resident participators. The deduction of tax from gain under s 13(7) is not available, for that relief applies only if the person disposing of the participation is the same as the person who paid the tax. That condition is not satisfied with non-resident trusts, for the trustees dispose of the participation and yet tax in respect of the apportioned gain is paid by the settlor in the case of s 86 and by the beneficiary in the case of s 87.

The application of the relief for distributions within two years to non-resident trusts is a matter of difficulty. The key point to remember is that the person paying the s 13 tax must be the same person as is taxed on the distribution. With this established, it is clear that s 13(5A) does give relief to the settlor if he is assessed under s 86 on the company's gain and then assessed either to income tax or under s 86 on the distribution.

With s 87 the position is much more complicated. The conditions for s 13(5A) relief appear to be as follows:

(1) The UK beneficiary receives a capital payment and is taxed on it under s 87 by reference to the s 13 gain. If there are other trust gains in the pool which exceed the capital payment, the Revenue will probably contend that the s 87 charge was not in respect of the s 13 gain at all.
(2) The company distributes an amount in respect of the gain within two years of its accruing.
(3) The person assessed under s 87 by reference to the s 13 gain is taxable on that distribution.

An interesting question is whether the distribution relief applies in s 87 cases where within the two years the company is wound up and then all the funds in the trust are distributed to beneficiaries. Absent s 13(5A), the trust gains allocated to the distribution to the beneficiaries would be doubled up, ie one gain under s 13 and another in respect of the liquidation distributions. However, s 13(5A) appears to prevent this.

Subsidiaries

At one time, there was an argument that gains in subsidiaries could not be apportioned to non-resident trusts. If this argument was ever good, it is no longer in point on account of amendments to s 13(10) introduced by FA 1996, s 174.

Double tax treaties

Prior to the enactment of TCGA 1992, s 79B, by FA 2000, there was debate as to whether tax treaties could prevent gains apportioned to non-resident trustees under s 13 from being charged on the settlor under TCGA 1992, s 86 or constituting trust gains for the purposes of s 87. The better view was that they could not (cf *Bricom Holdings Ltd v IRC* [1997] STC 19979). Section 79B has now put the matter beyond doubt for s 79B(2) is expressed in terms of a charge to tax arising rather than merely referring to tax being charged on the trustees. The phrase 'charge to tax arising' is certainly wide enough to catch liability under s 86, and also, it may be suggested, wide enough to catch tax on a capital payment under s 87 by virtue of the treaty protected gain.

Chapter 29

Offshore funds

Introduction

Gains accruing on roll-up funds are treated as income under TA 1988 ss 757–64. This legislation was originally enacted in 1984 when the top rate of income tax was 75%, and the rate of CGT was 30%.

This legislation is relevant to offshore planning for two reasons. First, offshore funds themselves represent a sheltering vehicle (see Chapter 9). Second, offshore funds are a likely investment for offshore holding companies and trusts. Material interests held by such entities are caught (TA 1988, s 762).

Material interests and offshore funds

Definition of offshore fund

The term 'offshore fund' is exclusively and exhaustively defined (TA 1988, s 759(1)). An offshore fund is a collective investment scheme constituted by:

(a) a company resident outside the UK;
(b) a unit trust scheme whose trustees are non-resident; or
(c) any other arrangements taking effect under foreign law, which 'create rights in the nature of co-ownership (without restricting that expression to its meaning in the law of any part of the United Kingdom)'.

The term 'collective investment scheme' bears its normal meaning, namely that given in s 75 of the Financial Services Act 1986. This is not the place to explore that definition in detail, but the following points may be noted:

(a) The investors do not have day-to-day control of the management of the investments, which are pooled or managed as a whole by the managers (s 75(2), (3)).
(b) The investors do not own any of the scheme's investments in specie and are not entitled to withdraw any particular investment (s 75(5)).
(c) The manager must operate the scheme by way of business (s 75(6)(a)).
(d) A company cannot be a collective investment scheme, and thus an offshore fund, unless it is an open-ended investment company (s 75(7)). This means the company must be an investment company. It must either give the

shareholders the right to have their shares redeemed or ensure the shares can be traded at net asset value.

Material interests

An interest in an offshore fund is charged only if it is 'material'. The definition of 'material' is allusive, for an interest is 'material' if, on acquisition, the taxpayer could reasonably expect to be able to realise its value within seven years (TA 1988, s 759). Realisation of value means realisation of value as a proportion of net assets of the fund. Quoted shares amount to a material interest if they are habitually traded at net asset value, but not if they only occasionally reach net asset value (SP 2/86, para 3).

An interest in a company is not material if (1) the holder of the interest has the right to have the company wound up; and (2) in the winding up he would be entitled to more than half the net assets (TA 1988, s 759(8)).

Non-qualifying offshore funds

Non-qualifying

A fund is 'non-qualifying' unless it is certified by the Revenue as a distributing fund (TA 1988, s 760). A distributing fund is itself defined and two conditions have to be satisfied. First, the fund must pursue a full distribution policy. Second, not more than 5% must be invested in another offshore fund, nor more than 10% in any one other company.

To pursue a full distribution policy, the fund must distribute an amount equal to at least 85% of both its income as per its accounts and what its income profits would be if computed for UK tax purposes (TA 1988, Sch 27 para 1(1)). A fund is deemed to pursue a full distribution policy if it has no income at all or if its income is 1% or less of the average value of its assets (ibid, para 1(2)).

Detailed rules amplify the basic requirements and relax them in specific situations, for example where the fund holds more than 5% in an offshore fund which is itself distributing. Certification is a matter for the fund and the Revenue. The taxpayer only becomes concerned if a fund has failed to apply for certification. In that event, he may apply to the Revenue who determine its status (TA 1988, Sch 27 para 18).

Whether a fund is a distributing fund has to be determined for each period of account during which the taxpayer holds a material interest in it, and it is only a qualifying fund if it is a distributing fund for each such period, or for each such period after 1 January 1984 if the taxpayer acquired his interest before then (TA 1988, s 757(7)(a)). Periods of account are the periods for which the fund makes up its accounts (TA 1988, s 760(9)), and, if the fund does not make up accounts, it is non-qualifying (TA 1988, Sch 27 para 1(3)).

Offshore income gain

What is called an offshore income gain accrues when a material interest in a non-qualifying fund is disposed of. For these purposes, 'disposal' bear the same meaning as for CGT purposes, but subject to two important exceptions (TA 1988, s 757). First, on the death of an individual there is a chargeable disposal at market value of any material interests which he holds (s 757(3)). Second, the CGT roll-over relief available on take-overs and reconstructions is disregarded. Accordingly, for offshore fund purposes, a share for share exchange or a reconstruction involves the shareholders in a disposal at market value.

The offshore income gain is the unindexed gain, computed as for CGT purposes (TA 1988, Sch 28 para 5). Where the taxpayer held the material interest on 1 January 1984, it is treated as acquired at market value then, if this has the result of diminishing what would otherwise be a gain (TA 1988, paras 4 and 5).

Offshore funds operating equalisation arrangements

Equalisation arrangements arise where an investor subscribes for an interest in an offshore fund during an income period, and the first dividend he receives includes a capital payment representing income accrued prior to the date of his purchase (TA 1988, s 758). This capital payment is debited to what is called the equalisation account. The converse of the purchaser's position is that of the seller who redeems an interest in the fund during an income period, for then the proceeds he receives include accrued income in capital form.

The legislation contains two main rules relating to equalisation arrangements. First, the income element in any redemption by the fund counts as a distribution, thereby preventing the fund's distributor status from being jeopardised (TA 1988, Sch 27 para 2). Second, if the fund is a distributor fund, this element is taxable as an offshore income gain, save insofar as it exceeds the investor's overall gain on the interest he is redeeming (TA 1988, Sch 28 paras 6–8).

The charge to tax

The basic rule is that an offshore income gain is treated as income arising at the time of the disposal and is chargeable under Schedule D Case VI (TA 1988, s 761(1)). This is subject to two important territorial limits:

(1) A person is only chargeable if in the tax year of the disposal he is resident or ordinarily resident in the UK or trading here through a branch or agency. This is achieved by applying to offshore income gains the territorial limits to capital gains tax in TCGA 1992, s 2 (TA 1988, s 761(2)).
(2) A resident individual who is not domiciled in the UK enjoys the remittance basis (TA 1988, s 761(3)). However, the rules are those applicable to CGT rather than to income tax, which means avoidance techniques such as cessation of source and segregating income from capital do not work. A tax charge is only avoided if the entire proceeds of the sale of the material interest are kept abroad.

The rule that an offshore income gain is income does not apply where the gain accrues to a non-resident trust (TA 1988, s 761(7)). This means it cannot be assessed as the settlor's under TA 1988, Part XV should the trust be a settlor-interested trust.

Should the offshore income gain accrue to a resident trust, the charge to tax is at the 34% rate for trusts (TA 1988, s 764). This is so regardless of the form of the trust.

As noted above most disposals of material interests are disposals for CGT purposes. Where this is so, double taxation is avoided by requiring the offshore income gain to be deducted from what is otherwise the consideration for CGT purposes (TA 1988, s 763(2)). This does not apply where the offshore income gain results from an equalisation element in a distributing fund, but here the normal CGT rule would apply of excluding the income element from the CGT computation (TCGA 1992, s 37).

Non-resident entities

In view of the territorial limits described above, offshore income gains accruing to non-resident trusts and companies would, in the absence of special provision, be outside the charge to tax. In fact a range of anti-avoidance legislation applies.

Non-resident companies

The rules for apportioning capital gains in TCGA 1992, s 13 are applied to offshore income gains (TA 1988, s 762(1)). This means that an apportioned part of the offshore income gain can be assessed on any UK participator provided the non-resident company is close and the participator and persons connected with him own more than 5% of the company if the participator is an individual it is necessary for him to be UK domiciled (see further Chapter 28). The application of s 13 also means that the offshore income gain can be apportioned to any off-shore trust which is a participator in the company.

There is obvious scope for double taxation if, after the offshore income gain is apportioned to a UK participator, the company pays the gain in dividend or is sold or wound up. The relief allowing the deduction of tax from tax where the gain is distributed within two years does not apply, for that relief is not extended to offshore income gains (TA 1988, s 762(1)(b) passim). The only relief available is that in TCGA 1992, s 13(7), ie if the participator disposes of his shares in the company he can deduct from that gain any income tax paid by him on the offshore income gain (TA 1988, s 762(1)(b)).

Non-resident trusts

The basic rule is that offshore income gains are subject to the remittance basis, regardless of the form of the trust. This is achieved by TA 1988, s 762(2), which applies the CGT capital payment rules in TCGA 1992, ss 87–97 (see Chapter 26). Accordingly, a beneficiary receiving a capital payment is treated as realising offshore income gains insofar as there are such gains in the trust.

This has the following implications:

(1) The territorial limits are those applicable to s 87, ie a charge is not made if the recipient beneficiary is not resident or not domiciled in the UK.

However, as with s 87 payment to such a beneficiary washes out trust offshore income gains.

(2) Since s 87 only applies to payments not charged to income tax, a capital payment is taxed to income tax under TA 1988, s 740 rather than as an offshore income gain if there is accumulated income in the trust and the conditions for the application of s 740 are otherwise met.

(3) Assuming s 740 is not in point, a capital payment must be taxed as an offshore income gain if there are unattributed offshore income gains in the trust (TA 1988, s 762(4)). Only if the offshore income gains are exhausted is it taxed as a capital gain.

In contrast to s 87 proper, the notional interest regime does not apply to the tax on offshore income gains (TA 1988, s 762(2) passim). This means that the rule attributing offshore income gains before capital gains works against taxpayers, for it delays the attribution of capital gains and thus potentially increases notional interest.

Section 739

Section 739 applies as if the offshore income gain was income accruing to the person resident or domiciled abroad (TA 1988, s 762(5)). This means that if s 739 otherwise applies to a trust or company, the transferor is assessable on the offshore income gain.

On the face of it this rule duplicates the rules described above. In fact it does not, for s 739 is described as applying only where an offshore income gain is not otherwise treated as having accrued to a person resident in the UK (TA 1988, s 762(6)). As a result, it may be suggested that s 739 catches offshore income gains only in two situations:

(1) Where a resident non-domiciliary is transferor in relation to a directly owned non-resident company. Here TCGA 1992, s 13 is precluded as it does not apply to non-domiciliaries, so s 739 applies, albeit on the remittance basis.

(2) Where the offshore income gain accrues to a settlor-interested trust (or to a company owned by such a trust) and it is not matched by a capital payment made in that or a previous year to the settlor or some other beneficiary resident in the UK. Here s 739 applies because in the year the offshore income gain is realised it is not treated as accruing to a person resident in the UK.

Three points may be made about this latter charge:

(1) There is scope for double taxation if a capital payment is made in a year subsequent to that in which the offshore income gain is realised. If the payment is to the settlor, the general s 739 rule preventing a charge where income taxed under s 739 is subsequently received may apply (s 743(4)). But if applicable at all, this rule only applies where the recipient is the transferor, so would not prevent the offshore income gain being attributed to a capital payment received by another beneficiary.

(2) Tax is avoided if the capital payment made in the same or a previous year is received by a non-domiciled resident beneficiary. As the recipient is resident, s 739 is precluded despite there being no charge to tax.

(3)   If the settlor is non-domiciled but resident in the UK, the effect of s 739 applying is that the offshore income gain is deemed to be his income but is not chargeable unless remitted (cf p 175). A question arises of whether a capital payment made to a resident beneficiary in a tax year after the offshore income gain is realised, but prior to remittance would prevent a s 739 charge on the remittance. It is suggested the answer is not, for s 739 deems income to be that of the transferor when it arises, albeit not taxed unless remitted. Here too, therefore, there is scope for double taxation, once when the offshore income gain is remitted and once if a capital payment is made to a resident and domiciled beneficiary in a tax year after the offshore income gain is realised. It may be suggested this would apply if the settlor is a beneficiary and it is he who receives the capital payment.

It will be noted that despite the incorporation of CGT concepts in the taxation of offshore income gains, TCGA 1992, s 86, the section attributing gains to the settlor as they arise, is not applied to offshore income gains. Section 86 cannot apply to an offshore income gain under general principles, for it is expressed as applying only to capital gains, and in computing the capital gain, the offshore income gain is deducted.

Section 740

Like s 739, TA 1988, s 740 applies as if the offshore income gain was income accruing to the person resident and domiciled abroad. This means that it is relevant income, able to be matched with benefits received by beneficiaries resident in the UK.

As with s 739, an offshore income gain is not deemed to be the income of an individual for the purposes of s 740 if it is treated as already having accrued to a person resident in the UK (TA 1988, s 762(6)). In relation to s 740 this rule is not elegantly worded, for s 740 deems the benefit received to be income of the resident recipient rather than the income of the non-resident. However, it seems reasonably clear that the rule applies if under TCGA 1992, ss 13 or 87 offshore income gains are treated as having accrued to the recipient.

Assuming that is right the scope of s 740 in relation to offshore income gains is as follows:

(1)   In the case of a directly-owned company it would apply to benefits received by a non-domiciled shareholder who is not caught under s 739 as transferor. In accordance with s 740(5), the charge would be on the remittance basis.

(2)   If a trust or underlying company has realised offshore income gains, a s 87 charge is avoided if an amount equal to the gains has been distributed to non-residents and thereafter that amount cannot be allocated to future payments for the purposes of s 87. But in this situation, a subsequent benefit conferred on UK beneficiaries the offshore income gains would be relevant income under TA 1988, s 740 in relation to a subsequent benefit conferred on UK resident beneficiaries for the offshore income gains would not otherwise have been treated under s 762 as having accrued to a UK resident.

What is interesting about this last point is that there is a gap. If the initial capital payment is to a resident but non-domiciled beneficiary, the offshore income gains are attributed to the payment but not charged. But here s 740 cannot apply on a subsequent distribution to a resident beneficiary, for, even if not chargeable, the offshore income gains were still treated under s 762 as having accrued to a UK resident.

Trust and company structures

Where a non-resident company is owned by a non-resident trust, the effect of applying s 13 is that the offshore income gains of the company become the offshore income gains of the trust (s 13(10)). As such they are allocated to any capital payment made by the trust and income tax is charged if the recipient is resident and domiciled in the UK.

In such structures there is scope for triple tax. For example if the trust is settlor-interested trust tax my be charged on the settlor as follows:

(1) Under s 739 when the offshore income gain is realised.
(2) Under TA 1988, Part XV if the gain is distributed as dividend by the company to the trust, or under TCGA 1993, s 86 if the company is wound up. This charge is not precluded by s 13(5A) if the distribution is within two years of the gain being realised, for s 762 does not deem tax under s 13(5A) to include income tax.
(3) Under the continued effect of TCGA 1992, s 13, as applied by s 762(1) and s 762(2) if capital is distributed from the trust to the settlor (assuming such distribution is in a tax year following that in which the offshore income gain accrues).

Deeming legislation in FA 2000

FA 2000 s 94, the section disapplying double tax relief where the offshore company has trustee shareholders, does not apply to offshore income gains. This is because that section operates by inserting TCGA 1992, s 79B, which s 762 does not incorporate. So too, TCGA 1992, Schs 4B and 4C, the schedules dealing with trustee borrowing, do not applying to offshore income gains, for they too are not incorporated into s 762.

Comment

The rules described above dealing with the offshore income and gains of non-resident trusts and companies are extraordinarily complex. There are both loopholes and double charges to tax. It would have been far simpler to have left ss 13 and 87 out and deemed offshore income gains to be income for all purposes of ss 739 and 740. In any sensible system such amendment would be a priority for a future Finance Act.

Chapter 30

Life policies

The UK has a special code for taxing life policies, namely TA 1988, Pt XIII Chapter II (ss 539–554). When first enacted this was principally concerned with onshore policies but amendments made in 1984 countered the peculiar tax-saving potential of offshore policies. The legislation was further amended in 1998 and, so far as offshore policies are concerned, the most important of those changes was the introduction of a special regime for one particular kind of policy, namely personal portfolio bonds. In this chapter the general legislation is considered first, and then the rules targeted specifically at personal portfolio bonds.

General rules

The general legislation in TA 1988, ss 539–554 distinguishes qualifying from non-qualifying policies and treats the former more generously than the latter. However, offshore policies are by definition non-qualifying. This is because a policy issued by a non-UK life office after 17 November 1983 is non-qualifying save insofar as the premiums are paid to a UK branch (TA 1988, Sch 15 para 24).

Chargeable events

The legislation taxes offshore policies as and when the policyholder realises value. The occasions of charge are referred to as chargeable events and they are defined in TA 1988, s 540 as follows:

(1) Death giving rise to benefits.
(2) Maturity of the policy.
(3) Complete surrender of the policy.
(4) Assignment of the whole policy for money or money's worth.
(5) Partial surrender or partial assignment for money or money's worth.

A partial surrender or assignment is only a chargeable event if it gives rise to a taxable gain. A taxable gain arises only if the total value of partial surrenders or assignments since the inception of the policy exceed 5% of the premiums paid for each year or part year of the policy's life (TA 1988, s 546). The calculation is done at the end of each policy year, a new policy year starting on each anniversary of the contract (s 546(4)). If as a result of this exercise there is a taxable gain at the end of any policy year, the cumulative 5% of premium and the partial assignments and surrenders used in calculating the gain are left out of account in making the calculation in subsequent policy years.

Amount of gain

The measure of liability on a chargeable event is the gain then realised. Computational rules determine the amount of the gain and these differ as between the different kind of chargeable event.

On a partial surrender or assignment the gain is simply the taxable gain, computed as described above (TA 1988, s 541(d)). On any other kind of chargeable event the base cost is the total premiums paid plus taxable gains on prior partial surrenders or assignments. On death the gain is then the difference between this base cost and the surrender value immediately prior to death (s 541(1)(a)). On assignment, maturity, or surrender the gain is the difference between the base cost and the proceeds (s 541(1)(b), (c)). But in each case, the surrender value or proceeds are increased by what are called relevant capital payments plus (in the case of assignment) the proceeds of any prior partial assignment. Relevant capital payments mean any sum or other benefit previously paid or conferred under the policy (TA 1988, s 541(5)(a)).

Certain points should be noted about these computational rules:

(1) The gain on death is not computed by reference to the proceeds payable on death. What matters is the surrender value immediately before death.
(2) Although partial surrenders are not taxed if they keep within the cumulative 5% limit, the tax is deferred rather than avoided. This is because a partial surrender constitutes a relevant capital payment and so is added to the surrender or maturity value when the policy matures or is surrendered.

Liability to tax: UK residents

Any gain on the policy is taxed as the income of an individual if either:

(a) he is entitled to the policy proceeds, or
(b) a trust created by him is entitled to the policy proceeds (TA 1988, s 547(1)(a)).

The gain is taxed as the income of a UK resident trust if the policy proceeds are paid to the trust and the individual who created it is either non-resident or dead (ibid, s 547(1)(d)). The gain is taxed as that of a UK company if the policy belongs to the company or to a trust created by the company (ibid, s 547(1)(b)).

Assuming the policy is with a non-resident life office, the gain is charged in full to income tax or corporation tax. The charge on individuals is under Schedule D Case VI and the charge on trustees is at the rate for trusts. Neither individuals nor trustees may take credit for basic rate tax unless the life office is taxed in a state of the European Economic Area at a rate of at least 20% (TA 1988, s 533(6)).

The following points should be noted about this charge:

(a) Top slicing relief may be available to individuals (TA 1988, s 550).
(b) Since the charge on individuals is under Sch D Case VI, non-domiciliaries cannot claim the remittance basis.

An individual who is non-resident throughout the tax year in which the chargeable event occurs is not charged. This is provided for by concession (ESC B53), for the legislation does not expressly so provide. Should the individual be resident at the time of the chargeable event, a reduction is made in the gain in respect of any period during the life of the policy during which he was non-resident (TA 1988, s 553(3)). This does not apply where the policy is held on trusts created by the individual unless all the trustees have been UK resident at all times since the individual became UK resident (TA 1988, s 533(5)).

Rules exist for apportioning the gain where a policy is in multiple ownership (TA 1988, s 547A).

Liability to tax: foreign trusts and institutions

Rules enacted in 1998 cover the position where the policy belongs to either:

(i) a foreign institution, which is defined as a company or other entity resident or domiciled outside the UK (TA 1988, s 547(13)), or
(ii) a non-resident trust whose settlor is either dead or non-resident.

In such cases, TA 1988, s 740 is applied as if the gain were income accruing to the trust or institution in the tax year in which the chargeable event occurs (TA 1988, s 547(10), (11)). This means that a capital distribution or other benefit received by a UK resident individual from the trust or institution can be taxed as his income by reference to the policy gain. Such taxation is however subject to the motive defence in TA 1988, s 741 (see Chapter 23). A non-domiciled beneficiary cannot claim the remittance basis under s 740(5) since that basis would not apply had the policy gain accrued to him directly.

Personal portfolio bonds

The tax charge on personal portfolio bonds is set out in regulations, namely the Personal Portfolio Bond (Tax) Regulations 1999 (SI 1999/1029). The enabling legislation is TA 1988, s 553C (as inserted by FA 1998, s 89). The legislation and regulations use the concept of the policy year as defined in TA 1988, s 546(4), ie the year starting on the making of the contract and each subsequent year starting on the anniversary thereof. No charge was made in respect of any policy year ending before 5 April 2000 (reg 1(2)).

Definition

Taxes Act 1988, s 553C(7) defines a personal portfolio bond as one including the following terms:

(i) The benefits under the policy must be determined in whole or in part by reference to the value of some form of property, or income therefrom.
(ii) The property may be selected by or on behalf of the policyholder or a person connected with him.

The regulations cut down this definition in two respects (reg 4). A policy is not a personal portfolio bond if the property able to be selected is either appropriated to an internal linked fund available to policyholders or a class of policyholders generally or is comprised within a list of collective investments which any policyholder or member of a class of policyholders can select.

A policy is a personal portfolio bond if the benefits are determined by reference to an index selected by or on behalf of the policyholder. An exception is made for the retail price index and stock exchange indices provided such are available to policyholders generally (reg 4(7)).

It is to be noted that these exclusions from the definition do not allow selection to be within quoted shares and securities and still less to be of unquoted shares or real estate.

The gain

If a policy is a personal portfolio bond, a gain is treated as accruing in each policy year. In the first year the gain is 15% of the premium. In the second year the gain is 15% of the premium plus 15% of the gain charged in the previous year, ie 15% of 115% of the premium (17.25% of the premium). In subsequent years the gain is 15% of the premium plus 15% of the amount of the gain charged in each previous year since the inception of the policy. In each case the amount to which the 15% is applied is reduced by the taxable gain on partial surrenders which have occurred in the prior policy year or any earlier year.

This formula is draconian in its effect, in that the gain is cumulatively rolled up. This is why personal portfolio bonds should now be avoided. In computing the gain in previous years for existing policies, it is necessary to go back to the inception of the policy rather than simply to the first policy year ending after 6 April 2000.

The charge to tax

The gain is treated as a chargeable event occurring at the end of the policy year. The rules described above in relation to the chargeable event code apply to determine to whom the gain accrues and at what rate it is charged. All such gains are deductible in computing any gain when the policy matures or is subject to a complete surrender or assignment (reg 6(3)). However, such gains are not deducted in determining whether there is a taxable gain on a partial surrender.

The practical result of these rules is to give personal portfolio bonds an unacceptable tax cost if held by a resident taxpayer or in an offshore trust with a living, resident settlor. Such bonds held by other offshore trusts or in a foreign company do not suffer the immediate tax cost, but the relevant income under TA 1988, s 740 is disproportionately inflated.

Transitional

The definition of personal portfolio bond is narrowed in the case of any policy which was issued before 17 March 1998 and has not been varied since 16 July 1998 so as to increase the benefits or extend the term. In such a case, the policy is not a personal portfolio bond if in addition to the range permitted generally it allows self-selection within quoted shares or securities (reg 3). A policy which does not meet even this wider rule would be varied so as to come within it before the end of the first policy year beginning after 6 April 1999. But such a variation is only effective if since the inception of the policy or if later since 6 April 1994, the self-selection has in fact been within the investments thereby permitted.

Immigrants

Personal portfolio bonds may prove to be a trap if held by an immigrant to the UK particularly as policy gains do not attract the remittance basis. A measure of relief is given in that if a variation would have been effective under the transitional rule just described such may be made at any time during the first policy year after immigration (ESC B53).

Part six

Sheltering business profits

Chapter 31

Offshore subsidiaries

Sheltering income profits

UK companies and groups can shelter foreign income profits through offshore subsidiaries. There are many business activities which can be carried on in a low or nil tax jurisdiction, particularly in jurisdictions where employees can be accommodated in the jurisdiction itself or across the border in an adjoining high-tax country. Typical activities include international sales operations, investment services, insurance, financial services, shipping, and holding company functions. If these activities are carried on by an offshore subsidiary, UK tax can in principle be avoided because the subsidiary is recognised as a separate entity by the UK tax code and UK tax does not attach to the foreign profits of non-residents (see Chapter 1).

Fiscal connection

Residence of subsidiaries

Since newly formed UK registered companies are ipso facto UK resident any offshore subsidiary necessarily has to be foreign registered (cf p 35). The residence of foreign registered companies is considered in Chapter 4. The matter is governed by the central management and control test and Revenue scrutiny may be expected where, as postulated here, tax avoidance is intended. In practice the Revenue view is that the test is satisfied if the directors of the subsidiary apply their minds to 'suggestions' from the parent and form an independent judgement. The position is otherwise if they merely rubber-stamp the parent's wishes (*International Tax Handbook* para 335). It is suggested that this practice accords with recent cases as described on pp 32–3.

In practical terms it is essential for the subsidiary to have a local board of directors who genuinely meet and give due consideration to all matters properly requiring decision by the board. It is obviously sensible for the directors to be people who are competent to and do in fact run the business. The UK parent's role should be confined to that of shareholder.

Avoidance of taxable presence

It is self-evident that an offshore subsidiary is only an effective shelter if a taxable presence in high tax jurisdictions is avoided. The rules as to taxable

261

presence vary from country to country. Local advice must be taken on the rules, and the offshore subsidiary's operations so structured that taxable presence in high tax jurisdiction is avoided.

In the UK, the issue of taxable presence turns on whether the non-resident is trading with the UK, in which case it is not taxable, or whether it trading in the UK, in which case it is. If as is normally the case a company trading in the UK is so trading through a branch or agency, the company is liable to UK corporation tax on branch profits and gains (TA 1988, s 11). The branch or agent is normally assessable as the company's UK representative and has a right to recover or withhold any tax it pays from the company (FA 1995, s 126 and Sch 23).

The test of whether or not a company is trading in the UK is a common law one. At one time the place where the contracts of sale were made was thought to be decisive (*Grainger & Son v Gough* [1896] AC 325, 3 TC 462). If the contracts of sale were made in the UK the trade was carried on in the UK and if they were not it was not. Now, however, it is clear that this is only the position where the trade is pure merchanting. The general test is where the operations take place from which the profits in substance arise (*Firestone Tyre and Rubber Co Ltd v Llewellin* (1957) 37 TC 111). Thus a manufacturing trade is carried on in the UK if the manufacturing takes place here and a trade involving the provision of services is carried on in the UK if the services are performed here (cf *IRC v Brackett* [1986] STC 521).

A recent Privy Council decision has given useful guidance on the issue of taxable presence. In *IRC v Hang Seng Bank Ltd* [1990] STC 733 at 739 Lord Bridge expressed himself as follows:

> 'The broad guiding principle . . . is that one looks to see what the taxpayer has done to earn the profit in question. If he has rendered a service or engaged in an activity such as the manufacture of goods, the profit will have arisen or derived from the place where the service was rendered or the profit making activity carried on. But if the profit was earned by the exploitation of property assets as by letting property, lending money or dealing in commodities or securities by buying and reselling at a profit, the profit will have arisen in or derived from the place where the property was let, the money was lent or the contracts of purchase and sale were effected.'

This case concerned the question of whether for Hong Kong tax purposes profits generated by dealing in certificates of deposit were arising in or derived from Hong Kong. But Lord Bridge's observations apply equally to the distinction between trading in and with the UK (cf *Yates v GCA International Ltd* [1991] STC 157 at 172 and *IRC v HK-TVB International Ltd* [1992] STC 723 at 729). In the latter case Lord Jauncey affirmed that the proper approach is to ascertain what were the operations which produced the relevant profits and where those operations took place.

Case law has established that two forms of activity do not amount to trading in the UK:

(1) Purchasing goods or services in the UK for use in the business abroad (*Sulley v A-G* (1860) 2 TC 149);
(2) Representative offices, sales promotion, or after-sale services, provided the contracts of sale and other trading activities are made or carried carried on abroad (*FL Smidth & Co v Greenwood* (1922) 8 TC 193, HL).

If there is trading in the UK, the Revenue accept that UK tax is chargeable only on the profits attributable to the UK trading activities (*Tax Bulletin* 18 (August 1995) p 238). Thus in the case of a product manufactured abroad and sold in the UK, it is only the UK selling profit that is subject to tax. Obviously there is scope for disagreement in determining what proportion of the overall profit is attributable to the UK. In practice the Revenue apply the same criteria as are laid down in the Permanent Establishment Article of Double Tax Treaties. Accordingly it is necessary to ascertain what the profits of the UK operation would be if it was a separate enterprise dealing on arm's length terms with the rest of the business (*Tax Bulletin* 18 (August 1995) p 238). Accordingly the transfer-pricing criteria discussed in Chapter 33 apply.

Profit diversion and transfer pricing

The essential tax function of offshore subsidiaries is to earn profits which would otherwise be realised by group members in high tax jurisdictions. There are two ways in which this is done. One is for an independent business activity to be carried on by the offshore subsidiary, most goods or services supplied to or from the subsidiary being supplied by or to independent third parties. The other is for the offshore subsidiary to provide services to other group members, or sell materials to them or buy finished goods from them for onward sale. In this latter event the offshore subsidiary is potentially diverting profits which would otherwise be realised by other group members in high tax jurisdictions, and transfer pricing rules have to be considered.

Transfer pricing

Transfer pricing is an international issue, and most sophisticated jurisdictions now have legislation allowing the Revenue authorities to substitute market value on connected party sales. The UK is no exception, and the relevant legislation is discussed in Chapter 33. Its practical effect is to make it difficult to divert profits from the UK if goods or services are supplied to a UK entity at an overvalue or supplied by it at an undervalue.

Effective profit diversion

Profit diversion is not, however, completely precluded by UK and international transfer pricing legislation. Two kinds of operation remain possible. The first is where the subsidiary provides genuine services for other group members, its profits being fair remuneration for those services. Thus the routing of materials purchased through an offshore subsidiary falls foul of transfer pricing if the offshore subsidiary is simply an invoicing company. But an offshore subsidiary may be an effective shelter if it is a purchasing company for the whole group, buying in bulk and selling on in small quantities as and when the materials are specifically required. Similar principles apply where the subsidiary is providing services such as marketing, group insurance, or finance, so long as the subsidiary's margin is comparable with those providing such services on an arm's length basis.

The other form of effective profit diversion is where goods or services are supplied to or from countries with less sophisticated tax systems without transfer pricing rules. Here it may be that goods and services can be supplied by a subsidiary in the unsophisticated jurisdiction to other group members at below world prices, or supplied to it at above world prices. In this event neither the UK nor most other countries' transfer pricing rules say that the benefit of the over or undervalue must be taken in the group members in the high tax countries. Indeed, the essence of transfer pricing adjustments is that it should not be, for it is market value and no more which is substituted. Accordingly, the under or over-value can be effectively sheltered by an offshore company, perhaps one formed specifically for dealings with the unsophisticated country concerned.

Profits which may be sheltered

As a result of transfer pricing rules it may be said that offshore subsidiaries may principally be used to shelter three kinds of profit:

(1) Profits from business carried on with unconnected third parties.
(2) Profits resulting from genuine services provided on arm's length terms for other group members.
(3) Profits resulting from transactions with group members located in jurisdictions without modern transfer pricing rules.

Avoiding the controlled foreign company legislation

Until 1984, company residence, taxable presence, and transfer pricing were normally all that had to be considered in deciding whether an offshore subsidiary was an effective tax shelter. Since then, a further factor has had to be allowed for, namely the controlled foreign company legislation (TA 1988, ss 747–756).

The controlled foreign company legislation is analysed in Chapter 34. It is targeted specifically at offshore subsidiaries which are not subject to a local rate of tax of at least three-quarters the equivalent UK tax. Its effect is to make the UK parent subject to corporation tax in respect of the subsidiary's profits. Fortunately, there are important circumstances in which the legislation is excluded.

Exempt activities

The most notable exclusion is where the subsidiary is engaged in exempt activities. To be engaged in exempt activities, the subsidiary must satisfy certain key conditions. Its business must not be a quasi investment business such as leasing and if the business is dealing, the subsidiary's trading partners must be unconnected and outside the UK. If the business is what the CFC legislation calls wholesale, distributive, or financial service, at least half its receipts must be derived from unconnected persons. Perhaps more important, whatever the nature of its business, the subsidiary must have proper premises in the offshore jurisdiction where it is based, together with adequate personnel there to effectively manage its affairs.

If a subsidiary satisfies all these conditions it falls fairly and squarely within the exempt activities exclusion and a charge under the CFC legislation cannot be made. It might be thought that relatively few subsidiaries would meet these conditions but in fact this is not so. The conditions could, for example, be satisfied by an international sales subsidiary not dealing with the UK, or by an independent insurance subsidiary insuring unconnected clients.

Other companies

Where the offshore subsidiary is not engaged in exempt activities, it used to be possible to avoid the CFC legislation at reasonable cost by making acceptable distributions. Now, however, the relief for acceptable distributions is much curtailed as it does not apply unless the subsidiary distributes at least 90% of its chargeable profits.

One method whereby a subsidiary not engaged in exempt activities can achieve a measure of sheltering arises if the UK parent has a multiplicity of overseas subsidiaries, including some in high tax jurisdictions. Here all the subsidiaries can be grouped under a single non-resident holding company, or 'mixer company' as it is called. When that company pays dividends, underlying and withholding tax paid by all its subsidiaries will be aggregated, and the aggregate will be a credit against the UK company's corporation tax. It is highly likely that the tax borne by subsidiaries in high tax jurisdictions will exceed UK corporation tax, and so dividends from offshore subsidiaries can be injected to bring the aggregate creditable tax on the dividend to the UK company down to 30% or less. These dividends then amount to acceptable distributions.

Mixer companies will cease to be able to be used in this way with effect from 31 March 2001. This is because as from that date the tax credit on any subsidiary's underlying profits will not be able to exceed corporation tax at the main rate on those profits (FA 2000, Sch 20 para 8). This applies insofar as the eventual dividend to the UK parent is paid after 31 March 2001.

TA 1988, s 801A prevents a mixer company from being used where the claim to credit relief is made as part of a tax avoidance scheme. This section appears to catch cases where the high tax subsidiary is acquired specifically with a view to obtaining credit for its high tax through the mixer company (s 801A(7)). It does not catch the insertion of a mixer company into an existing group or the acquisition of a high tax company for genuine commercial reasons (see *Tax Bulletin* 29 (June 1997)).

Repatriation of profits

As with all offshore sheltering it is not enough to simply shelter income profits as they arise. Thought also needs to be given to whether and if so how they will be repatriated.

Dividends and capital realisations

On the face of it all, offshore sheltering is only a deferral. The profits of an offshore subsidiary can only be realised by dividend or on the sale or liquidation of the subsidiary. In the former event the dividend is subject to corporation tax under Schedule D Case V. On a sale or liquidation the tax is corporation tax on chargeable gains, and if, as is common, the original formation or acquisition of the subsidiary was for nominal consideration, the value of the subsidiary will be a chargeable gain in its entirety. Effectively, therefore, the same tax attaches to offshore profits received in dividend as to those realised on a sale or liquidation.

In certain circumstances, sheltering through an offshore subsidiary can result in greater overall tax. This arises where the subsidiary's profits have suffered withholding or other taxes as they arise. Here such tax can be relieved by credit against UK income tax if the subsidiary's profits are paid out as dividend (cf TA 1988, s 790(6)). But such credit is not available against any CGT charged on a sale or liquidation.

Set-off against losses

One way round the difficulties of repatriation is to accumulate profits in the subsidiary until the UK parent has losses. The profits can then be distributed in the accounting period when the losses arise and loss relief claimed. Unfortunately, the saving thereby achieved is more apparent than real, for the losses will not be available to set against other profits, for example profits of future accounting periods.

Importing the subsidiary

There is one well known if somewhat artificial route of repatriating profits free of tax. This is for the subsidiary to become UK resident, and then pay a dividend (TA 1988, s 247). UK residence is achieved by appointing UK directors and holding the subsidiary's board meetings in the UK. The dividend is tax-free, for, as a distribution, it is excluded in computing the parent's taxable profits (TA 1988, s 208).

There are two difficulties in proceeding in this way. One is that making the UK company resident may give the Revenue grounds for arguing that the subsidiary was UK resident all along. The second is that the exercise may be vulnerable to attack under the *Ramsay* principle. If when the subsidiary becomes UK resident it is virtually certain the dividend will be paid, then the Revenue would have grounds for contending that the dividend should be treated as paid prior to assumption of UK residence (cf *Craven v White* [1988] STC 476, [1989] AC 398). In practical terms the real difficulty for taxpayers will be proving that it was not certain the dividend would be paid if payment does in fact follow the assumption of UK residence.

Mixing

The concept of mixer companies has been explained above. If dividends from the offshore subsidiary are paid up through a mixer company, UK tax otherwise payable on those distributions is obviated by the higher foreign tax payable by the subsidiaries in the high tax jurisdictions. The result is effective avoidance of UK tax on distributions from the offshore subsidiaries. The use of mixer companies for this purpose will cease to be possible from 31 March 2001 but first impressions of the new regime for onshore mixing indicate dividends from offshore subsidiaries will be within this regime unless paid to satisfy the CFC acceptable distribution test (FA 2000, Sch 30 para 21).

Sheltering capital gains

Offshore subsidiaries in quoted groups can be used to shelter capital gains as well as income profits. Indeed sheltering capital gains is normally more straightforward, for neither the transfer pricing nor the controlled foreign company legislation applies to capital gains. It should, however, be remembered that under normal CGT rules market value must be substituted on any transaction between the offshore subsidiary and the UK group (TCGA 1992, s 17).

TCGA 1992, s 13

There is one legislative obstacle to sheltering capital gains and this is TCGA 1992, s 13. Where this section applies it apportions gains realised by the subsidiary to its UK parent, the apportionment being by the extent of the parent's interest if the subsidiary has multiple participators. Gains can be apportioned through a chain of offshore subsidiaries if there is an offshore group structure.

Section 13 is considered in Chapter 28. For present purposes the important point is that it only applies if the offshore subsidiary would be a close company if it were UK resident. The definition of close company which applies for these purposes is the standard definition in TA 1988 (ss 414–417). Very broadly a company is close if five or fewer participators either control it or would be entitled to the greater part of its assets in a winding up. However, a company cannot be a close company if at least 35% of its shares are held by the public and dealt in on a stock exchange. More importantly a subsidiary is not a close company if its ultimate parent is not a close company.

The practical result of this definition is that the offshore subsidiaries of quoted groups are not close companies whereas the subsidiaries of privately owned groups generally are. Accordingly, offshore subsidiaries provide an effective CGT shelter for quoted UK companies or groups, but not for their unquoted counterparts.

Offshore subsidiaries as holding companies

Multinational groups often group their foreign subsidiaries under an offshore holding company subsidiary. Such a strategy represents effective CGT planning if the group is quoted, for it shelters any gains realised if the operating subsidiaries are sold or liquidated. Until 31 March 2000 a further advantage is that such a company may act as a mixer company as described above.

If it is not being used as a mixer company for dividends, such an offshore holding company normally has one drawback, in that the controlled foreign company legislation has to be considered. A holding company can, however, accumulate dividends from the operating subsidiaries if it satisfies the motive defence or the exempt activities test (see Chapter 34).

If these exceptions are not in point, profits can simply be accumulated in such operating subsidiaries as are not caught by the CFC legislation and realised in a sale or liquidation. This will be tax-free since the gain will be capital and accrue to the offshore holding subsidiary. Such an approach is, however, unattractive if the profits of the subsidiaries bear substantial local tax, for then the sale or liquidation will mean that tax cannot be offset against UK tax if the profits eventually reach the UK.

Criminal offences

Ever since 1951 the criminal law has had to be considered in relation to non-resident subsidiaries. Until 1988 it was a criminal offence for a resident company either to migrate or to transfer its business abroad without Treasury consent (TA 1970, s 482). The maximum penalty was imprisonment for two years or a fine of £10,000 and while prosecutions are not thought to have been brought, the criminal sanction was a powerful deterrent.

It is now no longer a criminal offence for a resident company to migrate or transfer its business abroad. But what is often forgotten is that the 1951 legislation created two other criminal offences, with the same penalties as described above, and these offences have not been repealed (TA 1988, s 765).

Continuing criminal offences

The present offences are directed not at companies migrating but at the subject matter of this chapter, namely resident companies with non-resident subsidiaries. The first offence is for a UK company to cause or permit a non-resident subsidiary to create or issue any shares or debentures (TA 1988, s 765(1)(c)). The second offence is for the UK company to transfer any shares or debentures in a non-resident subsidiary otherwise than to directors as directors qualifying shares (TA 1988, s 765(1)(d)). It is to be noted that whereas the issue offence extends to issues by sub-subsidiaries, the transfer offence does not catch transfers by the subsidiary of shares in sub-subsidiaries.

Treasury consent

As with the former migration offences, an offence is not committed if Treasury consent is first obtained. Treasury consent may be either a specific consent applied for in advance of the transaction concerned or one of the published General Consents.

The General Consents were reissued in 1988 (The Treasury General Consents 1988). Their wording is extremely complicated, so much so that some advisers ignore them and apply for specific consent in all cases. The main transactions permitted by the General Consents are as follows:

(1)   Shares or debentures may be issued by any non-resident subsidiary to unconnected parties for full consideration.
(2)   Shares or debentures may be issued by one overseas subsidiary to another if both are resident in the same country.
(3)   Irredeemable shares may be issued for full consideration to the UK parent.

(4) Debentures may in certain circumstances be issued to the UK parent.
(5) Shares or debentures in the subsidiary may be transferred by the UK parent to unconnected parties for full consideration.
(6) Shares or debentures may be transferred on any terms to other members of the UK parent's group.

Minor amendments were made to the General Consents in 2000 (Inland Revenue Press Release 26 July 2000 (see [2000] STI 1079; *Tax Bulletin* 46 (April 2000)).

Guidance notes for applicants for specific consent were published in 1988. The application should be made to the Treasury, and, in an emergency, to the Revenue. The commercial reasons for the proposed transaction should be explained and in practice these are weighed against any loss of tax to the UK which the proposal would entail.

European relief

Neither the criminal offences nor the need to obtain Treasury consent apply if the transaction is movement of capital between residents of EU Member States (TA 1988, s 765A). In such a case the Revenue merely have to be notified of the transaction within six months of it happening. It is to be noted that the EU does not include the Channel Islands or the Isle of Man. The relief does not apply to movements between Gibraltar and UK residents because Gibraltar and the UK are regarded as the same state (SP 2/92).

Chapter 32

Parallel companies

Introduction

Parallel companies are an alternative to group structures. Instead of forming an offshore subsidiary, the shareholders in a UK company incorporate an offshore company in their direct ownership, its shareholding mirroring that of the UK company. Parallel companies are only a practical solution where the UK company is unquoted and normally they are only formed where the company has one or a small group of family shareholders.

A parallel offshore company has one great advantage over an offshore subsidiary. The controlled foreign company legislation does not apply to it, for that legislation can only attribute profits to corporate shareholders. A further advantage is that the criminal offences under TA 1988, s 765 should not arise, for these can only be committed by UK companies.

Parallel companies are, however, subject to the same rules as subsidiaries regarding such matters as taxable presence and transfer pricing (see pp 262–3). They also bring problems of their own, notably over company residence, shadow directors, TA 1988, s 739, capital gains and the repatriation of profits.

Company residence

As with subsidiaries, parallel offshore companies have to be registered abroad, and their residence is governed by the central management and control test. This is discussed in Chapter 4, and while the position ought to be the same as with subsidiaries in practice it may not be.

The reason for this is that one or two controlling shareholders may be much more tempted to interfere in the affairs of a directly-owned offshore company than the board of a UK parent would be. Furthermore the Revenue may take more persuading that central management and control is not being exercised from the UK.

Practical steps to avoid the risk are discussed on pp 33–4. It is particularly important that a parallel company of the kind being postulated here, which is genuinely trading, has a board of directors who are competent to and do demonstrably run the business. The board should meet regularly in the country where the company carries on business. The shareholders should maintain a proper distance, and requests they do make to the offshore company should only be implemented after due consideration by the company's board at a properly minuted meeting. In theory there is no objection to a shareholder being on the Board, but only if it is clear on the facts that all top-level decisions relating to the business of the company are taken at genuine Board meetings in the off-shore jurisdiction concerned.

Shadow directors

Even if the dangers of company residence are avoided a UK shareholder may still find he is at risk of being a shadow director. This issue is examined in Chapter 19, and as there explained *Secretary of State for Trade and Industry* [2000] 2 All ER 365 has made a finding of shadow directorship more likely. If a UK resident is a shadow director he is taxable under Schedule E on benefits received from the company, whether in the UK or abroad (*R v Dimsey* [1999] STC 846). Such benefits should therefore be avoided.

Section 739

Section 739 is analysed in Chapter 21. There is no doubt that it can apply when a foreign company is incorporated, and further that trading profits count as income for the purposes of the section (*Latilla v IRC* [1943] AC 377; *IRC v Brackett* [1986] STC 521). Accordingly, in the simplest of all cases, it applies where the proprietor of a wholly owned UK company incorporates a tax haven trading company which diverts profits from the UK.

But s 739 does not apply in all cases. First there is the motive defence, discussed in Chapter 23. Here the UK shareholder has to show that the incorporation of the offshore subsidiary was a bona fide commercial transaction not designed to avoid taxation. There are certainly cases where the defence can avail, for example if there are good commercial reasons for having an operating company near where foreign profits arise, and yet exchange controls or some other factor make it preferable to base the company in a nearby offshore jurisdiction rather than in the actual country producing the profits. The case of *Carvill v IRC* [2000] STC (SCD) 143, which is discussed on p 195, represents a good example of this. Another situation is where a local manager or joint venturer is to have a stake in a foreign operation and it is a genuine term of his participation that the company is based in a specific low tax jurisdiction.

Section 739 does not apply if the UK individuals buy an existing company. Here s 739 is precluded because the transfer made by the individuals, namely the purchase of the shares, is not one by virtue of which profits accrue to the company (cf *Vestey v IRC* [1980] AC 1148, passim). This is a well recognised route for escaping s 739, but it must not be taken too far. The company must genuinely be a pre-existing company, and not one formed a few days before by professional advisers specifically for the purposes of being bought.

Capital gains

Directly-owned offshore companies give rise to CGT problems, for their capital gains are apportioned to the UK resident participators. The apportionment is under TCGA 1992, s 13 and is on the basis of the extent of each participator's interest. While apportionment only applies to non-resident close companies, it catches virtually all parallel companies of the kind postulated in this chapter, since it is difficult to envisage such a company which is not close. There is a particular sting in s 13, for, where it has applied, the gain apportioned is not deducted from any gain subsequently accruing on the shares in the offshore company. Only the actual tax paid may be deducted (s 13(5)).

Section 13 is discussed further in Chapter 28. In certain business situations it is not of great importance, for gains accruing on tangible property used in a trade carried on by the company outside the UK are not apportioned, whether the tangible property is land or moveable property. So too currency gains are not apportioned if the currency is held for trade purposes. Section 13 is also excluded if the company is resident in a jurisdiction with which the UK has concluded a double tax treaty, and the treaty gives the other country sole taxing rights over capital gains realised by its residents. This does not apply insofar as the shareholders in the non-resident company are trustees (TCGA 1992, s 79B; see pp 242–3).

If none of these exceptions avails and charges do arise under s 13, the element of double taxation at least can be mitigated. Credit relief is available if the gain is distributed within two years of being realised (s 13). The distribution may be by dividend or in a liquidation, and now that income and gains are taxed at the same rate, a timely dividend may be considered where a substantial gain otherwise within s 13 has accrued.

Repatriating profits

As with most offshore structures, profits sheltered in a parallel company are not without more at the disposal of the shareholders. Either the company must be sold or liquidated, or a dividend paid. In either event UK tax will be due. If a dividend is paid, the liability is under Schedule D, Case V. On a liquidation TA 1988, s 740 applies unless the s 741 motive defence avails, for there will indubitably have been a transfer of assets by somebody. Section 740 may not apply on a sale, but both then and on a liquidation any gain it does not catch is subject to CGT.

In many cases these liabilities mean that overall tax is greater than if the parallel company had not been incorporated at all. This occurs if the profits of the company have borne overseas tax, either directly or as withholding tax. In contrast to subsidiaries, there is no mechanism for crediting such tax against the UK tax on dividends borne by individual shareholders. Nor, obviously, is such tax credited against a s 740 liability or the CGT on a sale or liquidation.

The simplest means of bringing the sheltered profits to the shareholders without these charges is for the shareholders to emigrate permanently. Alternatively it may be possible to wait until they die, and then sell or liquidate the company with the advantage of the new CGT base value available on death (TCGA 1992, s 62). However, this strategy is only effective if the circumstances are such that TA 1988, s 740 is avoided, for that section applies to successors as much as to the original shareholders.

Trust structures

Advantages

Ownership through an offshore trust offers a means of avoiding some of the difficulties otherwise attaching to parallel companies. As is explained in Chapter 5, an offshore discretionary or accumulation trust from which the settlor and his spouse are wholly excluded should with appropriate care prevent liability arising under s 739. It follows from this that exclusion from s 739 may be achieved in relation to a parallel company if such a trust owns all the shares. Ownership through the trust also brings the further advantage that it is harder for the Revenue to contend that the company is UK resident (cf p 34). The risks of somebody in the UK being found to be a shadow director are reduced, but probably by not very much, so benefits to any such person should be avoided.

In the result, it may safely be said that in income tax terms, the ideal structure for sheltering foreign business profits is a non-resident company owned by a non-resident trust from which the settlor and his spouse are wholly excluded. Such sheltering of business profits may be part of a wider structure, in which the trust is also used to shelter investments, as is described in Part two. Indeed the business activities of the company may generate the funds from which the portfolio investments are purchased.

One matter which is not necessarily resolved by a trust ownership is how the profits are eventually to be repatriated. The problems in this area, and possible solutions, are discussed in Chapter 18.

In relation to capital gains TCGA 1992, s 13 operates merely to apportion the company's gains to the trust. This is not an advantage where the trust gains can be further attributed to the settlor under TCGA 1992, s 86 for then the gains attract tax on an arising basis (see Chapter 24). But where this is not in point, CGT does not arise unless and until a resident beneficiary receives a capital payment.

Exclusion of the settlor

There is a price which has to be paid for a trust structure of this kind and this is that shareholders in the UK company are normally settlors and so have to be excluded. In some cases this is not a problem, as where the shareholders are already wealthy. Alternatively the problem may be avoided if the initial capital settled in the trust comes not from the shareholders but from parents or even, if gains are to be sheltered, from more remote relatives. Such arrangements are discussed on pp 44–5 and are normally effective to prevent the shareholders from being treated as settlors (cf *IRC v Mills* [1975] AC 38 and *Butler v Wildin* [1989] STC 22). But it should be remembered that s 739 liability extends to procurers of the offshore arrangements (see pp 176–8). Accordingly, the UK shareholders should as far as possible be distanced from the setting up of the offshore arrangements, and certainly they should not indirectly provide funds for the trust. The extended meaning of 'power to enjoy' should also be kept in mind (cf pp 168–71).

The settlor as beneficiary

Despite these possibilities, there are undoubtedly cases where the UK shareholders must inevitably be the settlors and do not wish to be excluded from benefit. In these circumstances, the question arises of whether trust ownership still brings benefits.

The answer to this depends on whether s 739 will catch the company's profits. Prima facie it will, for the creation of an offshore trust, followed by the formation of an offshore company, does bring s 739 into play. Indeed, in cases such as this the chances of s 739 applying may be greater, for the creation of the trust is motivated by tax considerations, and thus in practice jeopardises any motive defence which may exist in relation to the company.

Fortunately, there is one situation in which a s 739 liability can be avoided. This is where the company is a pre-existing company, purchased by the shareholders in the UK company prior to the making of the settlement or by the trustees thereafter. As is described above, s 739 does not apply to the profits of such a company so long as funds are not injected into it. It would, of course, catch any dividends paid to the trust, but there is no obstacle to the indefinite retention of profits by the company. Eventually the profits can be brought to the trust as capital in a sale or liquidation, and if this is done no income accrues to the trust and so there is nothing to be taxed under s 739. There will, however, be a capital gain, and the question of attribution under s 86 would have to be considered at that stage (see Chapter 24).

Chapter 33

Transfer pricing

Introduction

Transfer pricing is principally an issue with multinational groups of companies, but it also arises whenever a UK taxpayer deals with an associated foreign entity. Often there will be no commercial significance in the prices at which the two entities do business, and there is scope for diverting profits so as to reduce the UK entity's tax liability. Until recently, arm's length prices did not have to be used in UK tax computations unless the Revenue gave a direction under TA 1988, s 770. TA 1988, Sch 28AA, however, contains a mandatory code which, in broad terms, requires arm's length prices to be used in all tax computations relating to connected party transactions. For corporate taxpayers, Sch 28AA has applied to accounting periods ending on or after 1 July 1999, the appointed day for corporate self-assessment (FA 1998, s 109(5)(a)). For non-corporate taxpayers, Sch 28AA has applied since 6 April 1999 (ibid, s 109(5)(b)).

This chapter is principally concerned with Sch 28AA, but it also includes two related general income tax principles.

The statutory rule

The rules in Sch 28AA apply if the following conditions are satisfied (para 1):

(1) Provision has been made or imposed as between any two persons. This provision is referred to as 'the actual provision' and the two persons are referred to as 'the affected persons'.

(2) The actual provision has been made or imposed by means of a transaction or series of transactions.

(3) The actual provision differs from what is called the arm's length provision. This is the provision which would have been made had the affected persons been independent enterprises.

(4) The actual provision confers a potential advantage in relation to UK taxation on one or both of the affected persons. A person so advantaged is referred to as 'the potentially advantaged person'.

(5) One of the affected persons participates in the management control or capital of the other or a common third party so participates in both.

Where these conditions are satisfied, the arm's length provision must be substituted for the actual provision in computing the profits or losses of the potentially advantaged person. In contrast to the previous legislation, the substitution is mandatory, and must be effected by the taxpayer in preparing his self-assessment return; there is no prerequisite of a Revenue direction.

An advantage in relation to UK taxation means smaller profits or income or larger losses or reliefs (Sch 28AA paras 5(1) and 14(1)). An advantage is ignored if the disadvantaged party is resident in the UK and within the charge to UK tax in respect of the activities concerned (ibid, para 5(2)). But this relief does not apply if the disadvantaged party is exempt from UK tax in respect of the activities concerned or if he is entitled to have any tax chargeable offset by double tax relief (ibid, para 5(3)(c), (4) and (5)).

The term 'transaction' has an extended meaning. It includes arrangements, understandings and mutual practices, whether or not legally enforceable (Sch 28AA para 3(1)). The term 'series of transactions' includes any number of transactions entered into under the same arrangement. It is not necessary for either of the affected persons to be party to such an arrangement, nor need there be any transaction in the series to which they are both parties (ibid, para 3(4)).

Common participation

Common participation in management, control, or capital is the fundamental prerequisite of Sch 28AA. Under para 1(1), the participation may be direct or indirect.

Direct participation

One person can only be treated as participating in the management, control, or capital of another if the latter person is a body corporate or partnership. The participation is direct if and only if the participant controls the partnership or body corporate concerned (para 4(1)).

Control does not bear its extended close company definition but the narrower meaning given by TA 1988, s 840.

Under s 840 a person controls a partnership if he is entitled to more than half its assets or more than half the income (TA 1988, s 840). Hence Sch 28AA can apply to transactions between an individual and a partnership in which his share is greater than half, or between two partnerships in each of which one individual enjoys more than a half share. It also applies to transactions between such partnerships and a company which an individual controls.

A person has control of a company under s 840 if (1) he can secure that its affairs are conducted in accordance with his wishes; and (2) he is able to secure that result by one of two methods. The first method is by the possession of share or voting rights and the second is by powers conferred by the articles (TA 1988, s 840).

Indirect participation

Indirect participation is a much wider and more menacing concept (ibid, para 4(2)). A person indirectly participates in the management, control, or capital of a company or partnership if either:

(a)   he would be a direct participant if a whole series of other rights or powers were attributed to him; or

(b) he is one of a number of what are called major participants in the enterprise of the company or partnership.

Attributed rights and powers

The rights and powers which may be attributed to a person in determining whether he is an indirect participant are as follows (para 4(3)):

(1) Rights or powers which he is entitled to acquire in the future or will become entitled to acquire.
(2) Rights or powers which are or may be required to be exercised on his behalf, under his direction, or for his benefit.
(3) Rights or powers exercisable by any person with whom he is connected, or by any person connected with such a connected person.

For the purposes of (3) persons are connected with each other if they are relatives or if one is the trustee of a settlement and the other is a settlor or a person connected with him (ibid, para 4(11)). Relatives include children, grand-children, parents, grandparents, and spouses (para 4(12)).

There are two particularly menacing features of these definitions:

(a) The chain of connection at (3) can go on indefinitely (para 4(6)). Thus if X is the son of Y, Y is the brother of Z, and A is the son of Z, X and A are connected. So too X is connected with any settlement of which A is settlor, and vice versa. Such connections would only cease if Y or Z died.
(b) It is unclear what is meant at (2) by rights which are, or may be, required to be exercised on behalf of a person or for his benefit. In particular does it mean that shares or voting rights held in trust must be attributed to a beneficiary? The argument that it does is that all powers vested in trustees have to be exercised for the benefit of the beneficiaries. The argument that it does not is that such powers have to be exercised for the benefit of the beneficiaries collectively rather than for the benefit of any one of them to the exclusion of the others.

Major participants

To determine whether a person is a major participant it is necessary to show that he and one other person control the company or partnership (TA 1988, Sch 28AA para 4(7)). It must then be established that each of those persons has at least 40% of those interests rights and powers which give them control (ibid, para 4(8)). In carrying out these exercises all rights and powers which can be attributed to a person under the tests referred to above are so attributed.

A difficult point of construction arises with the 40% test. Is it 40% of the combined interests, rights and powers held by the two persons who together control the company or partnership? Or is it 40% of the total of such interests, rights and powers whether held by those two persons or by anybody else? It was clear in an earlier draft of the legislation that the latter was intended (Consultative Document, 'Modernisation of the Transfer Pricing Legislation' October 1997). The better view is that this is the correct construction of the legislation as enacted.

The arm's length provision

Schedule 28AA does not define what it means by arm's length provision. Instead it requires that the schedule be construed so as to secure consistency with the OECD guidelines applicable to the transfer pricing article in Double Tax Treaties which follow the OECD model (Sch 28AA para 2). The OECD guidelines are published in looseleaf form under the title, 'Transfer Pricing Guidelines for Multinational Enterprises and Tax Administrations'. Effectively what Sch 28AA says is that these guidelines must be followed in determining what the arm's length provision should be.

Such a rule is admirable in securing international consistency. The difficulty is that the language of the OECD guidelines is often elusive and academic, with the result that clear rules can be difficult to identify. Nonetheless, when all is said and done, there is one overriding principle. If it is possible to identify similar transactions between unconnected parties, the price at which those transactions are done is the arm's length price. The aim of any transfer pricing exercise must be to identify this price, the comparable uncontrolled price, or CUP, as it is called.

Problems start when it is not possible to find similar transactions from which the CUP can be discerned. Often this is because the related party transaction is not one which independent parties would be likely to enter into, eg one party buying the whole output of the other. When this is the case other methods may be used, notably cost plus, resale minus or some formula for dividing overall profit relative to contribution. But in a sense all these are variants of CUP, for what has to be identified is the kind of margin or division that would be agreed at arm's length. Often two of these secondary methods are used to provide a cross check.

Compliance

A critical point about Sch 28AA is that tax computations must be based on arm's length prices insofar as the taxpayer has engaged in connected party transactions with persons who are not UK taxpayers. Essentially this involves one of two requirements, namely either:

(1)   the taxpayer must be able to show that the prices charged on the connected party transactions were such as would have been charged had the entities been wholly unconnected; or
(2)   insofar as this cannot be shown, an adjustment must be made in the tax-payer's self-assessment return where goods or services have been supplied to him at above market terms, or where he has supplied goods or services at below market terms.

An equally important point is that transfer pricing is part of the self-assessment regime. This has two important implications:

(1)   If the company's self-assessment return is not correct, interest and penalties may be charged on any understated tax.
(2)   The company must create and keep appropriate records to subtantiate the entries in its return.

These requirements mean not merely that a taxpayer must be satisfied that his connected party prices are at arm's length, but that he must adduce and keep sufficient evidence to prove this. In the case of a company, Board consideration with suitable documentation is required.

In *Tax Bulletin* 38 (December 1998) the Revenue indicated the approach they take. In practice the sort of procedures the taxpayer should adopt are as follows:

(1) identify connected party transactions or groups of such transactions as are within Sch 28AA;
(2) identify how the prices and other terms of the transactions were arrived at;
(3) satisfy himself that the prices accord with arm's length prices, ideally by comparison with comparable transactions with independent parties;
(4) if he is not so satisfied, ensure tax computations reflect an appropriate adjustment;
(5) ensure all the above is properly documented with full reasons.

In the case of a company a good method of achieving the above objectives would be a full report to the Board from a suitably qualified person, followed by properly minuted Board consideration and approval.

Should a return not comply with Sch 28AA it may be adjusted with interest on any enquiry. Should fraud or neglect be involved, the issue of penalties will arise. However, the Revenue have confirmed that the onus is on them to show fraud or neglect and that they will not look for penalties where taxpayers have made an honest and reasonable attempt to comply with the legislation (*Tax Bulletin* 38 (December 1998) p 603).

Practical applications

A point to stress is that transfer pricing is not restricted to trading companies. Schedule 28AA applies whenever a UK resident enters into transactions with a non-resident. Thus it can apply in particular to loans and other financing arrangements. The Revenue take the view that Sch 28AA can catch back-to-back arrangements, ie arrangements where a loan to a UK taxpayer is guaranteed by an overseas parent or backed by collateral deposited abroad (*Tax Bulletin* 37 (October 1998) p 581).

It is not, however, every transfer pricing issue which results in a tax charge. Thus, in back-to-back financing, it may well be that the money borrowed could be borrowed commercially without a collateral deposit or parent guarantee. But there would be a substantial risk premium and so the rate of interest would be higher. Accordingly, the arm's length transaction would result in a greater, not a lesser interest deduction. In many cases this may be the answer to Revenue attempts to use Sch 28AA to attack financing arrangements.

Some advisers have expressed concern that Sch 28AA could apply where a non-resident company owns a UK house and makes it available to a connected party. The argument is that the company should be taxed as if it had received a market rent. There are good technical arguments against this point and in practice the Revenue have confirmed that they will not pursue it.

Advance pricing agreements

Finance Act 1999, ss 85–87 enables taxpayers and the Revenue to enter into advance pricing agreements in relation to transfer pricing. Such an agreement allows the taxpayer to be sure that, to the extent that the agreement provides, transfer prices will be acceptable to the Revenue. Revenue guidance as to the making and operation of advance pricing arrangements ('APAs') is set out in SP 3/99.

General income tax principles

Two general income tax principles should be remembered in relation to transfer pricing, namely the 'wholly and exclusively' rule and the rule in *Sharkey v Wernher* [1956] AC 58, [1955] 3 All ER 493. Both are wider in ambit than TA 1988, Sch 28AA in that they do not require any element of common ownership between parties to a transaction. They are narrower in that they only apply in computing UK trading profits.

The 'wholly and exclusively' rule

Trading expenditure is not allowed in computing trading profits unless it has been incurred wholly and exclusively for the purposes of the trade. There is no requirement that the expenditure be necessarily incurred, but the expenditure must still be incurred for the purposes of the business and for no other purposes (*Mallalieu v Drummond* [1983] STC 665, [1983] 2 AC 861).

A series of decisions have established that trading expenditure is not disallowed simply because it is excessive. As Lord Reid said in *Ransom v Higgs* [1974] 3 All ER 949 at 958, if a trader is activated by nothing but a commercial motive the Crown cannot say that he paid too much. But where enhanced expenditure is incurred for profit diversion or general tax planning reasons rather than for trading purposes, it is not allowable (*IRC v Europa Oil (NZ) Ltd* [1971] AC 760; *Ransom v Higgs*, supra). The issue, therefore, is not whether trading expenditure is excessive, but why it is excessive.

A difficult point is whether, if expenditure is disallowed, all of it is disallowed or merely that part of it in excess of market value. Dicta in *Ransom v Higgs* suggest that the former may be correct. But the point was not argued in the case, and certainly, on general principles, dual purpose expenditure is non-allowable.

The rule in Sharkey v Wernher

In *Sharkey v Wernher* [1956] AC 58, [1955] 3 All ER 493, the House of Lords held that a trader who appropriates trading stock to his own use should bring it in as a market value receipt. But the substitution of market value was not restricted to appropriations to personal use. Lord Simmonds, [1956] AC 58 at 73, expressed it as applying whenever trading stock was parted with so that it was no longer stock in trade, and Lord Radcliffe, [1956] AC 58 at 85, referred to non-commercial disposals. Accordingly, market value has to be substituted if trading stock is dissipated or given away.

Of greater significance is the subsequent extension of the principle in *Petrotim Securities Ltd v Ayres* [1964] 1 All ER 269, [1964] 1 WLR 190. Here a tax avoidance scheme had been implemented and, as part of that scheme, Petrotim sold trading stock to its parent at one quarter its true value. The Commissioners found that the sale was not made in the course of Petrotim's trade, and this was upheld in the Court of Appeal. The Court of Appeal then decided that the amount at which the disposal should be entered in Petrotim's trading account should be market value.

The principle underlying these decisions is that market value is substituted whenever a non-trading or non-commercial disposal of trading stock occurs. It is a question of fact whether a disposal is capable of falling within these categories but it will normally do so if the undervalue is substantial and the underlying purpose is tax avoidance.

Chapter 34

Controlled foreign companies

Introduction

The UK legislation dealing with controlled foreign companies was first enacted in 1984 and was consolidated in 1988 as TA 1988, ss 747–756 and Schs 24–26. Periodic minor amendments were made over the ensuing years, and in 1998 more radical changes were made to accommodate the legislation within the self-assessment regime (FA 1998, s 112–113 and Sch 17).

The basic rule is that an apportionment of a foreign company's chargeable profits is made if the foreign company is a controlled foreign company ('CFC') and apportionment is not prevented by six circumstances specified in TA 1988, s 748. In offshore tax planning, most important of these circumstances is that the company is engaged in exempt activities.

The apportionment is made among those with interests in the foreign company. Tax is charged under the CFC legislation insofar as profits are apportioned to a UK company and the percentage of the profits apportioned to that company and persons connected or associated with it is at least 25% (s 747(4)).

In June 1999 the Revenue published Guidance Notes which both explain the legislation in its amended form and indicate how it fits within the self-assessment regime. They also include an extra-statutory clearance procedure. These Guidance Notes are lucid and should be referred to whenever issues arise as to whether and if so how the legislation applies. The Guidance Notes state that the Revenue's International Division will provide guidance wherever possible unless tax avoidance is involved (para 1.1.1).

What is a controlled foreign company?

A company is a controlled foreign company ('CFC') if three conditions are satisfied (TA 1988, s 747(1)):

(a) the company must be resident outside the UK;
(b) it must be controlled by persons resident in the UK; and
(c) it must be subject to a lower level of taxation in the territory in which it is resident.

Resident ouside the UK

The question of whether or not a company is resident in the UK is not dealt with in the CFC legislation. Accordingly the issue falls to be determined under the principles described in Chapter 4.

Controlled by persons resident in the UK

The original CFC legislation incorporated the close company definition of control (TA 1988, s 416). A point to note was that individual and trustee shareholders could be taken into account if they were UK resident, for these come within the meaning of the word 'person'.

FA 2000, Sch 31 changed the applicable definition of control with effect from 21 March 2000 and brought it into line with the definition applicable to transfer pricing (cf pp 278–9). The basic definition is now not that in TA 1988, s 416, but one that follows the looser form of TA 1988, s 840. Under a new TA 1988, s 755D(1), a person has control of a company if he has power to secure that its affairs are conducted according to his wishes and that power is secured in relation either to the company under review or any other company.

A further provision introduced by FA 2000, following the transfer pricing legislation, is that a company is deemed to be controlled by a UK resident person in certain circumstances where he and another party together control the company. The circumstances are first that the UK resident must own 40% or more of the interests rights and powers by which the two parties together control the company. The second is that the other party must own between 40 and 55 percent of those interests rights and powers (TA 1988, ss 747(IA) and 755D(3), (4)).

On its own the new definition of control is looser than s 416 but its ambit is greatly extended by subsequent provisions in s 755D which attribute to a persons powers and rights held by others. The most important is s 755D(2) which provides that where two or more persons taken together have the requisite interests rights and powers, they are taken as controlling the company. This means that once a group of UK persons could by acting together have the necessary rights and powers to control the company the company counts as controlled by UK residents. It is to be noted that any UK person can be taken into account rather than just UK companies.

Other rules based on the transfer pricing legislation are the following:

(a) These are attributed to a person any interests rights or powers held by any person connected with him who is resident in the UK and any interests powers and rights held by any person who is resident in the UK and connected with the connected person. This chain of connection can go on through any number of resident connected persons, but in view of s 755D(2) appears otiose in determining whether a company is a CFC save in relation to the 40% test.
(b) Interests, powers and rights which are or may be required to be exercised on behalf of a person, under his direction or for his benefit, may also be attributed to him.

The territory in which the company is resident

Although the CFC legislation does not lay down rules for deciding whether a company is resident in the UK, it does deal with the residence of a company which is not so resident. The basic test is that the company is regarded as resident in the territory where it is liable to tax by reason of domicile, residence or place of management (TA 1988, s 749(1)).

Of itself, this liability to tax test is unsatisfactory for often it will result in a company being resident in several territories. But when this happens the territory of residence is deemed to be the place of effective management, or, if there is no such place or the management is split between two territories, where the greater amount of the company's assets are situated (TA 1988, s 749(3)). If none of these tests produces a single territory of residence, the UK company or companies holding a majority interest in the foreign company may elect between the territories in question (s 749(3)(d)). Should no such election be made, the Revenue are empowered to make a designation on a just and reasonable basis (s 749(3)(e)).

The converse of the liability to tax test producing several territories of residence is that it produces none. Here the company is simply treated as resident in an unspecified territory in which it is ipso facto subject to a lower level of taxation (TA 1988, s 749(5)).

The term 'territory' rather than 'country' is used in determining where the company is resident. The term 'territory' includes jurisdictions which do not have full independent status such as the British Crown Dependencies or Overseas Territories. In the Revenue view federal states such as the USA are a single territory (Guidance Notes para 4.4.8).

Subject to a lower level of taxation

The lower level of taxation requirement is at the heart of the definition of a CFC. It requires the company's profits to be calculated, and then any local tax has to be ascertained, that is to say tax paid in respect of those profits under the law of the territory where the company is regarded as resident. Such tax takes account of any double tax relief given by local law (Guidance Notes para 4.2.10). If the local tax paid is less than three-quarters of the corresponding UK tax on those profits, the company is regarded as subject to a lower level of taxation (s 750(1)).

For these purposes the term 'profits' has the same meaning as for corporation tax purposes. Chargeable gains are excluded (TA 1988, s 747(6)(b)) as are UK dividends, for these are not taken into account in computing profits for corporation tax purposes (TA 1988, s 208; Guidance Notes para 5.2.1). Since the income tax rules apply in computing corporation tax profits, the effect is to require a computation by cases and schedules of the foreign company's income. Accordingly, its profits for the purposes of the CFC legislation is not necessarily as per its local accounts, with the result that strictly the local tax brought into account is not the local tax in fact paid but the local tax attributable to the profits as per the UK-style computation.

The profits, the local tax, and the corresponding UK tax all have to be determined by accounting periods. Very broadly a new accounting period begins when the previous one ends or when the company either first comes under the control of UK residents or first commences business (TA 1988, s 751(1)). The normal corporation tax rules apply to determine when an accounting period ends, in that it ends after 12 months or on an accounting date (s 751(3)). An accounting period also ends if the company ceases to be controlled by UK residents or if it becomes or ceases to be liable to pay tax in any particular territory by reason of its domicile, residence or place of management.

The corresponding UK tax is the amount of UK corporation tax which would be charged on the foreign company's chargeable profits were it resident in the UK (TA 1988, s 750(2)). TA 1988, Sch 24 requires certain assumptions to be made. Thus it is assumed that the company is neither a close company nor a member of a group, with the result that such matters as group income and group relief are not in issue. It is also assumed that the company has made all relevant elections and claimed all relevant reliefs but this assumption may be displaced if the UK company or companies holding a majority interest in the non-resident company so elect (Sch 24 para 4). In general, capital allowances and losses cannot be carried forward from periods before the company's profits were apportionable, but election to the contrary can in certain circumstances be made (Sch 24 paras 9 and 10). A further rule is that the relief for blocked remittances (TA 1988, s 584) is applied, on the basis of unremittability to the country of residence as well as to the UK.

In substance, Sch 24 simply predicates what the company's chargeable profits would be if it were in fact amenable to corporation tax. So far as currency is concerned, the chargeable profits are computed in the currency used for the company's accounts (TA 1988, s 747A). The conversion to sterling is effected at the exchange rate prevailing at the end of the CFC's accounting period (s 747(4B)). The currency used cannot be changed in subsequent accounting periods save by reason of conversion to the euro (Guidance Notes paras 5.2.14–16).

The assumption that the company is UK resident means that the transfer pricing rules in TA 1988, Sch 28AA apply (see Chapter 33). If the foreign company is disadvantaged, the rules are displaced if the advantaged party is a UK company or another CFC (Sch 24 para 20; Guidance Notes paras 5.2.10–11).

If on the assumption of UK residence the foreign company would qualify for the small companies rate of corporation tax, the corresponding UK tax is determined on that basis (Guidance Notes para 4.2.6). Double tax relief is allowed in respect of foreign tax paid otherwise than in the territory of residence and a deduction may also be taken for corporation tax borne by a UK branch or agency and basic-rate income tax deducted at source on UK source income (TA 1988, s 750(3)).

Some offshore jurisdictions have responded to the CFC legislation by offering what are called designer rate tax provisions. These effectively enable a company to agree with the jurisdiction a rate of tax, which in practice is fixed just high enough not to count as a lower level of taxation. But since 6 October 1999 such arrangements have been ineffective as a weapon against the UK CFC legislation, for a company is now deemed subject to a lower level of taxation if the local tax is determined by designer rate tax provisions (TA 1988, s 750A). The precise meaning of designer rate tax provisions is to be determined by regulations.

Exempt activities

Apportionment is precluded if the CFC is engaged in what are called exempt activities (TA 1988, s 748(1)(b)). The exempt activities test is the most important feature of the CFC legislation.

A CFC is engaged in exempt activities if its main business falls outside certain forbidden fields and it satisfies two conditions as to the way in which the business is conducted (Sch 25 para 6). The latter effectively require the control and running of the business to be situated in the territory where the company is resident, and thus it can be said that the exempt activities exemption is satisfied if the company avoids the forbidden businesses and genuinely operates where it is resident.

Forbidden businesses

The forbidden businesses fall into three categories (Sch 25 para 6(2)):

(1) investment business;
(2) dealing in goods for delivery to or from the UK or to or from connected or associated persons;
(3) wholesale, distributive, financial or service business if 50% or more of the gross trading receipts are derived from connected or associated persons or from persons to whom 25% or more of the company's profits would be apportionable.

The simplest of these categories is (2), which is clearly aimed at invoicing operations. Goods delivered where the CFC is resident are excluded in deciding what the CFC's main business is (Sch 25 para 10).

Investment business is exhaustively defined as follows (Sch 25 para 9(1)):

(a) the holding of securities or intellectual property;
(b) dealing in securities otherwise than as a broker;
(c) leasing of any description of property or rights;
(d) investing funds which would otherwise be available for investment by or on behalf of the persons controlling the CFC and those who are connected or associated with them.

As already noted, wholesale, distributive, financial and service business is only forbidden if more than 50% of gross trading receipts are received from connected or associated persons or from persons with a 25% assessable interest. In computing such receipts the cost of any property sold is allowed. Wholesale, distributive, financial and service business is defined as the following (Sch 25 para 11):

(a) wholesale dealing in goods;
(b) shipping and air transport;
(c) banking and similar financial business;
(d) administration of trusts;
(e) dealing in securities as broker;
(f) dealing in commodity or financial futures;
(g) insurance;
(h) the provision of any other form of service.

Special rules govern the application of the 50% of gross trading receipts test to banking and to insurance (Sch 25 para 11). Thus the gross trading receipts of insurance companies are restricted to premiums and commissions, reduced in any particular case by any return of premiums or reinsurance. In computing the proportion of receipts derived from connected or associated persons business local to the territory where the CFC is resident is ignored.

Prior to 21 March 2000, service business was not included save insofar as it fell within the terms wholesale, distributable and financial businesss (cf FA 2000, Sch 31 paras 5, 8 and 9).

Manner in which the business is carried on

As already indicated, a CFC whose business is outside the forbidden fields only carries on exempt activities if it satisfies two further conditions as to the manner in which its business is carried on. These are as follows (Sch 25 para 6(1)):

(1) the company must have a business establishment in the territory in which it is resident;
(2) its business affairs in that territory must be effectively managed there.

The rules which apply in determining where a company is resident are as described above (see pp 288–9). If these rules do not produce any territory where the company is resident, the company does not qualify for the exempt activities relief, save that if it has somewhere a place of effective management, then it is deemed for these purposes to be resident there (Sch 22 para 5).

The term 'business establishment' means much the same as permanent establishment in double tax treaties. There must be premises, but these can be a mine or long-term building site as well as the more conventional shop, office or factory. More important, the premises must be reasonably permanent and the company's business in the territory must be conducted from them (Sch 25 para 7). Shared premises could be sufficient provided they are available at all times (Guidance Notes para 3.3.11).

A company is effectively managed in a territory if it employs sufficient personnel there to conduct its business and if services performed for residents outside the territory are not in fact performed in the UK (Sch 25 para 8). More than any other condition, this provision requires the CFC to have a genuine commercial operation where it resides. Services performed by an entity liable to UK tax are ignored in deciding whether and if so what business is performed in the UK.

Holding companies

Three types of holding company are regarded as engaged in the exempt activities exemption. They are as follows:

(1) The local holding company. The salient feature of this type of company is that its business must consist of holding shares in trading companies which are its 51% subsidiaries and resident in the same jurisdiction (Sch 25 paras 6(3) and 12).
(2) The ordinary holding company. The requirement for this type of company is that its business consists of holding shares in trading companies, whether resident in the same jurisdiction or elsewhere, or in local holding companies (Sch 25 paras 6(4) and 12). Any local holding company must be a 90% subsidiary but the trading companies need only be 51% subsidiaries.
(3) The superior holding company. The business of this type of company must be owning local holding companies, ordinary holding companies or other superior holding companies (Sch 25 para 12A(1)).

To qualify for exemption the general rule is that at least 90% of the income of any holding company must be directly derived from companies engaged in exempt activities or from what are called exempt trading companies. An exempt trading company is any company which satisfies the motive defence (p 295) is not subject to a lower level of taxation or is resident in an excluded territory.

An additional requirement which applies to holding company income for accounting periods beginning after 21 March 2000 is that the income must either be non-tax deductible dividends or income which is sourced and received in the territory where the holding company is resident (TA 1988, Sch 25 para 6 as amended by FA 2000, Sch 31 para 7).

As with trading companies, a holding company can only be regarded as engaged in exempt activities if it has a business establishment where it is resident and is effectively managed there.

The superior holding company concept was introduced by FA 1998 and removed a gap in the original legislation whereby a holding company did not count as engaged in exempt activities if it derived significant income from other holding companies which were not local holding companies. Prior to FA 1998 this gap was largely filled by practice, as recorded in *Tax Bulletin* 19 (October 1995) p 249. The inclusion of superior holding companies means it is possible to have tiers of holding companies providing the various other conditions in the legislation are met.

The *Tax Bulletin* article also indicated that a holding company is regarded as within the motive defence if its function is to receive interest and dividends from overseas subsidiaries as a staging post in their reinvestment abroad. The *Tax Bulletin* article still applies insofar as not covered by legislation (Guidance Notes para 3.6.36).

Other cases where an apportionment cannot be made

Apart from exempt activities, the cases where an apportionment cannot be made are as follows (TA 1988, s 748):

(a)   acceptable distribution policy;
(b)   public quotation;
(c)   low profits;
(d)   residence in an excluded territory;
(e)   motive test.

Acceptable distribution policy

A company follows an acceptable distribution policy for an accounting period if dividends paid to UK residents are equal to or exceed 90% of the net chargeable profits (TA 1988, Sch 25 para 2). Net chargeable profits are income profits computed as for UK tax purposes, less any tax actually suffered on those profits (Sch 25 para 3(4A)). The dividend must not be paid out of specified profits and it must be paid within 18 months of the accounting period or such longer period as the Board may allow. It must be taxable in the UK, ie it must not be exempt under TA 1988, s 208 because the company has previously immigrated to the

UK. TA 1988, s 799 applies with the result that a dividend which is not paid for a specified period is treated as paid for the accounting period most recently ended.

It should be noted that the requirement is not that dividends exceed 90% of chargeable profits but that that limit is exceeded by dividends paid to UK residents. Accordingly, the prima facie rule is that a company with some non-UK resident shareholders has to pay more than 90% of its profits in dividends for its distribution policy to be acceptable. But this rule is relaxed and apportionment is possible where the company has one of two types of capital structure (TA 1988, Sch 25 para 2(4) and (5)). One type is where all its issued capital is represented by a single class of ordinary shares and the other is where the capital consists of a single class of voting ordinary shares and a single class of non-voting fixed-rate preference shares.

The 90% rule is also relaxed where dividends are paid through a series of foreign companies. A dividend is counted as paid to a UK resident if it is paid to another foreign company and that or another related foreign company pays the dividend on to a UK resident (Sch 25 para 4).

A UK company caught by the CFC legislation may not know when it files its return whether the CFC will make acceptable distributions. In such a case, it is entitled to file the return on the basis of what it thinks is likely to happen (s 754A). An amendment should be filed when the position becomes clear.

Public quotation

The public quotation exemption requires two conditions to be satisfied (Sch 25 paras 13 and 14). First, at least 35% of the company's shares must be owned by members of the public and be quoted and dealt in on a recognised Stock Exchange. Second, the voting power held by the company's principal members must not exceed 85%.

For these purposes the public is anybody who is connected or associated neither with the company nor a principal member. The principal members of the company are the five largest holders of voting power, or, if some such holders hold less than 5% of the voting power, all the holders of more than 5% of the voting power.

Low profits

The low profits condition is satisfied in any accounting period if the chargeable profits of the CFC are below £50,000 (TA 1988, s 748(1)(d)). As noted above, chargeable profits exclude capital gains, but otherwise are profits computed as per the assumptions in Sch 24.

Residence in an excluded country

This exemption is couched in terms of regulations. It applies if the CFC is resident in one of the territories specified in the regulations, and satisfies such other conditions as the regulations may specify. This exemption and the regulations made thereunder have replaced the former extra-statutory white list.

The regulations are the Controlled Foreign Companies (Excluded Countries) Regulations 1998 (SI 1998/3081). There are two lists, one of territories where all companies are excluded and one of territories where companies are excluded save for certain specific exceptions. There is an overriding further requirement which is that even if a company is resident in an excluded territory it does not qualify for exemption if its non-local source income exceeds £50,000 or (if greater) 10% of its commercially quantified income. These terms are defined in the regulations and essentially they prevent a company from being exempt unless its profits are local-source income in the territory where it is resident or in another excepted territory in which it has a branch or agency.

The motive test

This exemption applies if one of two motive defences is satisfied in the accounting period under review (TA 1988, s 748(3), Sch 25 paras 16–19). The first is that if any transactions reflected in the accounts of the period achieved a reduction in the UK tax such was not one of their main purposes. The second is that reducing UK tax by diverting profits from the UK was not one of the main purposes of the company's existence. This exemption is primarily intended to cover cases which ought to fall within the other exemptions but for some reason do not (Guidance Notes para 3.6.25). It is analysed in paras 3.6.1–3.6.35 of the Guidance Notes.

The consequences of apportionment

The questions of whether a company is a CFC, and of whether apportionment is precluded, have to be determined for each of its accounting periods. If in any accounting period the company is a CFC and none of the exemptions described above applies, then the apportionment is made and the tax consequences of the CFC legislation may be visited on the CFC's UK corporate shareholders.

Apportionment by interests

The result of a direction is that a CFC's chargeable profits are apportioned among the persons who had an interest in the company in the accounting period concerned. As might be expected, complicated rules exist to decide who has an interest and how the apportionment is effected.

Four categories of person are deemed to have an interest in a CFC (TA 1988, s 749(5)). The categories overlap and they are as follows:

(a) holders of share capital and/or voting rights;
(b) persons entitled to participate in distributions;
(c) any person who can directly or indirectly secure that the company's assets are dealt with for his benefit. This does not include persons whose rights are solely contingent on a default by the CFC;
(d) any other person who, alone or with others, has control of the company.

The last of these categories is the most significant and, indeed, in view of the wide definition of control (p 288), it probably embraces all the others. What it makes clear is that a person need not be a direct shareholder to have an interest in the CFC; he need only hold shares in an intermediate company which itself holds shares in the CFC.

The basic rule governing apportionment among the interest holders presupposes that they, and any intermediate holding companies, hold only ordinary shares. This is the normal situation and where it obtains the apportionment is in proportion to the shareholding (s 752(2)). In cases where this is not the position the apportionment is between interest holders on a just and reasonable basis (s 752(4)).

Particular problems are presented where the same interest in a CFC is held both directly and indirectly, as where there is an intermediate holding company. Here the apportionment is to whichever interest-holder has the relevant interest. Rules are laid down for determining which interest is relevant (TA 1988, s 752A). In broad terms any interest held by a UK company is relevant unless it is itself held through another UK company.

It is not just the chargeable profits of the CFC which have to be apportioned, but its creditable tax. This term effectively means first the double tax relief to which the CFC would have been entitled if UK resident and second the UK tax the CFC has in fact borne, whether by deduction at source or direct assessment (TA 1988, s 751). The creditable tax so computed is apportioned in the same shares as the chargeable profits.

The charge to tax

Tax is chargeable on each UK resident company to which chargeable profits are apportioned (TA 1988, s 747(4)). If the CFC's profits are computed in a foreign currency, the amount apportioned is converted to sterling at the rate prevailing at the end of the CFC's accounting period (TA 1988, s 747(4A)). The tax charged is corporation tax at the main rate; the small companies rate cannot apply to apportioned CFC profits (Guidance Notes para 6.1.4). The tax so charged is regarded as tax for the accounting period of the UK company in which the CFC's accounting period ends and is reduced by so much of the CFC's creditable tax as is apportioned to the UK company concerned.

An important exemption requires the ascertainment of the proportion of the CFC's chargeable profits apportioned to any given UK company and persons associated or connected with it. If that proportion is less than 25% of the CFC's profits, no tax is charged on the UK company concerned (s 747(5)). This exemption protects portfolio investment by UK companies, but the inclusion of connected and associated persons diminishes its impact.

An interesting issue arises if the CFC is resident in a country with which the UK has concluded a double tax treaty and the CFC's income includes income over which the treaty gives the other country sole taxing rights. The issue is whether the treaty operates also to preclude a charge under the CFC legislation. In *Bricom Holdings Ltd v IRC* [1997] STC 1179, the Court of Appeal decided the CFC charge was not so precluded.

Interaction with s 739

The CFC legislation prevents a CFC's profits from being assessable on a UK resident individual under TA 1988, s 739 (TA 1988, s 747(4); cf Chapter 21). This relief only applies insofar as a UK company is actually charged on the profits so apportioned.

Reliefs

Where a UK company has an insufficiency of profits against which to set any relief, it may claim to have its liability to tax on any apportioned CFC profits reduced by tax at the same rate or effective rate on the unutilised reliefs (TA 1988, Sch 26 para 1). The reliefs to which this applies are as follows:

(1) losses relieved against general profits;
(2) charges on income;
(3) expenses of management;
(4) capital allowances available for set-off against general profits;
(5) group relief;
(6) non-trading deficits on loan relationships.

Future dividends

A measure of relief applies if the CFC pays a dividend out of the apportioned profits (TA 1988, Sch 26 paras 4 and 5). The key concept in this relief is the gross attributed tax, which is simply the tax assessed on the UK corporate shareholders. The relief operates by treating this as tax paid by the CFC in the territory in which it is resident, with the result that it counts as underlying tax for the purposes of double tax relief. If only some of the CFC's shareholders are liable to tax under the CFC legislation, then, unless the dividend is paid out of specified profits, the gross attributed tax is treated as underlying tax borne by their notional share of the CFC's profits.

One problem with relief for underlying tax is that it and any local withholding tax on the dividends may exceed what the UK corporation tax thereon would otherwise be. In this event TA 1988, ss 796 and 797 restrict double tax relief to the amount of such UK tax. Where this happens there is an amount of wasted relief, which the CFC legislation, by increasing underlying tax, compounds. To some extent the CFC legislation recognises this, for it allows partial repayment of any tax charge under the CFC legislation to the extent that the wasted relief less than the withholding tax on the actual dividend (Sch 26 para 4(5)).

Future disposals

Relief from CGT is allowed where a UK company disposes of shares in a CFC whose chargeable profits have previously been apportioned to it (Sch 26 para 3). In these circumstances, any tax paid by the UK company on its share of the chargeable profits may be deducted in computing the chargeable gain on the disposal of the CFC shares, or, if there is an intermediate holding company, on the disposal of the holding company's shares. An apportionment of the relief is made if some only of the shares concerned are disposed of.

This CGT relief does not apply if the CFC has previously paid a depreciatory dividend out of the apportioned profit or a dividend attracting the underlying tax relief noted above. Equally, once shares have suffered a disposal attracting the CGT relief, they cannot found a claim for underlying tax relief in the hands of the new owner.

Compliance and clearance

A supplementary page to the corporation tax self-assessment return deals with CFCs. Any company which has an interest in a CFC must complete this page unless the CFC is within the Excluded Countries Regulations or the interest of the UK company and persons connected or associated with it is less than 25% (Guidance Notes para 21.2). In cases of doubt companies should complete the CFC page or consult the International Division of the Revenue. If it is clear that one of the exemptions applies, the company need merely make an entry to that effect (Guidance Notes para 2.1.4). So too if there is doubt as to whether the foreign company is a CFC, but one or more of the exemptions would clearly apply if it was, the UK company can simply submit the CFC page and claim the exemption (ibid, para 2.1.4).

CFC liabilities are governed by all the normal self-assessment rules as to record-keeping, enquiries, and penalties. However, the Board's sanction is required if the Inspector makes an amendment otherwise than with the tax-payer's agreement (TA 1988, s 754B). Penalties are not sought where the UK company has made a reasonable attempt to produce an accurate return (Guidance Notes para 2.3.13).

Any UK company with an interest in an actual or possible CFC may apply for advance clearance in respect of any aspect of the CFC legislation. Once given the clearance will remain valid so long as the underlying facts remain the same. Details of the scope and procedure to be followed in applying for clearance are given in paras 2.6.1–2.6.17 of the Guidance Notes.

Part seven

Migration

Chapter 35

Individuals

Introduction

Migration is seen by many as a means of avoiding tax. Sometimes individuals go abroad in order to avoid a specific liability, for example CGT on a substantial gain or tax on a large capital payment from a trust. More often an individual decides to work or retire abroad in any event, and then seeks advice on how his plans may be used to minimise UK tax.

A point to stress is that most industrialised countries now have tax rates higher than those obtaining in the UK. Furthermore, the hitherto lax enforcement procedures in many parts of the world are being tightened up. Accordingly, a migrant may well face higher overall tax if he goes to such traditional retirement countries as Spain or Portugal. To achieve a permanent reduction in tax it is necessary to move to a tax haven or to a low-tax jurisdiction. Some such jurisdictions, such as Jersey, restrict immigrants, but others, for example the Isle of Man, still welcome newcomers.

Some individuals overcome the problem of where to go by not becoming resident in any country for tax purposes. Most countries define residency by days spent there, and it is therefore possible to avoid fiscal connection with any country by spending limited time in several. Local advice should be taken on the residency requirements of each country involved and it should be noted that severing fiscal connection with the UK can require a longer absence if the migrant does not move to one particular place (see p 21).

Becoming non-resident

An individual who leaves the UK is fully non-resident for tax purposes if three conditions are satisfied, namely:

(1) he is not resident in the UK;
(2) he is not ordinarily resident in the UK;
(3) his absence from the UK is not for the purpose of only occasional residence abroad (TA 1988, s 334).

In law residence is determined for complete years of assessment, and accordingly all three conditions must be satisfied throughout a tax year before a taxpayer is non-resident for that year. By concession, however, the Revenue allow non-residence to be backdated to the date of departure if one of two conditions is satisfied (ESC A11):

(1)   the individual leaves the UK for permanent residence abroad, and becomes not ordinarily resident in the UK;
(2)   the individual goes abroad for full time service under a contract of employment. Both the period of absence, and the contract, must subsist over a period which includes at least one tax year.

The circumstances which make an individual resident or not resident in the UK are discussed in Chapter 2, as is the meaning of ordinary residence and occasional residence. The conventional view is that an individual should not be resident in the UK for at least three tax years if he is to be certain of being non-resident for all tax purposes. The basis of this view appears to be that shorter absences are capable of being for the purposes of only occasional residence abroad, in which case income tax liability attaches as if the taxpayer were still resident (TA 1988, s 334). Alternatively, it is said the taxpayer may still be ordinarily resident in the UK, although as noted on pp 15–16, it is difficult to reconcile this view with the case law.

There are two situations in which a taxpayer who is absent for a period including only one complete tax year should count as fully non-resident. The first rests on practice rather than law. It is the same as one of the circumstances where non-residence is backdated to the date of departure, namely where the individual goes abroad for full-time service under a contract of employment. All duties under the contract must be performed abroad, but the individual is allowed to spend on average 90 days per year in the UK (see further p 21).

The second situation is based on the decision in *Reed v Clark* [1985] STC 323. Here the taxpayer left the UK on 3 April 1978 and did not set foot here again until 1 May 1979. He retained accommodation in the UK, but throughout his period abroad, he had a permanent home and place of business in Los Angeles. Nicholls J held that on these facts the taxpayer was not resident in the UK and that his absence was not for the purposes of only occasional residence abroad. He also indicated that occasional residence is the opposite of ordinary residence, and accordingly it is implicit in the decision that the taxpayer was not ordinarily resident here either. Thus it may be said that a taxpayer is fully non-resident in a year of assessment if he does not set foot in the UK at all in the year and has a permanent home and place of business in one specific place abroad.

IR 20 indicates the Revenue accept *Reed v Clark*, for under para 2.10 an individual absent from the UK for just a single tax year is treated as non-resident if he has gone abroad for a settled purpose. Indeed, in contrast to *Reed v Clark*, such an individual can visit the UK for up to 90 days per tax year. The Revenue indicate that 'settled purpose' includes 'a fixed object or intention in which you are going to be engaged for an extended period of time'.

CGT planning

In law CGT is not chargeable if the taxpayer is neither resident nor ordinarily resident in the UK throughout the year of assessment in which a gain accrues (TCGA 1992, s 2). Accordingly, a taxpayer can completely shelter capital gains by emigrating permanently in one tax year and realising the gains in subsequent years. This is so whether the gains arise on foreign situs or UK assets, and it is fair to say that migration is the simplest and most effective avoidance technique for the individual holding assets with substantial latent gains.

Short-term migration

In general CGT is now only avoided if the migrant is non-resident for at least five complete tax years. This is because TCGA 1992, s 10A renders an emigrant liable to CGT if he is non-resident for a shorter period. In such a case the years of non-residence are referred to as 'intervening years'. Gains and losses realised during the intervening years are treated as accruing in the year of return.

This is subject to the following exceptions:

(i) It does not apply unless the emigrant has been resident in the UK for some part of at least four of the seven tax years preceding the year of departure.

(ii) The gains or losses treated as accruing in the year of return do not include gains or losses realised on assets acquired during the period of absence. This, however, does not inter alia apply to:
    (a) assets acquired from the individual's spouse;
    (b) beneficial interests under settlements;
    (c) new assets under roll-over and similar claims.

(iii) Section 10A(10) expressly states that the charge under the section is without prejudice to Double Tax Treaties.

No assessment is made unless and until the migrant returns within the five years, and provided the migrant remains non-resident for at least five complete tax years, gains realised in the first five complete tax years of non-residence are free of tax.

Perhaps the most interesting provision in s 10A is that it is without prejudice to Double Tax Treaties. The UK has concluded Treaties with about 100 states and most of these follow the OECD model and give the country of residence sole taxing rights over capital gains save insofar as they arise on land or assets used in a permanent establishment. It follows from this that a short-term emigrant can still avoid CGT if he migrates to a country with which the UK has concluded an appropriate Double Tax Treaty and ensures he is resident there under its domestic law.

The obvious caveat with such a procedure is that most Treaty countries themselves tax capital gains. However, this is by no means universal, and some countries have favourable computational rules, for example deeming assets to be reacquired at market value on immigration. A further point to note is that while s 10A(10) protects gains on disposals actually made by the individual, it may not extend to gains imputed to him, for example as settlor or beneficiary of an offshore trust. The Revenue's view is thought to be that s 10A(10) does not protect such gains.

UK branch or agency

A further exception to the rule that non-residents are not liable to CGT arises where the non-resident is trading in the UK through a branch or agency (TCGA 1992, s 10). In these circumstances gains are chargeable to the extent that they accrue on UK situs assets used for the purposes of either the branch or the trade. At one time the charge was restricted to trades carried on through a branch or agency, but since 1989 it has been extended to professions (s 10(5)).

A migrant may find he is trading in the UK through a branch or agency if he retains a UK business and runs it through a manager. Perhaps the most common example is farming but the problem can arise with any kind of business. A branch or agency trade also exists if the migrant is a partner in a UK partnership, for in law any one partner is the agent of all the others (Partnership Act 1890, s 5). Accordingly, the migrant is chargeable on his proportion of any gains realised by such a mixed residence UK partnership (cf TCGA 1992, s 59).

At one time, the charge on branch or agency gains could be avoided by removing the assets from the UK or by not disposing of them until after the branch or agency trade had ceased. These avoidance possibilities were blocked in 1989, and now a deemed disposal occurs if assets are removed from the UK or the branch or agency trade ceases (TCGA 1992, s 25(1)). Roll-over relief is not available on the disposal of branch or agency assets unless the new assets are also branch or agency assets (TCGA 1992, s 159).

Disposals in the year of departure

Gains accruing on disposals in the year of departure are chargeable even if the disposals occur after the taxpayer has left the UK. This is because CGT is chargeable even if the taxpayer is UK resident for part only of the tax year (TCGA 1992, s 2(1)).

In most cases ESC D2 used to exempt post-departure gains. This concession applied if in practice non-residence was backdated to the date of departure under the split year rules noted above. However, ESC D2 now only applies where the migrant was non-resident throughout at least four of the seven tax years prior to the year of departure. This effective withdrawal of ESC D2 took effect as respects departures on or after 17 March 1998.

Postponing disposals

CGT is avoided if a permanent emigrant delays any disposal until the tax year following that of his departure. The date of disposal for CGT purposes is normally the date of contract (TCGA 1992, s 28). Accordingly, if a disposal needs to be postponed until a subsequent tax year, no contract should be entered into until after the following 6 April.

It should be remembered that a contract can be oral, save where the asset disposed of is land in England and Wales. Save as respects such land, the Revenue may contend in provocative cases that there is an oral contract prior to emigration. Care should be taken to avoid giving a factual basis to support such a contention.

Delaying a binding contract can be unacceptable commercially, but in such situations advantage may sometimes be taken of two exceptions to the rule that the date of the contract is the date of disposal. These exceptions are, first, that a disposal under a conditional contract only occurs when the condition is satisfied, and second, that where an option is granted, the disposal only takes place when the option is exercised (TCGA 1992, s 28(2)).

In theory conditional contracts are the better means of postponing a disposal, for both sides are bound. Unfortunately it is often unclear whether a contract is in fact conditional. A contract is only conditional if (a) the condition is precedent to performance and (b) it is contingent in the sense that neither party covenants to bring it about (*Eastham v Leigh* [1971] Ch 871). The best example of a conditional contract is one whose performance is subject to an unconnected third party consent, for example the grant of planning permission.

The difficulties with conditional contracts mean that options are frequently used to postpone the date of disposal. Options can either be call options, whereby the purchaser is entitled to call on the vendor to sell the asset, or put options under which the vendor can require the purchaser to buy the asset. The disadvantage in both cases is that only one side is bound. Sometimes this disadvantage is overcome by using cross options, ie having both a call and put option. If these options are exercisable at the same price and at the same time, it was at one time thought the Revenue could argue they constituted a concluded contract, entered into when the options are granted. But such an argument is now virtually precluded by *J Sainsbury plc v O'Connor* [1991] STC 318, CA. It is on any view much less convincing if the periods of exercise for the options are successive and the price varies slightly.

In appropriate cases, cross options merit serious consideration. However, Revenue scrutiny should be expected, particularly as to whether, notwithstanding the documentation, there was a binding oral agreement prior to emigration.

Business assets

It is difficult for an individual to use migration to shelter gains accruing on the disposal of an unincorporated UK business. This is because once he migrates, the business will be a branch or agency trade, and gains on the business assets will accordingly remain in charge.

There are two ways round this difficulty. One is to sell the business before migration and invest the proceeds in the assets of a new business situate abroad. In these circumstances roll-over relief is available (TCGA 1992, s 152). That relief is not clawed back when the individual migrates, and indeed it is even possible for the new assets to be purchased after migration. Since the new assets are foreign situs, no branch or agency charge can arise on their disposal, and accordingly, so long as the migrant remains non-resident, the gain is completely sheltered.

The second avoidance technique is to transfer the business to a company as a going concern prior to migration. If the transfer includes all the assets of the business and shares in the company are the sole consideration received by the individual, the gains on the business assets are rolled into the company shares (TCGA 1992, s 162). Since the shares are not a business, they can be sold after migration without fear of a branch or agency charge. To avoid attack under the *Ramsay* principle, the transfer to the company should take place before the sale is negotiated (*Craven v White* [1988] STC 476). It should also take place before migration, since otherwise the cessation occasioned by the transfer could result in a branch or agency charge (TCGA 1992, s 25(3)), although the Revenue said in 1990 they would not take this point (*Taxation Practitioner* (May 1990) p 232).

Charges on migration

In contrast to companies and trusts, an individual does not suffer a deemed disposal of his assets when he migrates.

Certain charges may come into issue. One such arises if (1) the migrant has been the recipient of a gift and (2) a gain accruing on the making of the gift was held over (TCGA 1992, ss 165 and 260). If these conditions are satisfied, migration causes the held-over gain to be assessed on the migrant and charged at his marginal rate of tax (TCGA 1992, s 168).

Fortunately there are two important reliefs from this charge:

(1)   the charge does not arise if migration occurs more than six years after the end of the year of assessment in which the hold-over disposal occurred (s 168(4));
(2)   the charge is also avoided if the taxpayer goes abroad for full-time employment and returns within three years without having disposed of the asset (s 168(5)).

Another charge to consider is where the migrant has deferred a gain under reinvestment relief, the Enterprise Investment Scheme or the VCT scheme. In such a case emigration triggers a charge on the postponed gain, but only if it occurs within three years in the case of reinvestment relief (TCGA 1992, s 164F(2)(c) and (12)) and otherwise within five years (ibid, Sch 5B para 3(1)(c) and Sch 5C para 3(1)(e)). The charge is not made if the emigration is for less than three years and for full-time employment.

Income tax

Migration avoids UK tax on foreign-source income, ie income from foreign employments and income from foreign possessions and securities chargeable under Schedule D, Cases IV and V. As a general rule, non-residents remain liable to income tax on UK source income, for UK income tax is charged if the source of the income is in the UK or the taxpayer is resident here (see Chapter 1).

The basic rule is that non-resident individuals are chargeable both to basic and to higher rate tax on UK income. In general personal allowances are not available, but the benefit of the allowances may be claimed by Commonwealth citizens, nationals of the European Economic Area and residents of the Channel Islands and the Isle of Man (TA 1988, s 278(2); FA 1996, s 145).

Withholding taxes

For the most part the UK secures the basic or lower rate tax payable by non-residents by requiring deduction at source (cf TA 1988, s 4(1), (1A)). Where the non-resident resides in a treaty jurisdiction, deduction at source may be wholly or partially abrogated by treaty, but otherwise it is the prime means of recovering tax from non-residents.

The principal section requiring deduction at source is TA 1988, s 349. Section 349(2)(c) applies to yearly interest paid to a person whose usual place of abode is outside the UK. It requires the payer to deduct lower rate tax and account for it to the Revenue. If he fails to deduct, he is still accountable to the Revenue and cannot recoup out of future payments to the non-resident.

There are a number of exceptions to s 349(2)(c), of which the most important are directly paid bank and building society interest provided the non-resident gives appropriate declarations to the bank or building society (TA 1988, s 349(2)(c), s 481(5)(k) and SI 1990/2231, reg 4(1)(a)) .

Non-residents in receipt of UK dividends are not entitled to the tax credit enjoyed by UK residents (TA 1988, s 231(1)). However, non-residents are treated as having paid tax at the Schedule F ordinary rate (TA 1988, s 233(1); F(No 2)A 1997, Sch 4 para 6).

Excluded income

The basic rule that non-residents are fully taxable in respect of their UK income is displaced in the case of what is called 'excluded income'. Excluded income is defined in FA 1995, s 128(2) and principally consists of interest or other payments chargeable under Case III of Schedule D and dividends chargeable under Schedule F. The Treasury has power to designate additional categories of income but not power to prescribe that a category of income should be excluded. It should be noted that rental income is not excluded income.

The significance of excluded income is that a non-resident's tax liability on such income is effectively restricted to tax treated as paid or deducted at source. This has two prime consequences.

(1) Interest able to be paid gross to non-residents is free of UK tax altogether.
(2) Dividends and other interest are subject only to the tax withheld or treated as paid.

The mechanics of the relief are that the non-resident's income tax liability is capped (FA 1995, s 128(1)). It is not able to exceed the sum of tax withheld or treated as paid on excluded income plus tax on non-excluded income. In computing the latter no credit is given for personal allowances.

Business income

A migrant who has been engaged in a trade or profession in the UK is treated as permanently discontinuing the trade when he migrates (TA 1988, s 110A). If in fact the business continues it is treated as newly started up. The individual remains in charge to UK tax if the business operations continue in the UK, for then he is trading in rather than with the UK (cf p 164 and *IRC v Brackett* [1986] STC 521). If as is normal the UK business operations amount to a branch or agency, the branch or agent is assessable as UK representative (FA 1995, s 127). Losses of the period of UK residence are able to be brought forward (TA 1988, s 110A).

Year of departure

In the year of departure only a proportion of foreign source income is in practice charged to UK tax. The liability is on the smaller of (a) the income in fact arising prior to departure and (b) an apportioned part of the income for that year (IR 20, para 7.15). UK investment income is fully in charge, for the restriction of liability to withholding tax does not apply in the year of departure (ESC A11).

Inheritance tax

A person leaving the UK remains liable to inheritance tax until three complete tax years have elapsed after he has acquired a domicile of choice in a new country. As is described in Chapter 10, he only acquires such a domicile of choice if he fixes his chief residence in the new country with the intention of remaining there permanently, unless and until something happens to make him change his mind. In order to demonstrate that a domicile of choice has been acquired, ties with the UK should be severed and any UK property sold.

A migrant remains liable to IHT until three tax years have elapsed because for IHT purposes he has a deemed UK domicile during that period (see Chapter 15). Once the three-year period is up, the foreign situs assets of the migrant are removed out of the ambit of inheritance tax. UK situs assets are still chargeable, but this difficulty can be overcome by owning those assets through a foreign registered holding company.

Once a migrant considers he has acquired a foreign domicile for IHT purposes, it is prudent to establish the position with the UK Revenue in case the migrant subsequently has to return to the UK. Means of achieving this are described on pp 80–1.

Chapter 36

Migration of trusts

Introduction

The migration of a trust does not entail the UK trustees moving abroad, although if this happened, the trust would become non-resident. Instead, the UK trustees retire, non-residents are appointed in their place and the general administration of the trusts is moved abroad. As is described in Chapter 3, this makes the trust non-resident. For CGT purposes it is only necessary to have a majority of trustees non-resident (TCGA 1992, s 69(1)). In practice, however, all the new trustees should be non-resident, as this constitutes the trust non-resident for income tax purposes (FA 1989, s 110).

Can the trust migrate?

The essence of trusteeship is a personal obligation binding the conscience of the trustee. The courts of equity enforce the trust at the instance of the beneficiaries, but in order to do so, the trustees need to be in jurisdiction. These fundamental principles mean difficult issues are raised by the appointment of foreign trustees.

There is little doubt that the courts will in appropriate cases sanction the appointment of non-resident trustees. There are several cases where this has happened, and in view of those cases it necessarily follows that the appointment of non-resident trustees can be expressly authorised by a settlement. Most modern settlements do contain such authorisation, coupled with a provision preventing the removal of a trustee on the grounds of absence for more than twelve months. It is generally accepted that such provisions make the appointment of a foreign trustee subject to the same considerations as apply where a resident trustee is appointed.

No express power

Until recently the law where there is no express power is thought to have been summarised by Sir John Pennycuick V-C in *Re Whitehead* [1971] 2 All ER 1334 at 1337:

> 'the law I think has been quite well established for upwards of a century, that there is no absolute bar to the appointment of persons resident abroad as trustees of an English trust. I say "no absolute bar", in the sense that such an appointment would be prohibited by law and would consequently be invalid. On the other hand, apart

from exceptional circumstances, it is not proper to make such an appointment. That is to say, the court would not, apart from exceptional circumstances, make such an appointment, nor would it be right for the donee of the power, apart from exceptional circumstances, to make such an appointment out of court. If they did, presumably the court would be likely to interfere at the instance of the beneficiaries. There do, however, exist exceptional circumstances in which such an appointment can properly be made.'

Two points follow from this dictum. First, it is plain that an appointment of foreign trustees can never be invalid in the sense that it is void. Accordingly it is effective unless and until upset by the beneficiaries and thus, as they accept, binds the Revenue. Second, according to Pennycuick V-C, the appointment is improper unless special circumstances exist.

The following cases are material in deciding what special circumstances suffice:

(1) In *Meinertzhagen v Davis* (1844) 1 Coll 335 the court approved the appointment of US trustees where the beneficiaries were US domiciliaries moving to the US.

(2) In *Re Long's Settlement* (1868) 19 LT 672 the court refused the appointment of New Zealand trustees where the beneficiaries were about to go, but had not yet gone, to New Zealand.

(3) In *Re Smith's Trusts* (1872) 26 LT 820 the court appointed Canadian trustees where the beneficiaries had lived in Canada since 1858.

(4) In *Re Liddiard* (1880) 14 Ch D 310 the court appointed Australian trustees where all the beneficiaries lived in Australia.

(5) In *Re Seale's Marriage Settlement* [1961] 3 All ER 136 Buckley J sanctioned an arrangement under the Variation of Trusts Act 1958 involving the appointment of Canadian trustees and an advance into an identical Canadian settlement where the beneficiaries had lived in Canada for many years.

(6) In *Re Weston's Settlements* [1968] 3 All ER 338 the Court of Appeal refused to sanction a similar arrangement in relation to Jersey. The beneficiaries were young, had only lived in Jersey for three months and could easily move.

(7) In *Re Windeatt's Will Trusts* [1969] 2 All ER 324, Pennycuick V-C distinguished *Re Weston* on the grounds that the beneficiaries had lived in Jersey for nearly 20 years.

(8) In *Re Whitehead's Will Trusts* [1971] 2 All ER 1334 itself Pennycuick V-C approved the appointment of Jersey trustees where the beneficiaries had lived in Jersey since 1959.

Modern decisions

The effect of these cases is that in the absence of an express power the only circumstances in which it is established as proper to appoint non-resident trustees is if the beneficiaries live in the jurisdiction in which the proposed trustees reside. Certain unreported decisions, however, suggest that this approach is too restrictive (see *Capital Taxes* [1992] 81). The decisions are as follows:

(1) In *Re Chamberlain*, an arrangement was approved under the Variation of Trusts Act 1958 for the export of a trust to Guernsey. The beneficiaries were domiciled in Guernsey and Indonesia.

(2) In *Richard v The Hon A B Mackay* Millet J sanctioned an advance to a new Bermuda trust. The beneficiaries were all UK domiciled although some had Far Eastern connections.

(3) In *Re Beatty*, Vinelott J sanctioned the appointment of Jersey trustees of a Will trust, where one of the three principal beneficiaries lived in Australia and another was about to move to Spain.

In the latter two cases, both Millet J and Vinelott J drew a distinction between cases where the court is appointing new trustees and cases where the appointment is being made out of court. They suggested that in the latter situation Pennycuick V-C's language is too restrictive. All that is required is that the appointor can properly form the view that the appointment of non-resident trustees is for the benefit of the beneficiaries.

Millet J referred with approval to a decision of Mann J in Australia (*Re Kay, MacKinnon v Stringer* [1927] VLR 66). Mann J identified the two relevant considerations as being:

'First, that the proposed transaction should not put the trust fund at risk or deprive the beneficiaries of appropriate protection from a court armed with the necessary powers; and, secondly, that the transfer of funds or the appointment of foreign trustees is appropriate.'

Millet J then concluded:

'Certainly in the conditions of today, when one can have an international family with international interests, and where they are as likely to make their home in one country as in another, and as likely to choose one jurisdiction as another for the investment of their capital, I doubt that the language of Sir John Pennycuick is really in tune with the times. In my judgment, where the trustees retain their discretion, as they do in the present case, the court should need to be satisfied only that the proposed transaction is not so inappropriate that no reasonable trustee could entertain it.'

Where are we now?

It is tempting to conclude in the light of these three cases that Sir John Pennycuick's dictum in *Re Whitehead* can be disregarded. However, it is to be observed that none of the three cases concerned the typical and straightforward case where it is proposed to appoint non-resident trustees of an English trust, with exclusively UK beneficiaries. The three cases perhaps make it highly likely that such an appointment would, if challenged, be upheld as proper. But in none of the three cases was the point so decided on the facts, and the strong language of the Court of Appeal in *Re Weston's Settlements* must not be forgotten. For the present, caution should still be the watchword, coupled with a fervent hope that the issue will soon be concluded by a properly reported decision directly in point.

Form of migration

Section 37(1)(c) of the Trustee Act 1925 must be watched when a trust migrates. It provides as follows:

'it shall not be obligatory, save as hereinafter provided, to appoint more than one new trustee where only one trustee was originally appointed, or to fill up the original number of trustees where more than two trustees were originally appointed, but, except where only one trustee was originally appointed, and a sole trustee when appointed will be able to give a valid receipt for all capital money, a trustee shall not be discharged from his trust unless there will be either a trust corporation or at least two persons to act as trustees to perform the trust;'

A trust corporation is a corporation entitled to act as a custodian trustee by rules made under the Public Trustee Act 1906 (Trustee Act 1925, s 68). Under these rules it must be incorporated under the law of the UK or some EU country and have a place of business in the UK. Such a corporation, therefore, will not be found in offshore jurisdictions.

As a result, the practical effect of s 37(1)(c) on trust migration is that the resident trustees do not get a good discharge unless there are at least two non-resident trustees. Until 1 January 1997, the non-resident trustees had to include at least two individuals, but the law was changed by the Trusts of Land and Appointment of Trustees Act 1996, Sch 3 para 3(12). If there is no good discharge, the resident trustees remain trustees and the trust remains resident (cf *Adam and Co International Trustees Ltd v Theodore Goddard* [2000] 2 ITELR 634).

It is unclear whether s 37(1)(c) can be excluded by express provision in the settlement. It is widely felt that it can as Trustee Act 1925, s 69(2) provides as follows:

'The powers conferred by this Act on trustees are in addition to the powers conferred by the instrument, if any, creating the trust, but those powers, unless otherwise stated, apply if and so far only as a contrary intention is not expressed in the instrument, if any, creating the trust, and have effect subject to the terms of that instrument.'

The argument is that s 37(1)(c) is ancillary to the powers to appoint new trustees in the Trustee Act, s 36, and as such capable of being excluded. *Re Turner's Will Trusts* [1937] Ch 15 has established that provisions ancillary to powers may indeed be excluded or modified under s 69(2). Such an analysis is supported by the preconsolidation history of ss 36 and 37. Section 37(1)(c) was formerly s 10(2) of the Trustee Act 1893, and as such explicitly subject to a provision in the same terms as s 69(2) in s 10(5).

The difficulty with this argument is (1) it is far from clear s 37 is properly described as ancillary to s 36 and (2) even if it is, the powers in s 36 are conferred on the appointor of new trustees rather than on the trustees themselves. For these reasons, it is unwise to rely on any purported exclusion of s 37(1)(c) when a trust is proposing to migrate, although it is to be noted that in *Adam and Co International Trustees Ltd v Theodore Goddard* Evans Lombe J proceeded on the basis that s 37(1)(c) can be excluded.

The Revenue used to take a point on s 37(1)(c) prior to 1 January 1997 where two individuals were not appointed. It may be assumed they would now take the point if two persons are not appointed. They are thought to have accepted that s 37(1)(c) can be excluded.

Tax on migration

When a trust migrates the trustees are deemed under TCGA 1992, s 80 to have disposed of and immediately reacquired all the settled property at its market value immediately before the relevant time. The relevant time is the time at which the trustees become neither resident nor ordinarily resident in the UK. Since the deemed disposal takes place immediately before the relevant time, any gains on the deemed disposal accrue to the UK trustees rather than to their non-resident successors.

The deemed disposal does not extend to UK situate assets which immediately after the relevant time are branch or agency assets of a trade carried on in the UK by the trustees: such assets remain in the charge by virtue of TCGA 1992, s 10. Nor does the deemed disposal extend to assets if, before the relevant time, gains accruing on them would have been protected by a double tax treaty.

A further restriction prevents the trustees from claiming roll-over relief under TCGA 1992, s 152 if the new assets are acquired after the relevant time. An exception is made where the trustees are trading in the UK and the new assets are branch or agency assets.

Reliefs

Relief from the s 80 charge is available where the trustees of a resident settlement become non-resident as a result of the death of a trustee. This would happen if (1) the general administration of the trusts was already carried on abroad; (2) before the death there was an equal number of resident and non-resident trustees; and (3) the deceased trustee was resident. Where this relief applies the deemed disposal under s 80 is restricted to certain assets provided the trustees again become UK resident within six months, ie provided a non-resident trustee retires or a new resident trustee is appointed. The assets to which the charge is restricted are assets disposed of between the death and the resumption of UK residence and such assets (if any) as on the resumption of residence are protected from UK CGT by a double tax treaty.

Relief from the s 80 charge is also conferred where (1) the death of a trustee causes non-resident trustees to become UK resident and (2) the trustees again become non-resident within six months. In these circumstances the deemed disposal under s 80 is restricted to assets which the trustees acquired while resident and in respect of which a hold-over relief claim has been made.

Recovery of tax from past trustees

TCGA 1992, s 82 empowers the Revenue to recover CGT assessed under s 80 from certain past trustees. They are able to invoke this section if the CGT is not paid by the migrating trustees within six months from the time when it becomes payable. That time is 31 January in the following year of assessment (TMA 1970, s 59B).

The tax may only be recovered from a past trustee if two conditions are satisfied. First, he must have retired within twelve months of the migration. Second, at the time of his retirement there must have been a proposal that the trustees might become non-resident. A retired trustee who has to pay the tax has a right of recovery against the migrating trustees.

Section 82 must be remembered whenever the trustee of a resident trust retires. If the export of the trust is even remotely in contemplation, he will need to see that he is satisfactorily indemnified against liability under this section. The section is open to criticism, for tax is recoverable from a past trustee whether or not he personally retired with a view to facilitating migration. Its effect is particularly harsh where a trustee is involuntarily removed, as can happen under many modern settlements.

Other CGT consequences of migration

Disposals in year of migration

Gains accruing on disposals after migration but in the same tax year are fully chargeable. This is because gains are chargeable if the taxpayer is resident in the UK during any part of the year (TCGA 1992, s 2(2)). ESC D2 has never applied to trusts.

Capital payments

As is described in Chapter 26, the gains of a non-resident trust are attributed to beneficiaries who receive capital payments in the same year as the gains accrue, or who have received hitherto unallocated payments in earlier years. When a trust migrates it should be remembered that a capital payment is brought into account for these purposes even if it was received when the trust was resident. This is only avoided insofar as the payment was not made in anticipation of a disposal by the trustees when non-resident.

As explained in Chapter 26, capital payments include advances in specie and, in the Revenue view, the free use of property. Furthermore, a beneficiary is taxed even if the settlement is a single settlement divided into funds, and the gain accrues in a fund from which he is excluded. Thus a beneficiary who is paid out in full in the year before the trust migrates can be taxed in full on subsequent trust gains even though he cannot benefit from them.

Beneficial interests

As is explained on p 146, the exemption for disposals of beneficial interests under settlements does not apply if the trustees of the settlement are non-resident when the disposal takes place. TCGA 1992, s 85 gives a measure of relief where the settlement was formerly UK resident and has migrated. This relief applies to any beneficiary whose interest was created or acquired before the relevant time, that is, the date of migration. Where it applies, any gain accruing on a subsequent disposal of the beneficial interest is computed on the basis that the beneficiary acquired the interest at its market value at the relevant time. This does not apply if prior to being resident in the UK the trust was previously non-resident and at the relevant time it has unallocated trust gains within TCGA 1992, s 87 or Sch 4B (TCGA 1992, s 85(10)).

Trustee borrowing

So long as the settlement is UK resident and gains are not assessable on the sett-lor under TCGA 1992, s 77, outstanding trustee borrowing within the meaning of TCGA 1992, Sch 4B in immaterial. But this ceases to be so once the settlement becomes non-resident. Ideally the borrowing should be repaid before emigration or, if not, great care is needed to ensure the non-resident trustees do not make a transfer of value. This subject is discussed in Chapter 27.

When should a trust migrate?

In the 1980s many trusts migrated in order to shelter prospective gains from CGT. Migration has only occasioned a deemed disposal of trust assets since 1991: before then the only CGT consequence of migration was that any gain held over on the transfer of an asset into the trust became chargeable. Once the trust was non-resident, gains were free of tax on an arising basis, for it was also only in 1991 that the rules attributing gains to the settlor were introduced.

Since 1991 the migration of trusts has been much less common. The deemed disposal on migration means migration should generally only be considered in limited situations. The most important is where the trust assets are free of latent gains and future gains will not be attributed to the settlor under TCGA 1992, s 86 once the trust is non-resident. As is explained in Chapter 5, the latter condition could be satisfied by a settlement whose settlor is dead or non-UK domiciled. As a general rule migration is worthwhile in this situation for it shelters future gains and foreign income. Migration will not, however, be worthwhile even in these cases if capital is likely to be advanced to beneficiaries resident and domiciled in the UK. In such circumstances, the effect of migration will be to replace the 34% tax payable by resident trusts with the tax of up to 64% payable by beneficiaries in receipt of capital payments (see Chapters 18 and 26).

Another situation where migration may be considered is where the trust assets do show some latent gains but much greater gains are anticipated in the future. Acceptance of an immediate charge on the latent gains may be an acceptable price to pay for the sheltering of the future gains. But here too, this is only worthwhile if the trust will be outside s 86 once it is non-resident.

The third situation in which migration may be considered is if the trust assets show little or no latent gain and, while the trust would currently be within s 86, it will not be so when gains are realised. The latter could come about because the settlor will then be dead or non-resident. The rationale of immediate migration in such a case is that by the time the trust is outside s 86, the latent gains may be much greater, thereby rendering migration more expensive.

Chapter 37

Company migration

Introduction

A UK resident company migrates when one of two conditions is fulfilled:

(1) it becomes non-resident under the central management and control test; or
(2) it becomes dual resident.

A company can now only become non-resident under the central management and control test if it is foreign registered (FA 1988, s 66; see Chapter 4). For such a company migration can be effected easily and without uncertainty, for all that is required is for the directors to cease meeting in the UK and commence meeting in a foreign territory. Unfortunately, it is not always the directors who exercise central management and control, and in particular, where the directors are mere cyphers for a controlling shareholder, it may be the place where he resides or takes decisions which determines the company's residence (*Unit Construction Co Ltd v Bullock* [1960] AC 351). In cases of this sort, it may be unclear where a company resides and in particular whether it has at some stage been resident in the UK and subsequently effected a migration.

A company becomes dual resident if it is resident in the UK and some other country under their respective domestic laws, and under a double tax treaty between the UK and the other country it becomes treated as resident in the other country for the purposes of the treaty. A company becomes so treated if the place of effective management moves to the other country. Under this test both foreign and UK registered companies can become non-resident (p 35).

Until 1988 company migration without Treasury consent was an offence. Now consent is no longer required, but migration does occasion certain tax and compliance consequences.

Tax consequences of migration

The deemed disposal

A company is deemed to dispose of its assets for CGT purposes immediately before it ceases to be resident (TCGA 1992, s 185). The fact that the disposal is before rather than on migration is significant, for it means any gains belong to the accounting period which ends with the migration. The cessation of residence in the UK is one of those events which causes an accounting period to end (TA 1988, s 12(3)(d)).

The deemed disposal and ensuing reacquisition take place at market value, and they extend to all the company's assets. There is, however, one exception and this is where the company continues to carry on a trade in the UK through a branch or agency (s 185). In these circumstances assets situate in the UK and used in the trade or for the purposes of the branch or agency are excepted from the deemed disposal. But this exception is not as generous as it appears, for the assets concerned remain within the charge to CGT even after the migration.

Postponement of the charge

In certain circumstances gains accruing on the deemed disposal can be postponed. This is possible if, and only if, the migrating company is the 75% subsidiary of a UK parent (TCGA 1992, s 187). For the postponement to apply both the parent and the migrating subsidiary must give notice of election to the Inspector within two years of the migration.

If an election is made, all the gains and losses arising in respect of the assets deemed to be disposed of are aggregated. The resultant figure is then treated as a single gain and this is treated as (a) not accruing to the migrating company but (b) accruing to the parent if and at such time as one of three events take place:

(1) the parent itself migrates, or
(2) the migrating company ceases to be a 75% subsidiary of the parent by reason of the parent disposing of some or all of its shares in the subsidiary, or
(3) the parent disposes of shares in the subsidiary after the latter has ceased to be a 75% subsidiary otherwise than on a disposal of its shares.

The postponed gain can also accrue to the parent if the subsidiary disposes of any of the assets which were subject to the deemed disposal (s 187). But such disposals only trigger a charge if they occur within six years of the migration, and, where some only of the assets are disposed of, only a proportion of the postponed gain is charged.

In certain circumstances the postponed gain can be reduced (s 187). This happens where the subsidiary has allowable losses which have not otherwise been relieved and requires an election by both the parent and the subsidiary. This relief is of restricted effect because (1) allowable losses cannot accrue to non-residents save in respect of UK branch or agency assets (TCGA 1992, s 16(3); TA 1988, s 345(2)) and (2) any losses accruing prior to migration will have already been relieved by a reduction in the postponed gain. As a result the relief appears to operate only if the non-resident trades in the UK through a branch or agency and the losses accrue there.

Loss of roll-over relief

One of the quirks of roll-over relief is that new assets count as new assets even if the trader becomes non-resident before they are acquired (TCGA 1992, s 152 passim).

Unfortunately companies cannot take advantage of this, for when a company migrates no asset acquired subsequently can count as a new asset (TCGA 1992, s 185). The only exception is the same as that made for the deemed disposal on migration: an asset can count as a new asset if (a) the company trades in the UK through a branch or agency, (b) the asset is UK situate and (c) it is used in the branch or agency.

Dual resident companies

The rule that dual resident companies are non-resident took effect on 30 November 1993 (FA 1994, s 249). The tax due on any deemed disposals thereby taking place is postponed until 30 November 1999 or, if earlier, until the assets concerned are in fact disposed of (FA 1994, s 250(4)).

Compliance obligations

Although the criminal sanction preventing company migration has gone, some obligations still have to be complied with (FA 1988, s 130). These obligations are normal compliance obligations and failure to honour them results not in prosecution but in penalties.

Notifying the Revenue

The following conditions must be satisfied by the company before it migrates:

(1) It must notify the Revenue of (a) the time at which it intends to migrate and (b) the tax outstanding or payable in respect of accounting periods beginning before that time.
(2) It must make arrangements for securing the payment of all the tax and those arrangements must be approved by the Revenue. If a dispute arises as to the amount of the tax it is settled by the Special Commissioners. The tax outstanding or payable includes interest on tax and any corporation tax occasioned by the deemed disposal on migration. It also includes PAYE, and other tax deductible at source (s 130(7)).

The penalty for failing to comply with these obligations is a sum equal to the tax outstanding at the time of migration (FA 1988, s 131). This penalty may be recovered from:

(1) The migrating company itself.
(2) Any director of the migrating company or of any company which controls it.
(3) Any person who has instructed or directed the directors to cause the relevant obligations to be breached.

For a director or other person to be caught, he has to be a party to an act which to his knowledge will result in breach of the compliance obligations. But directors are rebuttably presumed to be parties to any act of the migrating company and they are also rebuttably presumed to know the effect of any act which in fact breaches the company's obligations.

Revenue guidance notes

In 1990 the Revenue published guidance notes for migrating companies, which explain how the compliance rules operate in practice (SP 2/90). The advance notification of migration should be sent to International Division (Company Migrations), Room 312, Melbourne House, Aldwych, London WC2B 4LL. Two or more months should be allowed. A resident solicitor or accountant should be appointed to act for the company after the migration and the unpaid tax should be secured by a guarantee from a bank or a suitable resident company. If the guarantee is to be unlimited, the tax liabilities do not need to be computed in detail, and as a result the approval will be speeded up.

Securing unpaid tax

The main method by which the outstanding tax is secured is by the compliance obligations just described (FA 1988, s 132). However, in case those provisions do not prove watertight, the Revenue have further powers to recover tax due from the migrating company. The following persons may be required to pay any unpaid tax:

(1)   Any company in the same group as the migrating company.
(2)   Any individual who is or was a controlling director of either the migrating company or a company which controls it. A controlling director is simply a director who controls the company concerned.

The Revenue may require these persons to pay the tax if the tax is outstanding more than six months after it is payable. Written notice must be served, specifying the amount of the tax and requiring payment within 30 days. No notice can be served more than three years after the amount of the tax has been finally determined.

Index

Introduction. The index covers Chapters 1 to 37. Index entries are to page numbers. Alphabetical arrangement is word-by-word, where a group of letters followed by a space is filed before the same group of letters followed by a letter, e.g. 'double tax relief' comes before 'double taxation'.

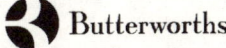